Laughing at Leviathan

CHICAGO STUDIES IN PRACTICES OF MEANING

Edited by Jean Comaroff, Andreas Glaeser, William H. Sewell Jr., and Lisa Wedeen

Also in the series

Laughing at Leviathan

Sovereignty and Audience in West Papua

DANILYN RUTHERFORD

THE UNIVERSITY OF CHICAGO PRESS   CHICAGO AND LONDON

DANILYN RUTHERFORD is professor of anthropology at the University of California, Santa Cruz. She is also the author of *Raiding the Land of the Foreigners: The Limits of the Nation on an Indonesian Frontier* (Princeton University Press, 2003).

The University of Chicago Press, Chicago 60637
The University of Chicago Press, Ltd., London
© 2012 by The University of Chicago
All rights reserved. Published 2012.
Printed in the United States of America

21 20 19 18 17 16 15 14 13 12   1 2 3 4 5

ISBN-13: 978-0-226-73197-1 (cloth)
ISBN-13: 978-0-226-73198-8 (paper)
ISBN-10: 0-226-73197-9 (cloth)
ISBN-10: 0-226-73198-7 (paper)

Library of Congress Cataloging-in-Publication Data

Rutherford, Danilyn.
    Laughing at Leviathan : sovereignty and audience in West Papua / Danilyn Rutherford.
        p. cm. — (Chicago studies in practices of meaning)
    ISBN-13: 978-0-226-73197-1 (cloth : alk. paper)
    ISBN-13: 978-0-226-73198-8 (pbk. : alk. paper)
    ISBN-10: 0-226-73197-9 (cloth : alk. paper)
    ISBN-10: 0-226-73198-7 (pbk. : alk. paper)   1. Papua (Indonesia)—Politics and government. 2. Sovereignty. 3. Hobbes, Thomas, 1588–1679. Leviathan.   I. Title. II. Series: Chicago studies in practices of meaning.
    DU744.5.R88 2012
    995.1—dc23

2011028476

♾ This paper meets the requirements of ANSI/NISO Z39.48-1992 (Permanence of Paper).

Contents

Illustrations

Preface and Acknowledgments

In his wise, witty, magisterial, and depressing book on the history of the conflict between the Netherlands and Indonesia over western New Guinea, the historian Pieter Drooglever (2009) describes the following incident. The year is 1960, and the conflict is coming to a head. Leaders in the US State Department have hesitated to confirm publicly the vague promises some administration officials have made to help defend Netherlands New Guinea in the event of an Indonesian invasion, although at least one of their Dutch counterparts is wishfully acting as if they had. Indonesia's charismatic first president, Sukarno, a champion of the nonaligned movement, is playing Cold War superpowers off of one another, reinforcing the Indonesian military with both American and Soviet arms. Even Australia, New Guinea's other colonizer, is softening its support for the Netherlands. The Dutch foreign minister and the diplomats negotiating in Washington are calling for restraint, while the governor of Netherlands New Guinea is calling for protection in the form of fighter planes and troops.

Dutch leaders know they cannot defend Netherlands New Guinea (and maintain their commitments to NATO) without outside aid. But they also know that the international community neither accepts nor really understands why the Netherlands is wasting so much breath on the "primitive" territory at a time when colonialism is going out of fashion. American policymakers need to know that their Dutch counterparts trust their assurances, but they also need to know that the Netherlands will fight to keep the colony if push comes to shove. And so Dutch leaders decide to send "the showcase of their navy," the aircraft carrier *Karel Doorman*, on a voyage to Dutch New Guinea intended, as Drooglever puts it, to "show their teeth" and "show the flag" (2009, 384).

The *Karel Doorman* sets out from Rotterdam in late May with two submarine chasers, a cargo of fighter jets, and an oil tanker for refueling.

The trip does not go well. Indonesia breaks diplomatic ties with the Netherlands upon learning of the scheme. Uneasy about the consequences of appearing to support the Dutch, the government in Madagascar cancels a planned visit. The stevedores' union in Fremantle, Australia, where the *Karel Doorman* is scheduled to dock, refuses to provide tugboat assistance. Only by using the fighter jets' engines to create lateral thrust is the crew able to maneuver the aircraft carrier into its berth. After a brief respite in New Guinea, the squadron heads north toward Japan, where the Dutch have arranged for a fleet visit to celebrate the 350th anniversary of Dutch-Japanese relations. Indonesia pressures the Japanese government, and the trade unions in Yokohama threaten to use force to prevent the ships from mooring. The fleet visit? Canceled. The squadron turns back to New Guinea then sails home via Cape Horn, calling at New Caledonia, Australia, Chile, and Brazil on the way. The *Karel Doorman* reaches Rotterdam in late December, nearly seven months after setting out.

This tale comes midway through Drooglever's exhaustive study, which the Netherlands Ministry of Foreign Affairs commissioned in 2000 to "provide sound information on the subject [of the decolonization of western New Guinea and the Papuans' right to self-determination] to a wide audience" (Drooglever 2008, 7). It appears in the midst of a detailed account of the twists and turns of what Drooglever calls "the dispute in international perspective" (Drooglever 2009, 310). Drooglever tells us of dealings within and among the various governments with a stake in the conflict, their representatives' constant effort to save face and save their jobs, the circulation of their utterances across genres and contexts, and the strategies they used to make one another perceive their respective countries' interests and animosities as the same. All this unfolded without the participation of western New Guinea's inhabitants, the putative beneficiaries of all this maneuvering, who were then known as Papuans, as they are again today. Even those caught up in what some Papuans called "*gila kedaulatan*," "sovereignty madness," found themselves excluded from the negotiations that were sealing their fate (Drooglever 2009, 540). Drooglever's description of this Cold War–era game of image management should have prepared me to see the voyage of the *Karel Doorman* for what it was: a carefully staged performance, designed with specific spectators in mind.

Yet as I read Drooglever's description of the ill-fated trip, I was struck by the strangeness of the enterprise. Picture that aircraft carrier, floating awkwardly in an Australian harbor, the air filled with the smoke and noise of jet engines. Picture the newspaper and television coverage of the crew's desperate efforts to turn the mammoth vessel around. One would think that a sovereign state would have the right to put its military hardware where it pleased within its own territory. But then there's the getting there, and the impression that getting there makes on onlookers, great and small. This book is the product of my fascination with such moments—moments when sovereignty makes an appearance, and in making an appearance, puts itself at risk.

All sorts of audiences have been involved in the making of this book. I conducted some of the research for it while pursuing my doctorate at Cornell University, a task that took me from 1989 to 1997. A summer internship with the Ford Foundation in Jakarta, which included a two-week visit to Irian Jaya, as western New Guinea then was called, paved the way for my eighteen months of fieldwork in the province, where I spent most of my time on Biak, an island off the north coast of the province. Before and after my fieldwork, I also conducted nearly two years of historical work, through periodic hunting and gathering expeditions to the Netherlands from London, where I was living at the time. In addition to visiting archives, libraries, and museums, I interviewed former colonial officials, both Dutch and Papuan, as well as more recent exiles from the province. I returned to Biak for two weeks in 1998. In 2003 I spent a month and a half as a visiting lecturer at Cenderawasih University in Jayapura, the provincial capital, and conducted a field visit that took me to Biak, then Nabire, a town on the north coast, and finally Enarotali, a government seat in the Central Highlands. I returned to the Netherlands in October 2002 and March 2003 for more archival research, interviews, and participant observation at Papuan nationalist events. Between 1998 and 2010, I also interviewed Papuan activists and community leaders in Bali; Jakarta; New York; Washington; Chicago; and Montpelier, Vermont, often while participating in advocacy and policy work as a board member of the Papua Resource Center and as the principal researcher of the West Papua Study Group for an East-West Center Washington project on Internal Conflicts in Asia. My domestic situation prevented me from spending as much time as I would have liked in what was by then known as Papua, which the Indonesian government barred to foreign researchers and journalists for much of this period. I did keep up with events through telephone calls and e-mail newsgroups. The Internet is not the only home of the contemporary struggle for sovereignty in West Papua. But I found it an important place to visit, given the phenomenon I set out to explore.

In the following pages I shall describe how some would-be sovereigns react not with anxiety but with pleasure to the sense they are being seen. This was certainly the case for many of today's West Papuan nationalists when it came to the publication of Drooglever's book. There is something thrilling about seeing through another's eyes and discovering something new about things one thought one knew well, including oneself. I have occasionally felt anxious about the imagined spectators who have perched on my shoulders during the many years that have passed since I began the essays collected here. But the thrill of discovery was never far behind.

Two of my teachers from Cornell have been a constant presence in my thinking. Chapter 2, "Laughing at Leviathan," is an expanded version of a class presentation I gave in Ben Anderson's remarkable course, The Plural Society, Revisited, in 1990. My dissertation chair, Jim Siegel, has never stopped helping me find something unexpected in my materials; my debts to him are great. I also still think of things I learned in Ithaca from Patricio Abinales, George Aditjondro, the late Donna Amaroso, Thanet Aphornsuvan, Coeli Barry, John Borneman, Suzanne Brenner, Meenakshi Chakrabarti, Nancy Florida, Marilyn Ivy, Audrey Kahin, Henk Maier, Rudolf Mrazek, John Norvell, Mary-Pat Olley, John Pemberton, Takashi Shiraishi, Steve Sangren, and G. G. Weix. In England, Fenella Cannell, Eva-Lotta Hedman, John Sidel, and Haru Yamada read and commented on my work in its earliest stages and remain fast friends.

At the University of Chicago, my home through some life-transforming times, I had many audiences: treasured colleagues and equally treasured students, who quickly became colleagues as well. I'd like to thank Nadia Abu El-Haj, Hussein Agrama, Andrew Apter, Gretchen Bakke, Lauren Berlant, Amahl Bishara, Rob Blunt, Dominic Boyer, John Boyer, Betsey Brada, Bill Brown, Summerson Carr, Manuela Carneiro da Cunha, Dipesh Chakrabarty, Jim Chandler, Anne Chien, Jean and John Comaroff, Shannon Dawdy, Robin Derby, Michael Dietler, Prasenjit Duara, Ben Eastman, Cassie Fennell, Jim Fernandez, Ray Fogelson, Arnika Fuhrmann, Rachel Fulton, Susan Gal, Mark Geraughty, Kate Goldfarb, Jan Goldstein, Kelly Gillespie, Peter Graith, Courtney Handman, Joseph Hankins, Mark Hansen, Nicolas Harkness, the late Olivia Harris, Jim Hevia, Brian Horne, Zada Johnson, John Kelly, Yongjin Kim, Alan Kolata, Averill Leslie, Claudio Lomnitz, Sarah Luna, Tanya Luhrmann, Saba Mahmood, Azande Mangeango, Debbie McDougall, Rob Moore, Kathleen Morrison, Sarah Muir, Nancy Munn, Shunsuke Nozawa, Elayne Oliphant, Stephan Palmie, Gretchen Pfeil, Elizabeth Povinelli, Justine Buck Quijada, Michal Ran, Malavika Reddy, Matt Rich, Rachael Rinaldo,

Tracey Rosen, Jonah Rubin, Marshall Sahlins, Richard Saller, Leslie Salzinger, Eric Santner, Robin Shoaps, Marsaura Shukla, Michael Silverstein, Dan Slater, Adam Smith, Kabir Tambar, Eli Thorkelson, Gabe Tusinski, Rihan Yeh, Benjamin White, Hannah Woodroofe, and Benjamin Zimmer. While in Chicago I received aid and comfort from many others as well: the late Marcia Adler, John Affeldt, Sarah Bade, J. P. Brown, Georg Buechi, the late David Buschema, Emily Buss, Rob Carriger, Romain Clerou, Annie Cuthbertson, John Davis, Julian Dibbel, Emlyn Eisenach, Eric Goldstein, Olive Holmes, Martha Kauffman, Bob Kylberg, Laura Letinsky, Amy Levine, Xiaorong Li, Cathy Mardikes, Janis McCormick, Bill McKenney, Dan Miller, Matt Nicodemis, Maire O'Neill, Mary-Pat Perri, Eric Posner, George Pratt, Sydney Robertson, Anne Rogers, Larry Ruth, Chris and Eunju Schonbaum, Julia Segre, Suzanne Siskel, Paul Strasburg, Mara Tapp, Tobin Weaver, Melissa Weber, and Bill Wyman. I owe a special thanks to Stephen Scott, who helped me with my research. I am particularly grateful for the cheerful assistance I received from my many writing group comrades, Danielle Allen, Jessica Cattelino, Jennifer Cole, Judith Farquhar, Kesha Fikes, Jacqueline Goldsby, David Levin, Sandra Macpherson, Joseph Masco, William Mazzarella, Deborah Nelson, and Jacqueline Stewart, and from my friends and colleagues at the Chicago Center for Contemporary Theory, including Jean Comaroff, John Comaroff, Leela Gandhi, Andreas Glaeser, Moishe Postone, Bill Sewell, Evalyn Tennant, Anwen Tormey, and Lisa Wedeen, whose discerning interventions along the way greatly enhanced my manuscript.

At my new home, the University of California, Santa Cruz, I'm quickly finding valuable interlocutors, including Mark Anderson, Karen Barad, Ted Biggs, Heath Cabot, Celina Callahan-Kapoor, Zach Caple, Chris Cochran, Don Brenneis, Melissa Caldwell, Shelly Errington, Diane Gifford-Gonzalez, Judith Haubicht-Mauche, Susan Harding, Colin Hoag, Dan Linger, Andrew Mathews, Carolyn Martin Shaw, Cameron Monroe, Megan Moodie, Olga Nájera-Ramirez, Triloki Pandey, Craig Schuetze, Noah Tamarkin, Megan Thomas, Nishita Trisal, Anna Tsing, and Matthew Wolf-Meyer. Mayanthi Fernando, Deborah Gould, and Lisa Rofel have joined me in a new writing group and provided useful advice on the introduction. In Vermont, where I spent a year and spend each summer, I received more cheerful aid from Vicki Brennan, Jennifer Dickinson, Emily Manetta, Jonah Steinberg, and Andrea Voyer, who helped me through the process of gathering up a bunch of fragments and turning them into a book.

This book would not exist were it not for the kindness and generosity of friends and colleagues in Indonesia, West Papua, and the Netherlands: Tom Beanal, Theo Bekker, Sary Burdam, Salomina Burdam, Cory Ap, Oppie Bekker-Kaisiëpo, Aryo Danusiri, Ien de Vries, Phil Erari, Sidney Jones, Nicolaas Jouwe, August Kafiar, Gershon Kaigere, Betty Kaisiëpo, Dolly Kaisiëpo, the late Markus Kaisiëpo, the late Victor Kaisiëpo, Arnold Mampioper, Willy Mandowen, Max Mirino, Arius Mofu, Sary Noriwari, Chris Padwa, Glenda Padwa, Hengky Padwa, Decky Rumaropen, Septina Rumaropen, John Rumbiak, Seth Rumkorem, Frances Seymour, Suzanne Siskel, Barnabas Suebu, Vience Tebay, Kiki van Bilsen, Frans Wospakrik, Philip and Tinuk Yampolsky, and many others. I am particularly grateful to Octovianus Mote, whose insights are scattered throughout these essays. Abigail Abrash, Steven Feld, Brigham Golden, and Ed McWilliams welcomed me onto the board at the Papua Resource Center. In the East-West Center Washington project on Internal Conflicts in Asia, I had the pleasure of working with Muthiah Alagappa, Edward Aspinall, Gardner Bovington, Kit Collier, and Carole McGranahan. Chris Ballard, Leslie Butt, Richard Chauvel, Mike Cookson, Piet Drooglever, Charlie Farhadian, Benny Giay, Paul Haenen, Karl Heider, Jelle Miedema, Mark Mulder, Ikrar Nusa Bhakti, Peter King, Stuart Kirsch, Rodd McGibbon, Titus Pekei, Mientje Rumbiak, Rupert Stasch, Agus Sumule, Jaap Timmer, Wilco van den Heuvel, David Webster, and my other fellow travelers in the field of West Papuan studies have taught me many things. I owe a special thanks to Eben Kirksey, who has generously shared his ideas, contacts, and adventures in the world of West Papua advocacy with me.

Over the years, I have also benefited from conversations with Joshua Barker, Anne Berger, Maurice Bloch, Tom Boellsdorff, Matthew Engelke, Ken George, Frances Gouda, Bill Hanks, Charles Hirschkind, Simon Jarvis, Jennifer Johnson-Hanks, Smita Lahiri, Bill Maurer, Fred Meyers, Rosalind Morris, June Nash, Joel Robbins, Rafael Sanchez, Bambi Schiefellin, Patricia Spyer, Mary Steedly, Ann Stoler, Eric Tagliocozzo, Mick Taussig, Matt Tomlinson, the late Annette Weiner, and Andrew Willford. I have presented parts of this book in various settings: Cornell University; Harvard University; Leiden University; the London School of Economics and Political Science; the University of Chicago; the University of California, Irvine; the University of Michigan; the University of Northern Illinois; and the University of Wisconsin. Various agencies saw fit to fund my research, including the Ford Foundation, the Social Science Research Council, the Wenner-Gren Foundation, the MacArthur Foundation Program on Global Security and Sustainability, and a University of

Chicago Social Sciences Divisional Research Committee Grant from the J. David Greenhouse Memorial Fund.

An anonymous reader and the indefatigable Webb Keane reviewed the manuscript for the University of Chicago Press. Their advice has improved this work immeasurably; I am grateful for their intelligent, careful interventions. David Brent not only shepherded the book through the publishing process, he also offered insightful suggestions of his own. Priya Nelson provided expert guidance in the final stages. I would also like to thank the editors of the publications where versions of some of my essays have appeared:

Chapter 2: "Laughing at Leviathan: John Furnivall, Dutch New Guinea, and the Ridiculousness of Colonial Rule," in *Southeast Asia over Three Generations*, ed. James T. Siegel and Audrey Kahin (Ithaca, NY: Cornell Southeast Asia Program Publications, 2003), 27–46. Reprinted by permission of the publisher. Also an expanded version in *Clio/Anthropos: Exploring the Boundaries between Anthropology and History*, ed. Andrew Willford and Eric Tagliacozzo (Stanford, CA: Stanford University Press, 2009), 50–87. © 2009 by the Board of Trustees of the Leland Stanford Jr. University. All rights reserved. Reprinted by permission of the publisher, www.sup.org.

Chapter 3: "Trekking to New Guinea: Dutch Colonial Fantasies of a Virgin Land, 1900–1940," in *Domesticating the Empire: Race, Gender and Family Life in French and Dutch Colonialism*, ed. Frances Gouda and Julia Clancy-Smith (Charlottesville: University of Virginia Press, 1998), 255–71. Reprinted by permission of the publisher.

Chapter 4: "Waiting for the End in Biak: Violence, Order, and a Flag Raising," *Indonesia* 67 (April 1999): 39–59. Also an expanded version in *Violence and the State in Indonesia*, ed. Benedict R. O'G. Anderson (Ithaca, NY: Cornell Southeast Asia Program Publications, 2001), 189–212. Reprinted by permission of the publisher.

Chapter 5: "Frontiers of the Lingua Franca: Ideologies of the Linguistic Contact Zone in Dutch New Guinea," *Ethnos* 70, no. 3 (2006): 387–412. Reprinted by permission of the publisher.

Chapter 6: "Nationalism and Millenarianism in West Papua: Institutional Power, Interpretive Practice, and the Pursuit of Christian Truth," in *Social*

Movements: An Anthropological Reader, ed. June Nash (London: Blackwell, 2005), 146–68. Also an expanded version in *The Limits of Meaning: Case Studies in the Anthropology of Christianity*, ed. Matthew Engelke and Matthew Tomlinson (Oxford: Berghahn Books, 2006), 105–28. Reprinted by permission of the publishers.

Chapter 7: "Why Papua Wants Freedom: The Third Person in Contemporary Nationalism," *Public Culture* 20, no. 2 (2008): 361–89. © 2008, Duke University Press. All rights reserved. Reprinted by permission of the publisher.

Then there is my family, some of whom have read my writings, or would if I asked them to: Brigitte Best, Karin Best, the late Dick Best, Alice Cummins, Gitta Dunn, George Fox, Jack Fox, Jo Fox, Nancy Fox Hoover, Kim Locke, Ron Rogowski, Donald Rutherford, Jim Rutherford, Marilyn Rutherford, Sandra Rutherford, Suzannah Rutherford, Tom Rutherford, Duke Spitzer, Marlis Ziegler, and Jack Ziegler. My delightful daughter, Melitta Best, has brightened my life for many years. Naima Bond, Erin Bresette, Billie Corrette, Bianca Dahl, Katie Flinn, Kate Goldfarb, Marilyn Landon, Amy Lebichuck, Iryna Martinets, Gabriella Navarrete, Chandra Rapley, Barnaby Riedel, Scott Richerson, Adriana Rivera, Tracey Rosen, Jeeranuch Sayjanyon, Deneale Steinvelt, and Helen Wang all cared for Millie; Adriana Coronado kept her busy and happy while I was finishing the revisions on this book. Finally, the men: my late husband, Craig Best, who knew how to laugh at Leviathan; our son, Ralph Best, who is quickly learning; and my dear friend, Tim Duane, who is always pulling down Leviathan's pants. This book is for them.

CHAPTER ONE

Looking Like a Fool

I often wondered whether any of the others grasped that I had done it solely to avoid looking like a fool. — George Orwell, 1950 [1936]

Each of the chapters in this book is an essay in the dictionary sense of the word: a "literary composition," but also an "attempt"—my attempt as an anthropologist to spur political thought by examining the uneasy relationship between sovereignty and audience. Sovereignty, according to the classic formulation of the sixteenth-century French jurist Jean Bodin (1992, 1) is "the supreme and absolute power over citizens and subjects." The seventeenth-century philosopher Thomas Hobbes agreed with Bodin that sovereignty implied supremacy, even as he stressed the human origins of sovereign power. For Hobbes, sovereignty began with the human capacity for what he called "prudence" (1998 [1651], 17–19). Before law and language, when individuals confronted one another and saw themselves being seen, prudence led them to anticipate one another's actions by imagining the situation from one another's point of view. According to Hobbes, prudence led first to preemptive violence then to the institution of a political order in which individuals exchanged obedience for protection against bodily harm (1998 [1651], 82–86). In this book, I both build upon and unsettle this view of sovereignty. Processes that Hobbes and others relegated to a timeless "state of nature," where fear of violence reigned supreme, appear in these essays in historical encounters pervaded by a range of sentiments, encounters of the sort that anthropologists are equipped to explore. Wielding instruments developed for the anthropological analysis of sign use, I dissect the play of gazes that incites and thwarts claims to sovereignty. I stress the interdependency that sovereignty always entails in practice, as governments turn to one another for resources and recognition of their legitimacy (see Cattelino 2008). But I also argue that audience infects the very concept of sovereignty: audience is sovereignty's basis and its bane.

I develop this argument by way of my work on West Papua, the name given by many of its indigenous inhabitants to the western half of New Guinea. A predominantly Christian corner of Indonesia, the world's largest Muslim-majority nation-state, West Papua is a rugged and impoverished region inhabited by 2.3 million people, roughly 35 percent of whom are settlers from outside western New Guinea (see McGibbon 2004b, 20, 25). It has long been home to people whom I call Papuans in this book, in part for convenience, in part because this is the name that most of them now use. They (and I) also draw finer distinctions among the region's hundreds of ethnolinguistic groups. There are Dani, Lani, Amungme, and Me, from the central highlands with their snow-capped mountains and fertile valleys; Asmat, Korowai, and Merauke from the swampy southern lowlands and coastal plains; Sentani, Serui, Biak, Waropen, and Arfak from the more accessible northern hills, islands, and shores; and Sorong, Teminabuan, Ayamaru, and Kaimana from centuries-old trading communities on the island's western edge. There are highlanders and coastal people, northerners and southerners, Catholics, Protestants, and a handful of Muslims: different "people" (Indonesian/Malay: *orang*), who trade, intermarry, speak in the Papuan dialect of Indonesian with one another, cooperate, and sometimes compete. Their homeland has gone by many names: Dutch New Guinea, West Irian, Irian Jaya, Papua, and, more confusingly, the adjoining provinces of Papua and West Papua, also known as West Irian Jaya. The Netherlands and Indonesia coined these terms in claiming sovereignty over this resource-rich region; West Papua is the term preferred by Papuan nationalists and the one I use in this book. The times covered by these essays span from the early nineteenth century to the present. I draw on historical and ethnographic research undertaken between 1990 and 2009. Many of the essays focus on Biak, an island off the north coast of New Guinea, where I conducted fieldwork from 1992 to 1994. Others range farther afield. This is not a definitive history of West Papua. My aim in each of these chapters is rather to use the analysis of episodes in West Papua's distant and recent past to illuminate how the pursuit of sovereignty inevitably entails an encounter with spectators: audiences in all their myriad forms.

West Papua is a setting that has forced me to expand my understanding of sovereignty beyond the limits set by Bodin, Hobbes, and other European thinkers. If the term, sovereignty, always speaks of supremacy, this supremacy can signal not only domination but also other, more generative forms of power. English speakers once spoke of medicines as sovereign — "efficacious or potent in a superlative degree" (Oxford English Dictionary 1991, 1839). Some Biaks envision the achievement of what they call "full sovereignty" (Indonesian: *kedaulatan penuh*) for their homeland as bringing them efficacy and potency. They imagine this achievement as occurring at a moment when the world's eyes turn to their homeland and they gain access to powers from afar. When their homeland is liberated from Indonesian rule, they will enjoy greater security and control over their livelihoods. Some go as far as to say that they will "eat in one place," the phrase they use to describe how they will live without toiling or traveling in a utopian world where desire and satisfaction merge into one (see Rutherford 2003). Speaking in their local language, they name this state "Koreri" (We Change Our Skin), an expression that derives from a myth recounting the transformation of Manarmakeri, "The Itchy Old Man," a despised and downtrodden figure, into a beautiful youth, Manseren Manggundi, "The Lord Himself." Biaks also refer to this state in Indonesian as "national sovereignty" (*kedaulatan bangsa*) or "independence" (*kemerdekaan*), the state of being "free" (*merdeka*), a word with multiple meanings (Giay 2000; Golden 2003; Kirksey 2012). Sovereignty in all these senses is a more or less unattainable ideal. Yet people like my Biak informants continue to reach for it. So do Indonesian diplomats, who have mounted a tireless campaign to ensure that other governments recognize Indonesia's territorial sovereignty throughout the enormous island nation. Near and distant spectators, including rivals and potential friends, have long figured prominently in the schemes of West Papua's would-be sovereigns. The value of these essays lies in the attention they draw to this aspect of the unending quest for sovereign power.

The sensibility that cuts across these essays—studies of topics ranging from colonial state building to the use of pronouns in nationalist texts— boils down to a preoccupation with a dimension of the quest for sovereignty that is blindingly obvious, when one thinks about it, yet infernally complicated in its workings and effects. International recognition is a key component of successful assertions of political sovereignty, and yet this dependence on others undercuts the "supreme and absolute power" to which a would-be sovereign, in the classic sense, lays claim. In the course of declaring independence, nationalists everywhere have found the force of imagined spectators impossible to evade. This is not to say that all imagined spectators hold equal weight. As Papuan activists know well, recognition from Vanuatu is one thing; recognition from the United States is another; recognition from Papuan friends and family for one's accomplishments is something else still. The West Papuan people would need the acknowledgment of powerful foreign allies to gain entry into the community of sovereign nation-states. Only some international actors have the economic and military muscle to act as binding arbiters in disputes.

But this dimension of the quest for sovereignty taps deeper springs. Sovereignty not only implies mastery over others; it also implies an exemption from the constraints of social relations—an ability to stand above the fray. But no one can command without anticipating a response, just as no one can give without getting some kind of return. As the philosopher G. W. F. Hegel (1977 [1807]) famously showed, the mastery gained through recognition is chimerical: the Lord is even more dependent on the Bondsman for "self-certainty" than the Bondsman is on the Lord. Like social action more generally, the assertion of sovereignty unfolds before the eyes of imagined others; every bid for power entails a confrontation with audiences of various sorts. I am using the term *audience* in an extended sense as shorthand for the varied kinds of interlocutors that social actors identify with or react to as they go about the business of social life. Audiences consist of others who elicit a response, even as they draw one into their ranks. Audiences participate in the "conversation of gestures" described by the philosopher and sociologist George Herbert Mead (1965, 210): the delicate dance of actions taken in anticipation of what others will think and do. One's dance partner is also one's looking glass, as social psychologist Charles Cooley argued: the mirror in which one sees oneself and sees oneself being judged (1983 [1922], 184). Audiences, strictly speaking, are never transparently available. One never exhaustively inhabits another's point of view, even when this other is standing in the same room. Preexisting expectations, categories, and frames shape one's response to interlocutors and, indeed, to every dimension of life.[1] Interlocutors identify with one another, yet never completely. Without a merging of perspectives, there could be no interaction, but if this merging were seamless, there would be no incitement to interact.

What's more, audiences always travel in more than pairs. What interests me most in these essays is the proliferation of audiences that elicit a response from would-be sovereigns, engaging them in a "conversation of gestures" that speaks to multiple interlocutors, yearned for or unwelcome, sequentially or all at once. Audiences are both imagined and imaginatively joined as people shift between perspectives. Audiences appear in various instantiations, from the more or less proximate interlocutor to the absent supervisor to the transcendent God, who holds the entire universe in His gaze. Audiences assume different stances on one's actions, from disinterest to critique. They are what sociologist Erving Goffman (1981, 146) called "ratified hearers," but they are also overhearers, witnesses to performances designed for other eyes. Size matters when it comes to audiences, as the anthropologist Marilyn Strathern (1988, 325, 337) implies in her reflections on Melanesian gift economies. When it comes to eliciting an exchange of perspectives, agents standing for collectives exert a more keenly felt force than agents standing alone. Evoked in informal conversations, represented in speeches, films, and books, embedded in bureaucracies and other institutions, audiences of different sorts and scales both enable and bedevil the political projects described in this book.

Some audiences, as we shall see, seem to possess a spectral sovereignty: an intangible ability to reframe a situation without actually appearing on the scene. Brought to mind through symbols, oratory, and the brandishing of cameras and microphones, such audiences can turn supposed "criminals" into dissidents and their arrest into a violation of international law. The spectral sovereignty associated with such audiences has haunted and inspired officials, bureaucrats, and activists in West Papua. The conjuring of such audiences has validated their claims to authority, but it has also brought into play what appear to some Papuans as transcendent—and hard to control—seats of power. One thinks of the role of the United Nations, the International Monetary Fund, United States foreign policy, and global corporations and investors in today's political struggles. In West Papua, as elsewhere, some of these international actors loom large in activists' conceptions of their struggle. Other international actors create the economic, social, and political conditions that impinge in less evident, if equally forceful ways on local worlds. But this situation has roots in the more distant past. Even Bodin (1992, 59) admitted that sovereignty was not entirely "indivisible": earthly rulers still had to bow to God (see also Engster 2001).

The proliferation of such audiences gives rise to passions, from identifiable emotions to the more elusive "feeling of having a feeling" that Brian Massumi (2002) has described as *affect*. These passions have political effects, as Hobbes argued and as my essays make clear. For those in pursuit of sovereignty, the sense that others are watching can spawn not only anxiety and embarrassment but also pleasure and hope. Much depends on where an audience is situated in relation to a would-be sovereign: audiences watching from beyond the borders of the Netherlands

Indies or Indonesia have inspired the most dramatic responses among the territory's rulers, as well as the ruled. It should come as no surprise that Papuan nationalists have responded with enthusiasm to the proliferation of audiences appearing to possess a spectral sovereignty, while Dutch and Indonesian politicians and bureaucrats have shied away from outside scrutiny. Outgunned and underfunded, Papuan nationalists are eager to recruit friends in high places who are willing and able to bring their adversaries to heel. But these passions are not just a side effect of political strategies—they are factors that can motivate the violent exercise of power. This is especially the case in colonized places, where the interplay between foreign and native gazes has proven discomfiting to would-be sovereigns. The ideal of popular sovereignty has sat uneasily with the conquest of peoples deemed incapable of being citizens, at least in their present benighted state (see Bhabha 1983; Mehta 1999).

In the chapters that follow, I describe how the uneasy relationship between sovereignty and audience has shaped the history of colonialism and nationalism in West Papua. I show how this uneasy relationship has played a direct and active role in the territory's colonial history and postcolonial fate. I focus on the multiple audiences sought out and confronted by would-be sovereigns, who are often caught off balance when the power they seek suddenly appears as dispersed across a shifting political terrain. The proliferation of these audiences opens opportunities for new claimants to partake in the dream of sovereignty, but, as we shall see, it also makes it difficult to sustain the illusion of being in charge. In the remainder of this chapter, I consider how my essays speak to questions raised by scholarly accounts of sovereignty as a concept and a practice. I explore some of the historical reasons why West Papua has proven such a fruitful site for rethinking what sovereignty means and how it is claimed. For capturing the approach to sovereignty that runs across these essays, fiction offers as useful a starting point as political theory or philosophy. And so I would like to begin with a short story: George Orwell's "Shooting an Elephant" (1950 [1936]), which provides this chapter with its name.

"The Real Motives for Which Despotic Governments Act"

I am certainly not the first scholar of colonialism to draw inspiration from Orwell (see Adas 1989, 387–88; Stoler 2009, 100). Orwell is best known for *1984* and his criticism of totalitarianism, but his earliest writings were scathing depictions of the British Empire, which he experienced firsthand as a middle level official in Burma (see Larkin 2005; Morris n.d.). In "Shooting an Elephant," Orwell describes an "unnerving" if "enlightening" encounter with an audience—or, rather, a plurality of audiences—that affords the story's narrator a "better grasp than I had had before of the real nature of imperialism—the real motives for which despotic governments act." Orwell's narrator is a subdivisional police officer in Moulmein, Burma. He is a man who hates the British Empire, but finds himself also hating its victims, in part because he sees little but disdain for himself and all Europeans in the faces of those natives whose cause he would like to plead. The narrator receives a call to "do something" when a domesticated elephant, afflicted with a fit of wildness that the locals call "must," goes on a rampage in a local neighborhood. He sets out for the native quarter to investigate. On the way he comes across a dead coolie, the elephant's first victim, face down in the mud and "skinned likse a rabbit." He sends for a powerful rifle. Yet when the narrator arrives, the fit has apparently passed. The elephant is calmly grazing, oblivious to the onlookers who have gathered. "I did not in the least want to shoot him." And yet the narrator finds himself compelled to do just that by what he experiences as the force of the natives' gaze.

> I decided that I would watch [the elephant] for a little while to make sure that he did not turn savage again, and then go home. But at that moment, I glanced around at the crowd that had followed me. It was an immense crowd, two thousand at the least and growing every minute. . . . I looked at the sea of yellow faces above the garish clothes—faces all happy and excited over this bit of fun, all certain that the elephant was going to be shot. They were watching me as they would watch a conjurer about to perform a trick. They did not like me, but with the magical rifle in my hands I was momentarily worth watching. And suddenly, I realized that I would have to shoot the elephant after all. The people expected it of me and I had got to do it; I could feel their two thousand wills pressing me forward, irresistibly. And it was at this moment, as I stood there with my rifle in my hand, that I first grasped the hollowness, the futility of the white man's dominion in the East. Here was I, the white man with his gun, standing in front of the unarmed native crowd—simply the leading actor of this piece; but in reality I was only an absurd puppet pushed to and fro by the will of those yellow faces behind. I perceived in this moment that when the white man turns tyrant it is his own freedom that he destroys. . . . For it is the condition of rule that he shall spend his life trying to impress the "natives," and so in every crisis he has got to do what the "natives" expect of him. (Orwell 1950 [1936])

As the narrator goes on to explain, the alternative to doing what he thinks the natives expect of him is to suffer their derision. "To come all this way, rifle in hand, with two thousand people marching at my heels, and then to trail feebly away, having done nothing—no, that was impossible. The crowd would laugh at me. And my whole life, every white man's life in the East, is one long struggle not to be laughed at." And so the narrator shoots the elephant—a "grandmotherly" figure, humanized, in contrast to the "skinned" coolie whom the beast has killed—and does so repeatedly, for the poor animal lingers over its death. Finally, the elephant, which had regarded the policeman so trustingly, is gone. Then the narrator retreats to face other audiences, including his European peers. "The older men said I was right, the younger men said it was a damn shame to shoot an elephant for killing a coolie, because an elephant is worth more than any damn Coringhee coolie." For his part, the narrator is "very glad the coolie had been killed; it put me legally in the right." But justice was merely the "pretext" for an act the story presents as interpretable from multiple perspectives: as an execution, as the destruction of an expensive piece of equipment, as the shedding of innocent blood. Indeed, "getting things into perspective" is something the narrator finds hard to do, both before and after shooting the elephant. Even his understanding of European opinion seems tenuous. To repeat my epigraph: "I often wondered whether any of the others grasped that I had done it solely to avoid looking like a fool."

The confrontation between the police officer, the elephant, and the native crowd recalls a tension at the heart of Hobbes's discussion of sovereignty. Hobbes, as we have seen, depicts sovereign power as the product of an implied covenant among individuals who exchange obedience for protection (from rogue elephants, for instance). Commonwealths present themselves as immortal. Their sovereignty is perpetual, Hobbes insists; there is no need for subjects to renew their vows. And yet Hobbes also depicts sovereign power as the product of impressions left by performances of sovereignty. Historically, commonwealths die when they no longer appear to the audiences of such performances to possess the capacity to protect subjects from one another and from outside threats (see Tuck 1991b, 153). The specter of dissolution haunts every commonwealth, Hobbes tells us. Orwell's short story tells us even more. The specter of dissolution arouses passions that can determine the form that performances of sovereignty take.

Implicitly, for Hobbes, and explicitly, for Orwell, the specter of dissolution stems from the proliferation of audiences confronted by the would-be sovereign. "Shooting an Elephant" reveals the causal force of the sensation of seeing oneself from multiple points of view. Pulled one way by what he thinks the natives expect, pulled another way by what he imagines as the Europeans' adjudicating gaze, the narrator strikes out against the least enfranchised party to the encounter, the elephant, whom he kills. But violence is not the only response to the play of multiple gazes the short story portrays. It is worth pondering Orwell's description of the faces in the native crowd "all happy and excited over this bit of fun." It is also worth pondering the object they are watching—the "magical rifle," an instrument that one is tempted to call "sovereign" in the sense that it is "efficacious and potent in a superlative degree."[2] The native spectators in Orwell's short story respond to the exchange and merging of perspectives not with shame and envy but with a certain joy—even "collective effervescence," as the foundational sociologist Émile Durkheim (1965 [1915], 260) might have said (see also Rutherford 2007; Mazzarella 2010). A native woman notices a neighbor watching something and looks to see what it is. Seeing a spectator, she becomes one, putting herself in her neighbor's shoes. Others catch sight of the onlookers and join the group. These "unarmed" spectators imaginatively wrest the "magical" rifle from the official; however fleetingly, his "sovereign medicine" becomes their own. This fleeting experience of collective potency leaves them with something they can offer to other audiences in the form of stories told to friends and family about this "bit of fun." In Orwell's story, the elephant pays the price of this pleasure. Still, as groups from Amnesty International to Witnesses for Peace make plain, audiences can prevent violence as well as inciting it. Audiences can enforce a norm, but the sense of being seen by new spectators, and seeing through their eyes, can also feed radical visions of change.

Features of Orwell's short story loom large in this book: the sentiments that pervade the scene of colonial domination, the struggle to justify colonial violence, the critics and rivals who haunt colonial scenes. Varied responses to audiences populate these pages, including, but not limited to, some Biaks' struggle to "eat in one place." I will be telling tales in which the actors involved, like Orwell's narrator, have difficulty "getting things into perspective." The Europeans, Papuans, and Indonesians featured in these tales have all in some sense "traveled far" and, like Orwell's narrator, find it hard to "trail feebly away." I will not take for granted the "will" of the natives or other audiences whom the protagonists in my essays sense they are confronting. I will not take at face value representations like Orwell's

stereotyped depiction of the dangers of the native crowd. But I will not
dismiss these representations out of hand. The mixture of racism and anti-
imperialism that dogs Orwell's narrator is not simply regrettable; it is also
telling. The narrator's ambivalent response to the audiences that confront
him seals the elephant's fate. Equally ambivalent responses, as prone as the
narrator's to lead to violence but also to less conventional expressions of
power, motivate the practices, projects, and dreams I shall describe.

Orwell's short story, along with my essays and so much historical and
ethnographic work, reveals colonialism to be an embarrassment—to European political theory as well as to officials like Orwell's policeman. As
such, the tale holds lessons for anthropologists and other social scientists
seeking an explanation for the actions of "despotic governments" and
those who oppose them, an explanation that doesn't stop at economic ne-
cessity, realpolitik, or rational choice. Like an ethnographer, or a scholar
who studies history in an ethnographic vein, Orwell illuminates the quest
for sovereignty by offering a blow-by-blow account of an empirical encounter. But the force of Orwell's short story is not merely methodological; as
I have suggested, it contains ingredients for a new way of thinking about
sovereignty. Scholars have long concerned themselves with what Bodin
called the "marks of sovereignty": the functions and attributes reserved
for those in charge (see Weber 1990a [1948], 1990b [1948]; Geertz 1981;
Anderson 1990 [1972]). By contrast, Orwell's short story, and the essays
that make up this book, approach sovereignty less as a set of functions and
attributes than as a value that social actors, for a range of reasons, seek to
have recognized as their own but never can fully possess. It is one thing to
act as an audience for the marks of sovereignty; it is another to analyze the
processes through which people conjure up and respond to a multiplicity
of such audiences in the course of seeking "supreme and absolute power."
It is still another thing to reconfigure our understanding of the nature of
sovereignty such that these processes, and the passions they arouse, are
intrinsic to sovereignty itself.

Sovereignty

Impassioned performances of sovereignty, like those described in these
essays and Orwell's short story, never occur in a vacuum. As Jessica
Cattelino argues in her (2008) ethnography of Florida Seminole gaming,
sovereignty is never simply an abstract theoretical category; it is a value that

lives and breathes in laws, institutions, government programs, and every-day practices, laying claim to the "political distinctiveness" of collectivities of various sorts. Nation-states are not the only political bodies to engage in what Cattelino calls, quoting Robert Warrior, "a process of asserting the power we possess as communities and individuals to make decisions that affect our lives" (2008, 129). In the United States, sovereignty is vested in multiple, overlapping political bodies, with states, the federal government, international organizations, and Native American tribes all claiming their share. Sovereignty is an ideal that has taken on a certain material reality in Indian country with the rise of gaming, which has given tribes the re-sources to back up their assertions. But the fact remains that this seeming supremacy only extends so far; many, if not all, of the decisions that tribes make are subject to reversal by Congress and the Supreme Court, and a decline in the market for gambling would narrow their choice of means for reproducing the "political distinctiveness" of their groups.

In the Netherlands Indies and Indonesia, the modern states that have laid claim to western New Guinea, sovereignty has taken forms as multi-farious and intertwined as those Cattelino describes. As I explain in chap-ter 2, the Netherlands Indies covered territory that initially came under Dutch control by virtue of a series of contracts entered into during the seventeenth and eighteenth centuries by the Dutch East India Company (Vereenigde Oost-Indische Compagnie, VOC) and local kings and sultans who became increasingly dependent on Dutch wealth and military might (see Taylor 2003). After the VOC went bankrupt in 1800 and the Neth-erlands turned its territory into the colony of the Netherlands Indies, the Dutch continued to rule through native elites. During the nineteenth cen-tury, the linchpin of the system was a pair of officials: a native regent (Ja-vanese/Malay: *bupati*), who dispensed justice and extracted taxes in cash and kind from the native population within his regency (Javanese/Malay: *kabupatan*), and a European resident who oversaw the bureaucracy and the European courts within the district. However unequally, each offi-cial exercised a form of sovereignty, with the regent deciding cases that fell under the jurisdiction of *adat*, or customary law, while the resident ran the European courts and a growing bureaucracy. There were other contenders in the quest for "political distinctiveness": the Chinese middle-men who controlled the opium trade; pirates, brigands, and traveling reli-gious teachers; and, in the early twentieth century, political and religious organizations with ties to global communities and trends (see Rush 2007 [1990]; Sidel 2003). The Japanese forces that occupied the Indies during

World War II dismantled the Dutch colonial bureaucracy and, in some parts of the colony, mobilized the native masses (see Kahin 1952; Kahin 1985). Lasting from 1945 to 1949, the Indonesian Revolution, which prevented the returning Dutch from reclaiming their colony after the war, still looms large in Indonesian memories as a time when popular sovereignty came effervescently to life: when farmers, workers, and urban youth took up arms under the battle cry *Merdeka!* (Freedom!) (see Kahin 2003; Siegel 1997).

In the aftermath of the revolution, Indonesia's new leaders built on the detritus of the Dutch system of governance. In the early 1950s there were still regents, but now they were elected, along with regency parliaments, which supervised various governmental agencies (see Malley 2003). Within the same administrative units, the central government ran a parallel bureaucracy consisting of branches of national ministries. A new addition to the scene was the military, which maintained a territorial command structure harking back to the revolution, when the Indonesian army consisted of a congeries of local militias. Soldiers were everywhere, with enlisted men and officers manning posts in every province, regency, and village. Wherever they served, soldiers supplemented the army's meager nationally budgeted salary with profits earned from businesses—often protection rackets—that varied in legality and scale. In 1965, following an aborted coup and anti-Communist massacres that left nearly half a million Indonesians dead, the military took control and Sukarno lost power to Suharto, a major general in the Indonesian army. Under Suharto's authoritarian New Order regime, which ruled Indonesia for thirty-eight years, the "political distinctiveness" of local communities became even more muted. A top-down system of government, focused less on expressing the voice of the "people" (Indonesian: *rakyat*) than on improving the quality of Indonesian "society" (Indonesian: *masyarakat*), took hold. Carefully orchestrated elections, with the government party's majority always hovering between 60 and 70 percent against a tightly regulated "opposition," put a democratic face on the regime for foreign observers (see Pemberton 1993, 1–10). Annual economic growth averaging 7 percent during the 1990s earned Suharto the title of "The Father of Development," despite the well-known fact that Suharto's family was enriching itself by taking advantage of his grip on power. Touted as the protector of national stability against the Communist threat, the military maintained the territorial command structure but took it further, with active and retired officers appointed as regents and governors in the majority of districts and provinces across the country (see Mietzner 2003). As in the Old Order, the military continued to fund itself locally through economic activities ranging from operating logging companies to smuggling endangered birds.

The New Order fell in 1998 under the weight of the Asian financial crisis and tensions within the Indonesian elite. Students occupied campuses and the national parliament, riots erupted, and demonstrators took to the streets demanding reform. In 1999 the national parliament passed laws that devolved authority and revenues to the regencies (see Malley 2003).[3] (A few years later, Papua and Aceh received "special autonomy" at the provincial level alongside "decentralization" at the regency level in an initiative intended to stem support for separatism in these troubled corners of Indonesia.) Today, locally elected regency legislatures once again choose their own regents, who have more resources and the right to act autonomously in many arenas. Yet the military's regional command structure survived US-backed demands for reform in the years immediately following the New Order's demise. Although officers no longer fill posts in the civilian bureaucracy, the military maintains its grip at the provincial, regency, and village level. Officers still run protection rackets and profit from their relationships with local elites, who in turn have depended on the military to secure electoral victories (see Mietzner 2003, 2006). The "people" are back, with political gatherings and demonstrations common throughout the country. Yet sovereignty remains shared among social actors, some of a decidedly shadowy sort.

In Indonesia, as in Orwell's Burma, sovereignty has always been internally disturbed: unsettled, inconsistent, fraught with contradictions, never quite as supreme as it may seem. The essays in this book relate sovereignty's internal disturbance to its uneasy relationship with audience. Would-be sovereigns depend on acknowledgment from others for their claims to be effective. This means their sovereignty is never equal to itself: sovereignty's spectators exercise a kind of sovereignty themselves. The French historian Michel Foucault and the Italian philosopher Giorgio Agamben offer reasons why contemporary would-be sovereigns are particularly liable to experience power as dispersed across multiple sites. Tracing the genealogy of European modernity to the seventeenth and eighteenth centuries, Foucault describes a shift in power's center of gravity away from the juridical, which was privileged by absolute monarchs who maintained their supremacy by demonstrating their "ancient right to take life and let live" (1991, 138). Discipline produces the docile bodies presumed by liberal political theory. Governmentality regulates populations and resources with the aim of promoting the orderly proliferation of "biopower," or organic life. Sovereignty is internally disturbed by its coexistence with these counterparts. In a world where power is "capillary," rather than unitary, productive, rather than repressive, no one element or actor is "supreme."

For Agamben (1998), sovereignty's internal disturbance derives less from its coexistence with discipline and governmentality than from the concept's reliance on the notion of the exception. Agamben's starting point is the German jurist Carl Schmitt's widely cited pronouncement: "Sovereign is he who decides on the exception" (2005 [1922], 5). The sovereign decides what (and who) will fall under the purview of the law and whether the law should be suspended altogether. This decision joins formal code to living case in determining whether a particular act is going to count as the token of a legal type. Agamben builds on Schmitt to bring into focus the target of the sovereign decision: a condition that Agamben calls "bare life." Sovereignty operates by taking bare life as its hostage; it gains a grip on those in its jurisdiction by virtue of the fact that they are living yet have been stripped of their political status and thus can be threatened with death. When a warden straps a prisoner into an electric chair, he is not an accessory to an act of murder; at least, say, in Texas, he is merely doing his job. By defining this pairing of bare life and unpunishable violence as sovereignty's "included outside," Agamben bridges the gap between sovereignty and governmentality. "Biopower" is "bare life" generalized to the entire population, which now exists in the "state of exception" once reserved for the condemned. Sovereignty has always been internally disturbed.

Foucault's and Agamben's discussions of the dispersed nature of modern power can tell us much about the conditions facing West Papua's would-be sovereigns. Life in Indonesia has long featured all three elements of Foucault's triad: the disciplinary production of national subjects, constant efforts to "improve" the nation's natural and human resources, the ever-present threat of lethal force. Indonesia has, to date, successfully stymied efforts to gain international support for West Papuan self-determination. In the postwar era, the international community has tended, at least in principle, to respect the territorial sovereignty of existing states unless exceptional conditions prevail, including, most notably, gross violations of human rights. It is no accident that Papuan nationalists devote much of their energy to documenting human rights violations. Some have tried to make the case that the label, *genocide*, is a legally defensible way of describing the Papuans' plight (see Brundige et al. 2004; Wing 2005). Whether they are the target of state terror or international intervention,

Papuan victims often only seem to matter to the degree that their role in the world boils down to the mere fact of living or being "abandoned" to death. Foucault and Agamben help us grasp why power might appear to would-be sovereigns as distended across multiple audiences, near and far, in a setting, like so many other colonial and postcolonial places, where "effective legal sovereignty is always an unattainable ideal" (Blom-Hansen and Stepputat 2006, 295; see also Sidel 1999; Comaroff and Comaroff 2004a, 2004b, 2006a, 2006b; Humphrey 2007; Nugent 2007).

Yet neither Agamben nor Foucault put their finger on the aspect of sovereignty that Orwell's short story makes plain—and that I am investigating in this book. There are plenty of audiences confronted and conjured in Foucault's description of sovereignty in *Discipline and Punishment* (1979), from the unruly crowds who attend executions to the regicide who contorts his body to look at his wounds. But in the end Foucault reduces these richly described scenes to symptoms of a historical rupture that transforms a complicated conversation of gestures into an apparatus of modern power. Agamben's writings on sovereignty hover above Foucault's level of historical detail, focusing instead on abstract structure. In the tradition of Claude Lévi-Strauss, Agamben presupposes the social but never gives it historical flesh.[4] "We must recognize," Agamben declares, "the structure of the ban [Agamben's gloss for the 'included outside' at the heart of sovereignty], in the political relations and public spaces in which we still live" (1998, 111). My approach to sovereignty, by contrast, requires us to look closely at processes of recognition themselves.

For this purpose, thinkers who have mapped the troubled relationship between sovereignty and recognition provide a helpful starting point. The French surrealist author and scholar Georges Bataille (1990, 1991) distinguishes between sovereignty and lordship, Bataille's shorthand for the figure of authority sketched out in Hegel's abovementioned discussion of the interdependence of Lordship and Bondage (see also Derrida 1978a). To be truly sovereign is to give harm or benefit without receiving anything, even recognition that one's act has occurred. In other words, it is to forego any relationship with an audience, including one's subjects, one's rivals, and even oneself. In a negative fashion, Bataille's account of sovereignty confirms the importance of the proliferation of audiences to the pursuit of sovereignty. Even if citizens and subjects do not answer back, foreign observers, real or imagined, still wait in the wings, not to mention one's conscience or one's God. As the German essayist Walter Benjamin also insists when he writes of a "divine violence" irreducible to any humanly recognizable ends, true sovereignty is impossible to achieve or even imagine (see Benjamin 1978 [1920–21]; see also chapter 4). The policeman in Orwell's short story may shoot the elephant, but he can't bring the play of gazes to a stop.

The European thinkers discussed in this section suggest why sovereignty might appear as internally disturbed in Indonesia, past and present, not to mention in Orwell's Burma. They depict sovereignty as constitutively troubled: by its coexistence with other dimensions of modern power, by "bare life" as its included outside, by its disavowed dependence on recognition. But their formulations do not quite capture the dimension of sovereignty's internal disturbance that concerns me in this book. To grasp how audiences, and the changes in perspective they elicit, have both furthered and disrupted the pursuit of sovereignty, I have had to dissect the performances of would-be sovereigns in the messy historical settings where they occur. An ethnographic method attuned to how people slip between voices, stances, and interpretive frames in the course of their interactions is particularly suited to my task.

Audience

In exploring the pursuit of sovereignty in West Papua, I have drawn on a rich vein of writing in the humanities and social sciences on ritual, spectacle, print, and the mass media and their relationship to the making of publics (see Warner 1990, 1991; Anderson 1991; Berlant 1991, 1996; Habermas 1991; Fliegelman 1993; Klima 2002; LiPuma 2002; Wedeen 2008). From Martha Feldman's (2007) exploration of the changes in opera that occurred with the transition from absolutist to liberal forms of rule in Italy, to Michael Warner's (1990) account of how the "Republic of Letters" gave rise to new reading publics populated by the bourgeois subjects who came to exercise sovereignty in the United States, much of this literature has focused on the tumultuous centuries leading up to the French Revolution and the founding of modern democracies. In these essays I follow this literature in linking the supremacy and potency associated with sovereignty with the feeling of expanded agency that people experience when they sense themselves adopting a widely shared viewpoint (see Warner 2005, 69, 105). But I go further. I stress not simply the sharing of viewpoints but also the movement across them that occurs by way of the communicative practices I consider. I am interested in how people's

attention both shifts and remains suspended between perspectives over
the course of a conversation, a performance, or a written or visual text.
In making sense of this process, I am using the term *audience* in a fashion
that bridges the distinction that Warner in particular draws between audiences and publics. For Warner, audiences are embodied, co-present, and
proximate to a performance, while publics maintain a shadowy existence
around a published work (see 2005, 67–68). I have found it necessary to
challenge the sheer line between absence and presence that Warner risks
drawing in distinguishing between these two terms. Even when a group of
individuals shares a patch of sidewalk, much work must be done to turn
them into addressees or over-hearers, let alone tellers of a tale. Alongside
the materiality of bodies, more or less available to a scene of interaction,
one must pay heed to the materiality of signs, be they etched in newspapers, lit up on computer screens, or pulsed through the air.

   In the essays in this volume, I make opportunistic use of terms and
methods developed by linguistic anthropologists and other students of semiotics, or sign use, to examine how people call to mind and imaginatively
become part of different kinds of audiences as they interact. Most useful
for my discussion of audience are approaches to linguistic interaction and
other semiotic practices that challenge the notion of what one might call
a sovereign speaking subject, an autonomous author of utterances who
freely says what he or she means without the words getting in the way.
Our mouths are always filled with the words of others, the Russian linguist
Mikhail Bakhtin (1981) insisted, capturing the inherently dialogic
character of discourse. Every utterance is at once a response and a
provocation in an ongoing history, reacting to interlocutors past and anticipating interlocutors to come (see also Vološinov 1986 [1973]). Anthropologists drawn to Bakhtin's insistently historical account of discourse
have also found inspiration in the work of the philosopher Charles Sanders
Peirce and his account of the sign as an object that represents another
object to a mind. They have been particularly taken by Peirce's discussion
of indexicality: the capacity of signs to call their objects to mind on the
basis of a presumed causal link (see Peirce 1986; see also Parmentier 1994;
Keane 1997).[5]

   Peirce's understanding of sign use has offered analysts a way of understanding a particularly eventful kind of utterance: what another philosopher, J. L. Austin, called performatives in his classic work, *How to
Do Things with Words* (1976). Performatives like "I promise," "I for-
give," or "I declare" carry a force different from that conveyed in what

Austin called "constatives," which consist of utterances like "The car is parked under the tree." Performatives seem to guarantee their own truth by virtue of the fact that they both index, or point to, and symbolize, or conventionally represent, what they will have accomplished by virtue of being said. Linguistic anthropologists have brought clarity to the analysis of performatives by introducing yet another vocabulary for describing how speakers do things with words. Michael Silverstein (1993) has shown how performatives operate by foregrounding the multifunctional—that is, multiply "doing"—character of sign use, an essential element of which is the "metapragmatic" power of all utterances and gestures to refer back reflexively to the work that these signs are in the midst of performing. We see that capacity at work in explicit performatives, (such as "I declare"), in pronouns, verb tenses, and deictics (like "here" or "there"), and in behaviors as subtle as a raised eyebrow or a conspiratorial tone.

This approach to sign use is central to my understanding of the concept of audience. Signs represent objects to minds, that is, audiences. Among these represented objects are often other audiences, that is, other minds. Like all sign use, language works in part by indexing or pointing. The things to which language points include what the sociologist Erving Goffman (1981) called "footing," the stance, alignment, or evaluative position a speaker is taking on the act of speaking (Irvine 1996; Woolard 1998; Dickinson 2007; Shoaps 2009). They also include addressees and possible eavesdroppers as well as distant audiences whose imagined viewpoints shape what a speaker says. This approach to sign use compels us to look closely for the conjuring of spectators whenever people make a bid for sovereignty, whether they are whispering to a neighbor during an official ceremony or chanting nationalist slogans on the street. This approach also compels us to watch for the shifting of footings and stances in the course of a conversation, speech, film, or book.

What's more, my deployment of this approach to sign use prevents us from reducing this conjuring or shifting to the intentions or strategies of a speaker. The meaning of our practices only becomes discernible by virtue of their effects as they emerge across the course of an interaction. Our identities are vulnerable to the "open-endedness and contingency of the future we share with others," as Patchen Markell (2003, 15) aptly points out. Indexing an audience is not something we knowingly set out to do; it is only by assuming another's viewpoint that we learn that this is what we will have done. This process is impassioned as well as interactive. As the anthropologist James Siegel (2006) has suggested, one way to respond to a

shocking or unsettling occurrence is to treat what has happened as a communication from a hitherto unimagined interlocutor. Conjuring and shifting are ineradicable features of sign use; sign users conjure a shifting array
of audiences every time they take up their pens or open their mouths.

Audiences come to crowd the scene of sovereignty-seeking through this
conjuring and shifting, which bring a multiplicity of perspectives into relevance, either sequentially or at the same time. Two examples from my essays help clarify how this conjuring and shifting works and why it matters,
when it comes to sovereignty. Picture yourself on a beach on the island of
Biak, gazing at the horizon where a Dutch warship surrounded by native
vessels is coming into focus. A rowboat lands, and some curious islanders watch from a safe distances as sailors erect a post. They nail a metal
shield embossed with the Dutch coat of arms to the wood. Once the deed
is done, a man in a uniform reads a declaration in Dutch. Now picture
yourself on the same island, over a hundred years later. This time, those
bringing the symbol of sovereignty come from a nearby bus terminal, not
the sea. Slipping past you, they climb the water tower that looms up over
the district capital that has grown up on this shore. Reaching the top of the
ladder, they climb onto the cistern and erect a pole. Hanging from it is a
West Papuan national flag. A man in a uniform reads a declaration not in
Dutch, but in Indonesian. Unlike the metal shield that marked the island
as belonging to the Netherlands Indies, the fluttering flag marks it as belonging to the West Papuan nation-state. But to whom and how?

Let's look more closely at the second event of sign use. As I explain
in chapter 4, where I consider this flag raising, which occurred on Biak
in 1998, the man in a uniform read an oath that stated, "We, the people
of West Papua, pledge to stay united, no matter what the circumstances,
under the flag of West Papua and the eastern morning star and pledge
to live and die for the flag of West Papua which has already flown over
an independent Papuan land" (Human Rights Watch 1998b). A classic
performative in Austin's sense, this utterance did what it said: it made a
vow and described that vow all at once. It also conjured into existence
an audience-turned-author: the "We, the people" who listened and identified with the perspective articulated in the oath. The philosopher John
Searle (1965) argues that the force of such an utterance depends on its
speaker's intentions. By contrast, Derrida (1982) reads Austin more radically to suggest that the very notion of intention depends on a performative's uptake. If an oath works—if it is "felicitous," to use another of
Austin's terms—it makes not only an act but also an actor into something

socially real: it shapes future events by positing a subject authorized to do these things with these words. This effect is the outcome of what Derrida (1982) calls the "iterability" of performatives; a performative must speak to an audience that recognizes it as such: in this case, in the first instance, the demonstrators who flocked to the site to flesh out the oath's West Papuan "we."

Who else did this performative conjure and speak to? If every sign serves multiple functions, as linguistic anthropologists have suggested, one audience is never enough. When I use an honorific—say, "your honor"—I elevate my interlocutor. But I also elevate myself by performing as the sort of person who would speak in this respectful fashion in this situation (see Errington 1998b; Agha 2007). In raising and pledging their allegiance to the flag, the protesters called into being a nation. They also presented themselves as the sort of people who would attempt such a feat in a setting where this act's felicity is far from assured. Directed at the Indonesian government, the flag raising was an act of refusal and provocation. Directed at foreign governments and the international community, the flag raising was an appeal for protection and authorization. Ideally these were to come from the United States and United Nations, which at the time were increasingly claiming a monopoly over the legitimate use of extranational force, including the peacekeepers, economic sanctions, and other coercive mechanisms that have allowed for the birth of new nations in places like East Timor and Kosovo. Directed at "God, the Son, and the Holy Ghost," whom the man in the uniform listed as witnesses to his pledge, the flag raising was an appeal for salvation—and justification—from even higher powers.

How did the flag raising achieve these effects? To answer this question, one would need to examine the verbal performances held in the course of the demonstration. From snippets of United Nations declarations to rumors that someone was filming the protest for CNN, verbal signs served to index distant witnesses to the event. Repeated in the midst of the protesters' negotiations with the authorities, the same signs indexed the demonstrators' capacity to attract global attention, should the police and military move in to take down the flag. One would also need to consider the other activities that made up the protest. People made a flag, they raised it, they gave speeches, and they chanted nationalist slogans and sang nationalist songs: these familiar ingredients indexed a genre of political action associated with particular kinds of spectators. In indexing this genre, the demonstration pointed not just to an abstract model but also to an eventful history of political protest in the province and beyond. By including prayers and hymns among their activities, the protesters indexed further genres of performance with their own eventful histories: church services, funerals, revival meetings, and, as I shall argue in chapter 5, millennial uprisings meant to overthrow colonial rule. Finally, one would need to discern subtler aspects of people's sign use, like tones, gestures, and expressions signaling irony, elation, or warning, which bring further interlocutors into play. Whether they occur in live performances, on film, or in books or treatises, all these means of conjuring are open to ethnographic investigation, as are the passions that participants show signs of experiencing as they slip between points of view.

I could offer an equally complicated depiction of the audiences conjured by the Dutch official who supervised the erection of the Dutch coat of arms. But this example from 1998 suffices to introduce the analytic tools used in the essays that make up this book. These tools are not neutral, as I hope I have made clear; the makings of a more insistently relational understanding of sovereignty lie at their heart. To dream of sovereignty is to dream of overcoming one's dependence on others. This is an impossible dream in a world where one's very ability to act presupposes resources, from bodies to money to words, that one can never fully control. In light of this predicament, one could argue that the metapragmatic capacity of signs—their ability to conjure a viewpoint that reflects back on itself from a higher plane—affords a fleeting experience of supremacy that may just feel like sovereign power. Don't be mistaken: it takes a strict set of geopolitical conditions to make a declaration of independence stick. But there is something seductive in voicing an utterance that creates its own truth, like "We the people declare." People who voice this nation-founding utterance have a chance to experience the flights of passion and imagination involved in taking a new stance on oneself. If I am correct, it is not just the promise of international intervention but often also the thrilling experience of moving between perspectives that accounts for the longstanding appeal of demonstrations like flag raisings. As one audience gives way to another, the quest for sovereignty continues, propelled by the passions that such performances spawn.

When we pay heed to the conjuring of spectators, we come up against questions of history. These questions have to do, first of all, with the history built into every use of signs. But audiences are themselves historical; they are always situated in time and space. My approach to questions of sovereignty and audience derives not simply from studies of sign use; it

draws on accounts of the workings of power and recognition in the Netherlands Indies and Indonesia, the states that have laid claim to the Papuans'
home.

Colonialism, Nationalism, the Indies, Indonesia

There are historical reasons why the colonial world, in general, and the
Netherlands Indies, in particular, have been places where the uneasy relationship between sovereignty and audience is particularly evident. Europe's
fraught involvement in Asia, Africa, and the so-called New World began
at a time when the dependence of earthly rulers for their authority on the
most transcendent of audiences—God and the Church—was beginning
to give way to what we now recognize as the modes of legitimation char-
acteristic of liberal citizenship and governmentality. But like the urban
networks and legal institutions that emerged in the late medieval period,
the doctrines promoted by the Church, which claimed authority over
religious matters within canon law, served as discursive resources for territorial polities such as the French absolutist state (see, e.g., Sassen 2006).

Focusing on changes within these doctrines, John Milbank (1990) has
argued that a new understanding of God accompanied the new concep-
tualization of secular power. Hobbes (1986) modeled his Leviathan on a
deity whose most important trait was his overwhelming might, as opposed
to his charity (see also Engster 2001). Rather than gratitude for the gift
of life, the Lord demanded obedience, on the one hand, and foresight, on
the other. Self-preservation was not just a right; it was also a duty, given
this new vision of power. Individuals were morally obligated to be pru-
dent, sacrificing their capacity for violence to the sovereign, who would
help them fulfill their duty to strive to survive. The same terms were available for rearrangement in the doctrines of popular sovereignty that soon
emerged, which still approached sovereignty as a self-preserving—and
justifying—power. Public deliberation, under John Locke (1993, 1997),
appeared as the most suitable way in which humans could use their God-
given capacity for reason—that gift of the "Wise Contriver"—in the
interest of their own maintenance here on earth. As historians and cultural
analysts of the period when Locke was writing make clear, power came to
be vested in a new kind of figure viewed by some as an improvement over
Hobbes's Leviathan: the subject of public opinion, the purveyor of reasonable assertions addressed to an audience of equally reasonable men.

Imperial sovereignty was not simply an exception to this new regime but a factor in its emergence, as Nicholas Dirks (2006) has argued in a study of the public scandals that accompanied the birth of British colonialism in India. Dirks's narrative begins at a time when officers of the British East India Company were taking control of vast expanses of the subcontinent on the basis of agreements with Mughal rulers and their retainers, turning limited trading privileges into the basis for British control over taxes, commodities, and land. Critics and supporters of this enterprise contended with the challenge of justifying the empire's "supreme and absolute power" over "subjects" who were not and would never be "citizens": a native population whose language, religion, and sense of justice appeared to stand in sharp contrast to the officers' own.

The "white man's burden" eventually gave empire an alibi: the British had a responsibility to the subcontinent's inhabitants to save them (and their culture) from their corrupt, abusive Mughal rulers. But on the way to this outcome, critics of the company presented a vision of India in which the corrupt, abusive rulers were the company's British employees. Dirks focuses on the impeachment trial of Warren Hastings, the governor general who oversaw the consolidation of British rule in India. Prosecutors accused Hastings of driving one ruler to revolt, confiscating the landed income and treasures of another, receiving illicit presents, and wrongfully conducting a war (Dirks 2006, 100). In taking up the cause of Hastings's supposed Indian victims, Hastings's critics also laid the groundwork for a defense of empire as a noble endeavor. Among these critics was the philosopher and statesman Edmund Burke, who addressed parliament over the course of weeks to a sell-out crowd. Scandals play for audiences, and the tale that Dirks relates identifies the spectators that some subsequent officials may have imagined watching over their shoulders. Dirks does more than simply reveal the theatrical character of empire; he shows how the multiple audiences imagined to be evaluating the enterprise determined the form and rationale of British imperial rule.

Dutch colonialism in the Netherlands Indies featured its own share of scandals. During the nineteenth century, the novel *Max Havelaar* (Multatuli 1987 [1860]) provided a sordid picture of the corruption of colonial officials and their aristocratic native counterparts, including the residents and regents of the coffee growing districts of Java. Grisly accounts of Papuan violence reached the Dutch parliament at the turn of the twentieth century, leading to a greater investment in the archipelago's administration and pacification. But Dirks's account of the role of scandal in the birth of the British Empire offers more than a ready comparison for the scholar of Dutch colonialism; Dirks's study provides us with clues concerning the context in which this history unfolded. Much like the British, company officers at once responded to and played up the threat of competition from other European powers in their efforts to secure a foothold in the sub-continent. Dutch East India Company officers in the Spice Islands, as the Moluccan Islands to the east of New Guinea were widely known, waged diplomatic and military battles to eliminate competition from the Spanish, Portuguese, British, and French (see Andaya 1993).

In 1811, following Napoleon's invasion of the Netherlands and subsequent defeat at Waterloo, the British took control of the Netherlands' holdings in Southeast Asia from the French before returning the colony to the Dutch in 1816. Although the Netherlands had once dominated the seas, these days were over in the nineteenth century; it was only under the protection of British sea power that the Netherlands was able to reap enormous profits from the Indies' so-called culture system, an arrangement of government monopolies aimed at the forced production of tea, sugar, cotton, and indigo on Java. The Netherlands was even more directly reliant on foreigners for the tax income earned later in the century from oil fields and rubber plantations operated by multinational corporations granted concessions in Sumatra and Borneo by the Indies government (see Stoler 1985). Dutch leaders sometimes seemed to labor under an inferiority complex of sorts, expressed in the adoption of policies and strategies distinct from those of their rivals. Unlike the English or French, the Dutch did not impose their own language upon the natives, preferring to rely on local vernaculars and the regional trade language, Malay, for use in schools, courts, and government offices. Representatives of an increasingly minor European power, Dutch colonial leaders nonetheless prided themselves on their colony's skillful management (see Gouda 1993, 1995). Dutch universities offered carefully crafted training programs in an effort to ensure that Dutch officials knew their natives' languages and customs better than their European rivals knew those of theirs.

Given the Netherlands' place in Europe, there are obvious reasons why the specter of outside scrutiny loomed large. But the specter of inside scrutiny—from the natives for whose benefit they supposedly ruled—also came to haunt Dutch officials as the scale of the colonial enterprise grew. Scholars who have analyzed the impetus behind the transformations that swept the Indies at the turn of the twentieth century have played up the importance of the emergence of new audiences for colonial rule. In 1913

Dutch forces finally managed to prevail in Aceh, on the western tip of Sumatra, where a war against the sultanate had dragged on for forty years. New resources became available to carry out what became known in the Netherlands as the "Ethical Policy": a set of colonial imperatives embraced under the assumption that it was only "ethical" for the Dutch to "repay" this land that had yielded such marvelous wealth (see Locher-Scholten 1981; Shiraishi 1990). The twentieth century saw the opening of schools, hospitals, and agricultural stations; the building of roads and railroads; an expansion in cash cropping; and, as we will see, increased involvement in more remote corners of the colony. Certainly, policy makers felt pressure to emulate the deeds of colonizers elsewhere, but changes in the composition of Europeans in the Indies also played an important role in the Indies' modernization. The opening of the Suez Canal and the dropping of restrictions limiting the number of European women allowed to immigrate to the Indies brought demographic changes to the Indies. Growing numbers of "pure-blooded" European men and their wives came to the Indies to work, displacing an older community made up of the mixed-race progeny of Dutch officers and their native or mixed-race wives (see Taylor 1984; Stoler 2009).

Better communications and transportation exposed these new Europeans to the limits of their understanding of the native worlds through which they passed. Ann Stoler (1995, 2009) and Elsbeth Locher-Scholten (1998) have described the concerns surrounding native servants that emerged at this time. Policies designed to reform European child care represented a response to the anxieties these intimate strangers provoked. Not unlike Orwell's narrator, Europeans in the Indies responded to the sense that the natives were watching them by seeking ways of confirming the Netherlands' "supreme and absolute power." Confirming this power entailed not only brutal acts of violence but also the cultivation of new forms of discipline and surveillance designed to bring the natives "from darkness into light."

The uneasy relationship between sovereignty and audience figures prominently in the stories historians have told of the Indies' modernization. It also figures in accounts of the rise of mass politics and the birth of Indonesian nationalism. In the early twentieth century, improved communications and transportation stimulated the growth of the vernacular press. Alongside serialized versions of traditional tales, the newspapers featured translations of writings from outside the Indies: works from authors ranging from modernist Muslims to Marx. James Siegel (1997) has

written of how native readers and writers overheard these global conversations and came to imagine themselves as possessing a power to "pass" for
someone new. Journalists and novelists were among the earliest leaders of
mass organizations during what Takashi Shiraishi (1990) has called an "age
in motion." For Siegel, Indonesian nationalism, which emerged in the aftermath of this period, represented a closing down of possibilities. The unsettling sensation that they were being addressed from afar led "natives" to
see themselves in new and unfamiliar ways. They overheard others' conversations—on colonialism, on nationalism, on religion, on class—and
imagined themselves participating in the debate. Indonesian nationalism
domesticated this sensation: the surprising new identity now appeared as
Indonesian, with national authorities recognizing a nationalized self.
Indonesian-ness was the unexpected essence that participants in the
movement discovered within themselves. Intimations of possibilities that
exceeded this new identity became harbingers of treason in the eyes of nationalist leaders and fellow citizens of the emergent nation-state. One was
national or one was doomed. In the writings Siegel analyzes, the discovery of
something hitherto unrecognized within the self could spell death—a death
that acted within one, a death that one's foreignness could attract.

Siegel (1998) has carried this analysis forward into the postcolonial period, focusing in particular on the years of New Order rule. On the one
hand, Suharto's authoritarian regime, which maintained a tight grip on
political power and the spoils of foreign investment, was the source of
recognition for Indonesian citizens. Seeing oneself from the perspective of
this powerful center became a way of protecting not only one's identity but
also one's ability to make a living and move up the social ranks. The force
of popular militancy, once embodied in Indonesia's revolutionary masses,
reappeared in the figure of the criminal, whose lethal power was "nationalized" by the regime (Siegel 1998; see also Barker 1991, 2001). According
to Siegel, the witch killings that followed Suharto's resignation in some
parts of Java and, arguably, the ethnic and religious violence that swept
other parts of the archipelago, occurred in reaction to the dissolution of
the center from which recognition and patronage once flowed (see Siegel
2006; see also Sidel 2006). The fall of the New Order created new opportunities for political mobilization and also a new sense of threat. Whereas
at one period in Indonesian history the proliferation of audiences gave
rise to a sense of pleasure, power, and possibility, now the loss of a stable
identity led some Indonesians to fear possession by a lethal form of otherness. Persecuting others became a way of suppressing the thought that one
might be the target of a witch—or even a witch oneself.

Siegel's discussion enables us to see how processes of recognition figure into the dispersal of sovereignty that becomes apparent when we consider Indonesia through Agamben's lens. Siegel portrays the excessiveness of the gift, the shock of the accident, and the surprise of foreign utterances as forces that are both within and beyond the law. The target of sovereign violence is not defined by what Agamben calls the "mere fact of living"; on the contrary, the victim is a spectral figure through which people seek to control experiences that cannot be captured in categories ready to hand. For Siegel, audiences are never simply given. In more or less evident ways, they are also conjured in response to unexpected events. The notion that such an event is a communication from somewhere—and someone—can enable its recipient to find his or her footing. To be recognized by a determined other is momentarily to feel secure in one's sense of oneself. This feeling of security quickly gives way to aggression among those who envision sovereignty as entailing a supreme and absolute power over citizens and subjects. In the quest for this supreme and absolute power over others, the sovereign must supersede observing audiences, such as that represented by the witch.

But as we will see, not all those who seek sovereignty react defensively to communications from afar. As my essays make clear, some people enjoy the sense that they are being seen in new ways. The audiences they imagine doing the seeing might include global powers. They might also include the most intimately local of interlocutors. Papuans have had reasons to experiment with both options, given their distinctive history and the racism they have long confronted. As audiences proliferate, those who feel compelled to see themselves from the derogatory viewpoint of Jakarta can switch perspectives and identify with the "international community" of nation-states and extranational institutions that have often stood in judgment of Indonesia. They also can switch perspectives and identify with friends and neighbors for whom their encounters with outsiders serve as a source of prestige. Like the history of the Netherlands Indies, the history of western New Guinea provides examples of the threat audiences can pose. But it also provides examples of the power, pleasure, and authority an encounter with potential spectators can bring.

Into West Papua

The essays that make up this book appear in roughly chronological order, yet none of them is limited in focus to a particular period in the past.

Rather, they are palimpsests: each tracks between historical moments, showing how a longer view of the territory's colonial experience casts light on predicaments faced by Papuans today. There are obvious ways in which Dutch colonialism set the stage for contemporary struggles for sovereignty in West Papua, as these essays and most studies of the conflict make clear.

Western New Guinea, the story goes, was only nominally part of the Netherlands Indies; Dutch intervention was limited to the coast throughout the nineteenth century (see Ellen 1986; Fraassen 1987; Andaya 1993; Vlasbloom 2004). It was not until 1898, well after Germany and Britain had gained a foothold on the eastern half of New Guinea, that the Dutch established a permanent post in the territory close to the mission station where Protestant Pietists from Germany and the Netherlands had been working since 1855. The first expedition to the interior occurred in the early 1900s; Biak, the coastal island where I have conducted much of my research, was not pacified until 1916. The Dutch had only just discovered the large population centers in the central highlands in the Baliem Valley and what were then called the Wissel Lakes when World War II broke out (see Vlasbloom 2004; Rutherford 2009). In the late 1930s, multinational corporations had just begun drilling for oil, and there were only the faintest indications of the massive reserves of copper and gold later exploited by New Orleans–based Freeport McMoran (see Leith 2003). A deposit discovered in 1936 on Ertsberg Mountain would later give West Papua a gross domestic product higher than that of many Asian nation states. Japan occupied all of western New Guinea except the southern town of Merauke from 1942 to 1944, when Allied forces led by MacArthur retook the island.

As I have mentioned, in 1945, on densely populated Java, in the colony's center, Indonesian nationalist leaders began a revolution that prevented the Dutch from returning (see Kahin 1952; Kahin 1985). In New Guinea and other parts of what the Dutch called the Great East, the Allies transferred power to a civilian administration headed by the Dutch. At the end of several years of fierce fighting and negotiating, the Dutch transferred sovereignty in 1949 to the United States of Indonesia, a federal polity that immediately morphed into the Unitary Republic of Indonesia. But the Dutch managed to exclude New Guinea from the agreement reached during the so-called Round Table talks, in which the United States, the United Nations, and Australia all had a hand. The giant territory's status was to be decided in negotiations to be held the following year. In the event, it was fourteen years before the Dutch and the Indonesians reached an agreement on the question. The "liberation" of West Irian, as Indonesian leaders dubbed the disputed territory, was a cause célèbre under Indonesia's first president, Sukarno (see Osborne 1985; Lijphart 1966; Chauvel and Nusa Bhakti 2004; King 2004; Fernandes 2006; Singh 2008). Arguably, western New Guinea's inclusion in the republic was key to Indonesian leaders' vision of Indonesia as a nation-state that transcended religion, race, ethnicity, and class. Toward this end Sukarno organized mass rallies and clandestine military operations and nationalized Dutch industries. Indonesian nationalism coalesced as a mass phenomenon in part around the goal of "freeing" the so-called Irianese from Dutch chains.

Just why the Dutch felt compelled to cling to this remote underdeveloped territory, whose natural riches were far from evident at the time, is a mystery addressed in the following essays. As I explain in chapter 3, the Dutch political scientist Arend Lijphart (1966) described New Guinea as a "fetish" replacing the enormous Asian colony the Dutch had just lost. My own explanation will focus on chronic concerns about sovereignty and audience that dogged Dutch colonials in this neglected land. For now, suffice to say that the Dutch experiment in Netherlands New Guinea during the 1950s did more than just provide a stimulant for Indonesian nationalism; it provided a context in which Papuan nationalism could emerge (see Drooglever 2005; Chauvel 2005). Dutch officials cultivated a tiny elite of educated Papuans to serve in the new colony's civil service. One of the initial rationales for keeping New Guinea harked back to a prewar campaign to designate the territory as a homeland for displaced Europeans, who would be given land and encouraged to farm. Some promoters of the scheme targeted Nazi sympathizers as potential settlers, but more had in mind the mixed-race Dutchmen then fleeing the Indies, whom some in the Netherlands were eager to keep from settling in the Netherlands itself. A tiny community of European agriculturalists eked out a living in New Guinea. As the decade wore on, though, concern over the Indo-Europeans' future faded, replaced by an insistence on the Netherlands' responsibility to prepare Papuans to govern their own sovereign state. On the one hand, like other "dependent" natives, Papuans had the right to self-determination. Yet on the other hand, their "primitive" condition militated against too quick a transition to self-rule.

Indonesia protested against the Dutch occupation of West Irian to the United Nations, and then threatened to invade. Fearing the growth of Soviet influence in Jakarta, the United States brokered a deal known as the

New York Agreement, which Indonesia and the Netherlands signed at
the United Nations on August 15, 1962, opening the way to the territory's transfer to the United Nations, then Indonesian control (see Saltford
2002; Drooglever 2009, 312). The United Nations Temporary Executive
Authority, which administered western New Guinea from October 1,
1962 to May 31, 1963, was the first transitional government under United
Nations supervision ever created in an experiment in extranational sovereignty that is arguably the ancestor of peace-keeping missions later
undertaken elsewhere in the world. Despite the fact that a plethora of
Papuan political leaders had emerged by this time, none—not even those
most loyal to the Dutch—were party to the negotiations that led to the
New York Agreement. The Dutch carefully watched Papuan leaders sympathetic to the Indonesian position on the conflict, some of whom landed
in jail. As historian Richard Chauvel (2005, x) has noted, there was more
support among educated Papuans for integration into Indonesia in the
early 1960s than there is today. The Dutch had allowed the newly formed
multiracial New Guinea Council to choose a flag and anthem for the West
Papuan nation to be in 1961; now the Netherlands withdrew support from
the nationalist cause. Gone too, following the transfer, were the subsidies
that had allowed for a relatively high standard of living for Papuan civil
servants. Their Indonesian counterparts, coming from a country facing
massive inflation, replaced Dutch, Indo-European, and high-ranking Papuans in the administration and reaped a windfall during the transition.
The Indonesian authorities ransacked New Guinea's infrastructure and
jailed Papuans who spoke out against the new regime.

In 1965, the same year as the anti-Communist massacres that brought
President Suharto into power, an armed organization, the Organisasi
Papua Merdeka (Free Papua Organization, OPM), was born after a group
of Dutch-trained Papuan soldiers broke into an Indonesian barracks
and stole some weapons, thus beginning a campaign of uprisings against
Indonesian rule (see Osborne 1985; Djopari 1993). The OPM's actions
prompted massive retaliation from the Indonesian military, but the rebellion could not change the outcome of the so-called Act of Free Choice,
the "act of self-determination" mandated in the New York Agreement,
which was to be carried out in 1969 by Indonesia with the United Nations' support (see Drooglever 2009, 500–501). In the event, a skeletal staff
of United Nations monitors was on hand for the act, which determined
whether western New Guinea would become an independent nation-state
or remain part of Indonesia (see Saltford 2002). The act took the form of

an Indonesian-style "consultation" (*musyarawah*), in which 1,022 hand-picked and carefully supervised Papuan leaders unanimously agreed that their homeland should remain part of Indonesia. The OPM responded to Indonesian rule with attacks on military outposts in the highlands and hinterlands, occasional outbursts of urban protest, and vociferous international lobbying in Australia and Europe as well as the Pacific and, in the 1970s, the newly independent nations of West Africa. Thus the Papuan nationalist movement survived, albeit often in fragments, throughout the long years of Suharto's reign.

The period when Suharto's New Order was in power saw a series of formative developments in West Papua (see Leith 2003; McGibbon 2004b; Chauvel 1998; Chauvel and Nusa Bhakti 2004; Butt 2005). These included the 1967 signing of the Memorandum of Understanding that launched Freeport McMoran's profitable mining operations in Tembagapura, which leveled one mountain before starting on another while destroying local communities and poisoning their rivers and streams; Papuan participation in the 1971 national elections, held in contrast to the Act of Free Choice according to the principle one man, one vote, an irony not lost on Papuan activists who recalled being told that the Papuans had been too primitive to participate in such a process just two years before; and a cultural revival led by Arnold Ap, a Biak anthropologist, and other Papuan intellectuals during the 1980s, which culminated in an uprising in 1984 in the province's capital, Jayapura, and a crackdown that cost Ap his life and led hundreds of Papuans to flee to nearby Papua New Guinea. They also included the flow of government-sponsored transmigrants from Java and Bali into the province, where they competed with Papuan farmers for land and a share of the market, and a flood of spontaneous transmigrants from Sulawesi, who dominated the economy in the province's towns; and increasing interest in the province from investors and speculators in Jakarta, Tokyo, and Seoul, who financed the building of factories and luxury hotels.

By the early 1990s, as I was told during my fieldwork on Biak, official policy had shifted from the "security" to the "prosperity" approach as Indonesian leaders grew more confident that the benefits of development were leading the Papuans to accept their status as Indonesians. But that didn't keep concerns about sovereignty from simmering under the surface. When land disputes broke out between Papuan villagers and Javanese or Sulawesian entrepreneurs; when Biak friends complained yet again about the mail service or the poor quality of Indonesian films, newspapers, and consumer goods; when they told yet another tale of the poor treatment

that a Papuan had received at the hands of Indonesian businessmen, bureaucrats, or soldiers, they tacitly spoke to a lingering question: who rightfully should be ruling this land?

The essays in this book reveal that this question of who should be ruling
West Papua is far from new. The reactions that it sparked in the past have
set the scene for the struggle for sovereignty today. When in May 1998,
President Suharto resigned and the New Order fell, elite Papuans who had
been trained under Indonesian rule and seemed to accept Indonesian sovereignty, suddenly came out in favor of Papuan independence—or, at the
very least, the holding of a referendum in which the Papuans could decide
their own future (see King 2004; see also Kirksey 2012). This development
seemed surprising to some observers, but it reflected the degree to which
the question of sovereignty remained open among Papuans, even those
with a personal interest in accepting Indonesian rule. History came explicitly to the fore in the post-1998 efflorescence of Papuan nationalism, led by
officials and activists who had seemingly prospered under the Indonesian
system. "Let's Rectify the Past" was the slogan for the movement's major
public gathering in May and June 2000. Papuan leaders have banked on
recent research that has criticized the United Nations' handling of the Act
of Free Choice to build international support for the West Papuan cause.
As my essays show, this may be a laudable strategy, but the current dispute
is also the legacy of a longer and even more twisted history, suffused with
its own anxieties and hopes.

Concerns regarding sovereignty have long taken the form of concerns
regarding audience in West Papua, for reasons that my essays explore.
Some of my essays focus on explicitly political projects: colonial state-
building, postcolonial nation-building, the moral justification of empire,
and the assertion of the right to self-determination. Others focus on missionization and the dynamics of Christian institutions in an effort to trace
connections among the interplay of audiences, ideas of language, and
ideas of God. There is a direct connection between these sets of topics.
West Papua is a place where discussions of sovereignty have long spilled
over from the political to the theological. This spillover is not surprising
if we accept Siegel's suggestion that people often conjure audiences in response to provocations that come from a place they cannot name. Dutch
New Guinea was a colonial contact zone filled with such provocations for
officials, missionaries, and natives alike. Missionaries were not the only
ones to claim that God was watching. In Papuan nationalist performances
and texts, divine spectators have rubbed shoulders with other specters,

from the international community to the Papuan masses who would exercise popular sovereignty should a referendum ever occur. By attending to the relationship among these specters, my essays shed light on a central dimension of the contemporary struggle in West Papua. They offer reasons why sacred images, narratives, and institutions have placed such a central role in Papuan nationalism, from its birth to the present day.

This book divides into two halves. The first half, "Geographies of Sovereignty," contains essays that map West Papua's changing political landscape, introducing the audiences, near and far, human and divine, appealed to through performances of sovereignty in the territory. "Laughing at Leviathan" builds on the work of the colonial critic and historian John Furnivall to analyze the place of the comic in the colonial, while showing how the concerns that fueled the expansion of Dutch rule in New Guinea at the end of the nineteenth century also fueled the Netherlands' retention of the territory after World War II. "Trekking to New Guinea" relates how mixed-race European political organizations and their right-wing supporters in the Netherlands promoted the idea of turning New Guinea into a homeland for mixed-race colonials and the Netherlands' urban poor. I trace the origins of this idea to the challenges facing the so-called Indo-European, a term that designates a language family in other settings but was broadly used for these hybrid colonial subjects in the 1920s and 1930s. Here multiple audiences again make an appearance: from the Papuan locals from whom the scheme's organizers sought to shield the would-be colonists to the pure-blooded Dutch newcomers who acted as the colony's new arbiters of European prestige. Again, an episode from a more distant past sheds light on a more proximate puzzle. How did Dutch policy makers come to envision New Guinea as a setting suitable for a separate administration—as a place in the Indies where Dutch sovereignty could continue unabated, even as it crumbled in the revolution through which the Indonesian Republic was born?

"Waiting for the End in Biak" surveys the contemporary political landscape in which today's Papuan nationalists are operating. This essay examines the relationship between violence and performance in the pursuit of sovereignty on the island where I did my dissertation fieldwork, revealing the two visions of politics that came into play during the aforementioned flag-raising demonstration of July 1998. In this chapter, I revisit the myth of Manarmakeri and the Koreri movement, which I have treated extensively in previous work, to provide a picture of a utopian viewpoint that broadens our understanding of the uneasy relationship between sovereignty and audience. I offer a glimpse of what some Biaks envision as the event of sovereignty's emergence: the conjuring of a supreme and absolute power manifested not through the taking of life but through a violent act of re-framing. However, I present this viewpoint as in tension not with a West-ern ideal type, but with a particularly Indonesian understanding of state authority, which turns violence to ends unlike those sought either by Biaks or by European thinkers. The past relates to the present in this essay, but the present is my focus: I seek to make sense of what Biaks were after when they raised the flag.

The second half of the book, "Signs of Sovereignty in Motion," delves more deeply than the first into the semiotic processes involved in the conjuring of audiences in West Papua. "Frontiers of the Lingua Franca" examines the linguistic policies and practices of the missionaries who set-tled in New Guinea in 1855. In an attempt to offer a new way of thinking about Malay, the administrative and trade language that was a precursor to the national language of Indonesia, I mobilize a concept from linguistic anthropology, "bivalence," which captures the capacity of multiple audi-ences to haunt an utterance that speakers recognize as belonging to more than one language at once. Focusing on the role of ideas about the lingua franca in the attempted conversion of "Noefoorsch"-speaking Papuans, my analysis makes sense of the linguistic vision of some Papuan national-ists in the early 2000s. They foresaw their nation as adopting three national languages out of the 250 spoken in Papua—"Malay Papuan," the heir to Malay; Tok Pisin, Papua New Guinea's national language; and English, the so-called language of global communication—each of which points to a different audience and a different dimension of what leaders depicted as the West Papuan national self.

"Institutional Power and Interpretive Practice," like "Frontiers of the Lingua Franca," reveals the lasting impact of Christian ideas and in-stitutions on political activism in West Papua. In this chapter, I am less concerned with concrete utterances than with the concrete interactions through which institutions and ideas about them are made. On the face of it, this essay engages in a dialogue with Talal Asad (1993) and others who have presented institutional power as determining interpretive practice. I add to this discussion by showing how interpretive practice can shape how people conceptualize and deploy institutional power. The uneasy relation-ship between sovereignty and audience may not seem to loom as large in this essay as in some of the others. Yet the force of imagined spectators re-mains palpable for the people I describe. An institution consists not only of technologies, buildings, and personnel, but also chains of command, held together by the flow of wages and a circulation of gazes given force by presumptions concerning where the true sources of authority lie.

In the penultimate chapter, "Third Person Nationalism," the implications of the Stone Age stereotype of New Guinea described in "Trekking to New Guinea" become evident. Of all the essays, this one most explicitly takes up the uneasy relationship between sovereignty and audience, arguing that extranational audiences have played a central role in nationalist projects not just in West Papua but also throughout the world. Like "Trekking to New Guinea," the bulk of this chapter consists of a close reading of documents. But here I focus on a different kind of text: *Why Papua Wants Freedom*, a video compact disc produced by the Papuan Presidium Council, a new nationalist organization that gained prominence in the post-Suharto period. Whereas "Trekking to New Guinea" examines how concerns over purity shaped New Guinea's future, "Third Person Nationalism" examines what Papuan activists gain by blurring the line between filmic points of view. My analysis provides an enlarged sense of the repertoire of semiotic practices through which audiences come into view. The final essay, "The Appeal of Slippery Pronouns," extends my analysis of the conjuring of audiences to the Internet while speculating on the insights my approach could provide into recent political developments in the United States. The *semangat*, or "spirit," that Papuans say they feel when they image outsiders witnessing and joining in their struggle accounts in part for how Papuan nationalism has survived and even thrived in a territory that Indonesia seems unlikely to relinquish anytime soon. A similar passion may well have contributed to Barack Obama's electoral victory following a campaign that mobilized its own slippery "we."

Political theory and philosophy have something to say about the uneasy relationship between sovereignty and audience. But in some respects, ethnography and works of fiction, like Orwell's short story, capture this relationship best. Ethnographers—and those who study history in an ethnographic vein—must by the very nature of their practice develop what the philosopher Ted Cohen calls "the talent for metaphor" (2009). Like all those who engage in social relationships, both ethnographers and fiction writers must be able to engage in the imaginative play of thoughts and passions that allow people to put themselves in another's place. West Papua presents itself as a unique case—even a limiting case—in these essays. But my findings have comparative implications. Sovereignty can be thought of as entailing pleasure as well as constraint; audiences can be

imagined as a source of hope and possibility as well as threat. It is tempting to project the assumptions underlying Western notions of sovereignty
onto others. But not everyone limits their understanding of sovereignty to
"supreme and absolute power over citizens and subjects." Not everyone
is afraid to be observed. Not everyone minds that unnerving sensation of
feeling drawn to see oneself through new eyes.

PART ONE

Geographies of Sovereignty

CHAPTER TWO

Laughing at Leviathan

One step above the sublime, makes the ridiculous. — Thomas Paine, 1795

Strictly speaking, we do not know what we are laughing about. — Sigmund Freud, 1960

Colonialism has rarely been called "ridiculous." Exploitative, yes; violent, of course; but rarely has it been presented as the butt of a joke. Yet if we believe John Furnivall, George Orwell's contemporary who also served in Burma, every study of the spread of colonial rule should bring precisely this quality to light. Furnivall begins *The Fashioning of Leviathan*, his 1939 study of the first decades of British colonialism in Burma, by reflecting upon why so little has been written about the birth of empires. Even Hobbes avoided the topic. Hobbes referred to "that great *Leviathan* called a Commonwealth or State" as "but an Artificial Man" (Furnivall 1939, 3). But when it came to describing Leviathan's birth, Hobbes recast the creature as a "Mortall God" and described the event in mythical terms.

> Hobbes is driven to myth, because Leviathan has this at least in common with the immortal gods that we know little or nothing of his childhood. This is not strange; for no god is quite immune to ridicule, and children cannot help being ridiculous at times: if Aphrodite had caught cold, when rising from the foam on her first birthday, she was already big enough to use her pocket-handkerchief without being told to do so by her nurse. A god must feel secure in his divinity to let himself be laughed at, and Leviathan is not sufficiently at home in heaven to allow it. (Furnivall 1939, 3)

John Furnivall understood very well the inherently ridiculous nature of the colonial state on the frontiers of empire. *The Fashioning of Leviathan*

is a comic masterpiece as well as an insightful foray into the violent underpinnings of modern colonial power. In this chapter I relate these two
aspects of Furnivall's study, showing how laughter and insight go hand
in hand. I apply the lessons implicit in Furnivall's humor to the imperial
frontier that long persisted in West Papua when it was known as Dutch
New Guinea and formed the easternmost hinterlands of the Netherlands
Indies. I show how phenomena that some might call "mestizo"—but
that Furnivall called "ridiculous"—were an unintended effect of colonial
intervention—and an incitement to bring the territory under greater
control.

My argument takes Furnivall at his word: I approach the comedy that
pervades *The Fashioning of Leviathan* as a means of diagnosing a central
feature of colonial practice. In excavating the ridiculous from the archives
of British imperialism, Furnivall does more than make fun of colonialism;
he reveals an aspect of the colonial situation that both dogged the apparatus and stimulated its growth. As such, Furnivall's method enables us to
build on the findings of more recent scholars who have called into question conventional explanations of European imperialism.

Consider Elsbeth Locher-Scholten's analysis of Dutch efforts to consolidate colonial rule within the Netherlands Indies' boundaries at the turn
of the twentieth century. This endeavor did not in any simple sense result
from the "economic interests of the metropole," "international competition," or the need to create a "diversion from internal problems" (Locher-
Scholten 1994, 93). At the same time, its impetus did not come from the
"periphery"—that is, the colony—alone. A new set of global imperatives, including "the expanding demands of economic privileges (tariffs
and mineral exploitation) and the task of the modern western state to
provide for the safety of European entrepreneurs, missionaries, and civil
servants," created the context for colonial expansion (Locher-Scholten
1994, 111). Paying heed to the interests and anxieties of the colonial administrators who called for increased intervention in areas under their jurisdiction, Locher-Scholten shows how a concern for "the prestige of our
nation among foreigners" in this increasingly fraught setting was a key factor in the launching of "pacification" campaigns. These campaigns began
when local officials felt that their authority had been called into question,
generally through the resistance of indigenous rulers to official incursions.
"Ethical imperialism," as Locher-Scholten dubs the phenomenon, giving
new meaning to a favorite Dutch watchword of the time, had enormous
effects. Twentieth-century state formation "resulted in foreign domina-

tion in many details of personal life, a process of westernization which in turn led to the forceful reaction of nationalism and at last to Indonesian national independence" (Locher-Scholten 1994, 111). Yet the potential for laughter lay at its origins. The intervention of local officials sparked a reaction that led Dutch authorities to worry about their regime's reputation in the eyes of the natives, no doubt, but also from the perspective of a global audience. "Ethical imperialism" began, in other words, with officialdom's fear of appearing as ridiculous: the opposite, one might argue, of having prestige.

Dutch New Guinea is a particularly good place to explore what we might learn from laughing at Leviathan. The history of this long forsaken corner of the colonial world can teach us how the conjuring of a particular kind of audience—an audience that laughs—can lead to concrete measures designed to tighten an empire's grip. Above I repeated part of Locher-Scholten's citation of an 1892 statement from the head of civil administration in Batavia. The full sentence reads: "The prestige of our nation among foreigners does not allow us to leave the population of Irian Jaya [that is, West Papua, then known as New Guinea or Dutch New Guinea, as I call it here] in their miserable and depraved condition" (Locher-Scholten 1994, 107; see also Bestuur 1897). From a distance, it was easy to blame the irregularities of colonial practice in New Guinea on the "depravity" of its Papuan inhabitants. Up close, in the North Moluccan town of Ternate, where officials responsible for administering the territory in the nineteenth century were based, intervention in New Guinea brought to the foreground vicissitudes that every colonial project to some degree shares. Called upon to create an impression of colonial sovereignty, at the lowest possible cost, these officials dreaded that others would discover the absurd nature of their claims. In the conclusion, I reflect on the implications of this aspect of West Papua's colonial history for the Netherlands' postwar decision to retain the territory as a separate colony when the rest of the Indies gained independence. The ridiculous, and the interplay among perspectives that gave rise to it, were directly implicated in the quest for sovereignty in Dutch New Guinea. In examining the effects of this interplay among perspectives—this colonial "conversation of gestures," to recall Mead's (1965, 210) phrase—this chapter introduces some of the audiences that populated the political landscape in which the agents of Dutch colonialism operated in western New Guinea. But before turning to this history, let us first consider Furnivall's insights on the logic and limits of modern colonial power.

Hobbes in Burma

The Fashioning of Leviathan focuses on a species of "Mortall God" for which, as Furnivall notes, the "searching light of truth" was likely to be particularly "embarrassing" (1939, 3). The study provides a "step by step" account of "the incorporation in the Indian Empire of newly conquered territory; the building up of a local administrative organization; the gradual adjustment and adaptation of this local organization to the mechanism of the central government; and, finally, the assimilation of the new province within the general imperial system, so that it could no longer be distinguished from the rest of India except by such accidents of geography as its peoples and products" (Furnivall 1939, 3–4). Furnivall constructs this narrative on the basis of letters written between 1825 and 1843 by Mr. Maingy and Mr. Blondell, the first two commissioners of the occupied zone of Tenasserim, the earliest outpost of what later became British Burma. At the time the letters were written, Tenasserim's future was far from certain. This narrow belt of coastal forest, accessible only by boat, had been won from the Thai by King Alaungp'aya of Burma some fifty years before the British assumed control. Viewed from the metropole, the occupation was but one variable in the British attempt to determine what sort of presence in the region would serve the empire's interests best. The commissioners thus faced a challenge: to make the territory pay, they needed investment, to get investment, they needed a commitment from the empire, to get a commitment from the Empire, they needed to make the territory pay. They had to do all this while instituting a political order entirely different in form and ideology than the polity that had come before.

The magnitude of this task becomes clear when we compare Furnivall's portrayal of the first commissioner's arrival in Tenasserim with the following description of his Burmese predecessor's eighteenth century campaign to capture the south.

> [King Alaungp'aya's] initial power came from his army, a force unparalleled in recent times, and grew as he developed a more complete array of hegemonic devices, including symbolic regalia and the means to manipulate ethnic identity. The momentum of his victories and the legends that swept around the new king provided him with an aura of supernatural power. By chain letters and sponsored ballads, he sowed fear among the population ahead of his armies, thereby weakening the will of his opponents and creating massive defections. In promising release from slavery, he won over additional groups of men. (Steinberg 1987, 101)

Enter Mr. Maingy on September 9, 1825, with four clerks, three translators and a pair of servants. Shipwrecked on his first attempt, the new commissioner finally made it to the port town of Mergui and posted his own "chain letter," a flyer that proclaimed his intention to provide Mergui's inhabitants with a "civil and political administration on the most liberal and equitable principles."

> Rest assured that your wives and children shall be defended against all foreign and domestic enemies. That life and property shall enjoy every liberty and protection, and that your religion shall be respected and your Priests and religious edifices secured from every insult and injury. Proper measures shall immediately be adopted for administering justice to you according to your own established laws, so far as they do not militate against the principles of humanity and natural equity. In respect to revenue and all other subjects your own customs and local usages shall be taken into consideration, but the most free and unrestricted internal and external commerce will be established and promoted. (Furnivall 1939, 5–6)

The new commissioner closed by promising that at "all hours and places" "even the poorest inhabitants" would be welcome to see him "on business" (Furnivall 1939, 6). Mr. Maingy did keep an elephant and seemed to have a sense of personal dignity, but he was hardly the stuff of ballads. One can hardly imagine a greater contrast between the commissioner's sporting efforts to legitimate his rule and the majestic aura his predecessor maintained.

Mr. Maingy fashioned his Leviathan, in good Hobbesian style, "by Art according to the rules of common sense" (Furnivall 1939, 136). His goal was to create a secure and lawful environment in which "liberal principles" (and commerce) could thrive. In Furnivall's chapter headings, one finds the colonial state stripped down to its essentials: jails and policing, road building and revenue, foreign policy. But Furnivall was keenly attuned to the questions of audience that are central to this book. The concern that propels Furnivall's inquiry is not how the inhabitants of Tenasserim were incorporated into the British Empire, but how someone like Mr. Maingy could think himself capable of such a feat. The answer lies in the internal workings of the colonial bureaucracy. For Furnivall, the archive is not simply a record of colonial practice (see also Stoler 2009). The very existence of an archive implies that officials had a range of evaluating others in mind whenever they designed or implemented a policy or reported on what they had done.

As such, the archive was a key element in the apparatus of colonial rule. By basing his analysis solely on the commissioners' official correspondence, Furnivall establishes the degree to which this apparatus both sustained the two men's confidence and controlled their fate. Mr. Maingy's letters ended up in "the Secret and Political Department of the Government of India where, apparently they were regarded as so inviolably secret that for some years they were filed unread" (Furnivall 1939, 19). Mr. Blondell, by contrast, had to answer to bureaucrats in Calcutta who were beginning to develop an institutional memory with regard to Tenasserim. Furnivall registers the ebb and flow of bureaucratic supervision by populating the study with multiple "Leviathans." On the one hand, the reader is invited to witness Leviathan's birth on Burmese soil; on the other, Leviathan is always already present in the form of Calcutta's meddling hand in the region's affairs.

Although Furnivall associates "common sense" with the rationality of a system "geared for profit and productivity," Leviathan's guiding principles turns out to be equally multifarious. There is local common sense, residing in the commissioners' expeditious responses to Tenasserim's limitations and opportunities. There is common sense in Calcutta and presumably in England, serving different sets of utilitarian needs. What counts as common sense changes what counts as what Furnivall calls "human decency." As "Leviathan Indicus" assumes control of Tenasserim, those who fashioned the local system with a "velvet glove" become the human grit in the machine. This is why Mr. Blondell, who instituted the "compassionate" policy of taxing tribal communities at six times the going rate, can end the book as a "conservative" and "nationalist" (Furnivall 1939, 134). However ironically, Furnivall anticipates the well-established insight that nationalism is a product of the administrative pilgrimages offered by the colonial state (Anderson 1991, 53–56).

Make no mistake: however serious Furnivall's conclusions might be, *The Fashioning of Leviathan* is incredibly funny. There are two ways of accounting for this feature of the text. Furnivall's first career was as a colonial official, serving in the south of Burma, where the study was set. But in 1939, when *The Fashioning of Leviathan* was published, Furnivall was part way through his second career, as a bookstore owner with close ties to the Burmese nationalist movement. On the one hand, Furnivall deploys comedy for a classical purpose: to demean an exalted institution. *The Fashioning of Leviathan* anticipates themes from Furnivall's monumental studies of colonialism, *Netherlands India* and *Colonial Policy and Practice* (see Furnivall 1944, 1956). In these decidedly less humorous works,

Furnivall elaborates a critique of colonial society, calling it "plural," that is, inhabited by ethnic and racial groups that only meet in the market. In a population utterly lacking the "common will" that Furnivall viewed as integrating functioning democracies, the "survival of the cheapest" is the rule that prevails. In *The Fashioning of Leviathan*, Furnivall notes, in a similar vein, that colonialism's "common sense" is often at odds with the "claims of life" (Furnivall 1939, 136). Obliquely, by taking up Hobbes's moniker to describe the colonial state, Furnivall calls attention to what he regards such a regime as missing—the "sense in common" or "common will" that is arguably a key element of Hobbes's understanding of the basis and outcome of the social contract (see Tuck 1991b). For Furnivall, who views the precolonial order as one where people were "fast bound to honesty by the ties of social life," it is the colonial system that inaugurates a life that is "nasty, brutish and short" (Furnivall 1939, 45). It is from the perspective offered by a liberal understanding of popular sovereignty that Leviathan appears as the butt of a joke.

On the other hand, the study plays on a potential for comedy that is intrinsic to the materials Furnivall cites. Take, for instance, Furnivall's account of the importation of convict labor from the subcontinent.

The Commissioner recognized that the jails were not very secure. But they were not meant to be very secure. He regarded the convicts as so much cheap labour imported to make roads; if he had to spend money on housing the labourers he might as well employ more expensive local labour on the roads. But the people in India who supplied the convicts looked at matters in a different light; when they were asked to supply convicts for Tenasserim, they thought it a providential opportunity to get rid of their hard cases. At that time the Government of India was engaged on rooting out the thugs, that strange caste of professional murderers. So it happened that among one batch of convicts sent to labour on the roads there were twenty five who had been "guilty of Thuggee and Murder,—part of a desperate gang of Thugs which had lately been broken up in Central India" and "whose safe custody was an object of paramount importance." Nasty fellows to build roads with, these, or to keep in confinement in a wooden bungalow with a thatched roof. It was hardly playing the game to send convicts of that type to a well-meaning officer who had quite enough trouble in building up his own little corner of the Empire. Mr. Maingy protested vigorously, but in vain. He asked for convicts and kept on asking; Thugs were convicts, so they sent him Thugs, and kept on sending. It is not surprising then to read of murders by Thug convicts who "not only confessed the murder, but gloried in the act and vied with each other in shouldering the guilt." Even that did not convince the authorities in India that thugs should not be exported to Tenasserim. For, many years later, a young missionary, destined to become famous as an educational pioneer in Burma, was sent to the hospital in Moulmain, seriously ill. But he found the hospital more dangerous than his disease. Left alone under the charge of a convict hospital assistant, apparently quiet and well mannered, he was alarmed by a sudden change in the man's demeanour. All was quiet in the hospital, and the convict was performing the usual duties of a sick nurse, when suddenly a ferocious glare lighted up his eyes and he sprang at the sick man's throat. Fortunately, for lack of practice, his hands had lost their cunning, and the noise of the struggle attracted help; the assailant was overpowered and, presumably, discharged from his duties in the hospital. He was a thug, one of the men sent in the early days to labour on the roads, and after all these years his lust for murder was not yet quenched. The missionary lived to educate Prince Thibaw, and to see his pupil massacre his relatives on a scale that would have done credit to the most devout of thugs. Still, it was rather a slur on the medical profession to appoint a professional murderer as a hospital assistant. (Furnivall 1939, 37–38)

The judicial system provides fodder for similar stories. In an attempt to respect his native subjects' own sense of justice, Mr. Maingy appointed a jury of local notables to render decisions, which included sentencing a man accused of rape to be paraded through town with his face blackened, despite the fact that they had just acquitted him (Furnivall 1939, 19). Mr. Maingy found the courts to be quite efficient—no lawyers were allowed, so cases sailed quickly through the system—even though there was room for improvement. "There might have been even less crime, if people understood what the English regarded as offenses" (Furnivall 1939, 30). Furnivall does not relate these details solely to amuse his readers. Rather, in detailing the absurd outcome of decisions that must have seemed reasonable at the time, these anecdotes illustrate the forces that led to Calcutta's intrusion into local affairs. In more neutral terms, one could describe Mr. Maingy's "ridiculous" policies as an effect of the "mestizo" qualities of the situation in Tenasserim (see Taylor 1984). After all, Mr. Maingy did try to draw on Burmese "law and order" in establishing his regime. Still, in suggesting a smooth confection of ingredients, the term does not quite capture Mr. Maingy's predicament. Mr. Maingy was compelled to envision the world he created from the perspective of distant others who shared his commitment to "humanity" and "natural equity." Yet this world took shape through his interactions with colonial "subjects" who no doubt interpreted his behavior in very different terms.

This scenario, in which one comes to perceive a situation from multiple perspectives, all at once, is essential to the comic, if we can trust Freud's formulations. The comic, like jokes and humor, derives from the "economy of expenditure" that results when one contrasts what one witnesses to more proper or predictable ways of acting. In the difference between the energy it takes to meet conventional expectations and that exposed by the comic figure one observes emerges the "quota" that one "laughs off" (see Freud 1960, 149, 234). A common form of comedy takes as its object the "naive," a person who devotes more effort to physical activities (e.g., walking or gesturing in an exaggerated way) and less to mental activities (e.g., reasoning with little regard for logic) than the observer imagines him or herself expending in a similar situation. But another form, more relevant for our purposes, entails a process of degradation, through which an esteemed person or institution is put into a comic situation or frame.

One way to render such a person or institution ridiculous is to make them "tally with something familiar and inferior, on imagining which there is a complete absence of any expenditure upon abstraction" (Freud 1960, 210–11). Furnivall's comparison of that abstraction *par excellence*, the colonial state, to a runny-nosed child, a devouring monster, and an out-of-control machine certainly fits within Freud's formulations. But another and potentially more potent component of *The Fashioning of Leviathan*'s comic vision lies in the nature of the materials on which Furnivall drew. The writings of European colonial officials, like Mr. Maingy, provide a fertile field for the "Janus-faced" experience of the comic. Two audiences jostled for attention in the minds of such officials; the very structure of this situation created a toehold for Furnivall's mirth. On the one hand, these officials had to present their actions as meeting the standards of a colonial regime whose objectives were framed in terms of abstract values. On the other hand, they had to appeal to local interlocutors, to elicit, at the very least, a simulacrum of consent. The fact that officials sought this consent against the backdrop of the threat of force did not resolve the interpretive dilemma faced by the state's agents; if anything, it made it even more difficult to gauge when the "natives" were making a mockery of one's rule. Colonial encounters brought to the forefront what Freud describes as key sources of pleasure in "innocent" jokes, the "illogic" that comes into focus when different forms of rationality come into contact, a fixation on the "acoustic images" of alien words. No doubt, this potential pleasure would have been a source of discomfort for officers responsible for reforming native ways.

We can learn much from dissecting this conversation of gestures. In *The Fashioning of Leviathan*, Furnivall uses laughter not only as a weapon, but also as a lens to bring into focus aspects of the colonial situation that might otherwise have remained obscure. It is no accident that this work is comic, whereas *Netherlands India* and *Colonial Policy and Practice* are not. In fact, the earlier and the later works are not as similar as one might think. Whereas Furnivall's account of the "plural society" provides a portrait of what one might call the horizontal dimension of the colonial system—as epitomized in the market, where groups maintain their distance, even as they interact—*The Fashioning of Leviathan* focuses on the vertical dimension.[1] The colonial official, unlike the colonial capitalist, cannot take difference for granted, for what is at stake is the validation of inequality. As Homi Bhabha (1983, 18–36) and others have noted, modern colonial discourse is inherently unstable. The colonial project is justified by the racist presumption that the colonizers are inherently more civilized and rational than those they colonize. But it is also justified by a vision of progress in which this disjuncture, however gradually, is bridged. The ridiculous emerges at moments like those described in *The Fashioning of Leviathan*, when officials come face to face with the estrangement that is a necessary component of the civilizing mission. The colonial market, at least as Furnivall describes it, does not stimulate this kind of self-consciousness; even the power of currency to erode differences, so stressed by Marx (1967) and others, fails to threaten colonial boundaries (see also Simmel 1978; Bohannon 1955).

Furnivall was clearly mistaken in presuming the existence of ethnic and racial identities that were as much the outcome of colonial practice as its object. But his formulations do open an interesting angle on the complexities of colonial consciousness, which we'll return to in other essays in this book. To complicate matters even further, one could argue that the ridiculous arises when the "vertical" meets the "horizontal." On the one side, we have colonial officials anxiously seeking an indication of the "natives'" recognition of their authority. On the other side, we may well have "natives" using their interactions with the state's agents to appropriate something of value from across a linguistic and cultural divide.

Furnivall is not the only writer to have found comedy at the heart of state power (see, e.g., Žižek 1993, 146; Mbembe 2001, 133). But *The Fashioning of Leviathan* provides a distinctive perspective on the colonial situation. To arrive at this perspective, one must move beyond Furnivall's understated wit, which follows the conventions of a particular brand of

British humor, to scrutinize those aspects of colonial rule that provided this sensibility with such fertile ground.[2] Approached in this fashion, Furnivall's study demonstrates why it is possible to read colonial reports against the grain as more than simply an expression of metropolitan ideologies. In the fodder for ridicule that lurks in these reports, one finds evidence of a range of alternative points of view. This interpretation of Furnivall's study provides the grounds for examining one way in which the uneasy relationship between sovereignty and audience shaped colonial policy and practice in Dutch New Guinea, a part of the Netherlands Indies where Leviathan's "infancy" was extended. I do not presume that one can simply map Furnivall's insights onto Dutch New Guinea's history: merely that this history reflects the same constant, anxious confrontation of colonialism with the absurdity of its claims. The Dutch officials whom I consider were not simply embarrassed; they were sometimes humiliated, often quite angry, and, in one case, even suicidal at the difficulty of creating anything resembling effective colonial rule in this far off hinterland. The anecdotes that follow may not be as funny as those that Furnivall recounts, but they prove equally revealing. In coastal New Guinea, as in Tenasserim, colonial expansion turned on the fact that Leviathan just could not take a joke.

Abstinence and Display

Western New Guinea became part of the Netherlands Indies early in the nineteenth century.[3] In 1828 and 1848, one will recall, the Netherlands Indies government drafted secret documents asserting sovereignty over areas of western New Guinea supposedly ruled by the North Moluccan sultanate of Tidore, as well as regions directly controlled by the Dutch. These documents were kept secret for the simple reason that their publication would have exposed the unstable basis of Dutch claims (see Drooglever 2002, 23). The first document rested on the right of first occupancy in the form of a hastily established, then abandoned garrison in southwestern New Guinea. The second document rested on the arbitrary inflation of Tidore's sphere of influence to suit Dutch needs. Although there is no doubt that the Tidoran sultans sporadically received tribute from the "Papuan islands," Tidore's authority was most tangible in the Raja Ampats, in the waters west of the Bird's Head peninsula (see Andaya 1993). What's more, this authority did not date back much further than the period of European expansion. Archeologist Pamela Swadling has argued that Tidore's neighbor and rival, the north Moluccan sultanate of Bacan, had "real influence" in the Raja Ampats before 1660, when the Dutch made their first formal treaty with Tidore (1996, 109–10.) Yet the colonial government ultimately used Tidore's dealings in the region as the basis for its claim to New Guinea's entire western half, which was made public in 1865. The very same documents that extended Tidoran sovereignty over large portions of New Guinea included a mechanism for dissolving it: there was a clause in the various contracts that the Dutch had the Tidoran sultans sign stipulating that the Netherlands Indies government could assume direct governance of the region at any time (Swadling 1996, 119). If indirect rule always rested on more or less fictitious foundations, when it came to New Guinea, Dutch officials were acutely aware of the fragile underpinnings of their rights.

New Guinea was scarcely the only section of the colony where Dutch authority existed more or less only on paper. During the nineteenth century, before the period of "ethical imperialism" described by Locher-Scholten, the Indies government "abstained" from direct involvement in much of the so-called Outer Islands. For much of the century, the administration concentrated its interests and investment on the "inner island" of Java, which forced cultivation of sugar, indigo, and tea transformed into one of the most profitable pieces of colonial real estate in the world. Dutch activities in the outer islands were overshadowed by a long and costly war in Aceh, a polity at the northwestern tip of Sumatra near the strategic Malakka Straits (see Goor 1986). This policy of abstention had roots in an earlier period of conquest and trade, when Dutch merchants worked through existing kingdoms and sultanates to gain access to lucrative exports, from bird skins to aromatic bark. Jean Taylor (2003) has described how the Netherlands East India Company (Vereenigde Oost-Indische Compagnie, or VOC), which the Dutch state chartered in 1602, came to assert sovereignty over indigenous polities like Tidore. Initially, the "Company" was but one of an array of foreign allies whom the region's leaders made part of their retinue; others included south Indian holy men, Portuguese mercenaries, and Arab scribes. But by providing aid to participants in the wars that shook Java during the seventeenth and eighteenth centuries, VOC leaders were able to negotiate agreements that were increasingly favorable to the Company. As Piet Drooglever (2004, 26) has pointed out, Hugo de Groot's principle of "equality between states" informed the VOC's dealings with local sultans, even if in practice the more powerful party set the terms of these relationships.

Later in the eighteenth century, the growth of British sea power and the erosion of the VOC's trading monopoly brought other principles into play. The VOC declared bankruptcy in 1799, leaving its assets and debts to the Dutch state. The British took control of Java, the Moluccas, and the Netherlands' other overseas territories when France occupied the Netherlands during the Napoleonic wars. In the conventions signed with the British in 1814 and 1824, the Dutch ceded territory in India, Ceylon, and mainland Southeast Asia in return for a consolidated colony in the Indies. The Dutch imposed a Napoleonic system of administration on newly recovered Java, dividing the island into sixty residencies overseen by Dutch officials appointed by the governor general (see Drooglever 2004, 25). Outside of Java, indigenous kings and sultans remained responsible for collecting taxes and maintaining order. The pursuit of sovereignty had long forced the Dutch to contend with multiple audiences: from the rulers who entered into agreements with the Company to the foreign competitors for whom such documents were intended to provide legal cover for Dutch profit-seeking. During the nineteenth century, new audiences turned their attention to the Indies, leading to a critique of native "despotism" and calls for more "ethical"—and intrusive—approaches to colonial rule. Officials in Batavia and The Hague reacted cautiously to outside scrutiny, as Drooglever notes. "Whenever an occasion for it arose, they took steps to make their claims clear to the outside world. They did this carefully, but purposefully" (Drooglever 2002, 26).

Within this wider context, what was peculiar about western New Guinea was not simply its size, not simply its isolation, but also the fact that it abutted the holdings of other colonial powers. This was also the case in Borneo, yet in New Guinea, the threat posed by foreign intervention—or even just foreign attention—seemed much more palpable. VOC leaders in Ternate regarded New Guinea as a buffer zone keeping foreign competitors from challenging their monopoly over the trade in cloves and nutmeg, which the Netherlands won through pitched battles against England, Portugal, and Spain (see Fraassen 1987; Andaya 1993). Their fears were realized at the end of the eighteenth century, when English and Papuan seafarers joined forces with a contender for the Tidoran throne, Prince Nuku, who invaded Tidore twice before seizing Ternate in a rebellion that only ended after the British replaced the Dutch (see Vlasboom 2004, 56).

The tangled history of Nuku's rebellion illuminates the different audiences involved in the pursuit of sovereignty in the region at the time—and the potential for ridicule generated by their juxtaposition. The uprising began when the Dutch resident of Ternate passed over Nuku when he appointed his brother, Prince Paku Alam, as the Sultan of Tidore. Nuku retreated to Patani, in eastern Halmahera, then the Raja Ampat islands, where he amassed a fleet manned by local Papuans as well as Papuan and Tidoran deserters from the Tidoran war fleet or *hongi*. The VOC official serving in Ternate reacted with vehemence—even paranoia, some might venture. First he deposed Paku Alam, whom he accused of supporting the rebellion. Then he declared direct Dutch rule. VOC leaders in the Company's headquarters in Batavia took issue with this strategy and appointed another of Nuku's brothers to the throne. Nuku was defeated, briefly retreated, then attacked Ternate again, this time with a fleet manned by nearly five thousand men, including the crews of two English ships from the Bengal East India Company (see Vlasboom 2004, 55). The Dutch had noticed other English ships scouting out the waters where Nuku and his Papuan supporters sailed. This time Nuku prevailed. When the VOC declared bankruptcy, he was occupying the Dutch post.

This was not the first such episode. A few years earlier, John Hayes of the Bengal East India Company had come to Doreh Bay, a popular trading stop on the eastern side of New Guinea's Bird's Head peninsula, with several other East India Company officers and a small contingent of Bengali soldiers (see Vlasboom 2004, 57). Apparently acting on their own authority, the men had built a walled compound, which they called Fort Coronation, and Hayes had declared himself the governor general of this colony-to-be, which he named New Albion. Compared to Nuku's rebellion, the Dutch made it through this crisis relatively intact. From Ternate and Batavia, Dutch officials sent letters of protest to the British government; luckily for them, poor health, hunger, and a devastating attack by local Papuans forced the English settlers to withdraw.

The inglorious final days of the VOC in Ternate would have remained fresh in the minds of nineteenth century officials and policy makers.[4] The Papuans they met no doubt called up old memories when they referred to the colonial government as "the Company," using a name also given to the VOC; up into the 1930s, Papuans in the highlands knew the Dutch colonial government by this name, no doubt having learned it from their brethren on the coast (see Rutherford 2009). Foreign visitors to New Guinea also called up old memories, with the Italian and Russian explorers penning lurid descriptions of kidnapping and slave trading in the 1870s, leading the government in The Hague "to fear the tarnishing of the international prestige of the Netherlands as a colonial power" (Campo 2002, 166). Then there were the British, whose opinions also weighed upon the Dutch.

Throughout the Indies, the Dutch had reasons to avoid antagonizing British leaders. The Pax Britannica imposed by the British navy enabled the Dutch to profit from the Indies without having to invest much in the colony's defense. In asserting Dutch sovereignty in New Guinea, Dutch officials leaned heavily on a British contract from 1814 that established Tidore's jurisdiction over the Papuan islands and four districts on the mainland associated with clans originating from Numfor Island. British leaders recognized the legitimacy of the Netherlands' right to the parts of New Guinea claimed by Tidore. But they viewed the rest of the island as up for grabs, although they agreed to inform their Dutch counterparts should they decide to establish settlements of their own. It was not until 1884 that Britain and Germany officially set the boundaries of their own colonies on the eastern half of the island. Throughout this period of uncertainty, there was little actual saber rattling, merely a vague anxiety on the part of the Dutch that outsiders might mistake the territory for unclaimed land.

During the nineteenth century, to assuage this fear, the government pursued what Smeele (1988) has called a policy of display. Through limited concrete measures, the Netherlands Indies government attempted to create the impression of colonial occupation in New Guinea. Fort du Bos, the garrison founded to buttress the secret document of 1828, proved short-lived; disease and attacks by hostile locals decimated the small settlement of Dutch and native soldiers. Undertaken in response to rumors that the British were contemplating establishing a similar post, the experiment was the last of its kind for years to come. Instead of establishing settlements, the Indies government dispatched war ships to erect and maintain escutcheons at intervals along New Guinea's coasts. Officers like the resident of Ternate, P. van der Crab, who toured the north coast aboard the *Dassoon* in 1871, set out "to investigate—and where necessary to confirm—the relations that exist there between the chiefs and the Sultan of Tidore" (Campo 2002, 163). Often accompanied by the Tidoran war fleet (Tidoran/Malay: *hongi*), the crews built or repaired bases for the metal shields, which were embossed with the Dutch coat-of-arms. Meanwhile, their commanders confirmed the appointment of local headmen, leaders who had received their Tidoran titles from various sources, ranging from the Sultan and his vassals, to European ship captains, to Papuan relatives and trade friends, who passed along such signs of investiture as gifts (see Ellen 1986). Each headman received a suit of clothing and a flag, which he was instructed to trot out whenever a foreign ship anchored near the village. The Dutchmen also distributed gifts of beads and knives to the natives, before loading up with food and water for the voyage to the next site.

Given its role in the regional slave trade, the Tidoran war fleet did little to ensure a warm welcome for the visitors. D. J. van Dungen Gronovius, a pensioned official, took on the task of investigating the extent of Tidoran influence along New Guinea's north coast in 1849. When van Dungen Gronovius's ship, the *Circe*, entered Doreh Bay in the company of the hongi, "women and children fled in all directions, taking with them anything of value, to escape the seafarers' lust for plunder" (Haga 1884 in Vlasboom 2004, 63). Jan van Eechoud, who served as resident of New Guinea after World War II, summed up the nineteenth century as "the time when our authority in New Guinea was established by nailing some iron escutcheons to trees, then for the most part rushing to find the boats to escape with life and limb" (Vlasboom 2004, 65).

Although the erection of escutcheons left sporadic evidence of Dutch sovereignty in the territory, it clearly did not solve what Dutch administrators referred to as the problem of peace and order—the government's failure to establish a monopoly over the legitimate use of violence. Given his responsibility for European security in New Guinea, the Dutch resident of Ternate was not pleased when two German missionaries associated with the well-known Dutch Pietist theologian, O. G. Heldring, approached him in the mid-1850s with plans to establish a post in Doreh Bay, a popular harbor on the northeastern tip of the Bird's Head (Kamma 1976, 50; see also chapter 5). Yet the resident soon found a use for the Protestant evangelists, who were well apprised of regional happenings, since they supported themselves by trading with the Papuans. The administration gave the "brothers" a monthly stipend for rescuing foreign shipwreck victims, whom the natives tended to kill. Eventually, the missionaries became a thorn in the government's side, with their grisly accounts of Papuan raiding and immorality, which usually ended with a plea for the administration to apply a firmer hand. In the meantime, by preventing the scandal that would have resulted from the death of foreign nationals, the missionaries helped keep the residents' superiors off their backs.

After the Berlin Conference of 1885, which made effective occupation a condition for the holding of colonial possessions, the stakes in New Guinea rose. As I noted in the beginning of this chapter, when in 1895 the Estates General in The Hague finally agreed to allocate funds for the placement of colonial administrators and police in New Guinea, lawmakers justified the measure not only in terms of the plight of the "deeply

sunken" population, but also of the Netherlands' reputation in the colonial world (see Locher-Scholten 1994, 107; see also Smeele 1988). This
was the decade when the government steamship line, the Koninklijk Paket
Maatschappij, or KPM, extended service to New Guinea. Greater access
to the Indies' farthest frontier only made the frailty of Dutch authority
more apparent to outsiders. In 1899, in a widely publicized incident, three
KPM passengers were "attacked, kidnapped, and probably killed" when
the crew of the *Generaal Pel* attempted to make contact with the inhabitants of Sileraka, a south coastal community not far from the British border (see Campo 2002, 175). In roughly the same area, attacks by Tugeri
tribesmen had led to complaints by the British, who had demanded that
the Dutch either control their Papuan subjects or move the border so that
the British could curb the raids themselves. In the north, spurred by a new
fashion in ladies' hats, a "feather boom" had brought scores of Malay,
Chinese, and European traders and hunters to New Guinea, where, with
their modern rifles, they had exacerbated the region's security problems
by starting a small arms race among the various tribes.

Between 1898 and 1901, the government founded permanent posts at
Manokwari, Fak-Fak, and Merauke. But the government's accomplishments never lived up to the expectations of optimistic observers, who
cherished hopes that New Guinea would not only cover the cost of its
own administration, but also actually turn a profit for the Dutch. Before
World War II, the Dutch divided the territory between two administrative
units: one based on Ternate and the other in the southern Moluccan city
of Ambon, with the exception of three years in the 1920s when the Dutch
took steps to turn New Guinea into a separate—and hence better subsi-
dized—administrative unit. The assistant resident posted in Manokwari,
the coastal town chosen as the new headquarters, committed suicide after
receiving news that the central government was aborting this experiment
(see Vlasboom 2004). Despite the introduction of a head tax and corvée
labor in limited parts of the territory, the Netherlands continued to follow
a policy of display, albeit by different means.

One could argue that the policy of display continued into the 1950s,
when the Netherlands retained this final fragment of the colony after the
rest of the Indies gained independence. The "Ethical Project" undertaken
earlier in the century in the Indies provided an administrative and philosophical model for the mission in post–World War II New Guinea (Baal
1989, 169; Drooglever 2009, 522–23). But the Dutch faced a very different international political landscape in this later period (see Drooglever
2009, 310–65). The founding of the United Nations created novel audiences

for Dutch politicians and diplomats to appeal to and contend with. The General Assembly was filled with delegates from the recently decolonized nations of Africa and Asia, who had little patience for the continuation of European imperialism and tended to sympathize with the Indonesian position in the dispute over "West Irian." The Security Council was somewhat less hostile to the Dutch, although the United States, which exercised veto power, was not inclined to support an old style civilizing mission in this new era, especially when it threatened its effort to win allies in the Cold War. Officially, Dutch New Guinea fell under the United Nations Charter as a non-self-governing territory. Throughout the 1950s, Dutch officials reported to a newly constituted 73E committee (named after the provision of the charter covering such territories), which issued yearly reports on the "quality of the administration" that was entrusted with western New Guinea (Drooglever 2009, 330). This arrangement appealed to Dutch diplomats since it "implied international recognition of continued Dutch sovereignty over the area" (Drooglever 2009, 330). But outside scrutiny did not always strengthen their sense of security. In addition to the view from United Nations headquarters, the Dutch had to contend with the view from Canberra, Jakarta, and, above all, Washington, where the Kennedy administration eventually called the Dutch adventure in New Guinea to a halt.

Given this political landscape, Dutch officials, diplomats, and ministers were keenly aware of the publicity value of initiatives undertaken to speed up the development of this "extremely backward" territory (Drooglever 2009, 330). But to understand the impetus behind the Netherlands' costly postwar project in New Guinea, one must attend to a prior series of colonial moments. To borrow Locher-Scholten's terms, the Dutch authorities were "pulled into the periphery" in coastal New Guinea not simply by the "resistance" of their Papuan subjects but also by the unexpected effects of their interventions. In the writings of officers charged with governing the territory, one detects a heightened awareness of the prospect of surveillance, not simply by their own superiors, not simply by other Europeans but also by the Papuans, who turned their encounters with authority to their own peculiar ends.

Encountering the Ridiculous

The best place to find the ridiculous in colonial documents concerning New Guinea is neither at the end nor at the beginning of an account.

Dutch officials who described their forays into the territory, not surprisingly, incorporated particular agendas into their reports. Naval lieutenant second class, G. F. de Bruyn Kops, wrote a chronicle detailing his experiences as the *Circe's* first officer during D. J. van Dungen Gronovius's 1849 expedition. Bruyn Kops wrote of the Papuans' "sweet, timid" nature, as part of a diatribe against the depredations of the Tidoran war fleet. "Under a civilized government, they would surely quickly attach themselves to the same and could demonstrate great service," Bruyn Kops concluded, in an effort to convince his superiors of the value of introducing direct Dutch rule. In 1888 the resident of Ternate, P. van der Crab, ended a description of a similar journey with harsh words on the Papuans' "disposition"—which was "in a word, bad"—to support his argument against greater investment in this god-forsaken land (Aa 1879, 131). The Papuans "are crude in their manners, cruel to one another, treacherous with foreigners and traders, little subordinated to their own chiefs and more than frank with Europeans," van den Crab fumed (Aa 1879, 131). But in the middle of these reports—and often in the middle of particular paragraphs or even sentences—one finds an indication of these same officers' awareness of imagined observers, above and beyond the official audience for which these texts were penned.

Take, for example, Bruyn Kops's description of the pleasure with which one group of Papuans greeted the erection of an escutcheon. In Doreh Bay, the natives

> took it with joy that the pole was a sign that the Dutch government had taken the place under its protection, because they hoped through this to remain free of the (visits) of the hongi. The upper chief was charged with keeping the pole in good condition, and, to the end of inspiring the people, they were told that it was an amulet for the village, the latter to their great satisfaction. (Bruyn Kops 1850, 195)

For Bruyn Kops, the natives' "satisfaction" indexed their almost instinctive affinity for their "civilized" Dutch rulers. The despotic Tidorans, by contrast, only enjoyed the appearance of Papuan loyalty; Papuan chiefs, Bruyn Kops notes, only put on their yellow costumes and acted like leaders when they learned that the *hongi* was close at hand. But certain details in the passage indicate that the Papuans' enthusiasm for the Dutch may well have rested on equally shaky grounds. The people were "inspired" because they took the escutcheon for an "amulet," called a *korwar* in this region. These small wooden statues, sometimes containing a fragment of a skull, served as the temporary container of a vaguely ancestral form of power (see Baaren 1968; Rutherford 2006). If nineteenth-century accounts are correct, when amulets ceased to work, the Papuans simply cast them into the sea. The details Bruyn Kops paints into this happy scene belie his wider message: the Papuans' "attachment" to the Dutch may not have been so solid after all.

In arguing that the Papuans' submission to the Tidorans was no more than a facade, colonial observers raised the question of whether the Papuans' submission to the Dutch might not be equally superficial. Needless to say, this question was made all the more pressing by the fact that Dutch expeditions of the period traveled with the *hongi* in tow. Clearly, one could read the signs of Dutch sovereignty—including not only the escutcheons, but also the Papuans' words and gestures—in multiple ways. An account of an 1858 expedition to Humboldt Bay ends with a long description of the joy with which the Tobati welcomed the raising of a Dutch flag over one of their "temples." At the flag's unfurling, "a cry of amazement and pleasure arose from the gathered crowd" (Commissie voor Nieuw-Guinea 1862, 100). The Tobati were eager for the Dutch officers to return and found a post—an observation that the report's author presents with remarkable confidence, given that no one on the expedition knew the local language.

Still, the 1858 report contains hints that the natives could be promiscuous in their affections. When the ship first arrived in Humboldt Bay, near the site of what is now the capital city of the territory, canoes soon surrounded the vessel, carrying natives whose necklaces reminded the Dutch visitors of the collars worn by French Legionnaires. The expedition members were quite aware that the French explorer Dumont d'Urville, sailing in the Astrolabe, had reached the bay in 1827 and named it after the famous Dutch scholar (Vlasboom 2004, 59). Among the Papuans' "screams," one word was discernable—"*Moseu*"—interpreted by the travelers as "*Monsieur*"—a reminder that the French had gotten to this bay first (Commissie voor Nieuw-Guinea 1862, 86). The casual way that Tidoran titles circulated among the Papuans—and were accepted from visiting traders—would have left Dutch officials somewhat uneasy. Other Europeans just as easily could have raised their flag on Papuan territory. Dutch officials may well have recalled that John Hayes, the self-proclaimed "governor general of New Albion," had done just that in the late 1790s. The Papuans may well have been equally "satisfied" by *any* European bearing gifts.

In fact, the most unlikely of characters did serve as agents of the Dutch colonial state. Confronted with a Papuan audience, Europeans not on the colonial payroll still faced a predicament: they felt both coerced by the natives and responsible for the exercise of sovereign power. Much like Furnivall's appropriately named Mr. Gouger, the merchant whom Mr. Maingy appointed as police superintendent, magistrate, and judge, these characters brought their own interests to the job (see Furnivall 1939, 23). The missionaries were particularly inclined to view local happenings through their own distinctive lenses, as we learn in the 1873 Memorandum of Transfer penned by F. Schenck, an outgoing resident of Ternate. Word reached Ternate in 1872 that a pair of Italian naturalists, O. Beccari and L. M. d'Albertis, would soon be visiting New Guinea (Overweel 1995, 58–59; see also Campo 2002, 165–66). (Beccari and d'Albertis were among the visitors who penned the lurid descriptions alluded to above.) At first, the government called on the resident to lend the visitors his support. But in May 1873, the resident received a secret missive warning him to watch the men carefully in connection with the Italian government's purported plan to establish a penal colony somewhere in the Netherlands Indies (Overweel 1995, 59). Fears of Italian intervention ran high in the Indies during this period. Dutch officials were beginning to despair of making anything of New Guinea near the start of the protracted war in Aceh, on the other end of the archipelago, where the Italians also showed interest. "There were even plans in Batavia to buy off the Italian plans for Acheh by dumping New Guinea on them: change in an imperialist cattle market," as historian J. à Campo dryly observes (2002, 164).

The resident had contacted the missionaries on the earlier occasion to ask them to help the Italians; now he asked them to spy on them. Woelders, the missionary serving in the area where Beccari and d'Albertis launched their investigations, responded to the conflicting instructions with skepticism. He quickly developed his own reading of the Italians' objectives: they were not simply spies; they were Jesuits, which in his mind was even worse! Convinced that the Italians were distributing rosaries to the Papuans, Woelders railed against the governments' tolerance in a letter reproduced in the resident's report.

> we Hollanders show such liberality with strangers, not least towards "other thinkers" (i.e., Catholics) who may one day lead us to regret it . . . the Jesuits, notwithstanding a centuries long history that warns us against it . . . we cannot bear to have men surprise us with such Satanic wiles and all faults and errors of description without apprising others of the danger. (Overweel 1995, 59)

While the resident notes that Woelders wrote "as a missionary," he appreciated the information; it was only through Woelders that he had learned that the Italians had come and gone.

In addition to the missionaries, visiting foreign nationals played a role in governing New Guinea, as another anecdote from Schenk's Memorandum makes clear. Rumors of the murder of crew members from an English pearl fishing vessel reached Ternate by way of four Papuan heads, who had met the foreigners in Sorong, on the western tip of the Bird's Head (Overweel 1995, 50–54). A further report from a Tidoran vassal on one of the Raja Ampat islands filled in the details. Having refused the King of Salawatti's help, the English captain had sent two sloops to Poeloe Jaar, a lonely offshore island, where the crew met some local people and communicated with gestures that they wanted them to go pearl diving. The local people obliged, then waited on shore until the crew was busy opening shells, upon which they set upon the men. The captain learned of the incident in Salawatti. After resolving the matter, the captain sailed on, leaving behind three letters: one for the first warship to pass through the area, one for the Prussian Consul General in Hamburg, and a third for the Sultan of Tidore, which thanked him for the King of Salawatti's assistance. In fact, the captain had forced the King of Salawatti to accompany him to the interior near Poeloe Jaar, where the hastily assembled "*hongi*" caught three men, including one in possession of rifles belonging to the dead men. The search party took the culprits back to the scene of the crime, where the captain ordered the King of Salawatti to pronounce judgment. The Englishmen then shot one of the culprits and hung his body from a tree as a warning. The captain left the other prisoners in Salawatti, having urged the king to execute them as well.

The King of Salawatti was understandably quite uneasy about his role in the expedition, given that the ban on *hongi* expeditions then in force. This was a space of overlapping jurisdictions, with many "minisovereigns" in the mix; the king had little way of knowing who was really in charge. Still, the resident was grateful. "Be that as it may, through this hongi expedition, lawful or not, but in any case compelled with a pistol on the chest and thus excusable, they took the law into their own hands, but at the same time bringing a good end to a thorny affair" (Overweel 1995, 54). The English captain's actions met the requirements of "common sense" in this place where Dutch officials were more worried about angering foreigners than the niceties of judicial process. Still, the little drama made it clear that Dutch officials were far from possessing a monopoly on "legitimate" force.

By the end of the nineteenth century, this dispersal of colonial authority
was beginning to grate. With the effort to consolidate Dutch sovereignty,
natives and officials alike began to act with reference to new sorts of imagined spectators. The colonial government gained greater importance in
the eyes of the Papuans. But the Papuans' interest took forms that could
be amusing or exasperating to Europeans documenting their experiences
in the territory, depending on the observer's reason for being there. In
1903 a Dutch writer traveling with a team of naturalists met a headman
on Biak, who was convinced that he had an official appointment from the
government on the basis of a letter "that had nothing to do with that and
contained the simplest matters." Another headman had somehow come
by a receipt from a photographer, which he used as a letter of appointment. "The letterhead of the receipt was printed with several medals that
the man had won at exhibitions, but these stamp-like marks gave the thing
its cachet" (Lorentz n.d., 195). Even in situations in which the "right" re-
galia were worn, headmen derived more than a sense of their role in the
assertion of colonial sovereignty from these signs. Above I suggested that
the ridiculous emerges when the "vertical" dimension of colonialism, that
is, the hierarchies of rule on which it rests, meets the "horizontal" dimension, characterized by the colonial market. The following passage by the
same Dutch writer captures this dynamic well:

> People once admonished us that we associated with them [DR: the Papuans]
> too familiarly and permitted them liberties that were not in fact proper. I be-
> lieve that these persons are very mistaken and have more in mind the inter-
> course between Europeans and Malays or Javans. One must not forget that the
> Papuans feel entirely free and independent and can live very well without us.
> Indeed, the only thing in which our government can be noticed consists of the
> fact that the korano is given a Dutch flag and a black jacket with gold lace. *He
> thus understands that at the arrival of a ship the bearer of the pretty jacket gets a
> double portion of the gifts in the form of tobacco and beads.* (Lorentz n.d., 31–32,
> my emphasis)

This Dutch writer seems to have found the Papuans' "familiar" relations with their European visitors refreshing. The officers dispatched
to bring New Guinea under an orderly administration at the turn of the
century had a far less sanguine view of this state of affairs—and were
far from pleased to see it publicized far and wide. While earlier officials
were clearly interested in the reactions of the Papuans, their requirements

were modest: they asked only that the denizens of particular, well-frequented trading stops be willing and able to express their awareness of Dutch sovereignty. Now the goal was to "enlighten" the Papuans. Where nineteenth century officials confronted the fear of being observed—and replaced—by foreign interlopers, early twentieth century officials faced the specter of appearing to the natives as the bearers of an alien, distinctly "unenlightened" power.

The writings of Lt. W. K. H. Feuilletau de Bruyn, the officer who "pacified" Biak in 1915, bear evidence of this danger. Feuilletau de Bruyn participated in the ambitious military expeditions into the interior of northern and southern New Guinea launched in the early twentieth century (see Langeler and Doorman 1918). During the same period, he helped to consolidate colonial authority on Biak, whose inhabitants had a long history of relations with Tidore. Feuilletau de Bruyn's campaign on Biak was part of a broader effort to bring Papuan "criminals" to justice. Instead of exacting collective retribution, the new generation of officials apprehended individuals and sent them to jail. The new policy was no doubt one factor in the mass conversion of coastal Papuans to Christianity. With the government holding them responsible for paying taxes and serving jail terms, the Papuans had good reasons for inviting native evangelists to settle in their villages: they benefited from their fluency in Malay, the Indies' administrative tongue (see chapter 5). After a Biak warrior killed one of the Ambonese "teachers" (Malay: *guru*) serving on the island, the government intervened.

Feuilletau de Bruyn's goal in Biak was not merely to track down the culprit; it was to institute a form of authority different from that exercised by the Tidorans. With people at such a low level of development, Feuilletau de Bruyn noted, one achieved more through "justice tempered with mercy" than with a "mailed fist" (Feuilletau de Bruyn 1916, 264). Nevertheless, in Feuilletau de Bruyn's description of the military campaign, one funds evidence of contending perspectives on the situation. In a chapter of his Military Memorandum of Transfer on native warfare, Feuilletau de Bruyn explains how Biak raiders would land their canoes some distance from an enemy village, so they could approach the waterfront houses from the rear. Almost in passing, the lieutenant admits that he and his troops deployed the same method "with much success" (Feuilletau de Bruyn 1916, 259). Feuilletau de Bruyn comes close to admitting that the detachment's surprise attacks recalled a long history of punitive raids. In order to compel the perpetrators to surrender, Feuilletau de Bruyn and his men took hostages, some of whom ended up at the government post in Manokwari. It was all the lieutenant could do to convince the locals that their loved ones had not been taken as slaves. As Feuilletau de Bruyn notes later in the report, it was relatively easy to collect taxes on the island. "Through the levying that Tidore in earlier days imposed, people are used to the idea that taxes are levied by foreigners *in order to prevent the punishment people know they would get, which the population (incorrectly) thought we would do as well*" [the italicized section is crossed out] (Feuilletau de Bruyn 1916, 360). The fact that Feuilletau de Bruyn felt compelled to eliminate the second half of the sentence in the published version of the text indicates the officer's vague cognizance of his predicament. Resembling a Biak war party, calling to mind the Tidoran *hongi*, Feuilletau de Bruyn, like Furnivall's poor Mr. Maingy, reproduced the "old" order on Biak through his very efforts to impose something new.

Feuilletau de Bruyn's writings offer evidence of the alterative audiences that jostled for attention in Dutch officials' minds, much as they did in the minds of the British officials described by Furnivall. As contrasting perspectives shifted and merged, the "civilizing mission" came to appear in an unexpected light. The fodder for ridicule offered by this interplay among audiences becomes even obvious in mission documents of the period. Although missionaries like Friedrich Hartweg, a German who served in Biak during the mid-1920s, should have been grateful to the government for suppressing native raiding parties and heathen feasts, the effects of the new policies did not always meet the brothers' expectations. On the one hand, the native administrators who replaced Feuilletau de Bruyn failed to enforce the new regulations.

> We have a so-called prohibition against dance feasts. And it is naturally not followed. We have a prohibition on palm wine tapping, and that is good, but it is also only on paper. They took Marisan, the notorious raiding party leader, to Ternate [to prison]—and he escaped. They took a pair or so of pirates (murderers) to Manokwari [the government seat]—and they escaped. They have brought three murderers of village heads to the same place—they have escaped. Several years ago, those who incited unrest in North Biak were sent to Manokwari—each getting eight to ten years—and they all escaped. Can you imagine the impression this makes on the Papuan? (Hartweg 1927)

Hartweg did not mention this, the Papuans' impression of the government's actions was no doubt further complicated by the fate of those who

did serve out their sentences: they often returned as Malay speaking village chiefs.

A missionary, Hartweg noted, somewhat disingenuously, should avoid
interfering in government affairs. But the Papuans themselves did not
draw sharp distinctions between evangelists and government officers—
they were all "pastors" (Malay: *pandita*), in their eyes—and government
policy had a direct effect on Hartweg's work. The enforcement of the head
tax had made it impossible for the missionary to carry out his duties without regular infusions of cash. "No Papuan is of a mind, now that he has to
pay taxes and pay them quickly or be hauled away with truncheons and
ropes, to work without receiving pay" (Hartweg 1927). Due to a financial
mix-up, Hartweg had become deeply in debt, not only to the Chinese traders living near the mission post, but also to the Papuans his predecessor
had employed. "You know how a few Papuans can be worse than a blood
sucker, but almost sixty Papuans have a claim to the 100 guilders [owed
by Hartweg's predecessor, Brother Agter, who was evacuated due to poor
health]. They can talk you to death . . ." (Hartweg 1927).

Hartweg had to answer to mission society leaders in the Netherlands,
whom he accused, in a particularly ill-tempered letter, of taking him to be
"a monarchist or a Bolshevik" after they took issue with his criticisms of
the government.[5] But he also had to answer to local interlocutors, as his
letters also make clear. We can only guess what was at stake for Hartweg's
Papuan interlocutors in their interactions with the missionary, but it seems
safe to suppose that it was not his recognition of them as colonial subjects.
Hartweg's letters are tragic, to the extent that we identify with his predicament, but comic, to the degree that within them, we sense how the potential for ridicule made itself felt.

The Ridiculous as Social Fact

The ridiculous is the consequence of colonial intervention in settings
where a systematic lack of shared understandings prevails. In other words,
it is the product of a meeting of audiences, each imagined to be scruti-
nizing those claiming sovereignty from a particular point of view. Such
settings are not in any simple sense the product of isolation. Elsewhere,
I have explored how a tendency to fetishize the foreign served to repro-
duce a mismatch between Biak perspectives and outsiders' points of view
(Rutherford 2003). Juxtaposed in the accounts produced by officials and

missionaries, one finds evidence that the Papuans have embraced Dutch authority—and the authority of the Lord—and evidence that they have turned their interactions with these outsiders to very different ends. But in this chapter, in the spirit of this book's broader purposes, I have approached this gap in understanding from a different angle, to shed light on the forces that fueled Dutch imperialism in this enormous, "neglected" land.

In assessing these forces, one should not underestimate the impact on Dutch officials of serving in this difficult corner of the Indies. In 1884, A. Haga, a resident of Ternate, ended his two-volume history of New Guinea on a despondent note: "Sovereignty brings heavy duties and great responsibilities and only over the course of an extended time will any great changes in conditions be foreseen" (Haga 1884, 435). Rather than governing New Guinea in this unbearably ridiculous fashion, some administrators suggested that the Netherlands should simply sell the territory off. But others, like Feuilletau de Bruyn, did not despair. In the 1930s, Feuilletau de Bruyn joined with former residents of Ternate, governors of the Moluccas, and right wing Dutch politicians in calling for a renewed policy in New Guinea, in part, as we shall see in the next chapter, as a way of opening the territory to Indo-European migration (Rutherford 1998). In essays published in *Tijdschrift Nieuw-Guinea*, a journal he edited for several years, Feuilletau de Bruyn backed the idea of imposing a penal sanction in New Guinea, which would provide jail terms to coolies who broke their contracts, and of limiting the Papuan's rights to land (see Feuilletau de Bruyn 1933, 1936–37). Feuilletau de Bruyn's draconian proposals were never adopted. But as we will see in chapter 4, the publications and institutions of the period set the stage for the Netherlands' retention of New Guinea by providing a justification for separating the territory from the rest of the colonial state.

This chapter has begun the work of mapping the geographies of West Papuan sovereignty by paying special heed to early efforts to govern the territory. I continue this work in the following chapter, where I look more closely at the abovementioned developments in the 1930s, a time that saw the emergence of new audiences for colonial policy and practice in this long "neglected" land. My findings in both chapters suggest that the Dutch decision to cling to western New Guinea after Indonesia gained independence in 1945 was not simply a symptom of the "trauma of decolonization," as the Dutch-born political scientist Arend Lijphart (1966) has suggested. More was at stake in this decision than the sudden loss of the Indies, including, as we will see, concern for the future of mixed race Europeans in an independent Indonesia. Fearing the dispute's repercussions for Dutch corporations with operations in Indonesia, in the 1950s and early 1960s, the Dutch business community remained cold to the idea of keeping New Guinea. But at least one top-ranking Dutch leader, J. H. van Maarseveen, who was Minister for Overseas Territories during the Round Table Conference, insisted that western New Guinea would be "highly profitable" one day (Drooglever 2009, 145). When Dutch New Guinea turned out to be more trouble than it was worth, among the last individuals to give up on the project were former colonial officials. A long history of frustration and dashed dreams fed their commitment to the ill-fated mission, even after the Dutch Reformed Church and many Dutch politicians withdrew their support (see Derix 1987; Baal 1989; Drooglever 2009).

Many audiences jostled for attention in the minds of the new colonial officials who served in Dutch New Guinea after the war: United Nations committees, Dutch parliamentarians, the Papuans, and the mixed-race Europeans whom they worked with and governed, not to mention friends and family back in the Netherlands. A memoir recounting the adventures of a minor official on Biak during the 1950s captures the comedy that sometimes ensued (Berg 1981). Several chapters in the slim volume are devoted to the tension between the "pseudo-perfectionism" of high-ranking officers in the air-conditioned seat of government in Hollandia, and the "imperfections" their subordinates faced on the ground (Berg 1981, 57–59, 91–93). Berg's recollections sometimes call to mind Furnivall's account of Leviathan's antics. At one point, he describes how drivers who wanted a license had to pass a test that entailed identifying the entire repertoire of traffic symbols, even though the island had only one, unofficial, sign (1981, 81–83). But Berg also uses humor to defend what he calls the "New Guinea dream" (ibid., 134). In a chapter titled, simply, "Colonialism?" he sets straight a rumor that Biak was home to colonial extremists, by recounting how an incident in which an employer chained a Papuan worker to a flagpole was simply an innocent practical joke (Berg 1981, 122–26). Still, if we follow Furnivall, it becomes clear that absurdity is no stranger to the violent exercise of colonial power.

Biaks have made their own jokes about the colonial experience. One I recorded described a suspect pursued by Feuilletau de Bruyn and his soldiers, who hid from the detachment by climbing a tree. When the Dutch officials were distributing tobacco to a group relaxing below, the suspect could not contain his excitement. "Hey!" he shouted to the startled soldiers. "I get some, too!" And so the poor man took his place in the long line of prisoners, bound by barbed wire wrapped around their necks. Here is a rather different account of the linkage between colonial sovereignty and "tobacco and beads" than that offered by the bemused Dutch writer whom I quoted earlier. This story turns on the tension between colonialism's horizontal and vertical dimensions, but from the perspective of those who bore the brunt of their society's "reform." As Feuilletau de Bruyn noted, "tobacco" was the "small change" of Biak's "economy"; it is the desire to extract something of value from the ordeal that fixes the poor victim in the soldiers' gaze. Furnivall may claim that the colonial state does not have a sense of humor, yet he knew that law and comedy, like law and violence, go together. *The Fashioning of Leviathan* teaches us how to approach imperialism from within the Leviathan—where the ridiculous becomes a social fact.

CHAPTER THREE

Trekking to New Guinea

"The Netherlands Indies will only really be the Netherlands Indies when New Guinea is populated by men and women of Dutch stock." So went a rallying cry heard during the 1930s.[1] Little did those who promoted Dutch New Guinea as a homeland for displaced Europeans know how ironically prescient this conceit would later seem. Dutch settlers never successfully populated New Guinea. By 1963 the Netherlands Indies was no longer the Netherlands Indies, if, indeed, it had ever been. To rehearse the broad strokes of a history I have already related, on December 29, 1949, the Netherlands Indies gained independence as the sovereign nation-state of Indonesia. Dutch negotiators managed to exclude the western half of New Guinea from the settlement, and it was an additional fourteen years before the Dutch government was willing to let the territory go. But finally, in the midst of the Cold War, American political leaders persuaded their Dutch counterparts to end the increasingly dangerous dispute with Indonesia by relinquishing the Netherlands' claims to Dutch New Guinea. Dutch New Guinea went the way of the Netherlands Indies. The world had become a very different—and tentatively postcolonial—place.

In 1966, three years after Indonesia took control of Dutch New Guinea, the Dutch-born political scientist Arend Lijphart wrote *The Trauma of Decolonization* to explain why it had taken the Netherlands so long to give up this remnant of the Netherlands Indies. Throughout the 1950s, the Dutch government devoted large amounts of money, manpower, and political capital to the mission of preparing the primitive Papuans for self-rule. In the wake of Indonesia's independence, as Lijphart pointed out, the Dutch invested New Guinea with a significance that far outweighed its material worth (Lijphart 1966, 288; see also Hill and Weidermann 1989, 7; Manning and Rumbiak 1989). In the previous chapter I discussed some of the other factors that played into the Dutch decision to keep New Guinea; still, even in his more measured history of this period, historian Pieter Drooglever concurs: "A sense of frustrated chauvinism, feelings of being misjudged, and suspicion towards the new Indonesia were continuously simmering beneath the surface of all Dutch deliberations and actions during this period" (2009, 144). The Netherlands' seemingly irrational attachment to western New Guinea confused world leaders. President Dwight D. Eisenhower went so far as to call the territory a "fetish of the old empire" at a National Security Council meeting in January 1959 (see Drooglever 2009, 364–65). A few years later, Lijphart followed Eisenhower's lead. As a replacement for the Indies, Lijphart argued, New Guinea functioned as a fetish, a symptom of the injury to the Netherlands' global image and national self-esteem.

Lijphart's diagnosis reveals the extent to which the uneasy relationship between audience and sovereignty motivated Dutch policy. In the eyes of Dutch leaders and the public at large, possession of a large colonial empire had long defined their nation's standing in the world. The challenge posed by the loss of this empire to the Netherlands' prestige among foreigners, to recall that phrase from the previous chapter, moved Dutch policy makers to react in dramatic—and expensive—ways. Lijphart provides us with a starting point for examining the deeper roots of the Netherlands' attachment to New Guinea. But we can take my revision of Lijphart's argument even further than I did in chapter 2. Not only was the postwar mission to develop New Guinea a product of imperial desires and anxieties, so was the category in whose name this mission took place. In the decade before decolonization, politicians and journalists shaped an image of New Guinea that would justify continued Dutch rule.

In the psychoanalytic theories to which Lijphart alludes, the fetish is depicted as appearing in the face of an uncertainty that poses a threat to identity (Freud 1963, 202–13; see also Smirnoff 1980). Fixing on the last thing seen before witnessing the mother's troubling "lack," the fetishist displaces a series of nervous questions: Does she have it? Do I have it? Could I lose it, too? In light of these formulations, Lijphart's description of the Netherlands' postwar obsession with New Guinea presents us with an odd kind of fetish: a figure with no apparent relationship to sexual difference. But the pre–World War II fantasies that set the stage for this obsession brought the question of sexual difference to the fore.

In this chapter I examine these pre–World War II fantasies, which transformed New Guinea into a homeland for orphaned Europeans. I extend my exploration of the geographies of West Papuan sovereignty by examining the hopes and anxieties that sparked an explosion of Dutch interest in the territory in the period between the world wars. A multitude of audiences—and ideas of purity—come to the fore in my analysis here as well, but in the course of a tale of the insecurities that haunted the upper echelons of Dutch colonial society. I do not imply—and neither did Eisenhower and Lijphart, for that matter—that these hopes and anxieties belonged to some kind of national or racial psyche that suffered from familiar pathologies, only writ large. Rather, this chapter attends to historically situated individuals who proved susceptible to the passions that a particular colonial predicament fostered—passions that became more widely shared as the decade progressed. Profound changes in Indies society gave rise to a movement to settle New Guinea in the early 1920s. Persisting throughout the 1930s, the movement yielded three roughly chronological visions of this new "fatherland," as it was called. In this late colonial context, I track the shifting place of gender in portrayals of New Guinea as a zone of national, racial, and bureaucratic purity. Moving through the series, I explore how an explicit concern with sexual control yielded to a general pursuit of prowess. By tracing a rhetoric of exclusion through these depression-era texts, I show how this virgin land came to shelter a manly figure of colonial power.

Those who promoted the new fatherland in the 1920s and especially the 1930s were not the first to associate New Guinea's (lack of) development with the Netherlands' threatened prestige. But they were the first to insist upon the territory's detachment from the Indies. Nothing happened in New Guinea to account for its changing place in the colonial imagination. When the dream began, advances in transportation were bringing this neglected periphery closer to the imperial center (see Campo 1986; Locher-Scholten 1994). Although the fantasy changed the future for New Guinea's inhabitants, the Papuans had little to do with its emergence. It started in the heartland of Dutch colonial society, in Java, far to the west.

The Threatened Europeans

Sometime in the 1930s a Dutch supporter looked back on the birth of the dream of trekking to New Guinea. "The Indo-European desires to remain European, despite the color of his skin, inherited from his mother, no matter how poor his economic conditions may be. And this desire was the father of the New Guinea ideal" (Winkler 1935). In the 1920s reformers examined the circumstances of the self-described "Indo-European" and decided his future was grim. This perception was a product of the significant changes that the twentieth century brought to the Indies. Between the 1870s and the 1930s, political, economic, and technological developments redrafted the colony's social contours. With the liberalization of migration policies and the opening of railways and shipping routes, new opportunities and improved conditions attracted Europeans to the Indies. A key factor in the transformation of the European community was the abolition of the Dutch monarch's control over the Indies. After 1870 Dutch persons wishing to enter the colony no longer needed a passport from the king. Between 1905 and 1930, the European population grew 167 percent (see Drooglever 1980, 5). During the same period, gender ratios shifted from 471.6 to 884.5 European women per thousand European men (see Nieuwenhuys 1982, 201). The full-blooded European housewife replaced the native concubine, and a wealthy, Western-oriented community of newcomers who had been born and raised in Europe (*totoks*) swept away a mestizo cultural world (see also Shiraishi 1990; Tsuchiya 1986, 1990).

These concubines' descendants faced an uncertain future. In the 1930 census 190,000 of the 240,000 persons counted as "European" were labeled as Indies-born settlers (Malay: *blijvers*), persons of either mixed or pure European blood who were born and raised in the Indies (Drooglever 1980, 5; see also Van der Veur 1955). The colonial state and private industry had initially promoted mixed-race liaisons by discouraging the migration of married Dutchmen to the Indies (see Stoler 1989a, 1989b). Thus for several centuries a large portion of the colony's officially defined elite had consisted of Eurasians. Unlike the Philippines' Spanish rulers, Dutch authorities in the Indies never created a distinct legal category for the progeny of unions between whites and natives or whites and persons of mixed race. If many Indo-Europeans (also known as Indos) were classified as "natives," those recognized by their legal European fathers enjoyed the same status under the law as pure-blooded Dutch men and women. Ranging from the impoverished children of soldiers to the wealthy descendants of Batavia's ruling elite, in the late nineteenth century these Europeans had found employment in private enterprise and an expanding colonial bureaucracy.[2] But around the turn of the century, persons of mixed race began to lose their standing with the growth of a *totok* (trueborn or full-blooded) Dutch community increasingly attuned to distinctions in language, lifestyle, and skin color. Luxurious neighborhoods sprang up in cities like Batavia, Medan, and Surabaya, along with new amusement centers, restaurants, clubs, and office buildings. Their inhabitants sped through native and mixed-race neighborhoods on newly improved roads, kept separate from the Indies' other communities by the windowpanes on their automobiles and first class trains. Residents born in the Indies gradually adopted *totok* norms, some shared *totok* tastes, but few enjoyed the *totoks'* status or wealth.

The newcomers did more than monopolize the bureaucracy's highest posts. Their arrival set in motion changes that threatened the older community from below. The transformations that allowed for the creation of a "white" community also gave rise to unease (see Pattynama 1998; Furnivall 1956 [1948]; Stoler 2009). Confronted with a native world shrouded in mystery, a new generation of Dutch officials attempted to pull Java's villages into the light of modernity. In essence, these officials sought to illuminate—and reform—the sentiments that lay behind the native faces, that audience of watching servants and subjects whom they encountered at every turn. By expanding the colonial school system, the reforms first helped then hindered many of the racially hybrid Indies-born residents, who found themselves competing with educated natives who hailed from the archipelago's feudal elite. The Dutch modernization program—called, as one will remember, the "Ethical Policy"—contributed to the birth of the Indonesian nationalist movement and the replacement of the locally hired Europeans by lower-paid native clerks (see Anderson 1991; Shiraishi 1990). Many Indo-Europeans lost their steady, if mediocre, income from positions in either the colonial bureaucracy or the private sector; what remained to distinguish such redundant clerks from their competitors was their superior legal status as Europeans. The Indies government acknowledged this trend by adopting a new salary scheme that divided low-paying jobs for natives from high-paying jobs for European emigrants, leaving middle-level positions for "circles in the Netherlands Indies of relatively small numbers, whose general living standards call for the presence of an accordingly higher salary" (Van der Veur 1955, 253–60). As the Indies education system improved, natives hired at the lower pay rate would gradually take over from this relatively small group.

The Agrarian Act of 1870, which prohibited the alienation of native land to nonnatives, played a key role in the New Guinea dream (see Van der Veur 1955, 253–60; see also Lev 1985; Stoler 1985; Zerner 1990; Peluso 1992). To save Eurasians from vanishing into the native community, attempts were made in the 1920s and 1930s to expand the provisions of the law that offered access to land to European paupers who wished to become smallholders. At a time when nationalist rhetoric appealed to the natives' primordial connection to place, "the Indo-European farmer," living off his own land, was imagined in an attempt to preserve a place in the Indies for this embattled group. Ironically, by attempting to give him roots in the soil, the reformers who spoke for the Indo-European challenged a boundary that defined his privileged status (see Tsuchiya 1986). To beat a system that only recognized peasants or planters, Indo-Europeans needed a space where they could remain European but at the same time claim a native's right to own land.

In a dream that reflected desires other than simply the Indo-European's, New Guinea became that space. Ann Stoler (1989a, 1989b, 2009) has shown how late colonial elites consolidated their position in a variety of settings by reforming or repatriating their "unseemly" compatriots. The plight of displaced Indo-Europeans posed a special challenge to the Dutch East Indies' white masters, who were not pleased by the prospect of mixed-blood colonial residents returning to the mother country in Europe. Obviously, the New Guinea dream's father had a father, too—its grandfather, if you will: the desire of powerful interests in the metropole to remain in control. The late colonial period saw the birth of a determined, if eclectic, nationalist movement among educated Indonesians. At first, Indonesians' political awakening pleased a Dutch colonial bureaucracy imbued with "ethical" fervor, because their native pupils appeared to be learning to play Western politics. But it frightened them soon thereafter, as they sensed their prerogatives coming under attack. The Great Depression, unleashed in September 1929, also played a significant role in this history. Provoking a wave of unemployment in both the Netherlands and the Indies, the worldwide downturn brought some newly arrived Europeans to their knees. For the generation of European-born Netherlanders around the turn of the century, danger had resided in the archaic native mysteries that Europeans' enlightened rationality could not penetrate. Twenty years later they faced the threat that enlightened natives might replace them at the top of the colonial world.

With economic crisis looming and radicals lurking in every corner, the image of a haven in the Indies for a threatened elite captured the attention of both Indies-born settlers and Dutch-born newcomers. It was not the first time that the Indies' masters tried to avert disaster by turning potential troublemakers into pioneers on the periphery of this colonial society. The dispatching of impoverished Javanese peasants to the Indies' outer islands dated from 1902. Dutch officials referred to Javanese workers transported to the rubber plantations in Deli, Sumatra, during this period as colonists (Stoler 1985, 38–39). They used the same term for Indonesian nationalists sent to Boven Digoel, an "isolation camp" established in New Guinea's southern lowlands in 1928 (Mrazek 1994, 130). "Colonizing" was the euphemism for the coolie and the exile's harsh "new existences." Colonizing New Guinea became the solution for Europeans who were losing their place.

The Trek Begins

In 1923, four years after the founding of the Indo-European Union, one of the organization's district chairmen had an exciting idea.[3] Speaking at the union's annual convention, A. Th. Schalk proposed the founding of a European agricultural colony in New Guinea. Evoking both the Mormons in the United States and the Boers in South Africa, the head of the Indo-European Union's chapter in Banyuwangi depicted a community grounded in the principles of "self-reliance." While Schalk's speech met with the approval of many members "inside and outside the Indo-European Union," the organization's colonywide leadership remained cool to the idea, which directly competed with its own colonization project in Sumatra (see Lijphart 1966, 71). Schalk's proposal was dropped until 1926, when A. R. Landsman founded the New Guinea Colonization Society (Vereeniging Kolonisatie Nieuw-Guinea, VKNG).

The New Guinea Colonization Society grew rapidly, opening branches throughout Java. In 1929, after a dispute with other leaders, Landsman and his group from the city of Malang in east Java broke off to found what would be the VKNG's staunch rival, the New Guinea Immigration and Colonization Foundation (Stichting Immigratie en Kolonisatie Nieuw Guinea, SIKNG). The VKNG and the SIKNG, racing to be first, established settlements on the northern coast of New Guinea in November and May 1930. The VKNG chose a site near Hollandia, the town that later became the capital of Netherlands New Guinea. The SIKNG colonists settled close to Manokwari, then the territory's main administrative post.

By 1933 over four hundred Europeans had settled in New Guinea, and their trek was a topic of debate on both sides of the globe. In the Indies those who joined the colonization societies in the discussion included members of the proto-parliament of the Netherlands East Indies, the

People's Council (Dutch: *Volksraad*). Founded in late 1918 as a "school of politics" for native leaders, by the 1930s the racially mixed proto-parliament had become a platform for two European political organizations in particular (see Wal 1965, 95–120, 175–202). One was the above-mentioned Indo-European Union, which has been characterized as "more Dutch than the Dutch" in its loyalties. Claiming to represent tens of thousands of indigent Indo-Europeans, the union had 13,200 members at its height—an estimated one-fifth of the colony's mixed-race European population—most of whom were middle-level officials (see Van der Veur 1955, 229). The other was the ultraconservative Patriot Club (Dutch: *Vaderlandse Club*), founded in 1929 to disclose the truth about the Indies to a public misled by the propaganda of the Ethical Policy. Said to include among its members one-third of the colony's Dutch residents—all men, since women did not receive the active franchise until 1941—with a membership that peaked in 1930, the Patriot Club attracted top business and government leaders (Drooglever 1980, 348). Meanwhile, in the Netherlands itself, the Hitler-inspired National Socialist movement also took an interest in New Guinea (see Van der Veur 1955, 319; see also see Toorn 1975, 13). Playing to fears of the potentially radicalized urban masses, the National Socialists encouraged the handful of New Guinea colonization societies while they lobbied the national parliament for financial support.

The Patriot Club and the National Socialists joined forces with the Indo-European Union, which finally came out in support of the New Guinea movement in 1933, more in defense of the maligned colonists than out of any particular enthusiasm for the scheme (see Handelingen Volksraad 1931–32, 873; Van der Veur 1955). Caving to pressure from these groups, the Indies government granted the societies a share of the proceeds from the colonial lottery and offered SIKNG and VKNG members free fourth-class passage to New Guinea on the government shipping line. Each colonist received a year's worth of aid from the Crisis Relief Committees, which relied on the societies to administer the funds.

In calling for this aid, supporters prescribed New Guinea's colonization as the cure for a wide range of social ills. The trek would alleviate European unemployment on crowded Java and open an escape valve for the Netherlands' urban poor. It would offer land and a decent livelihood to the settlers of this "unpopulated" place. New Guinea's development would confirm the Netherlands' control of the colony's border and keep foreign interlopers at bay. Rehashed and recycled among the different factions who pushed the colonization of New Guinea, these arguments cannot account for the fervor shown a cause that was regarded in some circles as "criminally insane" (Winkler 1935, 38). When enthusiasts pictured the new fatherland in New Guinea, what did they see?

One could regard the view of New Guinea that came into focus at this time as the product of the late colonial politics of race and sexual morality. In a variety of settings, the presence of white women, who formed a new audience surveying the social landscape, both occasioned and justified a new policing of the European self. The enforcement of middle-class mores homogenized the elite, limited its membership and deepened the divide between the rulers and the ruled. In a futuristic work of late colonial science fiction, New Guinea became a setting for the deployment of new technologies of containment. The empty land became a laboratory for the cultivation of a monitored class identity—the cloning of moral purity in a pristine environment. Through measures protecting the character, hygiene, and health of the colonists, sexual control was perfected as an instrument of colonial power.

However, a wider set of concerns coalesced in this scheme to colonize New Guinea. When viewed from another angle, science fiction was transformed into a nationalist romance that was enhanced by unambiguously gendered images. The imagined New Guinea fatherland became a robust surrogate for the colonist's frail native mother, anchoring his claims in purer soil. Turning the pauper into a hero, the trek appealed to the "sublimated eroticism" of the Netherlands' earlier "cults of masculinity" (Velde 1992, 151). In the 1880s Dutchmen had felt a kinship with the brave South African Boers; in the 1930s they identified with New Guinea's brave pioneers. Like the colonial soldiers who served the virtuous young Queen Wilhelmina at the turn of the century, loyal youth would defend this virgin land (Velde 1992, 78, 151; see also Mosse 1985).

If nationalism infused the enthusiasts' dreams, fascism gave form to their nightmares. The Indo-European Union and the Patriot Club, as well as both colonization societies, made no secret of the affinity that existed between National Socialism and their version of the colonial mentality (Nieuwenhuys 1982, 205; see also Van der Veur 1955, 232). For those who saw New Guinea through the right-wing lenses readily available at this time, the alternative to settling in this pure territory was sinking into a swamp of indeterminacy. In Klaus Theweleit's analysis of texts from the early phases of German fascism, the "communist flood" that threatened to engulf the "soldier male" was invariably feminine (see Theweleit 1987). The New Guinea fantasies drew their urgency from a range of colonial discourses that depicted the indigenous woman as the focus of dangerous desires. Descriptions of "the Indo" referred to the "voice" of the "native mother in his blood," who was responsible for his taste for idle pleasures (see Handelingen Volksraad 1935–36a). In the "trueborn" Dutch household, the intimate other took the form of native servants, carriers of alien customs and communicable diseases. Various fears found expression in novels that presented the native mistress as a disruptive force (see Nieuwenhuys 1982; Toer 1982). When propagandists referred to "the woman question" as the most important factor in "successful colonization," they evoked a whole range of threatening images. Far from the masses of native mothers, servants, and lovers, New Guinea became a refuge from the woman within.

Playing to different audiences, different elements of the movement presented New Guinea as a real and symbolic refuge from contagion. As the drama of colonization progressed, three visions of New Guinea came into view: first as the cradle of a nation, then as a crucible of racial purity, and finally as a refuge for a reinvigorated state. As we move from one vision to the next, note the nature of the native Papuan, who must accommodate each scene. In particular, take note of the Papuan audience—watching the settlers or, more commonly, interested in other things—posited in an effort to make this space seem safe for Dutch sovereignty. The third solution brings us closest to postwar New Guinea. In this virgin land a changing cast of imaginary Europeans seemed to flee the paradoxes of colonial rule.

Vision One: The Land of the Indo-Settlers

Our first New Guinea, promoted by the New Guinea Immigration and Colonization Foundation (SIKNG), was a space of purified hybridity. Its colonization was a deed that would unify the "Indo-Settler race" (De Nieuw-Guineaer 1931k, 3). New Guinea would solve the dilemma of European land rights quite simply: just as the Sumatran could claim Sumatra, the Indo settler would claim New Guinea by embracing a newly forged identity that tapped both his maternal and paternal roots. A circular logic made the act of claiming New Guinea the justification for its possession. "We Indos and Blijvers . . . may thank God that in these times New Guinea exists for us," the editors of the SIKNG newsletter proclaimed (De Nieuw-Guineaer 1931k, 3; see also De Nieuw-Guineaer 1931h).

We live on in, through, and for our children, and most of us do not sufficiently sense this truth. Now our existence as a nation is at stake. . . . We want regeneration, and we are ready to start from the beginning. We want to be and remain and Indo-Blijver nation. But a nation needs land. And land is to be had in abundance in New Guinea; there is enough for every one of us. (De Nieuw-Guineaer 1931k, 3)

In epic poetry and strident prose, on Dutch pages scattered with Malay, German, and English words, the SIKNG's newsletters celebrated the future birth of "the New Guineaer" and the regenerated nation that the Indo-Blijvers "wanted to be and remain." To the Zionists' "Say Yes to Jewishness," the SIKNG echoed, "Say Yes to Indo-ness!" Borrowing from Zionist appeals to Jews to embrace their ethnicity, the SIKNG urged its Indo supporters to recognize who they were.[4]

The New Guinea Immigration and Colonization Foundation charted a way for the Indo settler to go native without vanishing into the masses. The New Guineaer would be indigenous but with a difference: unlike the "stiffened" Europeans or the "ancient" Asians, he would be of vigorous mestizo stock. "Evolution needs new forms, new sorts of plants, animals, men, races. . . . Alas!! Neither the Dutch, as the active agent, nor the Native, as the passive element, appear destined to form a great new race in this region" (De Nieuw-Guineaer 1931k, 3). With the glories of nature bringing out his best, the Indo settler would become the future leader of an Indies federation. The process of settling New Guinea would fill him with masculine vitality. Scarcity would teach him the true value of things. Strengthened by hard work in the clear "glacial air," the young colonist would commune with the "powerful creation process" and come nearer to the "reality of Being: the fields and hills in which the free wind blows are what furnish our bread and our MEN" (De Nieuw-Guineaer 1931k, 3; see also De Nieuw-Guineaer 1931b, 1931j, 1931l).

The colonists left behind a diseased existence when they set out for New Guinea. In Java's cities, where Indo settlers lived as parasites on the system, insatiable desires and meaningless distractions were sapping the national will. The unemployed joined the "human waste" of poverty that fertilized Communism's evil weed (De Nieuw-Guineaer 1931c). The idle pleasures of the rich fed the resentment of the poor, which would explode in "bloody excess" when "the crisis" finally came. In a newsletter article titled "Our Leading Principle," an Indo pauper and a native peer through a window at wealthy legally recognized Indo-Europeans enjoying themselves

on the dance floor (De Nieuw-Guineaer 1932b). Thoughts of revenge
take shape in their minds. This prose portrait was part of a bitter polemic
against its rival, the VKNG, which, as we will see, attacked the SIKNG for
including "natives" in their colony. The SIKNG called for the inclusion
in the fatherland of "unrecognized Indo-Europeans," who were divided
from their more fortunate brothers only by their lack of European legal
status. In place of fratricide, New Guinea offered nourishment, stability,
and peace. There would be no hunger or conflict in this "land of un-
bounded possibilities," where apples and coconuts could thrive side by
side (De Nieuw-Guineaer 1931g).

Far from urban sites of excess and distraction, the SIKNG's New
Guinea could safely employ either local or imported native labor (see De
Nieuw-Guineaer 1931i). For the society's supporters contagion was not an
effect of exposure to natives; it was the result of performing native tasks.
If a colonist did not have coolies, he would become a coolie himself and
"lose the Indo's meager capacity to remain lord and master." If his Indo
wife did not have servants, she would become her husband's "slave," just
like the local Papuan women. And when she rejected this treatment and
retreated to Java, the colonist would be forced to replace her with a local
girl. Those who refused to associate with Papuan helpers—albeit as their
masters—would, according to this convoluted logic, end up with Papuan
wives. This reasoning suddenly raised the specter of a New Guinea teem-
ing with natives. By intermarrying, inevitably, the colonists would "assimi-
late . . . and disappear into the Papuan population" (De Nieuw-Guineaer
1931d).

Marked by the contradictions of this fetishized space—Is it empty?
Or is it full?—such a command to associate presented the Indo settler
with a paradox. His standing as New Guinea's first possessor rested on the
Papuans being scarce. It depended on New Guinea being a place where
land was "to be had in abundance," as the SIKNG newsletter editors put
it. But as this publication's photographs from the colony showed clearly,
he needed Papuan servants to remain who he was (De Nieuw-Guineaer
1931m, 5; see also De Nieuw-Guineaer 1931m, 6, 1932a). "Boar hunting for meat supplies" reads the caption under an illustration featuring a
colonist in a T-shirt crouched beside a dead pig, his fellow colonists in a
line behind him (De Nieuw-Guineaer 1931m, 6). Two bare-chested Papuan hunters stand at a respectful distance in the rear. Another features
a Papuan girl in Javanese native dress posing behind a clothesline. "Papuan beauty promoted to washer woman," the caption reads (De Nieuw-

Guineaer 1931m, 9). The colonists not only needed Papuan labor; they also needed Papuan land, as we also learn in the newsletter. SIKNG colonists had to pay local villagers to let them use their abandoned gardens in order to plant their crops (see De Nieuw-Guineaer 1931m, 5). When it came to finding suitable farming land in New Guinea's fragile ecosystems, there was not "enough for every one of us," it turned out.

On the horns of the dilemma of this dependency, SIKNG writers transformed these other "New Guineaers" into the colonist's evil shadow. Papuan women urinated in public and allowed their husbands to lend them to their friends. Naked and dirty, they did all the work, leaving the men to adorn themselves with shells, scraps of Western clothing, and other worthless "finery" (De Nieuw-Guineaer 1931a). These Papuan dandies lacked the "vitality" to last for long against the ravages of modernity. But that was no reason not to employ them before they died out.

In the SIKNG's fantasy about New Guinea as the home for Indo settlers, sexual difference figured as a difference in potency. Just as performing native labor would degrade the Indo settler, "manly" Papuan women feminized their men. The same dynamic that produced decadence among the Papuans accounted for the flaws of the SIKNG's other racial others, the Dutch-born newcomers. One contributor portrayed the Netherlands' founding fathers, the Batavians, as loafers who lived off their shrewish, bullying wives until an invasion by the Huns forced them to get tough.[5] "Oh Holland, our land of origin," another lamented, "if only there were a Mussolini among your sons!" (De Nieuw-Guineaer 1931e). Making identity an effect of recognition and will, the SIKNG offered New Guinea as the only place in the Indies where the hybrid Indo-settler could "honor his father and mother [races]" (De Nieuw-Guineaer 1931k, 5).

Vision Two: White New Guinea

Our next vision of New Guinea is very different. With its fascist supporters in the National Socialist movement in the Netherlands, the New Guinea Colonization Society (VKNG) presented a fatherland whose sons would always be Dutch. A "blank page," just like Australia at the dawn of its history, the VKNG's New Guinea offered marginal Europeans a fresh start. According to the society's leaders, the VKNG's goal in New Guinea was not a political but a socioeconomic one: to rescue "Indies Netherlanders" from Java, where they lived among strangers, and place them in their own

European milieu. Far from the servants of the "feudal Indies," the colonists would roll up their sleeves and take up farming, "the natural basis of all things" (Schijfsma 1936, 68, 70).

Unlike their rivals in the SIKNG, who would let nature run its course, the VKNG attempted to restore what was natural through a program of moral reform. Training camps on Java instilled prospective colonists with discipline and self-reliance. The trainers faced a challenge in the Indies girl, who had acquired an unnatural disdain for manual labor. Addicted to high heels, dance halls, and other urban pleasures, she "wavered on the threshold" of an agrarian future. But with time, she would shed her "affectations" and take her place at the pioneer's side. The Indies girl would become the happy spouse of an honest farmer or *boer*. A diligent housewife like the matrons of yore, she would savor her toils "in the midst of—and in harmony with—God's beautiful tropical nature . . . without becoming a peasant as some people [that is, SIKNG editors] might assume" (Schijfsma 1936, 73).

This vision of domestic redemption depended on New Guinea remaining a "totally different setting" than Java. The trek to New Guinea was an escape from the "mixed land," where the competition from cheaper Javanese labor was destroying Indies Dutchmen (Onze Toekomst 1933). For the VKNG's rescue mission to be effective, New Guinea had to remain pure. The VKNG strictly limited the use of Javanese or Papuan labor in its colony. This prohibition was meant to promote "self-reliance," but the measure also spoke of other fears. "Natural repugnance" was not enough to prevent miscegenation, a writer noted (Onze Toekomst 1935a, b). "The Papuans must stay off the colonists' farms!" The National Socialist movement's propaganda went even further in its tract on "White New Guinea." Exposure to the natives could have "fatal effects." The writer proposed placing the Papuans in special reserves where the government could suppress "customs in conflict with good morals and hygiene, such as head-hunting, cannibalism, and certain sexual practices" (Winkler 1935, 6, see also 55–56). Hygiene was an obsession in White New Guinea: the authorities would even sanitize the terrain.

The VKNG and its supporters fixed the scale linking gender to potency and race. On top was a "man at the peak of his powers." Manning the helm of the Dutch ship of state, the Indies-born Dutchman would ensure that colonization was a success (Winkler 1935, 58). Next came the "hearty young Hollander," then the "current stock of colonists," and below them the "wavering Indies girl." The "mixed land" lay morally beneath them all, far to the west in the colony's crowded center: a heterogeneous, decaying swamp. White New Guinea was a "barrier to an awakening Asia" and a "bulwark" against a tide of feminine impurity (Winkler 1935, 21).

Vision Three: The Bureaucrat's Crown Territory

The third vision carried this logic to a different plane. The Patriot's Club fantasy New Guinea did more than transform lax boys into strapping men (see De Kolonist 1933). It was the stage for a manly apparatus: an unencumbered colonial state. Presented in the People's Council in the capital of Batavia, our third vision of New Guinea reflected the interests of ambitious businessmen and frustrated bureaucrats. This vision originated with the Patriot Club's colonization study committees in the Indies and in the Netherlands, who offered an expert assessment of New Guinea's potential. The committee in the Netherlands included three ex-governors of the Moluccas and two military officers; its chairman was L. H. W. van Sandick, former governor of the Moluccas and east Sumatra and an ex-member of the Raad van Indie. Other members included J. C. Brasser, a former colonial military colonel and a participant in the Mamberamo expedition of 1915 and the Dutch-German Commission that set the border that divided the Indies from the German colony in New Guinea's northeast; V. A. Doeve, a former assistant resident at the disposal of the governor of the Moluccas and an ex-resident of the Sumatran territory of Riau; J. G. Larive, a former governor of the Moluccas; C. Poortman, a former resident of New Guinea and of Jambi; L. A. Snell, a participant in the Fransen Herderschee expedition to New Guinea's south coast and a former colonial military colonel; A. T. H. Winter, a retired professor and colonial military colonel and the Patriot Society's first chairman; and Dr. H. B. Vrijburg, formerly the chief of Batavia's veterinary service and the founder of De Friesche Terp dairy farm in Pengalengan on Java. Most of these individuals would have had firsthand experience of scenarios like those I depicted in the previous chapter: scenarios in which they confronted the absurdity of the existing system of colonial rule.

While Indo-Europeans' colonization remained the impetus for New Guinea's development, the project drawn up by these luminaries now called for massive investments. To prepare for a large influx of Netherlanders from both the Netherlands and the colony's heartland on the island of Java—that is, "the Greater Netherlands"—the government needed to

commission soil studies; build roads and harbors; and open office buildings, hospitals, and schools (see Handelingen Volksraad 1935–36b). This
frontier was animated by the functions of government, not the feats of
brave pioneers. It called for a new Ethical Policy of technological development, but this time not focused on improving the lives of the natives.
Instead, it would be performed for the glory of the Dutch nation and to
reclaim the integrity of the state.

Like the SIKNG and VKNG, the Patriot Club defined the New Guinea
of the future in contrast to the colonial present. But different features
vanished from its terrain. For the territory's development to succeed, New
Guinea would have to be "set free" from the "purely fictive" system of
indirect rule, free from the People's Council's meddling and the bureaucracy's red tape; if possible it should be set free from the Indies' corrupted
government altogether (Nederlandsch Indië 1934; see also Handelingen
Volksraad 1935–36a). This backwater should be made a new crown territory, administered and funded directly by the government in The Hague.
A "strong young governor" took the place of the intrepid young colonists
celebrated in the first two visions. Unchecked by the Indies' moves toward
self-rule, he would lead this gigantic land that "lay awaiting a heroic national act" on behalf of the Dutch crown (Nederlandsch Indië 1934).

Patriot Club writers turned their gaze from Australia to Australian
New Guinea to find a model for the new fatherland. Instead of emphasizing the "sinking" European, they depicted the woeful decline of the Netherlands' international prestige. Its shameful performance in New Guinea
was striking to anyone who glanced at the island's eastern half, which was
run by Australia and featured scores of productive mines and thriving
plantations (Handelingen Volksraad 1935–36a). The Netherlands could
only blame itself for its shortcomings, because the two sides of the island
were identical. Defined by contiguity, not analogy, Dutch New Guinea was
"Australian." Its Papuans (Melanesians) were not of an Asian race (see
Ontwikkeling van en kolonisatie in Nieuw-Guinea 1934, 55).

The Patriot Club vision of New Guinea's cultural essence justified a re-
instatement of the penal sanction in the territory, a measure proposed by
the now retired W. K. H. Feuilletau de Bruyn, whom we met in the previous
chapter (Feuilletau de Bruyn 1936–37, 169).[6] As had once been the case
for Javanese migrant workers, Papuan coolies who fled their employers in
the New Guinea of the future should be jailed. As the Australian rulers
of eastern New Guinea had learned, legally enforced labor contracts had
an edifying effect on these primitive workers. But this portrait did more

than deny New Guinea's natives the protection of ethical reforms. It mobilized a new discourse to keep its European colonists safe. Harking back
to the writings of Friedrich Engels, the Patriot Club's experts placed the
"nomadic" Papuans before the dawn of "private property and the state"
and declared them *res nulla*, thus without rights to land (see Handelingen
Volksraad 1931–32; see also Tucker 1978, 734–60). In the Patriot Club's
vision, New Guinea was distant and empty—far below Europe on the ladder of evolution and entirely empty of law.

   The VKNG and the SIKNG cleared New Guinea of native rights and
native seductresses by making the Papuans a race without a future. For the
SIKNG, the local population's inevitable demise would make room for the
New Guineaer nation. For the VKNG as well, this doomed population fell
outside the purview of plans for native autonomy. As the VKNG's leaders
almost cheerfully put it, nothing could emancipate natives who were dead
(see Onze Toekomst 1933b). This view left the imaginary colonists from
the competing societies with a shared dilemma: how should they deal with
the ghosts? The Patriot Club's solution, if apparently milder, more effectively neutralized the Papuan. The Papuan and the colonist could never
share the same language, desires, or media of exchange. They certainly
could not share the same women or jobs. Placing the colonists among natives who lived in their own cultural infancy, Patriot Club propagandists
forgot their fears of contagion. They suppressed the discomfort others suffered in the face of Papuan audiences. There was no need to imagine the
Papuans as their rivals or, indeed, to imagine themselves through these natives' eyes. A marginalized community found its salvation in the powerful
tools of an unencumbered state that would master a sublimely feminine
Nature. In this Stone Age land of slow evolution, racial hierarchies were
impervious to change.

From Fantasy to History

Of these three visions of New Guinea, the last left the deepest impression.
It is not difficult to imagine why. The Patriot Club's colonization study
committee in the Netherlands was but one in the series of institutions
dedicated to the scholarly examination of New Guinea, a few of which I
introduced in the previous chapter. Sandick, who chaired the Patriot Club
committee, also belonged to the New Guinea Commission. Feuilletau de
Bruyn, who authored the Patriot Club's evolutionary portrait of Papuan

land rights, went on, one may recall, to edit *Tijdschrift Nieuw-Guinea*, which featured articles focused on both sides of the island throughout the 1940s and 1950s. Feuilletau de Bruyn was also a prominent member of the New Guinea Study Circle in Amsterdam, which ran a library and a lecture series attended by retired officials and missionaries, businessmen, and prospective pioneers. The academic separation achieved by these institutions prefigured political divorce. A former governor of Netherlands New Guinea wrote in his memoirs that by the end of World War II, any officer "well-oriented in the literature" who observed the Papuans could see that they had nothing in common with the Indonesians (Baal 1989, 153). By then colonial scholarship had defined the Papuans as Melanesians, cutting them off from the ethnic groups to their west.

The question is not whether real differences divided the natives of New Guinea from the natives of other parts of the colony. Like "the Batak," "the Dayak," and other Indies subjects, "the Papuan" was born in a process of naming in which those designated as such had little part. The documents I have analyzed offer us little insight into what New Guinea's inhabitants made of the encounters that led to this outcome. They tell us little about the projects that Papuans pursued or the various audiences that jostled for attention in their minds as Dutch involvement in their homeland intensified. What is significant is not the truth of the category but the conditions and effects of its development. As the three visions have demonstrated, the Papuans' detachment from the Indies suited a clear set of rhetorical demands.

The 1930s visions infused New Guinea with a significance that was easily rekindled. There are straightforward reasons, I have suggested, why the Dutch selected New Guinea as the place where they would continue their civilizing mission after the rest of the Indies gained independence: the territory fell back into their lap as a result of the Allied campaign that recaptured New Guinea before the end of the war (see Rutherford 2003). But the choice bears a whiff of the contingency that Freud associated with the fetish. Arising at the twilight of empire, this homeland was, in some respect, the last thing that captured the attention of right wing Dutch colonials before the trauma of decolonization set in. For reasons one can imagine, the 1940s were rough on the groups described in this chapter. In the Japanese internment camps where many languished and died, as in the Nazi-occupied Netherlands and, later, in a colony in revolt, old nightmares of dissolution seemed to come true. New Guinea was more than simply a refuge for loyal colonials; its development was an act of national will. Conveniently, the primitive Papuans seemed to cry out for guidance and protection. In the wake of the Indonesian struggle for independence, Dutch nationals in Southeast Asia did not have to look far for an appendage to replace what they had lost.

The discourse that produced this fetish was anything but neuter. Engaging what Leo Spitzer (1990) has called the "sublimated eroticism" of nationalist sentiment, virgin New Guinea became a crucible for the making of men. The SIKNG's Indo-Blijverland (land for Indo-European Settlers) offered relief from the colonist's struggle for acceptance by creating a newfangled "race" that was neither native nor Dutch. The VKNG's White New Guinea completed the colonist's assimilation by erasing his native descent. The Patriot Club's Crown Territory reserved a space for a reinvigorated bureaucracy unimpeded by having to share political power with these particular natives, stuck as they were in a Stone Age past. Kindred subjects emerged in this untainted land, far from Java's distracting pastimes, competing natives, and meddling reformers: the white governor, the Dutch colonist, and the New Guineaer, all powerful, young, and male.

In the first two visions, the colonists' regeneration demanded the purging of a negative femininity. The SIKNG's fantasy traded Java's confusing seductions for the bounty of mother earth. Offering beauty and sustenance, New Guinea gave the Indo settler the determinate origin that the rest of the Indies could not offer. The VKNG's fantasy sought purity through "segregation (Dutch: *apartheid*). To ward off the horrors of the "mixed land" of "mongrel" Java, the colonists needed pure women as well as pure air. Haunting the sites of contagion at moments of doubt, Papuan women represented the return of the repressed. As the Indo's maternal ancestry, as the full-blooded European's native servants, or simply as the source of Indo-European settler indolence, women signified the ambivalence expelled in pure New Guinea. They raised the possibility that the other could, in fact, be the self.

These visions of New Guinea illustrate what has been called the "analytic slippage (in colonial discourse) between the sexual symbols of power and the politics of sex" (Stoler 1985, 636). But they also reflect concerns not captured under the rubric of "sexual control." As the distinctions produced by the colonial system began to blur, shaken Europeans looked to a gendered New Guinea for a "slice of eternity" (see Mosse 1985, 9). But if land and women stood for origins in this fantasy, they could only present the slippery guise of solid ground. This becomes obvious in the final vision in the series. New Guinea's master was a colonial bureaucratic machine: in fetishized form, the very system that the Indo settler had tried to flee.

And so it was for the Indo-European pioneer, who enjoyed a short revival in the early 1950s when the Netherlands had transferred sovereignty
of the archipelago to Indonesians, only to be erased again in the Netherlands' postwar plans. There was a wave of Indo-European migration to
New Guinea following the transfer of sovereignty over the Indies to the
Republic of Indonesia in 1949 (see Portier 1994). A shipload of would-be
colonists was forced to dump dining room sets, pianos, and automobiles
into Doreh Bay after discovering that Manokwari's port had no jetty. All
but a handful of the original colonists had perished when Japanese forces
invaded Dutch New Guinea in April 1942. Ironically, local Papuans had
saved a few of the VKNG settlers who had worked so hard to keep the
natives at arm's length (see Onze Toekomst 1947).

The specter of White New Guinea briefly rose from the ashes in a proposal to purify the Netherlands of the disease of National Socialism after
World War II. A postwar plan to deport convicted Nazi collaborators to
New Guinea reads like a reprint of fascist schemes conjured up in the
1930s. One proposal would have given collaborators a choice between jail
sentences and hard labor in New Guinea (see Tichelman 1946). Those
who helped to open land and roads would have received their own farms.
But the Indo-Europeans, having followed the old dream by escaping to
New Guinea after Indonesia's independence from the Netherlands was a
political reality, soon gave up farming to join an expanding bureaucracy.
Within a few years they found themselves caught between high-ranking
civil servants born in the Netherlands and Papuans being groomed for
self-rule (see Portier 1994, 143). Old debates on the use of different salary scales for different groups made the rounds in Dutch New Guinea,
where many politically minded Papuans had their hearts set on a nation
that would exclude the so-called Indies Dutch (see Drooglever 2009, 541).
Postwar New Guinea was a scene for imparting Europeanness to someone other than the Indo. Portraying the Dutch nation as the Papuans'
privileged protector, the new rhetoric was grounded in an imagined affinity between the natives and the Dutch (see Rooijen 1989, 24–38; see also
Rutherford 2009). When the New Guinea dream expired once and for all
in the early 1960s, most Indo-Europeans and scores of Papuans fled Indonesian rule and together made the Netherlands their home.

These gendered visions of a pure New Guinea mark a moment in the entangled history through which Dutch colonialism created both the Indies'
rulers and those they ruled. Ann Stoler has described colonial fantasies
like those described in this chapter as "not events but the 'negative print'

of what stirred official anxiety to which colonial agents responded with infeasible policies for implausible arrangements that could be neither carried out nor sustained" (2009, 22). Yet in the case of Dutch New Guinea, this description underestimates the impact that such fantasies could have. However implausible, these visions of New Guinea directly contributed to the Netherlands' postwar retention of New Guinea, an arrangement that was carried out, if not sustained. The people of West Papua have had to live with this legacy. The Netherlands' postwar promotion of Papuan nationalism planted the seeds of the independence movement that has waxed and waned in the Indonesian provinces into which western New Guinea now is divided. The Indonesian authorities in Jakarta have attempted to promote integration through programs that echo colonial policies and plans (see Manning and Rumbiak 1989). Instead of European colonists, Indonesian transmigrants have trekked from crowded Java to this promised land far to the east. In the mid-1930s a pioneer wife told a little joke after her home was shaken by an earthquake: "Feel that? My husband finally put his shovel in the soil!" (Drooglever 1980, 203). Dutch dreams have given way to Indonesian realities, but in "empty New Guinea," some things have not changed. In the words of Nietzsche, it is distance—"*Distance!*"—that gives woman her allure (in Derrida 1978b, 47). The maternal fatherland, the paternal fetish: up close, it never seems the same.

CHAPTER FOUR

Waiting for the End in Biak

A "Not Wholly Peaceful" Protest

On July 6, 1998, just before dawn, soldiers opened fire on some two hundred demonstrators in Biak City, on Biak Island, in Biak-Numfor Regency, in the territory that was once Dutch New Guinea but was then known as the Indonesian province of Irian Jaya, to list some of the other names by which West Papua has gone. For four days the demonstrators had been guarding a flag that flew a hundred feet above them on top of a water tower between the main market and the port.[1] The demonstrators had raised the flag before dawn on July 2. Later that morning, at an open forum attended by the head of the district government and commanders of the district military and police, their leader, a young civil servant named Filep Karma, read an oath of allegiance to West Papua, the name of the sovereign nation that Karma and others wanted Irian Jaya to become. "We, the people of West Papua, pledge to stay united, no matter what the circumstances, under the flag of West Papua and the eastern morning star and pledge to live and die for the flag of West Papua which has already flown over an independent Papuan land," read the first lines of the document, which took the form of a letter signed by Karma and forty-two other protesters.[2] On behalf of the Papuan people, Karma went on to urge United Nations Secretary General Kofi Annan to come to Biak to hear their case and named "God, the Father, Son, and Holy Ghost" as the witnesses to the pledge. That afternoon, when the security forces injured an older demonstrator while attempting to break up the demonstration, the demonstrators retaliated by attacking several policemen and burning a military truck. On July 5, after negotiations with the demonstrators broke down, the authorities issued an ultimatum. If the crowd did not lower the flag voluntarily, the troops would remove it by force.

The shooting is said to have lasted from 5:30 a.m. to 7:00 a.m. Just how many people were injured and killed in the operation remains unclear. Colonel Edyono, the Armed Forces commander in Biak, initially announced that there were twenty-one casualties and no fatalities (see Sydney Morning Herald 1998a). Other sources have put the death toll between five and a hundred; reports of torture and disappearances abound (see Human Rights Watch 1998b, 1998c). After the Indonesian Human Rights Commission investigated the incident, the military leader finally admitted that one man, Ruben Orboi, had been killed (see Cenderawasih Pos 1998b). Orboi's body had been carried out to the sea, the commander told reporters. Fearing further unrest, the soldiers had decided to conceal the death. Instead of releasing the corpse to Orboi's family for burial in the village cemetery, they hid it in a shallow, beachside grave. When I arrived in Biak in late July 1998 for a brief visit, bodies had begun washing up on Biak beaches. Although the government claimed to have proof that these corpses were victims of the tsunami that struck Papua New Guinea on July 18, the police ordered villagers to bury them immediately (see Cenderawasih Pos 1998c). When I left Biak in early August, Filep Karma remained in police custody, with gunshot wounds to both of his legs.[3] It seems likely that the lowering of the flag cost many more than one of his supporters their lives.

The "flag of West Papua and the eastern morning star," which the Biak demonstrators were guarding, was officially raised in Hollandia, Dutch New Guinea's capital, next to the Dutch flag on December 1, 1961, at a time when some Dutch leaders still believed they could avoid transferring the colony to Indonesia (see Osborne 1986; Drooglever 2009, 560). Inspired in part by the American stars and stripes, in part by Biak myth, Papuan elder statesman Nicolaas Jouwe, then a member of the New Guinea Council, designed the so-called Morning Star flag. On October 21, 1961, Jouwe and other Papuan leaders convened a National Committee of seventeen representatives from across Dutch New Guinea to adopt this new flag and other West Papuan national symbols. Along with the national anthem, "Oh, My Papuan Homeland" (Malay: *Hai Papua Tanahku*), the flag became a powerful symbol of resistance to Indonesian rule (see Drooglever 2009, 555–57). (The other symbol adopted was the West Papuan coat of arms, which featured a crested pigeon and the national motto, "Diversity in Unity," a reversal of the Indonesian national motto, "Unity in Diversity." This motto later became "One Nation, One Soul.") This was, one will recall, less than a year before the United States and Australia brokered the deal that set West Papua on the path to integration into Indonesia. Indonesia was then threatening to invade Dutch New Guinea, having built up its military in part with Soviet-supplied arms (see Drooglever 2009, 570–74).[4] For over a decade, Indonesian leaders had been calling for the liberation of the territory, which they renamed West Irian, using a Biak term coined around the time of the round table negotiations that led to Indonesian independence in 1949. The Dutch had promised to meet with their Indonesian counterparts within a year after the signing of the Round Table Agreement to decide who would gain sovereignty over western New Guinea. According to many in Jakarta, the outcome should have been a foregone conclusion: the West Irianese, as the Indonesians called the Papuans, should have been liberated from the Dutch—and joined the Indonesian Republic—in 1950, rather than 1963.

Notwithstanding the high-minded rhetoric voiced by Sukarno, Indonesia's first president, during the dispute, the conditions under which the territory finally changed hands proved brutal for the Papuans. In the years leading up to the transfer, Indonesian strategists had envisioned a scenario in which the Irianese would welcome their Indonesian liberators and rise up with them against the Dutch (see Drooglever 2009, 367–68). In the event, there was widespread resentment toward the new rulers. The Indonesian government quickly took over from the United Nations Temporary Executive Authority (UNTEA), which the New York Agreement established to oversee the transfer and to assist in preparations for the Act of Free Choice, that controversial "act of self-determination" held to determine whether the territory would become an independent nation-state. Indonesian officials initially toyed with canceling the act, which they viewed as an unnecessary measure (Drooglever 2005, 618). It soon became clear that Indonesia would not run the risk of losing West Irian as a result of the consultation, which, as we have seen, was scheduled for 1969 (see Saltford 2002).[5] Headed by Ali Moertopo, a Special Operation for West Irian led the campaign for integration, often resorting to coercive means. Moertopo's efforts ensured the "success" of the act: under the military's watchful eyes, the 1,022 tribal leaders had little choice but to opt for their homeland to remain a province of Indonesia. In the years leading up to the act, groups of urban Papuans staged demonstrations demanding genuine self-determination; others entered the forest and took up arms (see Tapol 1981). According to one account, it was the Indonesian authorities that gave the budding movement its name: the Free Papua Movement (Organisasi Papua Merdeka, OPM) (Djopari 1993, 100).

The OPM repeated the nation-founding ritual of December 1, 1961, on July 1, 1971, when Jacob Prai and Seth Rumkorem of the Papua National Army (Tentara Papua Nasional, or TPN) raised the Morning Star flag and proclaimed West Papua's independence in their guerilla headquarters near the Papua New Guinea border. Both Prai and Rumkorem now live in exile in Europe; from his home in Sweden, Prai is a particularly vocal participant in the online community of West Papuan activists. In an Indonesian-language speech commemorating the thirty-fifth anniversary of the declaration, distributed on a listserv to be read aloud at celebrations in West Papua, Prai explained why the guerilla leaders had taken this step.

> The West Papuan Independence Proclamation of July 1, 1971 was *the way* that was most correct, just, honest, excellent, beautiful, and rational, or, the solution that was most correct, rational, and just for the Melanesian people in this land of Papua; besides this, there was no other road open for trying to stop the expansion of the conflict between the colonial government of the Republic of Indonesia and the ordinary people of Papua, who were still weak and not strong enough in the political, economic, and military senses to fight in physical opposition to the Republic of Indonesia's army, which had modern weapons provided by the U.S., the E.U, Russia, and other countries on the face of this earth. (Prai 2006, 3)

According to Prai, at the time of the 1971 proclamation, as at the time of the 1969 Act of Free Choice, the Papuans "had already been free as our own country, that is, 'The Republic of West Papua of 1961–1962" (Prai 2006, 5). The 1961 flag raising had made a statement to the international community, inviting it to view the ceremony as an expression of West Papuan national will. In the same fashion, the flag raisings held in 1971 and throughout the following decades provided "ordinary people" who were "too weak" to vanquish the well-armed Indonesian military with a chance to recruit global allies in the struggle against what Prai, Karma, and many other Papuans regard as a colonial regime.

The July 1, 1998, flag raising on Biak coincided with demonstrations in other provincial cities: Sorong, Nabire, Wamena, Jayapura, and Abepura, the site of the provincial university. The twenty-seventh anniversary of OPM's Proclamation of West Papuan Independence fell a little over a month after the resignation of Indonesia's second president, Suharto, after thirty-one years in office (see Djopari 1993, 116; Osborne 1986, 55). The Indonesian province of Irian Jaya was born during the same decade as Suharto's New Order regime. Suharto commanded a military mission established in 1961 to lead the threatened Indonesian invasion of West Irian, four years before coming to power in the aborted coup and state-sponsored massacres that destroyed the Indonesian Communist Party and forced President Sukarno out of office. In Irian Jaya, Suharto's sudden abdication served to revive old hopes. Through radio and newspaper reports, as well as gossip, those who joined in the protests had no doubt heard of the riots that swept Jakarta and other major Indonesian cities in May 1998, as well as the peaceful student protests that preceded them. Those with computers or televisions may have seen images of the students who occupied the parliament building during Suharto's final days. Between rounds of chanting and singing, the protesters chatted with young soldiers, who smiled, their weapons idle at their sides. The brutal response of Indonesian troops to the proindependence protests in Biak and elsewhere provided a lesson in the limits of *reformasi*, as this brave new era in Indonesian politics was dubbed. "These people were not demanding reform; they wanted a separate state," the commander in Biak explained (Sydney Morning Herald 1998a; see also Reuters 1998a). Against such a "betrayal of the nation," added General Wiranto, the chief of the Indonesian Armed Forces, "firm action" was required.

One need not look far for a straightforward explanation of the flag raising and its aftermath on Biak. "This really isn't a new problem," said one Biak friend, voicing a sentiment widely shared in the province. "People want a fair referendum so they can decide their fate." Such a referendum would force the world to acknowledge what Papuan nationalists already know themselves to be: in Prai's words, "a nation that is free, sovereign, civilized, and glorious and is the master and mistress of this land where we spilled our blood" (Prai 2006, 4). It was not surprising that Indonesia's post-Suharto rulers have opposed such a proposal. Shortly after Suharto's fall, several members of the US Congress sent a letter to the new president, Bacharuddin Jusuf Habibie, who was vice president under Suharto and replaced him when he resigned, and Amien Rais, his most powerful opponent, calling for dialogue on the political status of East Timor and Irian Jaya. While Indonesia proved open to negotiations on East Timor, both Habibie and Rais indicated in July 1998 that they would draw the line at Indonesia's resource-rich easternmost province (see Sydney Morning Herald 1998b). In the fall of 1998, there was some softening of this stance, with plans going ahead for a "national dialogue" between provincial leaders and the Indonesian national government.[6] But when one hundred representatives from the province presented Habibie with a demand for independence on February 26, 1999, in Jakarta, the president told them to go home and think again. For their part, the Indonesian armed forces reacted predictably to the July 1998 demonstrations in Irian Jaya. Under the New Order, military officers had a stake in the designation of certain provinces as "unstable." Former commanders often lived out their retirement in such regions so they could reap the harvest of profitable business deals made in such areas, where they wielded increased political and economic clout. While the assault came later than it would have under Suharto—when flag raisings lasted minutes, not days—the brutal treatment of the demonstrators followed a familiar script in which soldiers protect the Republic from the enemy within.

I would not want to underplay the long history of broken promises, corruption, and discrimination that led Karma and his followers to demand an independent West Papuan state. Nor would I want to downplay the individual, institutional, and international interests that have colluded in the continuance of Indonesian rule. At the same time, I would not want to let this straightforward explanation deflect attention from the subtler, less self-evident forces that came together in this highly charged event. According to the commander in Biak, only fifty of the demonstrators were "hardcore" separatists; the other three hundred were "deluded" by promises of miraculous improvements in conditions and the belief that something religious was going on (see Cenderawasih Pos 1998b, 1). A critique of this attempt to explain away the "disturbance" must go further than asserting that religion provided a language for the protesters. An interpretation of the flag raising must pay heed to the metaphysical underpinnings of all modern states. As this chapter makes clear, when we pay heed to these underpinnings, the uneasy relationship between sovereignty and audience comes to the fore. So does the role of violence in nation-founding performances, like the Biak flag raising. Like all performances, the Biak flag raising created something new even as it resonated with the echo of prior events: the 1961 flag raising, the 1971 proclamation, and, as I argue in this chapter, other violent moments of rupture rooted in a local society with its own singular past.

Violence and Performance

In a report on the July demonstrations, Human Rights Watch notes that the proindependence actions in Irian Jaya were "not all wholly peaceful"

(Human Rights Watch 1998b). Those who gathered under the Morning Star flag in Biak would probably object to this description, and rightly so. At the hands of the Indonesian security forces, protestors who had done little more than dance, pray, and sing hymns suffered horribly for the so-called crime of peacefully expressing their views. In an interview with anthropologist Eben Kirksey, who was on Biak at the time of the attack and has written extensively about the incident, Filep Karma stressed how he had promoted nonviolence in the speeches he gave at the water tower. A published excerpt from the open forum held there on July 2 confirms this observation. "I call on the people to defend the flag armed only with the Bible and the Hymnal . . . if we are only armed with the Bible and the Hymnal, the police will not shoot us," Karma announced (see ELS-HAM 1999, 11). Karma is a man of faith, but he was also aware that the movement would be more likely to garner international support if the Papuans refrained from using force, even if—and, indeed, particularly if—the Indonesian security forces opened fire. In calling for a peaceful protest, Karma may have had in mind particular spectators: the US Congress members, but also a United Nations envoy who was then in Jakarta pressing for dialogue on the future of East Timor, which two American journalists thrust into the international limelight in 1991 when they released footage of a massacre of unarmed protesters (Democracy Now 2006). Be that as it may, Karma's followers took to heart his description of the potency of the Bible and Hymnal, even if, as we shall see, some interpreted his words more literally than Karma himself did. Yet if we define violence more broadly, the Human Rights Watch assessment confirms what upon reflection should seem obvious. Violence was not simply a means to an end in the raising and lowering of the flag; it was crucial to the very meaning of both gestures. Violence was intricately implicated in both these fraught performances, as were the distant audiences, earthly and divine, that the protesters and their opponents tried to welcome to this scene.

This is not to say that the Papuan protestors engaged in anything like the acts of atrocity perpetrated by the Indonesian soldiers. Rather, the violence I have in mind consists of the forceful reframing of a situation, such that the people, places, and practices at hand suddenly appear in a changed light. This kind of violence always entails actions addressed to audiences. It can, but need not, entail the giving of physical harm. The demonstration on Biak began with an act of violence defined in these broader terms. Much to the surprise of passers-by, the Morning Star flag materialized on the water tower: an apparition from a sovereign past and the harbinger of a hoped-for sovereign future. Like a lenticulated image—say, on a refrigerator magnet—that changes shape as one walks past it, the scene before these spectators suddenly morphed. "Irian Jaya" came into focus as "West Papua," and a dusty empty lot became hallowed ground.

This forceful reframing of the situation created a context for violent acts of a more conventional sort. What was at stake in that contested piece of cloth known as the Morning Star flag was Indonesia's sovereignty. Recognized by the international community, this sovereignty gave the Indonesian state a monopoly over the legitimate use of force (see Weber 1990b; see also Benjamin 1978). This monopoly was clearly challenged by the demonstrators' attack on the police on the afternoon of July 2. But it was also challenged by the flag's very appearance at the top of the water tower and by the oath that Karma read at the open forum earlier that day. The demonstration began with what J. L. Austin (1976) calls a performative: an utterance that created its own truth. Karma's oath literally did what it said: it made a vow and described that vow all at once. Like the OPM's 1971 proclamation, the oath Karma read forcefully reframed the situation by conjuring a sovereign subject—the West Papuan nation—in whose name he promised never to abandon the flag.

In making this argument, I am experimenting with a different understanding of violence than that of the French sociologist Pierre Bourdieu, who has written of "originary acts of constitution" like the Biak flag raising (1981, 208). Bourdieu influenced a generation of anthropologists and social scientists with his account of "symbolic violence"—"*censored, euphemized*, i.e., unrecognizable, socially recognized violence"—which Bourdieu defined in opposition to "overt (physical or economic) violence" (Bourdieu 1977 [1972], 191). Initially, Bourdieu located symbolic violence in "pre-capitalist" forms of domination that were "disguised under the veil of enchanted relations" modeled on the bonds of reciprocity and obligation that united kin (Bourdieu 1977 [1972], 191). Later, Bourdieu (1981) extended the reach of this analytic concept from the "gentle, hidden violence" of the strategic gifts given by patrons to clients to the "political fetishism" by which delegates usurped the power of the "dominated" individuals for whom they spoke. The Biak flag raising provides a classical example of the latter kind of symbolic violence. Bourdieu would endorse what, as we shall see, was the view of Karma's critics: Karma spoke "on behalf of and in the name of [the Papuans]," but he also spoke "in [the Papuans'] place," furthering his own interests by presenting them as identical with those of the would-be nation (Bourdieu 1981, 209). Symbolic violence consists of action recognized as legitimate—and even valorized—by the dominated, as well as the dominant: "credit, confidence, obligation, personal loyalty, hospitality, gifts, gratitude, piety" (Bourdieu 1977 [1972], 192). Yet behind the illusion of consent lies coercion—the coercion entailed in the social production of the habitual dispositions that lead the parties involved to misrecognize these acts of violence for what they are. It takes a critical observer like Bourdieu to recognize the violence inherent in a delegate's "usurpatory ventriloquism." The victims of symbolic violence rarely do.

Do not be mistaken: when it comes to the Biak demonstration, there are good conceptual and ethical reasons to draw a distinction between the protesters' actions and the soldiers' reactions. But this does not mean that we need to follow Bourdieu's lead when we set these two forms of violence apart. For Bourdieu, as for Durkheim and Hobbes, whom he quotes in this respect, "the principle of all recognized and recognizable coercion" is the "move from the individual to the collective" (Bourdieu 1981, 212). Symbolic (unrecognizable, socially recognized) violence is collective violence, the violence done to individuals by collective forces. Overt (physical and economic) violence is presumably something else. Bourdieu's account of violence is impoverished in ways that become clear when we think more carefully about the nature of violence. As this chapter makes clear, the "move from the individual to the collective"—or, rather, a multitude of such collectives, of audiences, let us say—forms the "principle of recognized and recognizable constraint" that accounts for the social efficacy of both the firing of rifles and the raising of flags.

I have come to this realization with help from the German essayist Walter Benjamin. In "Critique of Violence," Benjamin sets out to delineate the essence of the violent act, something obscured when analysts consider violence as a means to an end. Benjamin proceeds by first establishing the difference between "lawmaking" and "law-preserving " violence. Lawmaking violence is the violence of the revolutionary who aims to institute a new political order, whereas law-preserving violence is the violence of the police officer and executioner. Lawmaking violence creates the new ends that, in retrospect, it appears only to serve; law-preserving violence maintains the status quo. Examples that illustrate these two kinds of violence are easy to come by. One man's freedom fighter is another man's terrorist, as the long history of American imperialism makes clear. Significantly for my purposes, Benjamin lays bare the questions of legitimacy—what Bourdieu calls "recognizability"—raised by violence in all its forms. These are not simply questions for critical observers, as Bourdieu would have it;

they are questions for participants. They are questions embedded in what Benjamin seeks as the essence of the violent act, an essence left obscure when scholars, journalists, officials, and activists focus on causes and effects to explain and/or justify the use of force. Audiences—audiences that recognize—loom large in Benjamin's effort to conceive of violence as something other than a tool for achieving or preserving sovereignty. As a result of this attention to audiences, violence becomes a limit concept for Benjamin, much as sovereignty is a limit concept for Georges Bataille, whose formulations I have discussed. Even the lawmaking violence at the origins of a new political order still anticipates a future audience that will legitimate this founding act. Only divine violence, Benjamin insists, is unrecognizable—or, rather, it is only recognizable to God.

According to Derrida (1996), Benjamin's reflections on violence enable us to grasp the violence of performativity. Oaths like Karma's partake of a kind of "lawmaking" violence: pulling themselves up by their bootstraps, as it were, they preemptively create their own truth as world-transforming and subject-creating acts. One can never pinpoint this moment of world transformation and subject creation. The authorizing source of Karma's pledge—the "Papuan people"—only came into being by virtue of this pledge having been voiced; no one can say which came first. This is because sign-users never live purely in the present; they can only ever know what they are saying by anticipating what they will have said. Derrida (1986) relates this "undecidability" to a common component of nation-founding performatives: their tendency to appeal to the transcendent (see also Lee 1997, 328). "With the blessings and love of God, West Papua already achieved independence on December 1, 1961," Karma told his followers. "West Papuan independence is due to the love and blessings of God, not due to the accomplishments of any one person or humanity as a whole. And this independence we ask for from God" (ELS-HAM 1999, 11). Contending verb tenses rub up against each other in these lines from Karma's oath: independence existed in the past, it exists in the present, and yet it is something that will happen in the future. It is God, both the witness and the source of Papuan freedom, past, present, and future, who has the "supreme and absolute power"—the spectral sovereignty—needed to merge these contending verb tenses into one.

But as this chapter also proposes, we can take Benjamin's reflections on the relationship between violence and audience in the opposite direction as well: not only are performatives violent, violence is performative. Anthropologist David Riches (1991) has argued that the very term, *violence*, brings to mind multiple audiences, including audiences whose conception of the good is violated by the violent act. Among these violated audiences is the victim of violence. The "grandmotherly elephant" of George Orwell's short story, to recall chapter 1, is just as important a component of the scene of colonial violence as the "immense crowd" that compels Orwell's narrator to pull the trigger. The tension between the viewpoints offered by this victim and these witnesses is a key component of what Orwell calls "the real motive for which despotic governments act" (Orwell 1950 [1936]). Riches goes so far as to suggest that violence is always preemptive: in striking the other, one eliminates in advance the other's opposition to the violent act. Albeit in a negative fashion, by this formulation, violence implicitly responds to the sense that another is watching. Through a blow that immobilizes one's victim and suppresses his or her point of view, one puts one's own spin on the situation. One preemptively defines one's violence as a justified means, forcefully imposing this perspective on one's victim through the very act of delivering the blow. In this sense, every act of violence is "lawmaking." Every act of violence is a performative that "says" what it "does." This is because all human acts—including physically harmful ones—call for interpretation. More than one audience—and more than one set of what Bourdieu calls "predispositions"—are always in play, simultaneously and by turns defining and haunting the violent act. When the soldiers fired on the demonstrators, their violence consisted of the forceful reframing of a situation, a reframing that legitimated itself by suppressing certain perspectives and putting others in their place.

Approaching violence in this fashion has helped me gain a richer understanding of the uneasy relationship between sovereignty and audience. Acts of violence, both ordinary and sovereign, always presume an evaluating gaze, even when they target what Agamben (1998) calls "bare life." But it is not only this expanded notion of violence that I wish to foreground in my analysis of the Biak demonstration. I also wish to foreground the contemporary geographies of West Papuan sovereignty in which these demonstrators' forceful reframing of a situation took place. To borrow another of Derrida's ideas concerning performativity, this task requires attention to the "iterability" of the performances that made up the demonstration—that is, to the fact that these performances were only legible to the extent that they appeared as repetitions of what had come before (see Derrida 1982). Divergent histories shaped the expectations of those involved in the Biak demonstration, when it came to the multiple audiences that the protesters and soldiers addressed and conjured. Crucially, these histories also shaped their expectations concerning the questions raised by Bourdieu, Benjamin, Derrida, and Riches: questions about what violence is and what it does.

Later in the book, I will have more to say about the expectations of West Papuan nationalists concerning the extranational audiences and interlocutors who have long played a critical role in nation-founding performances (see chapters 7 and 8). Here I focus on another audience addressed by the flag raising, consisting of the Biaks who witnessed the demonstration on their way to and from Biak City's main market and port—and in some cases joined in. I also focus on a wider audience of Indonesian and Papuan spectators whose expectations were shaped by a long history of Indonesian state violence. My discussion so far provides the basis for a preliminary explanation of the relation between violence and performance in the demonstration. But this explanation only captures one aspect of the confrontation on Biak, which brought together a multiplicity of conceptions of the relationship of violence to order and origins, not to mention truth.

In the remaining sections of this chapter, I explore the intersection between these multiple conceptions. In charting the contemporary geographies of West Papuan sovereignty, I offer a tentative answer to a question that many on Biak found important: what gave these demonstrators, young and old, the courage to face up to armed soldiers? I seek a response not only in Papuan nationalism and the recent experience of Indonesian rule, but also in the long tradition of Biak millenarianism. In chapter 6 I will consider the relationship between this tradition, the history of Christian institutions in West Papua, and the role of Christianity in the Papuan nationalist movement. In this chapter, I focus more narrowly on how this tradition finds its basis in everyday practices that transform what is foreign into a source of value, authority, and prestige. Biaks have long tended to valorize objects and texts—from foreign porcelain to government slogans—that they take as traces of encounters with dangerous outsiders. Biaks posit the violence of a clash between worldviews in the course of creating their identities and seeking status and power. To recall my broader definition of violence, Biaks both quench and feed a yearning for the forceful reframing of a situation in the activities, ordinary and dramatic, that punctuate life in their homeland. This valorization of the foreign, taken alone, cannot account for the proindependence protests in Biak. Nevertheless, at critical moments, a distinctly millennial vision has shaped the way Biaks envision and pursue political change.

As Kirksey (2012) points out, multiple visions and desires came together in the Biak flag raising. The demonstrators all had grievances against the

Indonesian government, and few were satisfied with the Papuans' standing in the province. Some no doubt came to the water tower in pursuit of what Orwell called "a bit of fun." Still others, including the prayer group leaders who, as Kirksey reports, first proposed the flag raising, viewed the protest as enacting God's will. Some Biaks reportedly went even further. "God, the Father, Son and Holy Ghost" was really Manarmakeri, the Biak ancestor responsible for outsiders' wealth and power. However Filep Karma's oath may have followed a familiar model for the founding of a nation, in the very act of appealing to the divine, Karma may have allowed for a reframing premised on a very different audience, with different assumptions about the nature of power, space, and time. But if I approach the flag raising as a millennial moment, I also pay heed to the more conventionally violent narratives of transformation promulgated by the Indonesian regime. To set the stage for this analysis, I begin by briefly considering the broader forces that have encouraged Biaks to participate in the Papuan nationalist movement from its earliest stages to the present day.

Papuan Nationalism and Biak Cosmopolitanism

Rising from the Pacific at the mouth of the Cenderawasih Bay, roughly two hundred kilometers off the New Guinea mainland, three small islands and a scattering of atolls make up the Indonesian Regency of Biak-Numfor. Over the territory's colonial and postcolonial history, the inhabitants of these islands have sometimes appeared as exemplary of Papuan or Irianese identity, sometimes as the exception that proves the rule. As I have noted in previous chapters, Biak-speaking seafarers were among the first of New Guinea's inhabitants to confront European traders, missionaries, and officials by virtue of their long-standing tributary relations with the Moluccan Sultanate of Tidore. By 1920 the Netherlands Indies military had pacified the islands. By the early 1930s the vast majority of Biaks had converted to Protestantism, and almost every village featured a mission church and school. In the late 1940s one official observed that illiteracy was "virtually nonexistent" among Biak men below the age of thirty-five (see de Bruyn 1948, 7). At a time when, in western New Guinea's rugged highlands, the ancestors of today's Dani, Me, and Amungme had yet to encounter Europeans, Biak evangelists were spreading the Gospel along New Guinea's northern coast.

Often to the consternation of Papuans from other groups, Biaks still tend to think of themselves both as more sophisticated than the territory's other indigenous inhabitants, and as more qualified to represent the Papuans as a nation. Biak's long-standing experience with outsiders made the islanders fodder for early Dutch descriptions of the customs and character of the Papuan (see, e.g., Feuilletau de Bruyn 1936–37). In the 1950s, when the Dutch retained western New Guinea as a separate colony, Biaks and other coastal Papuans continued to play a central role in colonial representations of the territory's natives as well as in policies designed to cultivate an educated Papuan elite. Dutch propaganda featured before-and-after photographs, opposing scantily clad tribesmen from the highlands to smiling coastal workers (see Vademecum voor Nederlands Nieuw-Guinea 1956). Figures from Biak, Sentani, and other places with a long history of contact stood in for the modern Papuan whom this new civilizing mission promised to produce.

By making progress appear as the outcome of Dutch intervention, these images obscure the accidents of geography and history that have made places like Biak and Jayapura what they were in 1998: relatively urban, cosmopolitan, multiethnic sites in a vast, sparsely populated province. During World War II, when the war in the Pacific started to turn against Japan, the Occupation forces began building what is still the longest runway in Indonesia on Biak Island; the Allies completed the project during MacArthur's famous island-hopping campaign, after driving out the Japanese (see Smith 1953, 280–396). After the war, the Dutch expanded the airport and the surrounding settlement, building on the foundations of the American military base. In 1998, in addition to an international airport, Biak City boasted a port; a canning factory; a plywood mill; three markets; two supermarkets; numerous shops, hotels, restaurants, and karaoke bars; three military posts; and countless government offices. It was home to Makassarese and ethnic Chinese merchants; officials and soldiers from Java, Bali, Sumatra, Ambon, and other distant Indonesian islands; a handful of Western visitors; and a large community from other provincial tribes. Urban Biaks included everyone from the Regent to NGO directors to teachers, day laborers, taxi conductors (people, usually young boys, who hustle for passengers and collect fares on public minivan taxis), nurses, and low-paid government clerks. Among their numbers was a growing population of young, unemployed high school graduates and drop-outs, many of whom whiled away their days at the taxi terminal near the main market. Some were waiting for job openings in the civil service, which, despite its expansion under the New Order, could absorb only a fraction of those who applied.

In addition, at any one time, Biak City was a temporary home to scores of rural Biaks: fishermen selling their catch, subsistence farmers marketing their extra fruit and vegetables, seasonal construction workers, and children staying with relatives while they attended school. In the years leading up to 1998, the Indonesian government had extended roads and bridges to distant coastal villages, making it easier for villagers to travel to market and for elite Biaks to build retirement homes on their kin group's land. With luck, one could make it to Biak City from almost anywhere in the islands in less than five hours. (By contrast, to reach the nearest market or government office, many Papuans living in the highlands had to walk long distances or wait for rides from small mission planes that could not land unless the weather was clear.) In the early 1990s, when Biak was a refueling stop on the route between Los Angeles and Jakarta, Honolulu was less than twelve hours away. Biak bureaucrats and academics, traveling to Jakarta, Townsville, or Leiden, sometimes boarded these international flights.

Below, I discuss in detail the distinctive values that oriented Biaks' participation in social arenas extending far beyond the local setting. But at this point, it is worth noting how conditions in Biak brought into sharp relief grievances shared by other provincial groups. In 1998 Biak-Numfor was the most densely populated regency in Irian Jaya, and, with its upraised coral soils, one of the least fertile. Yet Biaks had surrendered land for a range of projects, from a satellite launcher to a transmigration site to a five-star resort. Biak fishermen complained of declining yields as commercial trawlers depleted coastal stocks. As elsewhere in the province, migrants from elsewhere in Indonesia dominated the urban economy, owning everything from the taxis villagers rode into town to the shops where they bought sugar and rice (see Garnaut and Manning 1974; Manning and Rumbiak 1991; McGibbon 2004b). Traders from Makassar, a coastal area in southern Sulawesi with a long history of male outmigration, monopolized the choicest stalls in the central market, leaving local producers to crouch along the outer aisles or in the dirt outside. Local residents also found themselves pushed to the margins in the competition for government benefits. To the consternation of Biak parents, the children of migrants from outside the province often won jobs and scholarships reserved for the locally born.

Biaks were well aware of the province's vast reserves of minerals and natural gas; some had seen the Freeport gold and copper mine firsthand. They were also aware that public services in the province were woefully inadequate. Even in this relatively accessible regency, classrooms stood empty, and clinics were understaffed and understocked. Above all, Biaks shared with others in the province indelible memories of state terror (see Ballard 2002a). Some still carried scars (and in some cases bullets) from the turbulent 1970s, when the Indonesian military attacked North and West Biak villages, in the more remote parts of the island, to flush out armed guerrillas. Under the New Order, activists who criticized government policies were often accused of harboring separatist sympathies. Biaks had learned from decades of extrajudicial violence that the label OPM could be the "kiss of death" (Tapol 1980).

But it is not enough simply to point to what the Papuan anthropologist and public intellectual Benny Giay has called a *memoria passionis*, "history of suffering," to understand why the dream of self-determination not only survived, but thrived in Biak and Irian Jaya more generally (see Hernawan and van den Broek 1998). The four decades of New Order rule introduced a range of shared experiences that made an independent West Papua imaginable for growing numbers of the province's inhabitants. On the one hand, one must pay heed to the unifying effects of provincial initiatives from Internet newsgroups to newspapers like *Cenderawasih Pos* and *Tifa Irian* to government-sponsored contests promoting provincial costumes and dances. These technologies account for how Irian's highly diverse population came to express a sense of shared purpose, despite the disunity that often plagued the OPM.

On the other hand, one must consider the circumference of the administrative pilgrimages taken by the provincial elite (see Anderson 1991, 53–56, 170–78). A popular slogan depicts the territorial state of Indonesia as reaching from Sabang, the farthest western town in the archipelago, located in Aceh province, to Merauke, the farthest east. No matter how much overseas training they received, the majority of provincial bureaucrats, soldiers, and academics pursued their careers in the space between Sorong, a town on the west coast of New Guinea's Bird's Head Peninsula, and Merauke—that is, within the borders of Irian Jaya. The same elite long sustained the Papuan nationalist movement, both in the province and overseas (See Tapol 1981, 5). Eben Kirksey (2012) has analyzed how Papuans have collaborated with the Indonesian system without losing their vision of liberation. While Biaks have had no monopoly on OPM leadership—or high-ranking government posts—suitable examples of the phenomenon described by Kirksey emerge from their ranks. Markus Kaisiëpo, West Papua's first president-in-exile, was a graduate of the Netherlands New Guinea School for Native Administrators, and Permenas Ferry Awom, leader of the 1965 Manokwari rebellion, was a member of the Papuan Volunteer Brigade. But Seth Rumkorem, the OPM/TPN brigadier general who joined with Prai to declare independence in 1971, was an officer in the Indonesian army, and Arnold Ap, a promoter of Papuan culture and martyr to the nationalist cause, was a lecturer in anthropology at the provincial university and the curator of a museum of provincial art (see Djopari 1993, 100–131; Sharp with Kaisiëpo 1994; Anderson 1991, 178). Although consultants I spoke with suggested that he acted without the involvement of established Papuan nationalist groups, Filep Karma, the organizer of the Biak flag raising, fits the profile of a typical Papuan nationalist leader. Son of the first Biak to serve as a regent, Karma was, until his arrest, a midlevel official in the provincial administration. Like so many nationalists before him, he is the product of the system that he risked his life to overturn.

The new imaginings made possible by contemporary modes of communication and institutions played a crucial role in the flag raising on Biak. But there is more to the story, as the rest of this chapter should confirm. I have already offered some thoughts on the performative dimensions of the July protest and the multiple things that the demonstrators did with their gestures and words. My understanding of the demonstration is based on the proposition that it is possible for people to invoke different identities and address different audiences, both across settings and in the course of a single social interaction (see Errington 1998b, 4–5). This proposition, as should be clear by now, is at the heart of all the chapters in this book. Whether one has in mind the reading of a newspaper or the raising of a flag, representations are always in some sense underdetermined (see Keane 1997). Although interpretations of a performance are always contextually based, no single context is ever exhaustive of all the possible meanings of an event. This is not to deny that some readings are more powerful or pronounced than others; the challenge is to consider how contrasting and even contradictory frameworks can intersect in historically grounded and systematic ways—and how their intersection itself can carry a force.

Among West Papuan nationalists, one sees evidence of such an intersection on the provincial level, where nationalist pronouncements reflect the influence of a long history of mission involvement. Papuan nationalists have often described themselves as members of a global order of nations, but they have also depicted their imagined community in explicitly Christian terms.[7] This is not to say that all Papuans view the struggle for sovereignty as equivalent to the struggle for salvation. Some want a bigger share in the province's enormous mineral wealth; others simply want to live in relative peace. Be that as it may, I have heard Papuan activists describe even their most modest political victories as minor miracles, events in which God has had a hand. In the case of the Biak flag raising, the very values that prompted the islanders to participate in provincial struggles underwrote a resilient set of millennial expectations. Sometimes, many Biaks did seem to envision themselves as part of a politically silenced Papuan nation advancing in "homogeneous, empty time." But there was and remains a broadly shared tendency to interpret international acknowledgment of this identity as initiating an eschatological transformation. From this perspective, independence appeared as the utopian moment when Biak would be revealed as the true origin of earthly power. At other times, Biaks downplayed this millennial/nationalist vision through practices that posited a very different sense of self. Nationalism is often depicted as involving the recognition of an interiorized locus of identity (see Pemberton 1994; Ivy 1995; Siegel 1997). That is, those caught up in nationalist fervor feel that their nationality is deeply essential to who they are. In Biak, this interiority stood in tension with the assumption that one gained status from being foreign: different from oneself and one's peers.

Later in this chapter I develop this argument by looking more closely at the character of Biak sociality. But first I attend to another force of critical importance in the flag raising and its aftermath: the Indonesian state. John Djopari notes that Papuan youths who have fled Indonesia finally feel free to express their convictions. "Perhaps when they are in Irian Jaya they restrain themselves," he remarks (1993, 151). With the end of the New Order, Biaks and other Papuans suddenly found themselves living in what they took to be a new and different land. Unfortunately, the changes were not as radical as they may have seemed at first—as I suggest in the following section, where I examine the logic underlying the military's brutal suppression of the demonstration. On Biak at least, state terror persisted into the post-Suharto period in uncannily familiar forms, as the New Order's history makes clear.

The New Order and the Ends of Violence

When one considers the conditions under which President Suharto ruled, it is surprising that his fall did not come sooner. The New Order's longevity, as John Pemberton has noted, did not rest solely on open coercion or threat. To account for the quiescence that reigned in much of Indonesia for the period of Suharto's rule, Pemberton looks not to a "culture of terror," but to a "relatively muted form of terror that might become culture: the repression of fear that customarily secures, over time, an appearance of normal life" (Pemberton 1994, 8). With fear transposed into anxiety over the specter of cultural incompletion, Indonesia's Javanese majority embraced the official virtues of order, stability, and progress. Seeing themselves from the perspective of the abstract authority of custom, they engaged in compulsive rounds of state-sanctioned rituals. Mobilized to create the impression of an imperishable order, the transcendent realm of culture bridged the ruptures of colonial and postcolonial history. Building museums filled with new heirlooms and improved versions of old monuments, the New Order subsumed old and new, originals and replicas, into an abstract topology of clearly demarcated regional cultures and selves.

When I was conducting fieldwork on Biak from 1992 to 1994, I found no dearth of expressions of the official narratives of culture and development that Pemberton so astutely dissects. The "security approach" had given way to the "prosperity approach," I was told, by officials committed to the revival of Biak "tradition" and the entry of the population into the ranks of orderly Indonesian subjects (see Rutherford 1996). But alongside official discourses that assured Biaks that order and progress was what they desired was another set of narratives with a more sinister message for those who might be tempted to stray from the path. While I was free to visit most parts of the island, I was warned against traveling to West Biak, a place that remained "disturbed" by the presence of an OPM commander who had managed to survive decades of counterinsurgency operations on the island (see Kirksey 2012). In 1990 Indonesian troops shot the guerrilla's nephew, who had fled to the forest after a flag raising in a West Biak village. Carrying their victim's severed head aloft on a pole, the troops marched home along the densely populated coast (Amnesty International 1991, 25). In this grisly spectacle, the soldiers took on the lethal power of the headhunters who once inhabited the island (see also Siegel 1998, 8, 90–119; Hoskins 1996, 31–37; Tsing 1993, 72–103). A particular audience gave meaning to such atrocities: it consisted of Indonesian national subjects, on Biak and elsewhere, who would learn something crucial about the sovereignty that New Order authorities sought to claim. On the one hand, this performance communicated a message about the state's power in a form that the "primitive" locals could understand. On the other, it displayed the state's capacity not only to annihilate the state's "primitive" rivals but also to tap their savage, excessive power.

The events of May 1998 decisively shattered the illusion that the New Order was eternal. But in the months that followed, the logic that linked that order and violence under Suharto was still not a thing of the past. Confirming rumors that circulated widely in Indonesia, evidence quickly emerged of military involvement in the rape and murder of ethnic Chinese Indonesians in Jakarta and other major cities in the weeks leading up to Suharto's fall (see Sidel 1998, 179–82). The riots could be read as an effort to repeat the violent moment of the New Order's birth, when certain factions of the military orchestrated an eruption of local animosities then intervened to restore the law. This violent moment was a performance directed to a national audience, seen as welcoming the eradication of internal sources of disorder. The military on Biak seems to have tried to follow a similar script. In the days following the flag raising, the provincial paper reported on a counterdemonstration carried out by villagers in West Biak (see Cenderawasih Pos 1998a; see also Tapol 1998). Other sources suggest that the military not only coerced West Biak villagers into protesting the flag raising; they also set in motion a plan to bring them to the site of the demonstration (see Human Rights Watch 1998b). Armed with axes and machetes, the West Biaks were supposed to start a battle with the demonstrators, giving the security forces an excuse to step in.[8]

Few Biaks reading of the counterprotests would have been ignorant of the heavy price West Biaks have paid for sheltering the last armed fugitive on the island. Equally few could have avoided hearing of the abuse suffered by the protesters and others unlucky enough to be near the water tower at the time of the attack. Two sets of narratives told different stories about the event, the first depicting the state's lethal power over its critics, the second assuring the faithful that chaos had been firmly, but gently, contained. These two sets of narratives worked together effectively to quell criticism—and even acknowledgment—of the killings. In the aftermath of the shootings, only a handful of families dared to report that their children were missing. The lack of complaints was used as proof that no abuses had occurred. The authorities' effort to explain the sea-borne bodies as victims of a distant disaster was more than an exercise in damage control. It was an explicit demonstration of the state's monopoly over the giving and taking of identities, as well as lives.

Clearly, the tsunami was a stroke of good luck for the authorities; it gave them a chance to cover the traces of the massacre by providing a natural explanation for any recovered victims. But the argument that the corpses could not be the demonstrators because they were *not* Indonesians suited the strange logic of Indonesian state terror and sharpened the point of the military attack. James Siegel has pointed out that Indonesians have tended to "kill in their own image" (1998, 1). Extralegal violence against separatists, communists, and criminals alike is not intended to purify the nation of alien elements, but to demonstrate the state's ability to appropriate its enemies' potency—that is, its ability to "nationalize death" (Siegel 1998, 108). The soldiers who shot the young Biaks acted on the assumption that their victims belonged within the Indonesian state. This is not to deny that outsiders of various sorts took part in the affair, including the US congressional delegates mentioned above, whose letter to President Habibie reached the province, where it circulated widely. The authorities presented themselves as defusing these disruptions by translating them into manageable terms. Just as the authorities reassured the alarmed villagers by determining the true identity of the foreign corpses, they clarified the true meaning of the foreign letter, which called for limited autonomy, not independence, they claimed. Against the public secret of the state's lawmaking violence, the official version made violence alien to the law.

Biak and the Ends of Order

Among Biaks, one encounters narratives and practices that draw a relationship among violence, order, and origins in a fashion that contrasts sharply with the New Order tendencies I have just described. A few months after I began fieldwork, I found myself talking with a new friend about her husband, a mild-mannered teacher I had met on several occasions. Jan was "*jahat,*" Fransina told me, using an Indonesian word meaning "wicked" or "evil." Just as surprising as Fransina's choice of words was the boastful tone of her voice. As time went on I met other Biaks who used the adjective, *jahat,* as a compliment. A *jahat* person, though for the most part reserved, was capable of outbursts of violent rage. This capacity for violence was not only admired in fisherman or hunters. Top officials liked to describe themselves as present-day *mambri,* the fearsome "warriors" for whom Biak was once renowned.

The other way that top officials liked to describe themselves was as *amber beba,* "big foreigners." A word referring to Westerners, Indonesian migrants, civil servants, and individuals with special skills, *amber* also functioned as an adjective to describe the outside realms where Biaks sought wealth and prestige. This Biak notion opens new insights into the colonial history depicted in chapters 2 and 3. From the first appearance of Biak-speaking seafarers in European records, one finds an association of the foreign with both violence and value. Powerful outsiders, ranging from the Sultan of Tidore, to whom Biaks delivered tribute, to the agents of the Dutch colonial state, attracted both fear and desire. The Biaks I knew during fieldwork recreated the linkage between violence and value in the most intimate arenas of everyday life. According to Biak kinship, they divided the islanders into patrilineal, exogamous kin groups known as *keret*. Whereas same-sex siblings tended to be rivals for *keret* resources, cross-sex siblings regarded each other with longing and love. Elsewhere I have analyzed the connection between this affection and the inflationary nature of Biak exchange (see Rutherford 1998, 2003). The status of a Biak brother—and his kin group, more generally—depended on his and his kin group's ability to give their affines more foreign valuables than they received as bridewealth. Children became "foreigners" by virtue of the gifts their mother elicited from her brothers, who acquired this surplus through ongoing "raids" on foreign lands. Biaks spoke of these gifts as motivated by a brother's "love" for his sister. But the aesthetics of the feasts that sisters hosted to elicit foreign valuables from their brothers portrayed the giving of these prestations as an act of force. Violence was an explicit element of these performances. Everything from the guests' noisy procession to the dance ground to the songs they sang when they arrived recalled the violence of an encounter with the new.

But it was not only at feasts that Biaks stressed the violence and value of the foreign. They confirmed these qualities in narratives recounting the origins of social groups. Many stories about the founding of lineages, for instance, focused on the actions of *mambri*, the warriors mentioned above. In the past, warriors offered themselves for hire to feuding kin groups. The offended party got the warrior drunk, then spat in his cup to insult him, before sending him off in the direction of the offending village. Like a detonated missile, the infuriated warrior killed the first person to cross his path. The victim's relatives avenged the death by hiring another warrior, thus keeping the violence in circulation. But what also circulated were alliances. Clients compensated warriors by giving them their sisters to marry; warriors gave their own sisters to their victims' kin groups to compensate for the loss of life. Through these unions—and the brother-sister bonds they mobilized—particular individuals and their descendants received special skills and prerogatives. A dangerous uncle and a random act of violence stood at the origins of a prestigious new line.

In recounting their *keret* myths, Biaks also drew connections between random acts of violence and the institution of new identities. An enterprising Dutch official collected several dozen of such stories (see de Bruyn 1948). Most of them began with a fight over a domestic animal or some other object of shared interest. A dog defecated inside a hilltop house, sparking an altercation between two *keret* brothers. A man caught a lizard; his brothers ate it; he exploded in rage. A bloody battle ensued, and then the siblings dispersed, naming features of the landscape as they descended to the coast. In their new homes the siblings founded new kin groups; eventually their descendants married. Exploding a sibling set consisting of competing equals, the lethal violence caused a migration that set up differences and provided a basis for exchange.

Village histories showed how a particular relation to the foreign underwrote the connection between violence and origins. In chapter 2, I described Lieutenant W. K. H. Feuilletau de Bruyn's experiences on Biak, where he arrived with a company of soldiers in 1912 (see Feuilletau de Bruyn 1916, 1920). While his mission was ostensibly to capture the murderer of an Ambonese teacher—who had strayed into a drunken warrior's path—he used the occasion to pacify the island's north coast. Feuilletau de Bruyn ordered his troops to sneak up to *keret* houses and take their occupants as hostages. Feuilletau refused to release the men, women, and children until their kin group turned over any warriors in their midst. Soon the company was traveling with a string of prisoners, bound together by wire tied around their necks. The lieutenant scarcely cuts an endearing figure in his report on the mission. But in the stories Biaks tell about the operation, they remember him with admiration, as well as awe. "Dekna," as they call him, may have been *jahat*, but he opened a new era on the island. His strategies call to mind those of the Indonesian soldiers who paraded the dead rebel's head in West Biak. Ostensibly out to bring an end to heathen justice, Feuilletau de Bruyn, through these stories, became a warrior himself.

Stories about Dekna are taken as relating a particularly treasured beginning in Biak: the dawn of Christian light in heathen darkness. Narrated in this fashion, the "evil" of Dekna vanquishes the "evil" of the pre-Christian Biaks; Christian conversion would have led the Biaks to rethink the value of being *jahat* in an increasingly "pacified" world. To be sure, it was in the

1910s that most Biak villages began the long history of mission schooling that accounted for the islanders' dominance in many arenas of provincial life. But while the flag raising undeniably could be emplotted in the colonial story of Biak's march to modernity, this story does not capture the full range of readings evoked by the act. For one thing, it cannot account for the ways that Biaks represented the military and bureaucracy as foreign: dangerous, yet available for present-day warriors who wanted to advance in the eyes of their peers. For another, it cannot explain the persistence of a view of national liberation as an abrupt and total transformation. As a fourth and final example makes clear, the violence and value of the foreign has stood not only at the beginning of Biak identities, but also at the end. This example shows how being foreign has translated into being sovereign at least according to some readings of Biaks' place in a global order. But this is a supreme and absolute power that provides not only dominance over others, but also an escape from hierarchy and an ability to enjoy the satisfaction of all desires.

Punctuated by a series of startling encounters and violent incidents, the myth of Manarmakeri, literally "the Itchy Old Man," lays out the origin of the foreign (see Rutherford 2003, 378–461). In the versions I collected during fieldwork, the story begins with the hero's discovery and loss of Koreri, which means "We Change Our Skin," a utopian state of unending life and pleasure also glossed by Biaks as "We eat in one place" (Biak: *Kan do mob oser*). Disappointed by his inability to return to the cave where he witnessed Koreri, Manarmakeri develops a skin disease that covers his body with itching, oozing sores. The hero becomes a migrating outcast, subjected to all manner of abuse. In the key incident in the story, he regains access to Koreri from the Morning Star, whom he surprises when the spirit is stealing the old man's palm wine. But the old man must take a detour in order to return to Koreri: Manarmakeri first gains the power to impregnate a woman magically and make her his wife. The woman turns out to be the local chief's daughter, whose newborn son outrages the villagers when he identifies the old stranger as his father. Rejected again, when his affines flee the misbegotten family, the old man sets about performing miracles. He conjures up a magnificent feast and a modern steamship; he turns himself into a beautiful youth and his skin into treasure by jumping into a raging fire. But even these deeds cannot win him his affines' acceptance. Disappointed, Manarmakeri travels west. Someday, he will return and "open" Koreri. This final union with the foreign will end the world as Biaks know it. There will be no more striving, suffering, and death.

Stories like this—and millenarian movements like Koreri—are common throughout West Papua and the rest of Oceania (see Giay 1986, 1995a, 1995b; see also Burridge 1960, 1969; Lawrence 1971; Lindstrom 1984, 1990, 1993; Tuzin 1997; Robbins 2001). Many people in the region tell the story of their colonial history as the tale of an exchange gone awry—an exchange that will be rectified when the millennium comes and the locals finally get their due. What I would like to call attention to, when it comes to the myth of Manarmakeri, is the way that encounters with audiences are central to the workings of the plot. Manarmakeri, who watches the star, is in turn watched by his affines; these spectators move the story forward through their reaction when something unexpected is revealed. This aspect of the story not only reflects a long history of contact with outsiders, it also holds the key to the myth's long-standing grip on Biak minds. The myth thematizes the hero's rejection by an audience. Redemption thus appears in the form of the hero's acceptance by an audience that suddenly sees the light.

At the Koreri movement's heart is hope for a particular kind of change: one that occurs with a sudden shift in points of view. Beginning as early as the eighteenth century, Biaks periodically gathered to welcome Manarmakeri (see Kamma 1972). A leader would arise, claiming to be in contact with the ancestor; followers would abandon their gardens and gather to sing, dance, and drink palm wine, sure that Koreri soon would begin. Compensating for that earlier audience that refused to recognize Manarmakeri as the Lord, the crowds saw themselves as inaugurating a radical transformation. While not every incident ended violently, the followers consistently posited a reversal in existing structures of power. An early prophet instructed the faithful to stop traveling to Tidore; instead, they should deliver their tribute to him (see Kamma 1972, 106). Closing the gap between Biak and the Land of the Foreigners, the return of Manarmakeri would spell the end of a social order based on the pursuit of exogenous sources of value and power. Where New Order narratives repressed all reference to endings, for Biaks, this eschatological moment was—and remains—a focus of longing and hope.

I am certainly not the first to suggest Koreri's importance to the interpretation of Papuan nationalism on Biak; prominent Papuan nationalists have done the same (see Sharp with Kaisiëpo 1994). An older generation of scholars who took millenarianism as a stage in the evolution of revolution made much of the mixture of political and religious rhetoric that Koreri prophets used to describe their quest (see Worsley 1968, 48; Lawrence

1971, 256–73; Adas 1987). The reading I would like to offer of the flag raising avoids the teleological premises of such an approach. I will not venture into debates on the millennial origins of the modern notions of progress that infuse classic accounts of millenarianism (see Bull 1995; Anderson 1990, 90–93). How the phenomenon looks depends on the perspective of the observer: the events of 1939–42 on Biak, called a cargo cult by some, coincided with a multitude of similar reactions that later found a place in the annals of the Indonesian revolutionary war (see Rutherford 2003, 485–87). If Koreri is central to my analysis, it is not because millenarianism is a precursor to "real" revolution. Using Koreri as a lens, we catch a glimpse of the eschatological limit that all revolutions in some sense evoke.

The Morning Star flag, which refers explicitly to an episode from the myth of Manarmakeri, first flew in 1942, during an uprising that coincided with the Japanese invasion and the collapse of Dutch colonial rule (see Osborne 1985, 51; see also Kamma 1972; Rutherford 2003, 525–65). While my information on the 1998 flag raising is admittedly incomplete—and I certainly would not want to downplay the significant differences between the two historical moments—what I heard in Biak and read in reports on the previous incident suggests certain parallels. My friends and consultants perceived these parallels, commenting on the flag raising in ways that cast it as an iteration not just of previous West Papuan nationalist performances but also of the most dramatic Koreri uprising that Biak ever saw. The most striking, of course, is the timing: the fall of a seemingly permanent regime. In both cases the rupture came at the end of a period of expansion in the scope and reach of the state.

A second parallel pertains to the participants. Planned by individuals with recent experience outside the islands, the World War II uprising drew people from all parts of Biak, with the prophets and their close relatives forming the core of the movement. It was launched by Angganeta Menufandu, a traditional singer and healer who had worked on the mainland as a coolie. After her arrest, the movement was carried forward by a group of young warriors who had just been released from jail. As I noted above, Eben Kirksey has suggested that those who first proposed raising the Morning Star flag on Biak in 1998 belonged to a prayer group (see Kirksey 2012). These religious men and women, seemingly of modest means, came together following Suharto's resignation to pray for West Papua's release. They recognized that the flag raising would need a skilled leader, and Filep Karma was ready to hand. Filep Karma, who then worked in the governor's office in Jayapura, had only recently come to the island to visit his

ailing father at the public hospital in Biak City. The scene under the water tower was initially quiet, but onlookers soon gathered. Surrounded by
prayer group members and relatives from his North Biak village, Karma
attracted followers ranging from the teenagers who loiter near the Biak
City terminal to older villagers who made special trips to town to see the
long-forbidden flag. As was the case in the earlier incident, some of the
curious ended up staying on.

A third parallel can be drawn in the activities undertaken during the
flag raising. At the camps set up by Angganeta and her successors, followers drank palm wine and danced in a circle, singing songs composed by
their leaders. They were performing *wor*, a nondiatonic genre of singing
once central to Biak ceremonies and feasts (see Yampolsky and Rutherford 1996). The leaders were helped by "peace women," as they called
male and female dancers who had been possessed by the foreign and the
dead. Christian imagery was central to the movement; people and places
received biblical names. The followers renamed one village Bethlehem;
the Queen of Judea was one of Angganeta's names. In July 1998 the demonstrators spent their days dancing around the water tower and singing
Biak and Indonesian songs. While they performed a contemporary genre,
in fitting with the youth of many of the participants, the allusion to Koreri
and Biak feasting was clear. Every hour, the entire group, led by Filep
Karma, dropped to their knees and prayed. It is said that Karma even bap-
tized the territory where the demonstrators exercised control. Although
I heard nothing about speaking in foreign tongues, people did describe
the reading of incomprehensible foreign documents: "proclamations" in
English and Dutch.

A fourth parallel concerns the stress the followers placed on the conjuring of a foreign audience for their endeavors. Elsewhere I have compared
the state-sponsored revival of *wor*, the above-mentioned song genre, in
the 1990s to a similar revival sponsored by the mission in the 1930s (see
Rutherford 1996). In the uprisings that followed, Biaks responded to the
sense that outsiders had found something unexpected in their identities.
In prison the young warriors who took over from Angganeta heard rumors of Japanese promises to honor native political parties. Upon their
release they drafted an elaborate charter for New Guinea's future, which
became the basis of the movement's subsequent phase. Like the warriors,
Karma and his followers acted on the belief that powerful outsiders had
recognized their plight. I mentioned above the letter from members of
the US Congress, which circulated widely on Biak.[9] Much was made of a

rumor that the protesters had appeared on CNN. As was the case in Koreri, this evidence of foreign attention brought to mind not only the gaze
of outsiders but also their impending presence, bestowing a legitimacy on
the Biaks' struggle. When one friend left for the port to meet a passen-
ger liner that arrived during the demonstration, his neighbor asked him,
in great excitement, "has the foreigners' ship arrived?" (see also Kirksey
2012).

A fifth parallel relates to the interconnections between violence and
order that became increasingly apparent as the demonstration progressed.
Angganeta, who called herself "the Peace Woman," gained authority from
her ability to provide convincing signs of direct contact with Manarmakeri.
Her successors gained prominence by claiming to represent the prophet-
ess, the "Queen," whose troops they vowed to command. In two sites on
Biak, they drilled divisions of the "New America" army. For reasons I
describe in chapter 6, teachers and evangelists were submitted to beat-
ings; a policeman and a Japanese commander were killed. As the Japanese
gradually assumed control of northwestern New Guinea, the new administration tried several different strategies to quell the movement, including
recruiting the followers of one leader to attack those of another. Finally, in
October 1943, the Japanese navy opened fire on a huge crowd of unarmed
believers. The bullets failed to turn to water, and hundreds of people were
killed. But that was not the end of the violence. A blood bath resulted
when grieving families, in line with local conceptions of justice, turned on
the kin groups who had led their loved ones to their deaths. Over a much
shorter period, the 1998 demonstration evolved toward a violent confrontation. Early in the protest, the protestors formed a security force of sorts.
Boys wearing armbands that read "Security Guard—OPM" manned
roadblocks around the water tower. Some demonstrators began to stock-
pile weapons after hearing rumors that the military had recruited villagers
from West Biak to attack the crowd. By the time the military itself moved
in, the protestors reportedly had abandoned these weapons at the urging
of several pastors, who met with them in hopes of ending the demonstration (see ELS-HAM 1999, 14). Alerted by lookouts that the troops were
converging on the site, Karma and his supporters used nonviolent measures to protect the flag: they formed a circle around the water tower and
recited Bible verses and prayed. One eyewitness credited his Bible with
saving him from a bullet when a soldier fired on him at point blank range
(see ELS-HAM 1999, 22). Yet others could not sustain this stance on the
conflict. When news of the shootings reached young sympathizers in outlying neighborhoods, they took revenge by burning down migrants' shops.

Perhaps the strongest indication that the narrative of Koreri was evoked in the flag raising comes from the comments I heard after its failure. Friends spoke of Karma's movement in the same tone they used to discuss Angganeta and the warriors'—the goal was valid, but the timing was wrong. "We can't chase it," sighed the wife of a high-ranking official, "God will give it to us in his time." Just as believers found post-hoc justifications for Angganeta's failure, they found reasons for the flag raising's tragic ending. As I suggested above, one could view the shootings as deliberately provoked by the protesters to gain foreign sympathy for the movement. By contrast, some of my consultants viewed the massacre as a tragedy that was nonetheless the component of a larger plan. Maybe God was on Karma's side, I was told, and the shootings were meant to happen so that more people would hear about the cause (see also Klima 2002). The same friend reported how, after the incident, an ethnic Chinese merchant had had a vision of angels dancing with the demonstrators around the flag. Although the Biaks with whom I spoke described independence in a variety of ways, most assumed that divine intervention would somehow be involved in its delivery. In 1998, as in the early 1940s, the violence that would end the status quo was imagined as entailing a congress with foreigners and a triumph of prayers—if not machetes—over guns.

The Future of the End?

From the perspective of day-to-day life, the return of Manarmakeri had to remain unpredictable. Prophets who dared to venture a forecast ran a risk. In the 1990s many Biaks still honored the memory of Angganeta, who turned her body into a receiver of messages from Manarmakeri. They had nothing but contempt for her successors, who actively directed the movement in her name. The comments I collected on Filep Karma seemed to range between these alternatives. Some spoke scornfully of this "big foreigner" who led others to ruin because he wanted to "make it"—that is, independence—all by himself. But others who implied that the movement was divinely ordained spoke of the "light" in Karma's eyes.

The ambivalence that Biaks expressed in their judgment of both movements' leaders reflects something of their ambivalent views on violence, which became evident during my fieldwork on the island. If one had in some sense to be dangerous to engage in exchange, when Biaks manifested their potency by inflicting bodily harm, the effect on social relations was devastating. When the plan to involve West Biak villagers failed, the

commander assigned Biak soldiers to lead the attack on the demonstrators; I was told that it would be years before the families involved mend
the rift. Still if Biaks generally asserted that violence should be less than
"real," their actions often suggested that it must refer to something more
than rhetorical—or even "symbolic," in Bourdieu's sense. The massacres
that followed the collapse of Koreri in 1943 suggest how easy it was to slip
across the line.

One way of grappling with the "not wholly peaceful" nature of episodes like the flag raising is to create taxonomies. F. C. Kamma, a Dutch
missionary who wrote a well-known study of Koreri, spoke of a conflict
between followers who truly longed for redemption and those who turned
this longing to earthly ends. But the comments of those who still remember the movement suggest a more complicated dynamic. Angganeta's
movement sought to collapse limits, but it also recreated them through
the brutal suppression of those who failed to follow Manarmakeri's com-
mands. In normal times, Biak justice had no room for an inexplicable
death; one's misfortune was always attributable to another's misdeed. The
leaders of Koreri violently suppressed this principle of retribution by calling for an end to all feuds. The vengeful relatives of the victims of the
Japanese attack forcefully reinstated Biak law. Koreri's violence was not
simply the outcome of repression or the schemes of "secondary leaders"
(Barkun 1996, 7; see also Adas 1987, 122–37). The violent suppression of
order elicited its violent reintroduction, in a dynamic that culminated in
the movement's horrific denouement.

There is little doubt that the wartime movement, like the flag raising,
involved what Walter Benjamin calls *lawmaking* and *law-preserving* uses
of force. But we get a better sense of what was at stake in Koreri by considering the end of "Critique of Violence," where Benjamin tells us that
violence can be either mythical or divine. Mythical violence resembles that
of the Biak warrior: violence not as a means, but as a manifestation, as
seen in a man, "impelled by anger . . . to the most visible outbursts of a
violence that is not related as a means to a preconceived end" (Benjamin 1978, 294). Without a preexisting program to guide it, lawmaking, as
"power-making," must take place in such a manifestation, a sign of the
"existence of the gods" (Benjamin 1978, 295). Like the blow of a warrior
or enraged *keret* brother, mythical violence institutes an order and produces authority by parading as an "alien" force beyond conscious, "local"
control. Divine violence looks more like the moment evoked in Koreri: the
utter annihilation of order through an imagined collapse of the distance

that divides the transcendent sources of value and power from everyday life. I say "evoked" advisedly, because even Angganeta could not convey a pure vision of eschatological destruction.[10] Indeed, one could argue that Angganeta's movement served to defer the transformation of Biak notions of authority by presenting the forces of change in a locally recognizable guise. For Benjamin, divine violence is an element of all revolutions, but it is never possible to capture the order-destroying moment. How can one depict the elusive instant when one regime ends and another begins? As Benjamin puts it, "The expiatory power of violence is not visible to men" (1978, 300).

But it may be that the power of Koreri lies precisely in the elusiveness of its object. At moments when Biaks have been drawn to see themselves from the perspective of outsiders, they have evoked this figure of a millennial limit. Koreri has portrayed the submission to other orders, if fully realized, as spelling the end, not of a worldview but of the world. On Biak the dream of Papuan independence proved remarkably resilient in the face of decades of repression. This was in good part due to the groundedness of Koreri's millennial logic in the practices of everyday life. By valorizing the foreignness of government slogans and schemes, Biaks satisfied the demands of New Order hegemony without accepting a New Order sense of self. But one should not assume that Papuan nationalism has been immune from the logic of Koreri, which would destabilize any identity defined by its place in a homogeneous order of nations. To assume such an identity is to take a transcendent perspective and then relinquish it, such that one locates oneself within a nation that is but one among other equivalent groups of the same type. Participants in Korei undertook the first reframing without submitting to the second; thus, they imaginatively monopolized the most "supreme and absolute"—even sovereign—point of view. Ultimately, this position was not sustainable. To dance around the flag is to dance with angels; it brings one into an unsustainable proximity with God.

While its roots extend deep into the colonial past, the Biak I have described in this chapter is a product of the New Order, which was itself the product of geopolitical and capitalist orders of a wider scale. Over the past decade the Papuan nationalist movement has evolved.[11] The course of events in Irian Jaya, which Indonesia's fourth president, Abdurrahman Wahid, rechristened "Papua" while celebrating the millennium in Jayapura, initially followed something like the plot discernible in the Biak flag raising, with the entire province engaged in a symbolic refashioning of space. A former critic of Suharto, Wahid became president in 1999 following the first democratic elections held in Indonesia since 1955. Upon taking office, Wahid promised to permit peaceful political expression in the province. The proindependence movement soon gained a self-proclaimed leader in the person of Theys Eluay, a charismatic tribal chief from Sentani, not far from the provincial capital (see Suara Pembaruan 1999). A former legislator and chair of the province's customary council, Eluay was one of the tribal leaders chosen to participate in the Act of Free Choice in 1969. Among his colleagues was Yorrys Raweyai, a controversial figure who will appear again in chapter 7. Raweyai was long the head of Pemuda Pancasila, literally "The Youth of the Five Bases," the Five Bases being Indonesia's official national ideology. This was not a boys' club but a nationwide paramilitary organization with underworld connections, which the New Order regime used to terrorize and discredit rivals (see Ryter 2001).

Eluay's activities began with the planning of a mass flag raising to occur in Jayapura and other cities on December 1. Some observers feared that the scheme was a trap, designed to justify a bloody crackdown (see Tapol 1999; Kilvert 1999). But while there were shootings in Timika, Jayapura, and elsewhere, the event went off peacefully, with security provided by the Satgas Papua, a loosely organized "task force" of uniformed youths. In February 2000, Eluay and Tom Beanal, a well-known leader from the Amungme tribe, the traditional landowners of the Freeport mine, became the cochairmen of the presidium convened to organize a Papuan National Congress, which was first discussed during President Wahid's New Year visit to the province. Wahid, who in addition to advocating the name change offered an official apology for human rights abuses in the province, supported the idea. Besides providing funding, Wahid went so far as to offer to open the Congress—an offer he later rescinded when it became clear that the proceedings were likely to result in a declaration of Papuan independence.

Attended by three thousand delegates from across the province and overseas, the Congress's stated goal was the "rectification" of western New Guinea's history. Although the event, which was held in Jayapura from May 29 to June 4, 2000, took place with a remarkable lack of unrest, its conclusion—that West Papua had become independent in 1961—evoked a strong reaction from Jakarta. In an abrupt about-face, Wahid disowned the Congress, which he criticized for not representing the opinions of the majority of the province's inhabitants (see Jakarta Post 2000a). Other politicians went further, calling for the arrest of the organizers for treason; and, indeed, Eluay and others from the presidium were summoned for questioning by the police (see Jakarta Post 2000b; Astaga.com 2000; Agence France-Presse 2000; Indonesian Observer 2000b). In August 2000 the Indonesian national legislature officially rejected the Congress's findings and demanded that Wahid take firm action to defend the unity of the nation. In response Wahid pledged to fight separatism, if necessary, by "serious measures" (see Xinhua News Service 2000; Indonesian Observer 2000a).

In the midst of these developments, the Morning Star flag became a prominent feature of the province's landscape. Following the Congress, President Wahid announced that flag raisings were to be permitted, so long as the Indonesian flag was raised alongside the Papuan flag, which should be smaller and lower than its rival (see Jakarta Post 2000c). This proclamation legitimized what was already in many ways the status quo. During this period the flag appeared not only atop flagpoles but also on stickers, posters, decals, and even radio aerials sported by Papuans from all walks of life (see England 2000b). Filep Karma, who was released from jail in 1999, reportedly showed up for meetings with the Morning Star flag affixed to his civil servant's uniform, thus combining the emblems of national and foreign power. But even in this time of tolerance, violence occurred. In Sorong, Genyam, Timika, Nabire, and Manokwari, the security forces confronted demonstrators, and protesters and bystanders were killed or injured (see Daley 2000; Woods 2000). Equally troubling were reports of clashes between Satgas Papua units and members of the Satgas Merah Putih, a new "task force" organized along the lines of the militias responsible for the atrocities that accompanied the referendum that led to East Timor's independence in 1998 (see Scheiner 2000). In August 2000, following the legislature's recommendation, Wahid announced that the permissive policy on flag raisings had ended and called for the lowering of all Papuan flags (see McDonald 2000). Just as the brief period of imagined sovereignty under the water tower was eventually cut short, a remarkable interlude in western New Guinea's history drew to a close.

In the rest of this book, I return to these incidents in the post-Suharto history of the Papuan nationalist movement. But I do so in the course of analyzing signs of West Papuan sovereignty in motion. These remaining chapters dissect the semiotic processes that have been involved in the pursuit of sovereignty in West Papua from the colonial period up until the present day. I focus on the aspects of sign use that not only allow but also force would-be sovereigns to contend with more than one audience at the same time. I also revisit Koreri in some of these chapters, but with an eye to the interpretive practices that have both facilitated and hindered the quest for what Eben Kirksey (2012) describes as "freedom in an entangled world." There is no way of knowing if the West Papuan quest for sovereignty will succeed, but it does seem likely that it will continue. Two quotes spring to mind that sum up what Biak eschatology can teach us about this situation. The first is borrowed from a Biak friend who borrowed it from Kamma's (1972) book on Koreri. The second is stolen from the title of an essay by Frank Kermode (1995). "The hope in people's heart may never die," but there is nothing so interminable as "waiting for the end."

PART TWO

Signs of Sovereignty in Motion

CHAPTER FIVE

Frontiers of the Lingua Franca

The Constitution of the "State of Papua"—As Envisioned

Supporters of independence for Indonesia's province of Irian Jaya—attending a landmark conference here—have already drawn up a detailed plan for an independent "State of Papua" [. . .] The text stipulates that the official language would be English, the common language [would be] Malay-Papuan, and the Melanesian Language [would be] Tok Pidzin, while all tribal and ethnic languages would have the status of local languages. Alarmed by the way the congress appears to be heading for some kind of declaration of independence, the Indonesian government reiterated on Wednesday that it would never let the former Dutch colony secede.
— Agence France-Presse, June 2, 2000

I begin my exploration of the signs of West Papuan sovereignty in motion with a simple question: in what tongues does West Papuan nationalism speak? In July 1998, during the demonstration discussed in the previous chapter, a visitor to the Biak water tower would have heard multiple languages. There would have been songs in Biak and Indonesian, speeches in Indonesian, documents read out loud in English and Dutch, even a quip or two in Dani, Sentani, Javanese, and Makassarese. Linguistic diversity and multilingualism are widespread in Melanesia—and Indonesia—and have deep historical roots, as linguists and linguistic anthropologists have attested (Sankoff 1977; Kulick 1992; Errington 1998a and b; Tryon and Charpentier 2004). But nationalists and scholars of nationalism alike have long presumed that sovereign nation-states need a single, shared language (see Herder 1966 [1772]; Gellner 1983; Hobsbawm 1990; Anderson 1991). Popular sovereignty requires a shared medium for what Jürgen Habermas calls "rational-critical public debate" (1991, 28), just as the newspaper readers described by Benedict Anderson require a shared medium to engage in this modern "substitute for morning prayers" (1991, 35). As the linguistic anthropologist Michael Silverstein (2000) has pointed out, accounts like these of the birth of the modern nation-state neglect to investigate the processes that draw clean borders around languages (see also Bauman and Briggs 2000). When we take seriously the uneasy relationship between sovereignty and audience, these clean borders dissolve and my simple question explodes. What if languages are just as distended across multiple audiences as sovereignty is? What if languages are just as dependent on the view from afar—or, more precisely, a multiplicity of such views—for their illusory coherence and their appearance as something that "belongs" to a group? What if the border between language and other semiotic channels is far from clean and bright? In the remainder of this book, I pursue this line of inquiry. I do so by investigating aspects of sign use that enable audiences to multiply and social actors to shift between points of view.

This chapter launches this investigation by focusing on a phenomenon that has received close scrutiny in certain quarters. Recent work in linguistic anthropology has yielded an unnerving proposition: no one, not even a linguist, can definitely determine where one language ends and another begins (Woolard 1998, 23; Van Staden 1998; Gal 1998, 320; Irvine and Gal 1995, 2000; see also Bakhtin 1981). As Kathryn Woolard (1998) points out, research on "codeswitching," the alternation between supposedly different languages across a stretch of talk, has documented but analytically neglected the use of elements belonging grammatically or phonetically to what might be commonly understood as more than one linguistic system. Woolard argues that this indeterminacy is, in fact, highly significant because it enables speakers to claim allegiance to multiple communities and social positions all at once. That is, to recall the theme of this book, to the degree that they are "bivalent," meaning that they potentially call to mind more than one language or code, these elements enable speakers to address multiple audiences at the same time. This line of analysis moves translingual phenomena from the margins to the center of attention and replaces the structuralist privileging of "either/or" contrast with attention to "both/and" simultaneity. It also calls for heightened reflexivity on the part of scholars. No longer can we presume the existence of discrete codes between which speakers switch. No longer can we ignore what linguistic anthropologists have referred to as the language ideologies of speakers (see Woolard and Schieffelin 1994; Gal 1998). Speakers' perceptions of what Woolard calls the linguistic contact zone, following Mary Louise Pratt (1991), may differ not only from those of scholars but also among themselves. Pratt defined contact zones as "spaces where cultures meet, clash, and grapple with each other, often in contexts of highly asymmetrical relations of power" (1991, 1). Even as people expect certain contexts—such as schools and courtrooms—to be relatively pure zones of standardized speech, they associate others with the pleasures and perils of impurity. Not only are discrete languages ideologically constructed—imagined into being through practices premised on their existence—so are the phenomena that cut across them. The lingua franca, the term I use for the translingual registers described in this chapter, is the outcome and object of socially situated practices and discourses, just as is the so-called mother tongue.

My aim in this chapter is to investigate ideologies of the linguistic contact zone that took shape in Dutch New Guinea: ideologies through which it was defined, ideologies born of it. My goal is to unearth the range of perspectives assumed by those who entered and reproduced this zone of interaction, which brought together, in an intimate and interested fashion, diverse social, racial, and religious groups. Scholars of Dutch colonialism have followed contemporary observers in associating the contact zone discussed in this chapter with Malay, which was long used by traders and travelers in areas of the Netherlands Indies far from the homelands of those who supposedly spoke the "high" version of the language (see Hoffman 1979, 66–67). Also using Portuguese and Dutch, Europeans in the colony spoke in a dizzying variety of "low" Malay registers with native rulers, soldiers, Christians, regents, railroad workers and maids, "Chinese" merchants and tax collectors, and fellow Europeans (Hoffman 1979; Maier 1990, 1993). From this lingua franca emerged Indonesian, the postcolonial republic's much celebrated national language (Siegel 1997; Toer 1982; Anderson 1991).

The fact that during the colonial period, people in Dutch New Guinea also spoke some Malay would seem to support Indonesia's claims to the troubled province against those of Papuan nationalists, who insist that the Netherlands Indies, the colonial predecessor that set Indonesia's current borders, had little real presence in the territory before World War II (see Alua 2000, 12; Raweyai 2002, 8). The epigraph reflects the Papuan nationalist vision: the provincial dialect of Indonesian becomes "Malay Papuan," and the reference to "Tok Pidzin" [sic], Papua New Guinea's national language, signals the would-be nation's Melanesian roots. A complex set of social and historical factors have shaped the linguistic practices and ideologies of today's Papuan nationalists, including the elite drafters of the "detailed plan." In this vast and linguistically variegated province,

Indonesia has different resonances in the highlands than on the coast, not to mention among people of different classes, clans, and tribes. Tok Pisin, which derives from the English spoken in the colonies on the eastern half of New Guinea, has little resonance in the province.[1] Still, if my findings from one important part of Papua are any indication, neither the Indonesian nor the Papuan side of this debate can do justice to the border-destroying nature of colonial interactions in the region. Some of the participants in these interactions challenged the very existence of Malay as a bounded object and the Indies as a bounded space. The very effort to police linguistic boundaries led to their blurring: as the examples discussed below should make clear, standardizing projects recreated the very indeterminacy they sought to redress.

In making this argument I build upon but also call into question current scholarship on colonial Malay. This scholarship may seem to focus on narrowly linguistic questions, but it delves into a dynamic at the heart of this book. To study this lingua franca is to illuminate the multiple audiences imagined and confronted by colonial actors who sought to consolidate Dutch rule. There has been a wealth of research on the communicative practices that have emerged in contact situations, including in Indonesia and the Pacific (see Mühlhäusler 1986; Dutton and Tryon 1994; Dutton 1995; Errington 1998a; Urcioli 1996; Spitulnik 1998; Schieffelin 2000; Garrett 2004; Tryon and Charpentier 2004; Siegel 2008). I am focusing on the work of literary scholar and historian Hendrik Maier because, like the best of this research, he explicitly challenges the tendency to regard a language like Malay "more or less unproblematically . . . as a discrete code" (Garrett 2004, 48). As depicted in Maier's influential essays on the topic, Malay embodies the linguistic indeterminacy that Woolard describes.

According to Maier, where were Malay's frontiers? Nowhere and everywhere. On the one hand, Malay was a medium that united "a mixed and fragmented society, in ethnic, linguistic and cultural terms, a confusing network of groups and castes held together by a certain degree of tolerance and indifference" (Maier 1993, 46). To describe this situation, Maier uses Mikhail Bakhtin's term, "heteroglossia," the presence of heterogeneous languages, registers, and worldviews coexisting and contending with one another within a society or artistic work. Malay was a medium that bridged, yet did not homogenize, disparate outlooks and forms of speech. Living, as Maier puts it, "in the shadow of a center strong enough to impose some kind of political and economic unity, but too weak to impose a distinct cultural hegemony and produce a well-defined ideology to express it," those who spoke the lingua franca "did not have a strong awareness of borders and frontiers" (Maier 1993, 46). On the other hand, conversations in Malay entailed mutual mimicry, Maier suggests, since no one claimed authority to define proper usage (see Maier 1990). Those who spoke the language keenly felt the "force of the medium," as James Siegel (1997, 16) puts it; standing in the middle, Malay was nothing but frontier. Of course, this question—where were Malay's frontiers?—troubles Maier far less than it did the modernizing colonials he describes. These functionaries worked to domesticate the heteroglossia they found in the Indies by fixing linguistic, racial, and ethnic boundaries. Maier's goal is to track the "creation" of Malay, Dutch, and the Indies' myriad local languages through discourses and institutions oriented to a new object: the "standard civilized" version of a tongue (Maier 1993, 54; see also Errington 2001).

But there is another way to phrase this question of frontiers. Maier posits a lost space of heteroglossia, marked by an almost Edenic obliviousness to difference, that modernizing colonials discovered and ordered. By contrast, I follow Bakhtin (1981) in suggesting that heteroglossia is indestructible: the proliferation of linguistic heterogeneity and indeterminacy is a never-ending process (see also Zimmer n.d.). This is because every utterance originates dialogically, both borrowing from and responding to another's words (see Bakhtin 1981; see also Vološinov 1973). Dutch New Guinea is a particularly suggestive site to examine the role of the uneasy relationship between sovereignty and audience in the creation of heteroglossic translingual forms. The Netherlands Indies may have laid claim to western New Guinea in 1828, but the colony's effective border in the nineteenth century took the form of an uneven zone of contact. Within this zone were scattered traces of coercion and exchange: a tattered flag or rusting escutcheon, the treasured remnants of an Indian textile, a few Malay words incorporated into a Papuan tongue (Rosenberg 1875; Haga 1884; Smeele 1988; Elmberg 1968; Miedema 1984; Haenen 1991; Swadling 1996). Foreign words entered circulation through the same channel as the wealth used in the gifts through which Biaks and other coastal people produced valued persons (see chapter 4). In describing Malay's uses and meanings in this unpacified territory, one is forced to confront the divergent interests and imperatives through which a program of political and economic unity in the absence of hegemony made itself felt well into the modern colonial period. One becomes aware of the factors that prevented a single imagined audience from dominating how people from different ethnic and racial groups understood and evaluated their interactions with

one another. To the degree that these interactions were an integral ingre-
dient of Dutch governance, to raise the question of Malay's frontiers in
New Guinea is to bring under scrutiny the frontiers of colonial sovereignty
itself.

In focusing on details of language use, this chapter thus furthers my
investigation of the uneasy relationship between sovereignty and audience in West Papua, past and present. In the following pages, I delve into
the practices of the Protestant missionaries who settled in New Guinea
in 1855, close to fifty years before the establishment of the territory's
first permanent government post. At a time when Dutch officers visited New Guinea annually at best, the missionaries were already settled
at a popular trading station among speakers of a language they initially
called "Mefoorsch" or "Myfoorsch," but later knew as "Noefoorsch" or
"Nuefoorsch." These migrants from Numfor, along with their linguistically related counterparts from Biak and other offshore islands, raided
and traded along New Guinea's western shoreline and farther afield. They
occasionally delivered tribute to the north Moluccan Sultans of Tidore,
whose dealings in western New Guinea, as we have seen, provided Dutch
colonials with the basis for their territorial claims (see Haga 1884; Kamma
1947–49). My analysis focuses on mission efforts to inculcate the Papuans
with a uniquely Christian image of the colonial order. But I also scrutinize
the historical conditions under which this project unfolded, examining the
assumptions that oriented the missionary's interest in the Papuans' utterances and the Papuan's interest in the missionaries' words.

Central to my story is the missionaries' ambivalent relationship to Malay. I show how the missionaries reproduced the dangers they associated
with Malay through their very efforts to cultivate a Christianized Papuan
tongue. In arguing for the use of the natives' own indigenous languages
in church and school, mission writers and orators projected onto Malay
a particular set of dangerous pragmatic features and functions: all those
nonreferential dimensions of utterances they saw as interfering with the
transparent communication of the Word. Like the anthropologist Webb
Keane (2007), I pay close attention to the assumptions about sign use that
Europeans brought to this mission encounter. While these missionaries'
negative representations of Malay may have shaped their interactions with
potential converts, they provided, after the fashion of all language ideologies, a vision of discourse that was partial at best (Woolard and Schieffelin
1994; Kroskrity 2000; see also Silverstein 1976).

Pursued among people whose practices were oriented by an alternative ideology, one that valued foreign words as a source of authority and pleasure, the missionaries' dream of linguistic-cum-spiritual purity was decidedly utopian. One finds among the Papuan communities considered in this chapter a stress on precisely those aspects of language that the missionaries sought to suppress: its concrete qualities, its capacity to evoke encounters in distant worlds. These features of Papuan practice are not simply exotic anomalies: they bring to light dimensions of sign use that both confound and enable social action, wherever it occurs. As such, they illuminate the semiotic basis of an aspect of the situation that I described in chapter 2: the meeting of the vertical and horizontal dimensions of colonial relations in the interactions between Papuans and their would-be rulers and shepherds. Two conflicting audiences converged in these interactions: one that loomed over these benighted natives and another that stood at their side. In the conclusion, I reflect on the implications of the missionaries' colonial-era dilemmas for Papuan nationalists, who dream of their own utopian future when there finally will be firm linguistic barriers between West Papua and Indonesia. But first, let us consider the evangelical vision of the lingua franca that informed Protestant policies in this outpost of the colonial world.

The Christianization of a Language

On March 15, 1916, the celebrated and well-connected missionary linguist, Nicolaüs Adriani, gave a speech for a group of Protestant students and "mission lovers" in the Dutch university town of Leiden. Son of M. A. Adriani, the director of the Utrecht Mission Society, which was the sponsor of New Guinea's main group of Protestant missionaries, and nephew of J. W. Gunning, the head of the Netherlands Missionary Society mission school where many of these missionaries were trained, Adriani was heir to the Pietist currents in nineteenth-century Dutch Calvinism that gave rise to a plethora of religious societies and organizations outside the organized churches (see Rooden 1996). Along with his partner, Albert C. Kruyt, Adriani was an early promoter of a mission methodology known as the "sociological method," which married the tenets of the Ethical Policy then being pursued in the Indies with those of Ethical Theology, an anti-Enlightenment line of Protestant thought on the relationship between Christianity and culture that was then gaining prominence (see Schrauwers 2000, 51).[2] The sociological method called for the "inculturation" of

Christianity, an aspiration that, as anthropologist Albert Schrauwers has explained, "sprang from the revivalist emphasis on the emotional bond between the believer and God; personal piety could emerge only where Christianity was not perceived as an alien imposition" (Schrauwers 2000, 53). Eager to pursue this project, Adriani had left a doctoral program in theology to join the Netherlands Bible Society, which posted him among the "Bare'e-speaking Toraja" of central Sulawesi, who lived on a sparsely populated island between Java and New Guinea. Adriani's research on this group of what he and Kruyt famously called "animists" had earned him a doctorate from Leiden University in East Indian Languages and Literatures in 1893. The title of his 1916 talk—one in a long line of public addresses—was "The Christianization of a Language." Establishing the proper relationship of Malay to the "heathen" vernacular, and of both to God's word, was a crucial component of this task.

Adriani began by wondering aloud where in the Indies one might find such a thing as a "Christianized language." Although an earlier generation of bible translators had chosen (or, better, invented) the high Malay of the Malacca Straits and the islands of Riau, in the far west of the colony, to play this role, Adriani rejected this option as overly obscure to his interlocutors (see Hoffman 1979, 69; Maier 1993, 45).[3] In the colony's east, Minahassa, a region in North Sulawesi, and Ambon, a Spice Islands trade center in the Moluccas, which were home to the oldest communities of native Christians, seemed like more obvious places to begin the search. Yet the language of neither of these communities really qualified. In Minahassa, missionaries had neglected the local vernacular, focusing instead on "Minahassa Malay," which was "not so much a language as a 'modus loquendi' among people who don't speak each other's languages" (Adriani 1916, 102).

> The native has no opportunity to learn Dutch and the native language is too difficult for the European. In its place, he uses a language that he himself has mastered. This is naturally not the language of the Malays, for that language is just as difficult as every other Indonesian language, and to speak it purely, one would have first to work and live among the Malays [that is, in Riau]. The European Malay serves as a way of avoiding the difficulty of the vernacular (*landstaal*). It is put together (*in elkaar gezet*) in good part from his Dutch and thus displays, when used in the service of Christianity, the same character Dutch has in the same case. Such a language cannot be called a Christianized language; it can only be compared with a not very finely wrought translation. (Adriani 1916, 102)

The situation in Ambon, where Malay had become a vernacular, was equally unsatisfying. Here the influence of Christian discourse was strongly felt—especially in love letters. Adriani provided an example:

> If, indeed, my love can unite with me in words of peace, will you then answer with a heart full of love, saying "yes." Then shall I rejoice with the people of Zion; Hosanna, Hosanna, blessed are the tidings that come in the name of the Lord. (Adriani 1916, 103)

The shallow, Europeanized nature of Minahassa Malay went with the absurdity of the Ambonese appropriation of a Christian idiom to amorous ends; both lacked "difficulty" and hence "depth." To produce a Christianized language, one had to produce a Christianized society. Both tasks had to take as their starting point the mastery of a vernacular with roots in the heart of heathen life.

Although the Christianization of a language was the work of "centuries," not "years," Adriani's experience in central Sulawesi had given him a sense of what the process entailed. Adriani's first step was to learn the Torajan vernacular, which was not an easy task. The missionary linguist and his famous partner, Albert C. Kruyt, initially made mistakes that went uncorrected by the natives, who "viewed them as a peculiarity of the missionaries that they simply had to swallow" (Adriani 1916, 108). But eventually the missionaries mastered enough of the language to begin preaching to the Toraja and to gain an understanding of their animist beliefs.

In order to teach the natives, Adriani and Kruyt first had to learn from them; but the point was not to establish equivalences—or even in Haun Saussy's (2001) terms, a "workshop of equivalences"—through which Christian concepts could be expressed in the natives' language. Conversion was less a process of matching Dutch and native words than of provoking the natives' recognition of what their heathen language and thus conceptions lacked. In other words, it was a matter of cultivating an audience: the natives had to come to see what their language was missing when viewed through Christian eyes. First of all there was the lexicon, which lacked words for Christian values, like forgiveness, as well as a term for a single all-powerful and loving God. Adriani and Kruyt resorted to Malay words to fill the holes, yet the process of Christianization went much further than that. Adriani used the metaphor of the "roads" built by their ancestors. The missionaries' task was sometimes to create detours, sometimes to extend dead ends, but above all to reveal the need for repairs.

In a 1908 speech given for the Dutch queen and queen mother, Adriani's uncle, J. W. Gunning, described how Kruyt gave a sermon in one settlement after another on the Good Samaritan, which retold the parable as the story of an encounter between a Torajan and an injured foe. Kruyt could tell that the story had finally hit home when someone blurted out, "That's a lie!" Persuaded by the missionary that he would not have come so far to tell them untruths, the Torajans were forced to reflect on the transformation that would be required for such a story to seem plausible. "For such a thing to happen," one of them concluded, "our hearts would have to totally change" (Gunning 1908, 18). Conversion involves an ambivalent kind of identification in this anecdote. Even as they reject Adriani's sermon, the Torajans imagine what it would be like to join an audience for whom the parable would make sense.

Implicit in this vision are also particular assumptions about the nature of discourse, in general, and the difference between Malay and the vernacular, in particular. To effect a true conversion—the kind that produces congregations that are Christian "in more than name"—evangelists had to transcend the friction associated with what one might call the surface of language so that they could deploy, to their advantage, the friction between ideas.

> The Christianization of a language does not occur by imposing upon it a Christian treasury of words. Rather than furnishing a people coming to Christianity with a series of strange words, which will tend to dominate their usage and accustom them to parroting us, their evangelists, we must guard against the thoughtless use of Christian terms in the place of words that express animist ideas, without the latter thus disappearing. (Adriani 1916, 119–20)

The injudicious use of loan words led to the trivialization of the Christian concepts they were supposed to convey, as when heathens referred to a wild boar, called a "pig of the spirits" in their language, as a "pig of Jesus Christ" (Adriani 1916, 119). Adriani viewed the use of Malay as particularly dangerous in this regard, presumably because this "modus loquendi" lacked the proper grounding in an authentic speech community that would stabilize the meaning of its words.

But Malay was also prone to slippage, according to Adriani, because the heathens regarded the mere use of the language as a source of prestige. Multiple audiences haunted Adriani's description of mission work: the hypothetical Christians evoked by the Torajans and now the heathens who made a display out of the missionaries' language rather than spreading their Good News. If one used Malay for evangelical purposes, Adriani notes, the vernacular remained a "heathen language."

> And this adjective must be understood in the original sense of the word: "pagan," rustic, provincial. The vernacular is thus reduced to a bumpkin language, while Malay becomes the vehicle for progress, and where most education in the upper levels of school is in Malay, then the natives will happily be spoken to in Malay, because it elevates them in their eyes. Among people who are still animists, religion is tightly interwoven with the customs and mores of daily life, such that people see Christianity as a field of knowledge. By becoming Christian, people advance in knowledge; people thus should speak in the language that one always speaks with all the Europeans and which gives an entry to all kinds of knowledge that is never conveyed in the vernacular. For many natives, the difference between Malay and Dutch is not entirely evident. (Adriani 1916, 106)

By using Malay for evangelical purposes, missionaries distracted the natives and prevented Christianity from fully penetrating their daily lives. Potential converts ended up paying less heed to the content of the missionaries' message than to their code.

It is easy to imagine how Adriani and Kruyt's endeavors could have led to a bounding of local culture, analogous to the boundary-building work undertaken in colonial scholarship on "customary" (*adat*) law (see Schrauwers 2000). But it was not simply the value of the local that Adriani sought to confirm by "Christianizing" the vernacular; rather, he strove to make the native vernacular serve as a conduit to a wider world. By "cultivating" the local language—making it suitable for Bible translations and the production of edifying literature—missionaries could demonstrate to young Christians "that their language is just as good as others, and that it can continually win them new terrain" (Adriani 1916, 107). Note how Adriani projects onto Malay traits associated with the nonreferential functions and material qualities of discourse: its ability to index status, its underdetermined nature, all those things an utterance does above and beyond communicating knowledge. The vernacular, by contrast, is depicted as perfectly transparent, a window onto modernity and the native soul.

Adriani's project relied on the possibility of distinguishing between the pure and hybrid versions of a language. It also relied on the possibility of telling the difference between a purely referential use of words and one deployed to bring its speaker prestige. In Adriani's rhetoric, Malay served a critical purpose: it acted as a repository for dimensions of discourse that make these borders impossible to defend (see Derrida 1974, 1981; Bakhtin 1981; Silverstein 1996). Highly influential in mission circles throughout the Indies, Adriani's ideas had an impact on the "brothers and sisters" who served in New Guinea, whose views echoed his own. F. J. F. van Hasselt, whom we will meet momentarily, thanked Adriani for his encouragement in the preface to a 1905 Noefoor grammar (Hasselt 1905, 4). In a 1926 report on "Malay in our schools," another New Guinea missionary cited Adriani in warning against the "word worship" and "superficiality" caused by the use of Malay for evangelical purposes (Utrechtsche Zendingsver-eeniging 1926). By the time Adriani arrived in Sulawesi in 1890, Protestants like F. J. F. van Hasselt's father, J. L. van Hasselt, had been active in New Guinea for close to fifty years. "Let the Papuan remain a Papuan," an early missionary proclaimed in 1876, anticipating Adriani arguing against the "sacrilege" of giving Papuan children non-Papuan names (Kamma 1976, 274). Adriani was no doubt aware of these missionaries' trials and tribulations. The dilemmas that fueled Adriani's call for a Christianized vernacular were thus particularly evident in this field.

The Creation of Noefoorsch

On February 25, 1855, a trading ship from Ternate, the Moluccan town and sultanate adjacent to Tidore and the nearest government seat, dropped off some unusual cargo at a well-frequented trading stop on Mansinam Island at the mouth of Doreh Bay. In addition to the beads, knives, and porcelain the ship carried to exchange for bird skins and forest products, the vessel was transporting two unsalaried Christian Workmen, Carl W. Ottow and J. G. Geissler, who had come to New Guinea to ply their trade and preach the Word (see Kamma 1976; Rutherford 2005). The two men were proté-gés of O. G. Heldring, the Dutch Pietist theologian mentioned in chapter 2, who was a leader of the early nineteenth-century Dutch Protestant "awakening" known as the Reveil, and Johannes Gossner, a defrocked German priest, who together had founded a small mission sending Dutch and German craftsmen to the Indies. As we have seen, a variety of vessels passed through New Guinea's coastal waters during this period, from the outriggers in which coastal Papuans traded, raided, and delivered trib-ute to Tidore, to the *hongi* fleets sent by the sultan to punish rebellious subjects, to American and European whaling vessels and warships. The Dutch officials who sporadically toured the region, usually accompanied by a Tidoran prince, did not cherish high hopes for the success of the mission. But these officials soon realized that the missionaries had their uses. For one thing, the missionaries helped the government by ransoming foreign shipwreck victims captured by coastal natives. For another, they helped to guard a coal depository on Mansinam, so that government steamships could refuel there and complete more extensive tours. In addition to trading with the local Papuans, Ottow and Geissler survived on the small payments they received from the administration in Ternate for serving as the government's eyes and ears.

Ottow and Geissler quickly took steps to learn the languages spoken on Mansinam. European traders already knew some of the vernacular, which they called Mefoorsch or Myfoorsch, after the names then given to Numfor, an island a day's paddle to the east of the Bird's Head, not far from Biak (see, e.g., Goudswaard 1863). The Mansinam islanders had not been in Doreh Bay for many generations, by most accounts; their arrival had coincided with the transformation in regional politics that accompanied the Netherlands' changing colonial relations with Tidore. By the nineteenth century, the Dutch had little use for the Tidoran sultans other than as figureheads to justify the Netherlands Indies' claims to western New Guinea and its outlying islands (see Smeele 1988). With the rise of private markets caused by increased shipping to the region, seafarers from Biak, Numfor, and related communities came to play a prominent role in the trade in bird skins and slaves from the Bird's Head interior (see Miedema 1984, 3–17; Haenen 1991, 12–14). The "Meefoorsch" speakers at Mansinam were also particularly active in the sale of slaves from Amberbaken, a fertile area on the northern tip of the Bird's Head where they also acquired rice to meet the missionaries' rising demand.

Ottow and Geissler, who had just spent two years serving a congregation of Chinese Christians in Batavia, the Indies' cosmopolitan capital city, initially preached and taught school in Malay (see Beekman 1989; Kamma 1976). Their congregation at this point consisted of the handful of Ternatan carpenters who had been sent to New Guinea to help them build a house. A local headman spoke fairly good Malay, and he may well have helped Ottow with the production of a Malay-Mefoorsch word list, which the missionary passed on to a visiting official in 1858 (see Commissie voor Nieuw-Guinea 1862). But the missionaries soon switched their efforts to the vernacular. They reportedly were led to this decision by the action of local parents, who forbade their children to attend school after they learned that the missionaries were teaching their pupils to count in Malay. For the Papuans, albeit for different reasons than for the missionaries, a rather frightening audience was associated with this tongue. Supposedly, they feared that the missionaries were preparing the youngsters to be sent to the Netherlands as slaves with a trading ship then anchored in Doreh Bay (see Hasselt n.d.a, 43–44).

The first Mefoorsch publication was a hymnal that came out in 1860; in 1865 Geissler produced a grammar of the language, using notes left by Ottow, who died in 1862 (see Hasselt 1888, 61). A year later, Geissler published the first "Mefoorsch-Hollands" dictionary (Hasselt 1888, 62). In 1867 Geissler completed a translation of a catechism question book and a schoolbook in Mefoorsch, and by 1870 he had translated Zahn's Bible History and the Gospel of Mark (Hasselt 1888, 63). With the arrival of a new crop of missionaries from the Utrecht Mission Society, which took over the field in 1863, the rate of publication quickened. Although not all of the dozen or so missionaries sent to New Guinea during the nineteenth century settled among Mefoorsch speakers, most of their translations and compositions appeared in that language, even though the Dutch mission-aries often seemed uncertain as to its status and reach.

The multiple names assigned to Mefoorsch reflect this uncertainty. The missionaries, like other observers, knew that it could not be described as *the* Papuan language. Yet it was the only one most of the missionaries knew (see Hasselt 1888, 57). The missionaries were also puzzled by the language's relationship to Malay. The dictionaries published in the nine-teenth century each end with a list of Malay words, which include not only the usual suspects, like *adat* (custom), but also words like *nangi*, suppos-edly a "bastardized" version of *langit* (sky) (see Hasselt 1876, 119; see also Hasselt 1893). A similar skepticism surfaces in the reports of visiting colo-nial officials who insisted on correcting the Papuan's "mispronunciation" when they wrote down words they imagined had originated from Malay (see, e.g., Commissie voor Nieuw-Guinea 1862, 147–48). Thus, *rum sram*, the word for the men's house on Mansinam, appears as *rum slam* or *rumah Islam* in an 1862 report, in a gesture toward "Islamic priests" believed to have introduced the institution (Commissie voor Nieuw-Guinea 1862, 151–52). This uncertainty as to Mefoorsch's origins (and the originality of Papuan customs) culminated in a debate between the nineteenth-century philologists F. Max-Müller and H. Kern. The latter used the missionaries' word lists and dictionaries to demonstrate that the language was a mem-ber of the Malayo-Polynesian family of languages, notwithstanding its speakers' primitive race (see Kern 1916, 1917). In formulating this theory, which survives in the classification of Biak-Numfor as an Austronesian language, Kern left open the question of whether the Malayo-Polynesians had taught these savages how to speak (1917, 76).

Academic squabbling aside, the missionaries' ability to operate in Mefoorsch steadily improved. By the early twentieth century, F. J. F. van Hasselt oversaw the revision of school texts in what he now called "Noefoorsch" and the production of a body of edifying works. Among the extant texts I have inspected are two editions of Mrs. J. L. van Hasselt's Noefoorsch song book, which includes hymns and seasonal songs, such as "For Mr. Resident" (*Faro Toean Resident*), composed for touring officials and sung to the tune of "Those Whose Blood Is Dutch," the first Dutch national hymn (see Anonymous 1887, 27; see also J. L. van Hasselt 1885; Anonymous 1886). For his part, F. J. F. van Hasselt composed Noefoorsch readers and brief renditions of biblical stories as well as a version of La Fontaine's fables, which incorporates flora and fauna presumably familiar to his Papuan flock (see Anonymous 1911). But his *The Book in Which We Learn about Insulinde* (*Soerat ko farkoor ro Insulinde*), published in 1900, demonstrates most vividly Noefoorsch's power to play the role of a properly Christianized vernacular—that is, to "win" its readers to the "new terrain" that Adriani described. In this text, we get a distinctly utopian view of the Papuan Christian audience for whom the missionaries wrote.

Some seventy pages long, the book begins with an explanation of the meaning of Insulinde—"Many islands" (*Meos naboor*)—then launches into a journey. The trip begins in the east; "because we love the land of Papua, why don't we begin our study of Insulinde with that land, our land!" For reasons that will become apparent momentarily, in the excerpts that follow, Malay-seeming words appear in bold.

> On the maps we can read the name of our land, New Guinea, or "New Guinea" [Noefoorsch: **Guinea Babo**]. The Portuguese and Spanish were the first white people to come to the land of Papua, and when they saw the people in the land, they said, "They look just like the people of Guinea, Africa!" So they called the land New Guinea. (1900, 4)

Because "not all of New Guinea obeys the **Young Queen** of Holland (**Nonna Radja** Wolanda)," the narrator will just treat the western half.

> The Papuan people don't have just one tradition or set of **customs** (*adat*). In one place things are a bit good, in another place they are more evil, in one place they

plunder a lot, in another place they do not fight with one another. . . . I won't tell you about the customs or houses of the Noefoor, because you already know much more about that than I do. (Ibid., 5)

Instead, the narrator takes his readers to Humboldt Bay, named "out of **respect (*hormat*)** for **Mr. (*Toean*)** van Humboldt, a German gentleman who saw many lands and peoples" (ibid., 5). Humboldt Bay's inhabitants "walk around totally naked" and worship idols (*korwaar*). "Alas! They don't yet know what we read in Psalms 127:1: 'If the Lord doesn't **guard** (*djaga*) a house, men guard it in vain. They ask wooden [Gods/figures] to guard their houses, but wood doesn't see, doesn't hear; **safe (*slamat*)** are we who know to pray to the Lord God" (ibid., 6). The narrator proceeds to the west coast of New Guinea, then Ternate and Tidore, whose inhabitants, we learn, rejected the Spanish and Portuguese, but welcomed the Dutch people's offer to **help (*betoelong*)** their rulers in wars. The tour continues in a similar vein through the eastern part of the colony, before finally reaching Java, "a really nice island," where the text dwells for a disproportionate amount of time.

The ship drops anchor at the port of Tandjoeng Priok, in Batavia, the Indies' capital. The narrator describes Batavia's "many villages" (*mennoe naboor*) (ibid., 49). There is much to see in Batavia: the Governor General's house, "a big person made of copper" (a statue of Jan Pieterzoon Coen, Batavia's seventeenth-century founder), "men and women **wearing all sorts** of clothing (*bepaké sansoen roepa-roepa*) (ibid., 49). "If we are tired and the road is long, we call for a carriage, many of which we've seen in Batavia, and we pay some money and it takes us where we want to go" (ibid., 49–50).

The tour next takes us to Depok, the school founded by a minister who "thought it would be good if black people were taught by black men helping the Dutch missionaries" (ibid., 50). We witness a geography lesson and watch the students playing their musical instruments—"soon we are deafened by the great noise" (ibid., 51). Leaving Depok, we pass through tea plantations, visit the "very nice" village of Bandung (a major city in West Java), and take a trip up the famous volcano, Tankoban Prahoe. But the Christian villages and hospitals founded by missionaries are a key focus of our travels. In these places, "we see the power of the Lord Jesus. His power is greater than that of Mohammed, and we believe (*kiaar*) that all the Javanese people will soon **believe (*bepersya*)** in Jesus Christ" (ibid., 62).

After another imaginary geography lesson ("Should they ask you, 'Name the Great Sunda Islands,' you should name: 'Borneo, Sumatra, Celebes, and Java'"), a chapter on Sumatra, and a short discussion of the colony's new steamship service, the book ends with a hymn:

> On the mountains, in the valleys,
> Everywhere is God.

> At sea, on ships, in canoes,
> There is God.

> I speak, I believe the prayer,
> God watches me.
> […]
> You, the Gospel, you are so very powerful!
> You travel quickly, you are victorious!

> Great king! Oh, you give me blessings.
> You make your house all over the world.

> And all the hearts receive Salvation,
> Unite in single purity! (Ibid., 70–71)

Noefoorsch readers are invited to occupy a peculiar point of view by the narrative, which uses a "Papuan" language to insert them into a series of "non-Papuan" places. Their perspective is constructed to mirror that of a gentleman Christian traveler, who takes steamships, trains, and carriages, remarks on the colony's racial diversity, and dwells upon Java's tiny communities of native Christians. The hymn at the end describes and then addresses the Lord. In doing so, it points to the source of this remarkable ability to transcend geographic and racial boundaries: a God who is "everywhere," a Gospel that "travels fast." The text adheres to Adriani's prescription for the Christianization of a language; by way of what seems most intimate—what Adriani called the "language of the land" (*landtaal*)—readers gain entry into an expansive colonial world.

This entry into an expansive world is really an entry into an expansive audience: the reader imagines the colonial world from a new point of view. The Papuan jumps from the bottom of the Indies' ladder of civilization to the top, assuming the gaze of the colony's European rulers and their power to bridge distances in space and time. He sees the Indies through the lens provided by the map and a colonial history in which everything of import begins with "white gentlemen" who "saw many people and lands." In this, the utopian nature of the imagined Papuan audience becomes evident. For this audience, reading functions as overhearing: listening to comments intended for another—the gentleman Christian traveler—then putting oneself in this other's shoes. Adriani's account of the Torajans' reaction to the parable of the Good Samaritan springs to mind. The book is written for Papuan readers whose hearts have, indeed, "totally changed."

Yet there is something about the text that does not fit Adriani's model. It is riddled with what Woolard would call bivalent elements: scraps of text that belong to more than one language. It is here that yet another audience—of the heathen rather than Christian sort—intervenes. Consider the items written in boldface in the preceding description. One might expect to see Malay terms for God and Jesus (*Allah, Jesus*), although contemporary speakers of the related language, Biak, have their own gloss for the Lord (*Manseren*). Even the term, *bepersya*, (**believe**), could perhaps be accounted for; the Noefoorsch alternative, *kiaar*, also present in the text, may not have captured the nuances of Christian faith. But then there is *hormat* (**respect**), *soesah* (**difficult**), *ro waktoe* (back **in the days**), *buk prenta* (give **orders**), and *i bejaga ko* (he **guards** us).[4] These apparently random substitutions seem less the outcome of targeted borrowing than an indication of the author's tendency to speak in a fashion that simultaneously belongs to more than one language. In other words, the author speaks to multiple audiences simultaneously, including interlocutors who took pride and pleasure in their mastery of these bivalent features. F. J. F. van Hasselt built on the work of predecessors—including his parents—who worked very hard to police the boundaries between Malay and Noefoorsch/Mefoorsch. Yet his composition bears witness to a tangling of tongues.

Here is the irony, given Maier's formulations: these Protestant language workers not only failed to domesticate heteroglossia; their practices promoted it. From one perspective, the geography text plays to the dream of Noefoorsch as a Christianized language. But from another perspective, *The Book in Which We Learn about Insulinde* bears the marks of what Adriani depicted as the "bad" lingua franca. Recall what Adriani had to say about Minahassa Malay, this language without an authoritative center, "put together" on the fly. The dangerous thing about Malay was not simply its lack of cultural origins but also its appeal for natives who associated it with foreign wealth and power. If we consider the historical setting in which this mingling of Malay and Noefoorsch emerged, we find ourselves confronted by both of these characteristics. Mission Noefoorsch, as one might call this translingual register, was a language that emerged through imitation, a language whose possession brought with it a certain prestige.

Consider first of all the speech community, narrowly defined, in which the missionaries' version of Mefoorsch/Noefoorsch was spoken. At the end of J. L. van Hasselt's 1893 edition of the Noefoorsch-Dutch dictionary, one finds "a list of Malay words that have currency in Noefoorsch or at least are understood (*particularly by the Christian Papuans*)" (1893, 38, my italics). At that point the community of Christian Papuans was miniscule, consisting overwhelmingly of slaves, mostly from the Karon or Kebar regions of the Bird's Head interior. Officially outlawed, the slave trade persisted throughout the nineteenth century. Many war captives ended up in Moluccan ports, but a growing number were brought to Doreh Bay, where the missionaries redeemed them with silver and guns. The missionaries referred to the redeemed slaves as their foster children and kept up to thirty in their households at any one time. When they grew up, the former slaves married one another and remained in the vicinity of the mission posts in Mansinam and nearby settlements, where they founded small Christian villages. Theoretically, the foster children were free to leave; but in practice, they had little choice but to stay close to their Dutch "parents": freeborn Papuans were quick to recapture them if they strayed too far from their masters' homes.

With very few freeborn Papuan captives to boast of, the brothers and sisters filled the inspirational literature they produced for audiences back home with stories about these foster children. In books like J. L. van Hasselt's 1909 memoirs, *Nacht en Morgen*, we get a sense of the imagined readers for whom F. J. F. van Hasselt wrote his geography. We learn of Elli, a slave from the supposedly cannibalistic Karon tribe who was redeemed when she was three. Although Elli had the bad habit of biting other children (!), she grew up to be an excellent student and affectionate daughter. J. L. van Hasselt describes Elli's joy at her adopted family's return from home leave by quoting her tearful expressions—all spoken or written in Dutch (1909, 30–31). Then there is Johan, son of Jonathon and Paulina, two slaves captured in Koeroedoe. Johan traveled with J. L. van Hasselt to Ternate, where he impressed the missionary's friends by reciting the communion formula in Malay (1909, 36). Sent to a Malay-language school on Java to prepare for entering the seminary at Depok, Johan amazed his teachers with his versatility in their tongue. Perhaps the most vivid portrait of such a scenario comes from the pen of J. L. D. van der Roest, who learned Noefoorsch in Mansinam before traveling to his post in Windessi, whose inhabitants spoke what came to be described as a different language. When a smallpox epidemic hit the village, his predecessor's dying foster child—a woman from the community—amazed him with her piety: she sang a Noefoorsch verse: "I'm Jesus's **sheep**; My heart is happy" (*Aja Jezus **domba** ja, a marisein ornema*) (Roest 1912, 28–29). The New Guinea missionaries' published writings are full of direct quotations designed to give Dutch readers a sense of the magnitude of these Papuans' inner transformation. But at the same time these texts reveal a mobile, heteroglossic community. Noefoorsch was the lingua franca for a tiny social world.

The missionaries' writings also provide evidence of the other aspect of the lingua franca described by Adriani: its valorization as a source of prestige. In this, the specter of alternative audiences comes clearly into view. Accounts of failed conversions are particularly revealing of the difficulties this valorization of foreign words posed to the missionaries. We hear of an old heathen lady who uttered a devotional verse while looking at a biblical print—then laughed when the missionary's wife asked her if she had found faith (see Kamma 1977, 495). We learn of a Mansinamer who asked a missionary for a monopoly on a story so he could take it to Amberbaken to sell for rice (see ibid., 130). Elsewhere I have described how visitors from Biak and Numfor treated the missionaries' words as booty. Much as a valued trade good might demonstrate a traveler's prowess, so could his or her memory of an outsider's speech (Rutherford 2005).

Over the centuries, Noefoorsch-speaking Papuans had learned to profit from their interactions with dangerous outsiders. Parents in Mansinam may have associated Malay with slavery in the case of their children; but for local leaders, fluency in Malay was critical to their ability to capture wealth from distant worlds. When a Dutch warship approached, coastal villagers would flee. But in keeping with the government's policy of display, a headman with a Tidoran title and some knowledge of Malay remained to greet the visitors, running the risks and reaping the rewards that such dealings could bring (see chapter 2). The free Papuans who became involved with the missionaries tended to be precisely these intermediaries, like the old Korano who helped J. L. van Hasselt by repeating his Noefoorsch sermons word for word (see Hasselt 1909, 22). Although the world of the mission household was clearly different from the world of these Noefoorsch leaders, some "foster children" developed a similar sense of the prestige to be gained from contact with outsiders. A student sent to the seminary in Depok in 1900 returned with visiting cards to pass out to all his friends (see Kamma 1977, 573).

By Adriani's measure, the Papuan vernacular cultivated by the missionaries on this frontier of colonial authority was no less a "bad" lingua franca than Malay. It was a register born of linguistic contact to serve a diverse and often divergent set of ends, a register that brought the nonreferential functions of discourse prominently into view. A few years after the publication of F. J. F. van Hasselt's geography, the context that produced this "Christianized" language dramatically changed. A post at Manokwari, not far from Mansinam, opened in 1898, and the permanently settled Dutch controller immediately made his influence felt. Instead of responding to local feuds by launching surprise attacks on unruly settlements, the controller made individuals culpable for what had suddenly become crimes (see Roest 1912, 37). The new regime thus offered new dangers, but also new opportunities. In a small settlement on the mainland, a few days paddle from Manokwari, "three Papuans, one of whom spoke good Malay, asked to be appointed as Korano, Sanadi and Major" (titles given to government-appointed native chiefs in the region)—and the controller immediately complied (Anonymous 1995 [1898], 90). When coastal communities converted to Christianity en masse in the first few decades of the twentieth century, it was not simply the sense that the world was dramatically changing that gave rise to a keen interest in the religion. Papuans also converted to gain better access to Malay by way of the teachers and evangelists the missionaries imported from Ambon and elsewhere to meet the growing demand. Given their dependence on local communities for food and housing, these mission employees felt compelled to speak for the villagers when the government intervened to collect taxes, impose corvée labor, or settle a dispute (Feuilletau de Bruyn 1916, 244). On Biak, disputants would "buy" an interpreter to represent them in legal proceedings. By this view, when a Biak leader petitioned the missionaries for a teacher or an evangelist, he was after a Malay-speaking advocate, not the Holy Word.

This is not to say that the missionaries were ready to abandon Noefoorsch in the early decades of the twentieth century. Non-Papuan teachers, like the missionaries who began work during this period, were expected to learn Noefoorsch quickly so they could begin teaching and preaching in the language. This was the case even when the people they served spoke what later appeared as another dialect or even another mother tongue

(Starrenburg 1916, 5; see also Utrechtsche Zendingsvereeniging 1926; Hasselt n.d.a). In fact, it was the vast expansion of mission schools that brought
to the missionaries' attention the fact that Noefoorsch was not as widely
distributed as they had assumed. Nineteenth-century missionaries, who had
fleeting encounters with seafarers from places like Biak, thought that all
these people spoke the language they had learned in Doreh. As Feuilletau
de Bruyn explained, "Before 1915, the great difference [between Biak
and Nuefoorsch] escaped the younger van Hasselt, something that was a
result of the fact that when someone spoke to a Biak in Nuefoorsch, he
did not answer in his own dialect, but in Nuefoor" (1947–48, 189; see also
Hasselt 1936–37, 116). The contradictory nature of this situation becomes
clear in letters written by F. W. Hartweg, the aforementioned missionary
who served on Biak in the 1920s. Hartweg was adamant about the need
to produce separate materials "in the Biak language (better: dialect)," arguing that this is really what is spoken throughout the area. At the same
time, the "alien" character of Noefoorsch did little to limit local demand
for publications in the language. When the news spread that Hartweg had
received a shipment of Noefoorsch hymnals from the Netherlands, "hundreds of people" came to buy the "little books" (Hartweg 1926).

Perhaps in response to complaints like Hartweg's, when F. J. F. van
Hasselt revised and enlarged his father's dictionary, he included dialectal
variants (see Hasselt and Hasselt 1947).[5] But in the face of van Hasselt's
efforts to map the vernacular, heteroglossia arguably prevailed. Just as
some natives—pace Adriani—could not tell the difference between Malay and Dutch, it seems possible that Malay and Noefoorsch did not always
seem sharply distinct. The government promoted the former; the mission
promoted the latter—but then the difference between these two sources
of power, wealth and mobility, was often less than clear. As Hartweg noted
in the letter I cited in chapter 2, "The Biakkers call a *bestuurs assistant* or
a *gezaghebber* a *pandita*, just as quickly as they do us" (Hartweg 1926).
Whereas *bestuurs assistant* and *gezaghebber* are Dutch terms for lower-
level colonial officers, *pandita* is a Malay word, used in Noefoorsch, meaning "minister" or "preacher." For Papuans who sought mission teachers to
serve in their villages, access to one language spelled access to the other,
as we have seen.

In the last 1930s, when, as we have seen, some Dutch colonials proposed administering New Guinea separately from the rest of the Indies,
there was discussion of promoting Noefoorsch as a "language of unity"
(Hasselt 1936–37). But after the war, when Netherlands New Guinea was a

freestanding colony, its "language of unity" was Malay, by then also known as Indonesian, despite interested Dutch assertions that the Papuans and the Indonesians had nothing in common. Noefoorsch no longer exists in the form described in this chapter. Yet the language's peculiar connection to colonial authority is tacitly recalled. In the early 1990s, people in Biak did not describe their language as a version of Noefoorsch; rather, they referred to the Biak spoken in Mansinam and other migrant zones. In this they were supported by the work of recent linguists, who have taken "Bahasa Biak" as the phenomenon to be described (Soeparno 1977; Fautngil, Rumbrawer, and Kainakaimu 1994). When pressed, a friend in North Biak explained that Noefoorsch was the Biak's *kromo*, borrowing a Japanese term to describe the "refined" register of the vernacular. But the same friend was quick to echo what others had already told me: it was the Dutch missionaries who spoke this register best. Biaks called Indonesian—the successor to Malay—*wos amber* (foreign speech). But their comments suggested that the mother tongue, imagined to exist in its purest form in the utterances of Dutch pastors, was in some sense foreign as well. In the connections drawn by contemporary Biaks, one detects the lasting effects of mission practice. In this distant corner of the Indies, both Malay and the Christianized vernacular provided a way of capturing the value associated with foreign worlds.

Sovereignty in the Linguistic Contact Zone

Bivalency is arguably a feature of all semiotic practices. The effort to purge language of its others can never succeed. But it can take a confrontation between ideologies in the high-stakes context of colonialism to bring the perils and pleasures of indeterminacy to the fore. In the linguistic contact zone that developed in Dutch New Guinea, the uneven, sporadic exercise of colonial authority made the divergence between ideologies and audiences particularly sharp. Tidoran princes and their Dutch partners interpreted the Malay words uttered by local headmen as evidence that some form of colonial sovereignty existed in the region. Dutch officers were tormented by the question of how coastal New Guinea might appear to other European powers and took comfort in the vaguest indication that the Papuans might present themselves as members of the Indies world. For their part, coastal leaders turned their possession of the language of dangerous strangers into a local source of authority.[6] The arrival of the missionaries

complicated this mix, given their efforts to develop a Christianized vernacular that brought Papuan souls into communion with a transcendent
God. Yet the missionaries found themselves in a similar predicament to
that faced by colonial officials. They could never suppress the possibility
that the Papuans would fix upon the fact of language, rather than its meaning, the surface of Noefoorsch, rather than its soul. The Koreri movement
gave the missionaries a sharp sense of how their good tidings could run
astray (Kamma 1972; see chapters 4 and 6).

Which takes us back to the epigraph at the beginning of this chapter,
which highlights the conundrums born of the overlapping colonial histories that gave rise to Indonesian and West Papuan nationalism. In 2000 the
framers of the proposed West Papuan constitution seem to have taken a
page from Gellner (1983) and Hobsbawm (1990); for their movement to
fit the models developed by these scholars, Papuan nationalists must conjure an indigenous intelligentsia, discriminated against by a state whose
language differs from their own. The fact that, in practice, Indonesian is
the working language of Papuan nationalism presents a predicament; and
like the missionaries before them, Papuan nationalists dream of a clear
linguistic break. One possibility would be to define Papuan Malay as a
separate national language, analogous to Malaysian. Yet this answer, for
Papuan nationalists, can only be "temporary" (see Alua 2000, 44). The
ultimate solution described in the epigraph is decidedly creative. There
will be Papua New Guinea's Tok Pisin, which seems incontestably Melanesian, and there will be English, the language of global conversations. The
culturally particular will commune with the universal. This is Adriani's
vision, but with a twist: these are languages that many in the province
have yet to learn. In valorizing these tongues for the social worlds they
promise to open, Papuan nationalists embrace the dilemma that dogged
the missionaries. To this day, these "transcendent" registers serve as a local source of prestige.

In the following chapter I continue my exploration of the signs of West
Papuan sovereignty by looking at another legacy of the mission encounter in western New Guinea. In addition to visions of language, visions of
Christian institutions proliferated in this contact zone. By exploring the
interaction among these visions, I explain some of the reasons why Christianity remains a central factor in the pursuit of sovereignty in West Papua
today. Dutch New Guinea was surely a setting where, to paraphrase Maier,
the colonial state held political and economic power without being able to
enforce its hegemony. Yet it was never a zone free of ideology. It was never

a zone free of the multiple audiences that would-be sovereigns, like speakers everywhere, could not help but address. The contentious perspectives on linguistic practice discussed in this chapter did as much to produce heteroglossia as to suppress it. On this frontier of colonial authority, some of the Indies' inhabitants may well have felt the force of the lingua franca even in the absence of Malay words.

CHAPTER SIX

Institutional Power and Interpretive Practice

What is the relationship between people's experience of Christian institutions and the meanings they attribute to Christian texts? Anthropologists have offered a straightforward answer to this question. Christian missions, schools, and churches promote particular interpretations of scripture and ritual in an effort to produce particular kinds of believers (see Asad 1993; Rafael 1988; Comaroff and Comaroff 1991; Cannell 1999; Schrauwers 2000; Aragon 2000; cf. Bowen 1993; Foucault 1979). Christian institutions achieve this "disciplinary" outcome because they are dense sites of power, "the effect of a network of motivated practices" ranging from brute force to spiritual and material sanctions and incentives, from ecclesiastical law to routinized habits of self-cultivation and control (Asad 1993, 35). Yet this straightforward answer does not offer us a way of accounting for the mixture of Christian images and references deployed by Papuan nationalists fighting for sovereignty over their land. Throughout the predominantly Christian province, proindependence groups have resorted to texts, practices, and technologies associated with Christianity and the colonial and postcolonial state. To understand the conditions that have made it possible for Papuan nationalists to read the Bible for signs of God's support for their struggle, we need to understand the history of Christian organizations in the province. But we also need to understand how such institutions can come to feature in people's lives and imaginations as something other than a disciplinary force. During the Koreri movement of 1939–42, Biak prophets accused foreign evangelists of tearing a page from the Bible—the one that accounted for the wealth and potency wielded by outsiders (see Kamma 1972, 161). When it comes to the linkage between institutions and interpretations, our own approaches may be missing a page.

Take Talal Asad's (1993) critique of the approach to ritual and religion promoted by Clifford Geertz (1973) and others who have read social practices for their symbolic meaning. Asad foregrounds what Geertz takes for granted: the institutions through which a ritual's purposes, and what counts as religion, are defined. Asad offers evidence of a transition in the West from the monastic use of prayer and other practices as disciplinary techniques toward a more modern sensibility that searched for the meaning behind public acts. Asad shows how the medieval church set the boundaries of proper worship through "authorizing discourses," which at the same time represented the clergy's measures "as instruments of God" (1993, 35). But he neglects to explain how institutional power might become the object of alternative interpretations: ones that undermine, rather that uphold, the official monopoly on the truth. In other words, he neglects to attend to the multitude of audiences that bear witness to the practices and performances through which institutions exert their power.

Roy Rappaport's (1999) account of the universal problems addressed by ritual misses the point from the other direction. Rappaport distinguishes between the "highest order meanings" embedded in what he calls a religion's "Ultimate Sacred Postulates" and the concrete politics involved in the enforcement of the "lower order" rules. Institutions may derive legitimacy from conceptions of the sacred, but the vector only runs one way. The historical contingencies of social life seemingly exist on a different plane from the species-level threats to social order that religion supposedly evolved to address. Edmund Leach (1983) comes closer to bridging this gap by showing how particular institutional arrangements relate to particular understandings of power and mediation. Leach's argument turns on an analysis of the threat posed to early ecclesiastical authorities by the Arian heresy, which held that Jesus Christ was the human receptacle of the divine. Still, in sharply contrasting the church to the heretical millennial movement, Leach fails to account for how the trappings of orthodoxy can come to serve heterodox ends. What is missing from these approaches can be stated plainly: people's treatment of the Christian message is surely related to the specific ways in which they have negotiated the traffic in people, practices, goods, and, often, violence, opened by organizations acting in the name of God. This is because institutions, sovereign and otherwise, are literally made of audiences, as much as they are made of buildings, documents, and personnel. Institutions impose interpretations, but they also depend on interpretations, and interpretations can always run astray.

In this chapter, I explore this underexamined aspect of the link between institutional power and interpretive practice in the context of the episodes in western New Guinea's checkered history: the Koreri movement of 1939 to 1943 and the campaign for West Papuan independence that continued in the wake of the Biak flag raising and other demonstrations of 1998 (see chapter 4). The conventional threats to coherence described by Geertz (1973) certainly figure in my analysis: as we have seen, death, suffering, and injustice loom large in West Papua. But I intend to focus on dilemmas inherent to the institutions that disseminate Christian texts and rituals and attempt to control their meaning and use. I use the term *institution* to refer to what Max Weber called "compulsory organizations" (1978, 52). For Weber, these included the church, which exercised "psychic coercion," and the state, which claimed a monopoly on the legitimate use of force. Like Weber, I view the actions undertaken by these organizations as fueled by a combination of abstract ideals and concrete motivations and constraints, including the collective interest of functionaries in a "secure existence" and the resources at their disposal for pursuing this end (1990a, 199). But unlike Weber, I do not hold the "ideological" and the "functional" purposes of an organization in stark opposition. "Ideas such as 'state,' 'church,' 'community,' 'party,' or 'enterprise'" only exist to the degree that they are evoked in social practice," Weber wrote (Weber 1990a, 199). Purposes, including "functional" ones, are never simply given: these values and the subjects who pursue them are discursively produced.

As such, institutions are subject to what Webb Keane (1997) calls the "risks of representation": organizations depend for their authority—and their social reality—on instances of social interaction involving words, things, and forms of behavior that people can use in multiple ways and see from multiple points of view. In the course of a Christian ritual, one such point of view might fix upon the officially sanctioned symbolism of an utterance, gesture, or object. Another perspective might foreground the ties between these phenomena and broader contexts and enabling conditions: the Sunday school or seminary where the participants learned these verses and movements, the money that paid for this bread and wine. A further perspective, which comes into focus in the cases I consider here, would highlight the links between the Christian institutions that introduced these texts and practices and other "coercive" organizations, including the colonial and postcolonial state. However official doctrine treats these ties—with some Protestant forms of Christianity doing their best to obscure the believer's dependence on established social forms—Christian genres of practice always index, that is, derive from and potentially point to, broader institutional orders (see Bauman 1983; Collins 1996; Mertz 1996; Shoaps 2002; Keane 2007). That is, they welcome multiple audiences to every sacred act. Potentially a threat, but also a resource for believers, this aspect of Christian ritual elicits interpretation, figuring in local struggles for authority derived from the divine.

These struggles are local because, as I hope to make clear in this chapter, historically particular understandings of the nature and powers of coercive organizations shape people's participation in Christian rituals and their interpretation of Christian texts.[1] One effect of such participation might be something akin to a phenomenon discussed in chapter 4: the consciousness born of the "bureaucratic pilgrimage" (Anderson 1991, 55–58). Through their involvement in a translocal institution, colonial officials develop a sense of "connectedness" and "interchangeability" with one another as they traverse the same administrative space. In the context of Christian institutions, which are almost always translocal and often transnational, a parallel instance might entail a situation in which participants, in imagining their global peers as equivalent "brothers and sisters in Christ," experience a sort of "practical transcendence" that calls to mind the divine transcendence of an otherworldly God (see Rooden 1996, 71). But other possibilities exist. Participating in a ritual can appear as a means of demonstrating one's access to wealth and potency from beyond the reach of local worlds. The coexistence of these alternatives presents a dilemma to institutions whose pretensions to universality require them to extend personnel and resources across political boundaries. By virtue of an institution's role in the pursuit of status within a particular social context, Christian texts can appear as evidence of a limited good: a treasure possessed by outsiders, a stubbornly inscrutable truth, whose revelation unleashes extraordinary power.

Ever since European missionaries set foot in western New Guinea, the region's inhabitants have attempted to seize the potency of Christian institutions by laying claim to the truth behind official doctrine (see Kamma 1972; Giay and Godschalk 1993; Giay 1986, 1995a, 1995b; Timmer 2000; Rutherford 2000, 2003). My discussion of this dynamic begins with an analysis of Koreri and its relationship to the islands' history of conversion and colonization. In chapter 4, I turned to the Koreri movement to illuminate a way of thinking about violence, order, and origins that contrasts with that associated with the New Order state. In this chapter, I attend to what we can learn from the ways in which the movement's participants understood and replicated the colonial institutions that at the time were increasingly impinging upon their lives. I then revisit the resurgence of Papuan nationalism in the province. Among Papuan nationalists, as among those who participated in Koreri, a particular orientation to officially sanctioned institutions has created a space for the pursuit of decidedly unsanctioned ends. I end this chapter by exploring the wider implications of these findings. But first, let us consider a case in which the link between the power of Christian institutions and the secret meaning of Christian texts comes particularly vividly into view.

Koreri and the Power of the Foreign

In chapter 4 I set the long tradition of Biak millenarianism, which dates back to the earliest days of colonial contact in New Guinea, in the context of the practices through which the people of these islands have pursued value, authority, and prestige (see also Rutherford 2003). In arenas ranging from marriage to the performance of sung poetry, Biaks have reproduced an image of the so-called Land of the Foreigners as a source of excessive wealth, pleasurable surprises, and inscrutable texts. Under the New Order, this aspect of Biak social life had a corrosive effect on the identities the regime imposed on the islanders. The islanders suppressed the referential meaning of official rhetoric by deploying it as evidence of a speaker's proximity to distant sources of wealth and power. This valorization of the foreign, I have suggested, is the product of this region's history on the frontiers of powerful polities, beginning with the Moluccan sultanate of Tidore, where Biaks delivered tribute in return for trade goods and titles.

This dynamic found its limits in Koreri. Drawing on a myth that made a Biak ancestor, Manarmakeri, into the source of foreign potency, Koreri occurred at moments when Biaks were drawn to adopt the perspective of powerful outsiders on their society. Signaling a collapse in distances and differences, this recognition sparked expectations of Manarmakeri's imminent return among some Biaks past and present. Whereas pastors in the early 1990s presented their sermons as translations originating in an encounter with a sublimely alien original, Koreri prophets claimed to have discerned the Bible's secret significance: it was a rendering of Biak myth. Jesus Christ was really Manarmakeri, "The Itchy Old Man," that abject hero whose potency resides in his scaly skin. This revelation heralded Manarmakeri's return and the opening of Koreri, a utopian state of endless plenty, which, as we have seen, literally means "We Change Our Skin." Koreri prophets thus drew upon and superseded the strategies of Biak orators who used translation as a means not of overcoming, but rather of positing difference, that is, of creating the very foreignness that was the source of their prestige (see Rutherford 2000; 2003). But there is another way to look at Koreri, one that locates the movement in the context of the region's colonial institutions, which took a particular form.

This form bore the mark of the peculiar conditions under which the colonial agents of church and state operated in western New Guinea. The first missionaries to work in the region were the Christian Workmen, whom we met in chapter 5, Carl W. Ottow and J. G. Geissler, who settled in Doreh Bay, on the Bird's Head Peninsula, in 1855. Their presence in New Guinea owed much to religious developments back in the Netherlands. The Reveil, which I mentioned in chapter 5, supported a "romantic, anti-rational, emotional kind of religious experience" along with "social work for the benefit of outcasts" (Koopman and Huusman 2007, 192). A strong distrust of official institutions was what led O. G. Heldring and his partner, Johannes Gossner, to hit upon the idea of sending unpaid craftsmen to the colonies to spread the gospel as they plied their trade. Ottow and Geissler were cabinetmakers. But as we have seen, they did less building than bartering. The local Papuans had little use for cabinets, but they did want trade goods, which the missionaries supplied in return for food and forest products. The missionaries collected these local goods for a merchant based in Tidore's sister polity, Ternate, seat of the residency that included western New Guinea. When the Utrecht Mission Society took over the field in 1863, its leaders pushed for the elimination of this practice. But the brothers in New Guinea found they needed to trade to attract the Papuans' attention. Very few Papuans converted to Christianity during the first fifty years of the mission; those who did were manumitted slaves like the "foster children" whom I described in chapter 5. But coastal natives did take an interest in the mission post. Biak seafarers came to Sunday services, where they received tobacco and trade goods, along with snatches of sermons, which they repeated verbatim in their home communities or even sold for rice.

This tendency to turn Christian words into "booty" exasperated the missionaries. Even worse, would-be converts declared that Jesus belonged to the "Company," that is, the colonial state. That Papuans associated Jesus with the colonial government should come as little surprise, given the conditions in which the missionaries operated. Missionaries, one will recall, played an active role in the Netherlands Indies government's policy of display. The officials responsible for New Guinea relied in part on the missionaries to create the impression of Dutch authority. Occasionally, the Resident of Ternate launched punitive expeditions, often to placate the missionaries, who kept the government informed of the Papuans' "evil" acts. The remarkable security enjoyed by the Protestants in this "unpacified" land attests in part to the value attributed to the commodities they traded, in part to their association with a violent colonial state.

By the end of the nineteenth century, the missionaries that succeeded Ottow and Geissler had become convinced that their efforts would never bear fruit until the government applied a firmer hand in New Guinea. Protestant pressure in the Netherlands contributed to the Dutch Parliament's decision to fund the expansion of the colonial bureaucracy into New Guinea, which I discussed in chapters 2 and 5. When at the turn of the twentieth century, new victories for the mission accompanied the establishment of permanent government posts, the missionaries worried that the great awakening of interest in Christianity might signal another round of Koreri, whose "prophets" they had battled in the past. In fact, as we have seen, this awakening seems to have signaled local people's desire for Malay-speaking advocates to cope with an increasingly intrusive colonial state. At the same time, conversion gave Biaks access to Christian narrations, which they incorporated into Biak myth as a means of interpreting their changing experience of colonial power.

The Biak communities that requested evangelists got more than they bargained for. The first native teacher to visit Biak was a manumitted slave who had attended a native seminary in Java with a handful of other Papuan "foster children" (see Hasselt n.d.b). But Papuan evangelists soon found themselves outnumbered by native Christians from Ambon and Sangir, whom the mission imported in large numbers to staff their government-subsidized school. Natives from other parts of the Indies also monopolized the lower ranks of the colonial bureaucracy. The officials and teachers worked hard to suppress local practices, including "heathen" feasts and song and dance genres, which the missionaries associated with warfare, licentiousness, and other heathen "sins." The missionaries tried to impose a division between the affairs of church and state. But even in the 1920s, the two remained interchangeable in the local imagination. Colonial officials and mission teachers were not only known as "pastors." They were also known as *amberi*, the Biak term meaning "foreigner" that is also used in such expressions as the Land of the Foreigners, *Sup Amber.*

At the same time, the intensified experience of colonial rule and mission guidance gave rise to new opportunities for the pursuit of status in Biak. One Papuan nationalist told me how his father, an evangelist trained in the 1930s, had managed to marry his mother, the daughter of a titled village chief.[2] Such a woman could only marry the son of a man with a similar Tidoran title unless the suitor was a teacher, whose association with the mission and government gave him equivalent rank. The remarkably high literacy rates observed for Biak in the 1930s and 1940s indicate the attraction of these new ties (see de Bruyn 1948). Even coolies, stevedores, and mission carpenters enjoyed a certain cachet. Biak workers spent some of their wages buying the imported cloth and porcelain that circulated as bridewealth along with silver bracelets made from colonial coins (see Rutherford 2001). Commodities and money, often regarded as instruments for dissolving distinctions, became evidence of encounters in distant lands.

The World War II outbreak of the millennial Koreri movement must be set in this context in which the colonial institutions that Biaks confronted appeared as sources of both violence and value. I have argued elsewhere that the mission contributed to the movement by reviving *wor*, a forbidden song and dance genre, for use in church (see Rutherford 2003, chap. 6). This surprising act of recognition occurred at a time when the colonial landscape was quickly changing. The Japanese occupation of the Netherlands Indies led to the destruction of the colonial administration. On Biak, as elsewhere in the Indies, local people responded by attacking the elite natives through whom the Dutch had ruled (cf. Kahin 1985).

Angganeta Menufandu, the former plantation coolie who started the movement in 1939, was deathly ill when Manarmakeri appeared to her in a vision and explained his plans for her and "Papua," as he called her homeland. Angganeta miraculously recovered and soon was healing others, who gathered around her on a nearby island. In the first phase of the movement, she called for people to perform *wor*, the formerly banned genre, and drink palm wine, which was still forbidden. The faithful had to trade their imported clothing for loincloths and follow food taboos derived from the myth of Manarmakeri, who soon would return to his chosen land. The encampment grew quickly, and soon thousands had gathered to drink and sing and dance to *wor* songs. While these practices reflected a certain "nativism," a closer look complicates the picture. For reasons I explore elsewhere, *wor*, which had attracted so much foreign attention, served as a privileged method for providing evidence of encounters with new and startling things (see Rutherford 1996; 2003, chap. 3). Angganeta spent the nights crouched in what her followers called a "radio room," where she received transmissions that she turned into songs, which her followers repeated. Carried along by the music, some participants went into a trance and spoke English, Dutch, and Japanese, channeling the voices of outsiders and the dead. At a later stage, those who spoke in tongues earned the right to serve as the representatives of Angganeta and her successors: they were the *bin dame* (peace women) mentioned in chapter 4, who were deputized to spread the movement and punish (perhaps "pacify") those who opposed it. Like Angganeta, their authority derived from their power to embody alterity. Their incomprehensible words made present absent worlds.

As the uprising progressed, its leaders increasingly laid claim to the authority of foreign institutions, as the *bin dame* example suggests. Angganeta, now known as the "Queen," held court in her hut, where Tidoran etiquette prevailed. The recently released Biak warriors who took over from Angganeta after her arrest and execution began by writing by-laws for the movement. In jail they may have heard rumors that the Japanese had promised to recognize existing nationalist organizations. Among other things, the by-laws designated an upside-down Dutch tricolor as the new Papuan flag. In addition to establishing an "army," one of the warriors founded a "city" where people from different communities followed a strict schedule of activities. Word spread that this warrior owed his power to a tiny Bible, which, according to his relatives, he received in a colonial prison from Sukarno, the future Indonesian president, who spent much of the 1930s in captivity. Another leader built a replica of an airplane, around which his followers drilled, danced, and prayed.

Along with this recourse to objects, texts, and practices associated with the colonial church and state—and their Japanese and Indonesian opponents—went a radical reversal of colonial hierarchies. When Koreri came, the prophets proclaimed, all the *amberi* would be Papuans, and all the Papuans would be *amberi*. An Ambonese teacher later described to the mission how a huge band of believers had confronted him (see Picanussa n.d.). After beating him up, they forced the teacher to listen to a statement, which began with an announcement: "Our movement is called the New Religion and the New Government." The statement went on:

- Our Manseren has returned from Holland, so the Dutch people are now poor and the Papuan people are going to become rich. Queen Wilhelmina is now wearing a loincloth and we Papuans are going to be wearing fine clothing. We also have a clothing factory. The Dutch people now have to work in the garden planting cassava, sweet potato, taro and so forth, and we Papuans are going to be eating the food Dutch people usually eat.
- You *amberi* from Ambon, Java, Menado, etc. who still remember and follow only the Dutch Government, now we are going to imprison all of you just like the Japanese have imprisoned the Dutch. Now we want to chase away all the Dutch people and other *amberi* from our land because they have oppressed us too much. Now we want to be free and stand on our own.
- We want to become our own government [Dutch: *Bestuur*], our own local head of government [Dutch: *HPB*, acronym for *Hoofd Plaatselijk Bestuur*], our own teachers [Malay: *Goeroe*] and preachers [Malay: *Pendeta*].
- The Dutch people and you *amberies*, you have deceived us Papuans. You have hidden many secrets from us.

On the face of it, this effort to clarify the Bible's secret meaning seems at odds with Angganeta's radio transmissions and her followers' outpourings of foreign words. Where the crowd questioning the elder focused on the significance of foreign discourse, the singers and dancers highlighted its material qualities: its startling effects, its strange sounds. Yet if we view interpretation as itself a social act, the paradox disappears. Both sets of practices demonstrated Angganeta and her successors' privileged access to Manarmakeri and proved that the Biak ancestor soon would return. In this way these prophets compelled their followers to see themselves from a new perspective. At this critical juncture, as in the other episodes of West Papuan history depicted in this book, these leaders' bid for sovereignty entailed the conjuring of an audience that recognized something new in the Papuans. In this case, it was the capacity for freedom. The Papuans now saw themselves as possessing the potential to form a government and chase all the foreigners away.

The missionaries who served in New Guinea envisioned their Papuan converts as submitting to a similar operation. For these Pietists, Christianity's significance lay in its implications for "existing individuals" and their "eternal happiness," not in the abstract, communicable logic of a doctrine (see Kierkegaard 1992 [1846], 385). Suddenly subjected to the gaze of an invisible, inscrutable Other, the new Christians were supposed to forgo worldly ties for spiritual treasures stored up in an otherworldly realm (see

Derrida 1995; Kierkegaard 1985 [1843]). As I suggested in chapter 4, the myth of Manarmakeri thematizes this transformation. It describes startling moments of recognition and the "leap of faith" required to sacrifice old obligations on behalf of the new. But the Biak narrative results in a productive sort of failure: Manarmakeri leaves New Guinea after Biaks reject his offer of prosperity and eternal life because these changes would eliminate the conditions underlying Biaks' pursuit of prestige. Through Koreri, Biaks acknowledged a force that they had obscured by making the church and state into sites to raid. Refracted through a myth that deified the most degraded of characters, Biaks caught a glimpse of themselves as these institutions' official ideologies defined them: as ignorant and sinful, yet subject to salvation. But this acknowledgment could only occur at a millennial moment, spelling the end of the (colonial) world.

Koreri thus offered an account of biblical truth that laid bare an imperative embedded in the prewar mission and colonial government. The movement marked the limits of an approach to these institutions that made their foreignness into a source of value and prestige. Not surprisingly, Koreri left a lasting mark, not only within Biak society but also on the organizations established in its aftermath. With the Indonesian revolution raging in distant Java and Sumatra, postwar officials banned all "paraphernalia" associated with the Koreri movement and once again prohibited the performance of *wor* (see Galis 1946). After the Netherlands transferred sovereignty over the rest of the Indies to Indonesia in 1949, a new understanding of Koreri emerged among Dutch officials. They cited the movement as evidence that the "Melanesian" Papuans had an innate aversion to Indonesians—but not to continued Dutch colonial rule (see de Bruyn 1948, 22; Baal 1989, vol. 2, 167).

In August 1962, when the Netherlands submitted to United States pressure and agreed to transfer Dutch New Guinea to the United Nations, then Indonesia, this new reading of Koreri came to the foreground. Some of the Papuan nationalist leaders from Biak who emerged during the tumultuous period leading up to the Act of Free Choice presented Koreri as part of an age-old tradition of Papuan resistance (see, e.g., Sharp with Kaisiëpo 1994). But this vision of Koreri was not universally shared, as I learned in a conversation with Seth Rumkorem, a Biak who long served as commander of an armed wing of the Free Papua Organization (Organisasi Papua Merdeka, or OPM).[3] Koreri was a "false religion" (Indonesian: *agama palsu*) that could only lead to death—as it had on a massive scale when the Japanese military finally wiped out the movement. Rumkorem had spent much of his time in the forest fighting similar "false religions," movements led by people loosely affiliated with the guerrillas who suddenly became convinced that they themselves had become the embodiment of a divinely liberating force.[4] Rumkorem had little patience for such nonsense—or for fellow exiles who have talked of reviving Koreri as part of the official culture of Papuan nationalism. Rumkorem's opposition to Koreri is not surprising given his personal background; his father was one of the Biak teachers that the crowds attacked.

Clearly, when Papuan nationalists tap the power of the province's Christian institutions, they are doing so in a fashion different from that of their millennial predecessors and competitors. But rather than following Rumkorem in distinguishing between "true" and "false" religions, we need to pay heed to the range of interpretive strategies that can coexist within a particular social field. The fact that both the Koreri prophets of 1939–42 and Seth Rumkorem have mobilized the term *religion* (Indonesian/Malay: *agama*) indicates that they all, in some fashion, have sought to tap this official category as a source of legitimacy (cf. Timmer 2000; Giay 1986, 1995a, 1995b; Giay and Godschalk 1993). Today's elite Papuan nationalists have faith that someday Jesus will free the Papuans. But unlike the prophets, few have dared to declare how and when this will occur.

Something like the millennial truth of Koreri may well provide the horizon toward which contemporary nationalist performances gesture. In the second half of this chapter, I explore this possibility by examining the more recent history of Christian institutions in western New Guinea. I focus on the Evangelical Christian Church (Gereja Kristen Injili, GKI), heir to the Protestant mission whose authority Koreri leaders sought to supersede.

Papuan Nationalism and the Power of Prayer

In a 1973 study of the GKI, Ukur and Cooley (1977, 27–29) point out that the Koreri uprising of 1939–42 is in part to be thanked for the speed with which the native church gained autonomy during the 1950s. The Koreri movement traumatized the Protestant missionaries by showing them how quickly the local schools and congregations they had created could crumble. Before World War II, the missionaries failed to delegate any of their responsibility for performing Christian sacraments. When the Japanese military rounded up the European missionaries and sent them to distant camps, no one was on hand to baptize infants and serve communion or, even more importantly, to determine who would be allowed access to these rites. The Protestant mission's response to Koreri's call for a reversal of colonial hierarchies was to attenuate prior relations of inequality. As a result, growing numbers of Papuans did become *amber*, albeit without a radical transformation of the colonial conditions under which they lived.[5]

These changes entailed the expansion of opportunities for participation in Protestant institutions on all levels (see Ukur and Cooley 1977; Kamma 1977). In 1918 the Utrecht Mission Society funded a school to train Papuan evangelists and teachers at the mission headquarters at Doreh Bay. In 1925 the mission moved the school to Miei, at the base of the Bird's Head, where it remained in operation until the 1950s under the guidance of Isaak Samuel Kijne, a missionary from the mainline Dutch Reformed Church (Nederlandse Hervormde Kerk), which took over the New Guinea field from the Utrecht Mission Society after World War II. When Jan P. K. van Eechoud, the first Resident of Netherlands New Guinea after the war, began the task of cultivating a small corps of Papuan colonial officers, he recruited the school's best students (Derix 1987, 133–56). Eventually, the school for teachers faced competition from the new educational opportunities offered by the colonial government and the Catholic Church, which began working in Merauke in 1905. Jesuit, Augustinian, and Franciscan missionaries moved into the mostly Protestant north in the 1930s when the colonial government lifted territorial restrictions on evangelization. After World War II the Catholics opened training centers for Papuan lay leaders and eventually established dioceses in Jayapura, Sorong, Merauke, and Agats (see Mewengkang 2001; Hadisumarta 2001). But Protestant institutions still provided a privileged avenue to social advancement. The Protestant mission began ordaining Papuan ministers in 1952, beginning with a handful of experienced teachers and evangelists, then turning to graduates from a school of theology founded in 1954 (see Ukur and Cooley 1977, 29–30). Although Ambonese and Sangirese church workers remained prevalent, Papuan pastors began to appear in greater numbers.[6] Among these early pastors was a Biak named William Rumainum, the son of an evangelist trained on Java who became the first chairman of the GKI.

At the same time, on a local level the church created new possibilities for involvement. Before the war, mission evangelists and teachers exercised a great deal of control over the Papuan congregations. The congregations in turn were divided into resorts, each overseen by a European missionary who answered to the chairman of the mission convention, the

most senior Dutch pastor on hand. In 1956, when the GKI gained autonomy, this form of governance gave way to a Presbyterian system, in which
a board of elders and male and female deacons governed a congregation
(Ukur and Cooley 1977, 45–46, 53–72). Elders shouldered a range of responsibilities, from visiting the ill to leading Sunday services to enforcing
policies laid down at higher levels of church organization. Local congregations elected their elders, who chose representatives to make up the parish
governing body, which in turn sent representatives to the synod council,
which met once every three years.[7]

Yet even if the mission satisfied, however partially, desires associated
with Koreri, the missionaries who implemented these measures did so in
the hope that the New Order would undermine some of the presupposi-
tions on which the movement rested. Even as the church's Dutch advisors
introduced new avenues to authority for Papuan villagers, they sought to
deny that authority was primarily at stake. A booklet written by the mission anthropologist, F. C. Kamma, author of the seminal study on Koreri
mentioned in chapter 4, reflects this contradiction. "Eldership is a form of
service," as Kamma (n.d., 3) puts it at the beginning of the text, which contains frequent references to the Bible. "To serve means: to help, to provide
everything that people need. Thus although eldership must also be called:
a *position* or even often a *rank*, its meaning is *not* to command people, to
seek or demand to be served, but rather just the contrary" (Kamma n.d.,
3). Despite the fact that a congregation selected its own elders, these servants should always remember that their true source of authority lay elsewhere. "Elders are appointed by Jesus Christ through the intercession of
the Congregation. Because of this, the choice is prayed for, so that Christ
will use the Congregation to designate His servants. In this way, elders become the instruments of Christ. Christ governs the Evangelical Christian
Church (GKI) by way of these office holders" (Kamma n.d., 6).

A similar publication for deacons makes much of the example provided by Christ, who served his disciples food—and even washed their
feet—behavior the booklet insists was utterly degrading at the time (see
Teutscher 1961, 1). In Biak, and perhaps elsewhere, this effort to control
the meaning of Christian "service" may well have had ironic effects. Here
is a context in which Pierre Bourdieu's (1981, 209–14) discussion of the
"self-consecration" of the delegate seems apropos. The very effort to limit
the church officers' authority may well have provided a means of enhanc-
ing it, through proximity to Jesus, the ultimate foreign power. A similar
possibility lies in the booklet's advice on conducting home visits, which

are presented as occasions to comfort the suffering and reprimand sinners. The elder should bring along a list of suitable Bible verses to read to the household, rather than speaking in his own words (see Kamma n.d., 52–55). Such a displacement was key to the strategies of New Order–era Biak leaders, who sought to be recognized as purveyors of foreign words.

Perhaps in response to this possibility, Kamma insists that the elder should neither present himself as a "spiritual policeman" (Malay: *polisi rohani*) nor as a "Christian magician" (Malay: *tukang hobatan kristen*), who in a heathen (Malay: *kafir*) fashion presents himself as holding the monopoly on a community's religious resources; rather, every father should lead his family in prayer (Kamma n.d., 49–50). Again, this advice opens the way to its own subversion. The very move that would have the institution's authority penetrate ever more deeply allowed for the dispersal of spiritual skills. The long-term effects of these policies were evident on Biak in the early 1990s, when lay people regularly mounted the pulpit to deliver sermons, and everyone, myself included, was expected to be able to lead a prayer (see Rutherford 2003, 125–26). The democratization of Protestant rituals also carried with it the danger that entrepreneurs, like the prayer group leaders who planned the 1998 Biak flag raising, could emerge outside the institutional boundaries of the church.

A further set of productive contradictions comes into focus if one considers the way in which Christian institutions responded to a changing political context during the postwar period of Dutch, then Indonesian rule. In July 1956, during the same year the GKI was founded, the General Synod of the Dutch Reformed Church issued a Call to Reflection on the New Guinea question (Generale Synode der Nederlandse Hervormde Kerk 1956; see also Henderson 1973, 84–85; Drooglever 2009, 388–92). The statement urged Dutch Protestants to carefully scrutinize the motivations behind the Dutch decision to retain western New Guinea, which, rather than serving a greater good—the Papuan's right to self-determination—could be read as a concession to Dutch national pride. But aside from the higher purposes a negotiated settlement with Indonesia would serve, the Call appealed to more practical imperatives. The dispute threatened the Dutch Reformed Church's ability to operate in Indonesia, including in the Christian villages and hospitals mentioned in chapter 5. With President Sukarno stoking anti-Dutch sentiment, the church's leaders feared for the safety of their Dutch and Indonesian personnel, especially in Indonesia's heartland, and for the future of Indonesian Christianity more generally. For Dutch missionaries working in New Guinea and their Papuan flock, the event revealed the risks that went along with the benefits of belonging to an organization that could channel resources from afar.[8]

In the aftermath of western New Guinea's transfer to Indonesia, the GKI's close relationship with the Indonesian Council of Churches, which was a legacy of the episode, helped the church survive in tumultuous times (see Ukur and Cooley 1977, 210, 295). Many Papuans in the colonial administration lost their jobs in the 1960s, when scores of Indonesian officials flocked to the new province of West Irian. In contrast, the departure of Dutch missionaries vacated positions in the GKI hierarchy that were filled by the Irianese, as the Papuans were now called. These Irianese pastors presided over a growing, increasingly multiethnic flock, thanks to the Council of Churches' policy of encouraging Christian migrants to join the GKI instead of founding branches of their home churches in the new province.[9] Similar pressures on the Catholic Church did not yield the same windfall for the indigenous faithful. European priests, many of whom became Indonesian citizens, were more willing to weather the change in administration than European pastors. Given the strict standards imposed for ordination, there were very few Papuan priests qualified to staff the dioceses, so the Europeans who did leave ceded their posts to Javanese and Eastern Indonesian colleagues (Hadisumarta 2001). Under Indonesian rule, the relatively stronger European presence in the Catholic Church—and its relatively more formalized links to the outside world—provided Catholic leaders more leeway to criticize the government. But both the GKI and the Catholic Church moved within a space of possibility that depended on their playing the role of mediator between the government and the population, rather than acting as the champion of either. Both institutions pursued this role not simply in the name of "peace," but because their institutional survival was at stake.

Official Indonesian state ideology played a key role in setting the rules of the game. In an effort to stem the growth of pro-Indonesian sentiment, Dutch propagandists had warned the Papuans that if Indonesia gained control of western New Guinea, the Indonesian government would force its inhabitants to convert to Islam, Indonesia's majority religion (see Ukur and Cooley 1977, 285). In fact, a generalized "belief in God," rather than Islam per se, was and remains the first pillar of Indonesia's official state ideology, Pancasila (the Five Bases mentioned in chapter 4), which was introduced by Indonesia's first president, Sukarno, and revised by Suharto (see Kipp 1993, 107–8). Several months before the attempted coup and massacre of communists that brought Suharto to power, an Indonesian brigadier general explained to religious leaders from West Irian that "to pray for God's help and blessings for the good of mankind and the prosperity of the State is the essence of the Indonesian personality in everything they [*sic*] do" (Sutjipto 1965, 10). Under Suharto's so-called New Order regime, "belief in God" was more than a description of the Indonesian national character—it was prescribed. All Indonesian citizens had to list an approved world religion on their identity cards, or risk being labeled communists. The central government's promotion of *agama*, that Indonesian term for institutionalized religion, served the regime's purposes (see Kipp 1993; Spyer 1996). Religious-based identities tempered the grip of those associated with ethnicity or residence and suppressed allegiances based on class.

As a result, in Irian Jaya, as western New Guinea was once again renamed in 1973, Christianity provided a safe refuge for indigenous leaders and provided a passage into national networks through which New Order patronage freely flowed. Many members of the Papuan elite participating in today's nationalist movement have ties to Christian institutions: they include church officials, the rectors of schools of theology, graduates from Christian universities, and staff members from church-backed NGOs (see chapter 4; see also Mote and Rutherford 2001). Since colonial times, Indonesian Christians have claimed more than their share of positions in the national elite by virtue of the opportunities for social mobility and alliance building offered by participation in church-based institutions.[10] Under the New Order, these pathways led in just one direction: to the center, where the regime used its control over export earnings, foreign investment, and military power to harness religiously based *aliran*, or "currents." Indonesians came to view the center as holding a monopoly on the sources of their livelihood and status as legitimate social actors (see Pemberton 1994; Siegel 1997, 1998). But Irianese participation in the Catholic and Protestant "currents" seems not to have resulted in this level of submission. The churches in Irian Jaya operated in a different political environment from that found in other parts of Indonesia. Elsewhere, the lingering threat was communism; in Irian Jaya, it was the specter of Papuan separatism that haunted the Indonesian nation-state.

The GKI came to occupy a particularly fraught position between the administrative and military apparatus and an often-rebellious indigenous population. Intelligence officers attended church services during the 1960s to monitor the messages issued from the pulpit.[11] The authorities expelled some foreign pastors, including a German Lutheran who reportedly gave a sermon in which he touched on the question of whether West Irian might in fact be God's chosen land. The government soon found uses for indigenous pastors, who risked being imprisoned, tortured, or worse if they misspoke. Early on during the Indonesian period, the church distributed letters to local congregations, reminding the members of their duties "as Christians and citizens of the Indonesian Republic" (see Ukur and Cooley 1977, 295). On the eve of the Act of Free Choice, the GKI played an active role in promoting the Indonesian position. Many pastors served on the consultative councils that took part in the heavily manipulated event. One of the speakers at the GKI's Fifth Synod Convention called on the delegates to rise above any "personal disappointment" and place their trust in Jesus. After all, "Jesus already endured a choice that was free: to be crucified at Golgotha. Christ is the implementer of the *Act of Free Choice*: for the salvation of people with faith" (Ukur and Cooley 1977, 295; italicized words are in English.)

In a similar spirit, the GKI participated in military operations in which church officials distributed leaflets urging those who had joined the OPM to return to their communities and families (Ukur and Cooley 1977, 289–90). But on occasion the church's authority was directed against the Indonesian military as well, as when one pastor saved some four hundred captured "rebels" from execution by begging for forgiveness, then kneeling to pray in front of the commanders and their troops (Ukur and Cooley 1977, 290; see also chapter 8). In addition to Protestant rituals, the GKI itself sometimes appeared to be up for grabs. This point was brought home to me when Seth Rumkorem, the OPM leader mentioned above, turned from "false religions" to speak of his own view of the place of faith in the struggle.[12] In the forest, he told me, the guerrillas always held Sunday services, divided according to denomination. Whether they were Catholic, Protestant, Seventh-Day Adventists, or Pentecostals, all the freedom fighters worshiped God in their own (institutionally) sanctioned ways. In the mid-1970s, Rumkorem went so far as to send a letter to the chairman of the GKI, urging him to send an official delegation to confer with the armed separatists. The pastors and guerrillas would pray together, and if God indicated that the Papuan nationalist cause was just, then the GKI would agree to support the struggle openly; if not, the OPM would give up the fight.[13] New Order ideologies and imperatives clearly could not fully define Christian institutions in the eyes of the province's inhabitants; the churches' power still remained, in some sense, at large.

Perhaps for this reason the post-Suharto period in Papua has yet to see the religious violence that has plagued other parts of Indonesia. Else-where, the sudden collapse of the institutional networks that connected local communities and the national center has given rise to intense anxie-ties about identity. A key theme in the nationalist literature analyzed by James Siegel (1997) is the fear that one could be a traitor to the nation without knowing it. Under the New Order, one was either recognized as a proper Indonesian, or one stood with the forces of disorder and death. These anxieties arguably account for the ferocity of conflicts in Indonesian cities like Ambon and Poso, where, under conditions of democratization, being Muslim or Christian entails membership in potentially threatened political "currents" (see Klinken 2001; Sidel 2003). But in Papua, the pos-sibility of seeing something unexpected in oneself is not unwelcome: Pap-uanness is what has suddenly come (back) to light.

This moment of recognition has not resulted in the suppression or re-placement of existing institutions. Instead of founding a new religion, the current movement's leaders have recontextualized the old, turning the churches and practices associated with them into a source of legitimacy for a new national order. It was the churches that instigated the formation of the Forum for the Reconciliation of Irian Jaya Society (FORERI), which sought to open a dialogue between provincial leaders and the central government following the flag raisings of July 1998. A FORERI member who accompanied the Team of 100 to Jakarta in February 1999 described what the delegates did during the hours before their meeting with Presi-dent Habibie. Conferring in secrecy, they drafted the statement in which they would startle Habibie by announcing that the province's popula-tion wanted to secede. But reportedly, the delegates' main activity was prayer, including a service led by a famous Indonesian evangelist (Mote and Rutherford 2001, 126). Upon their return to the province, the del-egates "socialized"—that is, broadcasted and explained—their message by urging their constituents to pray for the nonviolent movement's suc-cess. Prayer was in abundance in June 2000 at the Second Papuan National Congress in Jayapura (see Van Den Broek and Szalay 2001, 89–90; King 2004). The event's emotional climax was the raising of the Morning Star flag and the singing of the national anthem, "Oh, My Papuan Homeland." For many, the Morning Star flag recalls the myth of Manarmakeri. But Nicolaas Jouwe, who designed the flag, told me that the flag also recalls the Christian virtues of faith, hope, and love, with the star representing hope.[14] In the case of the West Papuan national anthem, the connection to Christian institutions is even more direct. Composed by Isaak Samuel

Kijne in 1923 and widely sung in Protestant schools, the anthem begins with a pledge and ends with a prayer (see Drooglever 2009, 557). Throughout the Congress, each day's session opened with a representative of one of the provinces' religions and denominations leading a brief devotion. Although most public meetings in Indonesia begin with a similar ritual, for my Papuan consultants this is anything but an empty gesture. The secretary of the Papuan Presidium Council, the executive branch confirmed during the Papuan congress, is a Papuan Muslim who, I have been told, prays for West Papua's liberation along with everyone else.[15]

I have heard rumors of strange occurrences associated with the contemporary Papuan nationalist movement. As Eben Kirksey (2012) has reported in his study of the movement, a group of Papuans near Wasior, where an attack on a military-controlled logging concern led to harsh reprisals and many civilian deaths, supposedly have been keeping the "original" Bible safe in an undisclosed location. But the movement's institutionally sanctioned invocations of Christianity are worthy of scrutiny as well. Those who organized the congress seemingly followed the lead of Indonesian ideology in deploying a generalized notion of religion as one of the "pillars" established to represent the new nation's bases of support (see King 2002, 101). But at the same time, like the Koreri prophets, they gave new meaning to Christian practices and texts. As one Papuan colleague told me, "All the people pray for independence, the Presidium, everyone. They also hope and depend on God. They always pray for this. They have the hope, the faith, that someday it will arrive. Faith that what they are struggling for is right, and because it is right, God is on their side."[16] Speaking in English and Indonesian, he concluded by calling this faith a "force within the heart of every Papuan" that "military weapons" would never "kill." Papuan nationalist prayer evokes the checkered history of Christian institutions in the province. But in doing so, like Koreri's millennial rituals, it gestures toward the moment when God's true intentions will be revealed.

The Politics of Transcendence

This chapter contains a different portrait of the effects of missionization than one finds in some recent work in the anthropology of Christianity. Bambi Schieffelin has written of how the Kaluli of Papua New Guinea's embrace of Christianity is "changing the ways Kaluli would interpret events, establish facts, convey opinions, and imagine themselves" (2000, 294).

It is worth emphasizing that those who introduced Christianity in Papua New Guinea regarded their own culture as superior and the local society as in need of civilizing, in all respects inferior. Furthermore, the local people, confronted with missionaries, their goods, their stories, and their clear connections to wealth beyond local imagination, came to question their own society and, in many cases, came to regard it as morally and technologically inferior. (Schieffelin 2000, 294–95)

Reflecting a trend in recent anthropological writing on Christianity, Schieffelin's essay provides a useful corrective to earlier ethnographies that narrowed research on the topic to the study of "syncretism" (see also Coleman 2000; Robbins 2004; Cannell, ed. 2006; Engelke and Tomlinson, 2006; Keane 2007; Engelke 2007; Elisha 2008; Tomlinson 2009). Joel Robbins (2007) has rightfully criticized what he describes as "continuity thinking" in anthropology for preventing scholars from appreciating the real changes that Christianity can bring. But as Fenella Cannell (2006) has pointed out, these changes can vary dramatically, given differing historical circumstances: in some cases, people can "forget" their conversion altogether (see Gow 2006).

I do not have space to offer a detailed comparison of the respective historical circumstances that have shaped the outcome of mission encounters in West Papua and Papua New Guinea. Such a comparison would need to take into account the relationship between religious and political institutions in these two very different places. It would need to take into account the different sets of audiences confronted and conjured by would-be sovereigns on New Guinea's eastern and western halves. As the next two chapters shall make clear, in their pursuit of sovereignty, some West Papuans have taken pleasure and gained prestige by playing audiences off of one another. Biaks in particular rarely describe Christianity as a force that makes them feel inferior to westerners. They are much more likely to describe Christianity as a resource that makes them feel superior to the non-Christian Indonesians with whom they deal. It is only in the myth of Manarmakeri that we find evidence of anything like the sense of inadequacy expressed by the Kaluli and other Papua New Guinea Christians (see Robbins 2004). And in the end, Manarmakeri will have no need to be ashamed. The tables will turn when the world finally recognizes the Biak ancestor as the true source of wealth and power.

In painting this portrait I have dwelt upon the conditions that have enabled Papuan leaders to turn Christian texts and rituals toward their own ends. These conditions include the materiality of institutions—their dependence on concrete acts and objects—and their embeddedness within wider social and political fields. In paying heed to these aspects of institutions in a context that has brought them to the fore, I have sought to illuminate how institutional power can be appropriated. But at the same time my findings shed light on some of the ways in which institutional power is produced. The traffic in authority between official institutions and unofficial practices runs in both directions, as anthropologist Steve Caton (2006) suggests. By turning Christian prayer into a separatist weapon, today's Papuan nationalists have reinforced the churches' authority, even as they have run foul of these organizations' officially neutral stance. In the same fashion, Indonesian leaders have created a resource for Papuan nationalists through their own deployment of Christian practices and texts. Even the practices of Koreri prophets, who radically rejected the mission's legitimacy, had a constitutive effect on the province's religious institutions. As I have suggested, coercive organizations owe their authority—and their very existence—to such concrete practices and evocations. Institution, after all, is a word with two meanings: an instituted order and the instituting processes through which such an order, however provisionally, comes into force (see Weber 2001a).

The interpretive practices described in this chapter have played a critical role in shaping Papua's religious institutions as sites of contestation. Human rights workers who visited OPM groups still at large in the province in the early 2000s report that their commanders were spending much more time preaching than planning attacks.[17] Against these guerrillas-turned-pastors, the Indonesian authorities were deploying their own version of Christian truth. A crackdown against separatists followed the relative openness that prevailed at the time of the Second Papuan National Congress. On Biak in 2003, the followers of an aging OPM leader were given three months to turn in their weapons and insignia, or else face the full force of the law.[18] The Indonesian police "socialized" the call for surrender by way of the island's Protestant congregations. The letter inaugurating the operation ended with three Bible verses: Matthew 5:9 ("Blessed are the peacemakers, for they shall be called sons of God"), Hebrews 12:14 ("Strive for peace with all men, and for the holiness without which no one will see the Lord"), and Psalms 34:15 ("The eyes of the Lord are toward the righteous, and his ears toward their cry") (see ELS-HAM 2003).

With the US-led "war on terror" reshaping global realities, the future looked grim for Papuan nationalists in 2003. This is not to say that when it came to the true meaning of the Bible, the Indonesian authorities had the final word. I hope I have made one thing clear in this chapter. Institutional power both shapes and is subject to interpretive practices. Institutions depend on and are subverted by the multiplicity of audiences that such practices bring into play. This is why, long after Koreri, the forces capable of making West Papua a reality still go by the name of the Lord.

CHAPTER SEVEN

Third-Person Nationalism

My discovery was not significant, but it was curious, for I had discovered that there simply is no repetition, and had verified it by having it repeated in every possible way. — Søren Kierkegaard, 1983 [1843]

The Strange Bedfellows of Nationalism

In this chapter I address a question that has preoccupied recent writers on nationalism: does nationalism repeat itself? Is every assertion of national identity, no matter how intimately singular each may seem, merely the recurrence of a general form? Scholars have criticized Benedict Anderson for conceptualizing nationalism as a "modular" phenomenon, a mode of consciousness born in the eighteenth century and repeated identically, without remainder, across time and space (see Chatterjee 1986; Kelly and Kaplan 2001; Duara 2003). Some have focused on the role of such factors as decolonization and the Cold War in shaping, relatively late in the game, what is taken as the national norm. My aim in this chapter is somewhat different. I want to rethink the very notion of modularity by way of an investigation that focuses on a subtle aspect of national discourse: its pronouns. As we shall see, these are among the more important of the signs of West Papuan sovereignty in motion today. Instead of tracking deployments of the first-person plural—the nation as *we*—I explore the significance of references to the nation made in the third person—the nation as *he, she, they,* or even *it.* These references appear in the utterances of would-be citizens—in particular, elite would-be citizens—who adopt the voice of outside commentators to describe their people's legitimate and legitimating desires. I undertake this inquiry in a setting where pronominal usage has particularly fraught effects: West Papua, which, as we have seen, is a region whose inhabitants have long sought, but rarely enjoyed, a voice in their own fate.

When it comes to nationalism, I shall argue, Kierkegaard's dictum holds: there simply is no repetition, yet nationalisms verify this discovery by repeating it in every possible way. This is because nationalisms always speak to a plurality of audiences: audiences presupposed and entailed in nationalist texts and practices, audiences that multiply, merge, absorb each other, and fragment. Over the centuries, nationalist discourse has mobilized an array of expressive genres and registers, old and new, linked to historically specific institutions, viewpoints, and landscapes of power. Shifts between genres and registers leave their mark wherever the nation appears in the third person to an extranational *we* that looks back from beyond the nation's pale. When one heeds the proliferation of audiences, subjectivities, genres, and registers signaled by the play of pronouns, nationalism stops looking like an abstract ideal endlessly expressing itself across an infinity of cases; instead, it becomes the focus of a different kind of repetition, one "forcibly assigned a place in space and time" (Deleuze 1994, 12; see also Weber 2001b). Variably conceived and addressed, transcendently extranational interlocutors have played a constitutive role in nationalist documents everywhere. There simply would be no nationalism without strange bedfellows of a historically particular sort.

In the case of Papuan nationalism, these strange bedfellows have played a particularly dominant role. As we have seen, outsiders have tended to view the inhabitants of western New Guinea as far too primitive to act as the mature, rights-bearing subjects of popular sovereignty that liberal thinkers placed at the heart of the modern nation form. As a result, Papuan nationalists have gone to especially great lengths to conjure extranational agents to endorse their claims. Consider the following scene from my fieldwork on the contemporary Papuan nationalist movement. The date was October 12, 2002, and I was seated in a conference room at a sports complex south of the Dutch city of Utrecht. It was an odd moment to be hearing a Javanese accent. In the chairs around me were nearly a hundred Papuan men and women, members of an Indonesian minority who generally have little good to say about the Javanese majority that dominates Indonesian political and cultural life. PaVo, the Papuan People's Organization, was holding a meeting to commemorate the fortieth anniversary of the New York Agreement, the US-brokered deal that led to the transfer of the western half of New Guinea from the Netherlands to

the United Nations and then to Indonesia in early 1963. Some in the audience belonged to the Papuan elite the Dutch had groomed for self-rule in
the 1950s. Many had gone into exile during the 1960s in the years leading
up to the Act of Free Choice. Others on hand included Dutch veterans,
the children of Dutch missionaries, and scholars with an interest in West
Papua, as this Papuan elite had dubbed their nation-to-be before Indonesia renamed the territory West Irian and then Irian Jaya, only recently
settling on Papua in the spirit of "reform."

There was no shortage of languages and dialects at the meeting. The
organizers provided a running Dutch translation of speeches delivered in
the Papuan dialect of Indonesian by guests, including Agus Alua, secretary of the Papuan Presidium Council, which coordinated the nationalist
movement in the early post-Suharto period (see chapter 6).[1] But despite
this linguistic cacophony, *Why Papua Wants Freedom* (Mengapa Papua
Ingin Merdeka), the video shown at the start of the meeting, still came as a
bit of a surprise. The lights dimmed and an opening credit appeared on the
television: "The Papuan Presidium Council Presents." After a long title
sequence featuring racialized images of "Stone Age" Papuans, a narrator
began to speak. "Papua," he intoned gravely, "often known as the land of
birds of paradise, spirits, and orchids." I was sitting with a fellow anthropologist, and she whispered to me, "That narrator is Javanese."

At the time I disagreed. But later, when I interviewed Willy Mandowen,
the presidium moderator who assisted in the video's production, I learned
that my friend had been right. Not only was the narrator Javanese, but so
was the entire production crew. All were acquaintances of the aforementioned Yorrys Raweyai, the leader of the notorious gang-cum-"youth organization" mentioned in chapter 4, Pemuda Pancasila, a man with a Papuan
mother and Sino-Indonesian father who, somewhat implausibly given his
ties with Suharto, had reinvented himself as a loyal supporter of Papuan
nationalism (see Ryter 2001; Mote and Rutherford 2001). The presidium
had chosen the Javanese production team on purpose, to make the video
seem more "neutral." The narrator had never even been to Papua. His was
an extranational voice referring to Papua in the third person. According to
my consultant, this was not a weakness; it was a strength.

Unexpected alliances and affinities have pervaded the recent resurgence of Papuan nationalism. Readers of the previous chapters will be familiar with the factors involved. Home to the largest gold and copper mine
in the world, operated by New Orleans–based Freeport McMoran, Papua
faces a host of social problems, from urban unemployment to high rates of

infant-maternal mortality to an emerging AIDS epidemic (see Leith 2003; Butt 2005). Human rights abuses have recurred throughout the period of Indonesian rule, with the most extreme violence occurring in the context of counterinsurgency campaigns against the Free Papua Organization, or OPM, the scattered yet tenacious guerilla army founded in 1965 (see Osborne 1985; Chauvel and Nusa Bhakti 2004; Chauvel 2005). Many Papuans have suffered under Indonesian rule; at the same time, as I argued in chapters 4 and 6, Indonesian institutions and social networks have shaped the fortunes of members of the Papuan elite (see also Rutherford 2003; Kirksey 2012). At the time of the Second Papuan National Congress, the mass gathering that gave birth to the presidium in 2000, the movement's two most prominent figures were Theys Eluay, the Sentani tribal chief who was one of the thousand-odd representatives bribed and threatened to vote for integration in 1969, and Tom Beanal, the Amungme leader from the main tribe displaced by the Freeport mine, who was a long-time critic but is now a commissioner of Freeport Indonesia, a subsidiary of Freeport McMoran. Equally striking as these institutional and personal ties is the movement's apparent compulsion to repeat Indonesian nationalist documents and discourses. Presidium resolutions generally begin with long lists of supporting documents, including not only UN resolutions but also the Indonesian constitution (see Alua 2002a, 47). Well before the Papuans began their struggle for independence, *merdeka* (freedom) was an Indonesian revolutionary call to arms (see Siegel 1997, 214; see also Kahin 2003).

Papua has provided fertile ground for conspiracy stories, not all of which are without basis. Presidium members themselves have wondered in retrospect whether the public events of 2000, which proceeded more or less unimpeded by the military and enjoyed some shadowy financial support, might well have been part of a scheme to discredit then President Wahid and detract attention from former President Suharto's crimes (see Kirksey 2012; Davies 2001). Still, it would be a mistake to presume that Papuan nationalism's strange bedfellows can be so easily explained away. The unexpected alliances and affinities of Papuan nationalism signal something significant not only about the nature of politics in post-Suharto Indonesia; they also bring to light the limits of our approaches to every nation's extranational roots.

Papuan nationalism's strange bedfellows have left calling cards in the form of the movement's remarkable use of pronouns. Building on my previous fieldwork in Papua, I have examined this use of pronouns in political documents, e-mail discussion groups, books, videos, and the press, as well as in conversations within and outside of the region.[2] My findings have contrasted with those of scholars who have examined nationalist usage in better-known sites. Recent scholarship has located the conditions for the eighteenth-century emergence of an American nationalist *we* in the rise of what Habermas (1991) famously called the "bourgeois public sphere" (see also Warner 1990). In light of this research, what is perhaps most striking about the texts of Papuan nationalism is the relative paucity of the first-person plural.[3] Although there are places where the phrase "we the Papuan nation" appears in documents and reports, and this kind of *we* is certainly a feature of rumor and other kinds of informal talk, the movement's leaders more commonly write of their nation in the third person: in this regard, *Why Papua Wants Freedom* is an exemplary text.[4]

Taking this decidedly third-person production as my focus, I set this feature of Papuan nationalism in the context of the territory's peculiar history and current plight. Following the devastating tsunami of 2004, foreign news crews invaded Aceh, another would-be breakaway region of Indonesia; in the aftermath, the Indonesian government halted military operations in the province and negotiated a peaceful settlement with the Free Aceh Movement. During the same period, the Indonesian government prevented foreign journalists, researchers, and aid workers from entering Papua while the security forces jailed demonstrators, hounded human rights workers, and retaliated against rural communities suspected of aiding the OPM (see Human Rights Watch 2007). The Indonesian authorities, like their Papuan critics, have reasons to respect the power of those who call the Papuans "they." In a setting where the extranational looms large as both a promise and a threat, one's choice of pronouns, I argue, is more than merely a matter of grammar; it bears on matters of life and death. But first, I consider how the third-person nationalism so evident in West Papua directs us to the inherent historicity of all nationalisms—and, indeed, all social forms.

The Politics of Pronouns

The multiple repetitions and citations of extranational voices that pervade the vignette I just recounted stems less from the "derivative" character of West Papuan discourse than from the iterability intrinsic to all nationalisms (see Chatterjee 1986; see also chapter 4). What is repeated always retains the memory of another scene, an origin that is only discernible as such after the fact. As I have stressed throughout this book, whenever we speak or engage in social practices, we both respond to and repeat others' utterances and actions. Learning to do something is always learning to do it again, under the pressure of another's gaze. Repetition is a function of the irreducible relation to the Other. Although this "haunting" is an indestructible feature of social life, it becomes particularly apparent in certain contexts (see Bauman and Briggs 1990; Bakhtin 1981.) In a world where diplomatic acknowledgment is the sine qua non of legitimate statehood, nationalists are particularly dogged by the specter of iterability. A nation comes into existence only when its members can imagine themselves becoming recognizable to outsiders. In the rituals, writings, and practices associated with nationalism, the undertow of alterity is particularly strong and problematic, while the stakes of recognition are particularly high. Rendered so explicitly in the case of West Papua, the tensions at the heart of contemporary nationalist movements are not simply the outcome of globalization. As Gilles Deleuze (1994, 1) might put it, these tensions are "repeated in advance" even in the seemingly most exemplary of nationalist texts.

We can detect these tensions in these exemplary texts' deployment of pronouns. Émile Benveniste (1971) described pronouns as linguistic resources that allow individuals to use language meaningfully by anchoring general categories in the here and now of a particular instance of speech. In other words, pronouns are "shifters," to use Roman Jakobson's (1971) helpful term (see also Silverstein 1993). Metapragmatic, in the sense that their meaning refers back to aspects of their own use—*I* being "the individual who utters the present instance of discourse containing the linguistic instance *I*"—their deployment endows a certain "reality" to language, to the degree that after the fashion of performatives, those who utter them seem to be doing what they say (see Benveniste 1971, 218; see also chapters 1 and 4). When one says "I pledge allegiance" or "I declare," as nationalists are wont to do, one accomplishes the very act one depicts. As in the case of performatives, there is, of course, a catch, because as elements of language, pronouns are negatively defined by opposition within a structure.

For Benveniste, the third person is really a "nonperson": a form excluded from the "human reality of dialogue" (1971, 201). And yet it is implicated in the first two persons in two respects: as the site of distinction by which the other two persons are defined as "personal," and as that which passes between them in the form of utterances about the world. This intervention of the "nonpersonal" into the "human reality of dialogue," which potentially destabilizes all identities, is prior to the further complications that Benveniste associates with the passage from "*I*" to "*we*."[5] In languages like Indonesian, a distinction is drawn between the inclusive (*I* plus *you*) and exclusive (*I* plus *he*, *she*, or *they*) forms of the first-person plural. In English and other languages that draw no such distinction, "'we' is not a quantified or a multiplied 'I'; it is an 'I' expanded beyond the strict limits of the person, enlarged and at the same time amorphous" (Benveniste 1971, 203). Analysts of the national *we* have made much of these expansive, absorptive capacities, but they have not always probed the full range of ways in which grammatical "persons" interact within nationalist texts.

It is not only in West Papua that the third person haunts the first. Consider, for example, Greg Urban's (2001) treatment of the American Declaration of Independence, the canonical text for analyses of the national *we*. Urban criticizes Jacques Derrida (1986) for arguing that the Declaration's "signatures invent the signatory," the national "we the people" that is the subject of this performative and the basis of its legitimacy (Urban 2001, 94). According to Urban, this people already existed in the form of a *we* familiar to the colony's inhabitants from their participation in a "circulating discourse of discontent" (2001, 97). What the Declaration did, through its poetic regimentation, was to codify and stabilize this discourse by promoting the proliferation of a more sharply defined version of this first-person national form.

Urban's argument, however ingenious, rests on the presumption that the Declaration was addressed primarily to a national audience, which it did not create, but rather incited to "rise up." But as Michael Warner points out, Derrida is less concerned with the founding of an "empirical public" than he is with a conundrum inherent to the "founding act of an institution" in a particular historical setting: one in which law was coming to be defined "by its derivation of authority from itself" (1990, 104, 106). In accounting for how the Declaration accomplishes this feat, Derrida focuses on more than the document's explicitly performative statements—its signatures and repeated "*we declares.*" He also insists on the importance of the Declaration's "constative" elements, which consist of utterances that describe an established state of affairs, rather than creating one anew. Hence, Derrida's focus on the *is* and *ought* of the final statement—in which "we the representatives of the United States of America . . . solemnly publish and declare that these united colonies are and of right ought to be free and independent"—brings out a dynamic necessary to the foundational act. As Warner points out, this act's "legality rides on the inability to decide whether the people constitute the government already—that is, in fact—or in the future, as it were by prescription" (1990, 106).[6]

This duality of modes, which arguably pervades all performatives—with utterances that "say" what they "do" always in some sense being constative and performative, all at once—also applies to the distribution of utterances across the Declaration. Statements referring to "the people" in the third person are central to the logic of the text. These statements include not only the Declaration's famous opening words, "When in the course of human events," and its explicit references to God, the laws of nature, and "self-evident" truths, but also less lofty lines:

> he [i.e., King George] has refused his assent to laws the most wholesome and necessary for the public good.

> he has dissolved representative houses repeatedly for opposing with manly firmness his invasions on the rights of the people. (Fliegelman 1993, 204).

Voicing the "view from nowhere" (Nagel 1986), these parts of the Declaration address an audience transcending the colonies, an implicit *we* that would be the *we* of rational, moral humanity, a site of "rational-critical debate," but now unencumbered by national allegiances. Perhaps this aspect of the text is so obvious that analysts see no need to stress it, yet it should be clear that the complex foundational drama described by Derrida and others is designed for more than local consumption. After all, the Declaration declares at the very start what it is up to: demonstrating "due respect to the opinions of mankind" by declaring "the causes that have impelled them [the American people] to separation." The performative creation of the American nation entails the conjuring of a transcendentally extranational point of view. The Declaration functions, at least in this respect, in the same way as the presidium video. "Why America Wants Freedom" could be its name.

If analysts of American nationalism (not to mention American presidents) have found it easy to presume a perfect overlap between the national and the universal, an analyst of Papuan nationalism is faced with the legacy of a colonial insistence on their disjunction. In fact, it was on the basis of this disjunction that the Dutch made the case for keeping western New Guinea after Indonesia gained independence. As the previous chapters have made clear, this case was made at a very different historical moment than that of the US Declaration. The transcendental perspective first posited in the American founding document had recently gained new institutional heft with the establishment of the United Nations, whose conventions made self-determination a right to be defended by representatives of the international community, thus displacing a priori emphasis on popular will (see Kelly and Kaplan 2001; Niezen 2003). The Papuans' right to self-determination supposedly rested on their status as a culturally and racially distinct population. But across this diverse population, the one unifying feature that presented itself was the Papuans' "primitiveness," a quality that disqualified the Papuans from having any say in their fate. The Papuans had the right to self-determination, but—and because—they did not have the right kind of selves.

In previous chapters I have recounted the prewar colonial history that made the Papuans such suitable candidates for a repetition of the Netherlands' civilizing mission, speeded up and in miniature, after the rest of the Indies gained independence. Although western New Guinea's economic prospects seemed far from bright to most observers at the time, and the territory was expensive to govern, Dutch officials came to see this place and its people as offering the Netherlands an opportunity to start over and do colonialism right. The idea of dividing New Guinea from the rest of the Indies, and continuing to administer it, did not immediately spring to the minds of Dutch policy makers during the Indonesian Revolution (see Chauvel 1998). As one will recall, the Round Table Conference of 1949 resulted in a settlement granting Indonesia sovereignty over the former Indies, with the exception of western New Guinea, whose status was to be decided within a year. Dutch leaders cut short further negotiations by proclaiming the founding of Netherlands New Guinea as a colony under the Dutch crown. In the name of universal principles, the Dutch pursued an anachronistic project: the establishment of a colony in the era of decolonization. Like a pleat in history, an extended period of Dutch oversight would cause the Papuans to emerge from the Stone Age into the world of nation-states. Indonesia's leaders responded by rallying together behind the developing consensus that new nations should assume the shape of their colonial predecessors (see Duara 2003, 18). They argued that the people of West Irian, as Indonesia renamed the territory, had already exercised their right to self-determination when Indonesia proclaimed its independence in 1945.

The Papuan Presidium Council returned the compliment in June 2000, when the Second Papuan National Congress issued a resolution proclaiming that, appearances notwithstanding, West Papua had been independent since 1961 (see Sekretariat Presidium Dewan Papua 2000, 49; King 2002,

108–9). This was the year before the First Papuan National Congress, held from September 14 to 20, 1962, in Hollandia by the Papuan National Front to give representatives from the colony's various regions a chance to respond to the newly signed New York Agreement and to develop a strategy for handling the stipulated act of self-determination (see Drooglever 2009, 593). On December 1, 1961, when the New Guinea Council first presented the flag, anthem, coat of arms, and motto for the new nation-to-be, many Papuans believed they would someday live in a sovereign West Papua. But at that time, the conflict between the Netherlands and Indonesia prevented West Papuan independence from occurring in the present tense. A deep mistrust of Papuan loyalties and capabilities runs like an undercurrent through Dutch colonial reports of the period. Dutch officers carefully monitored pro-Indonesian tendencies, real or imagined, and tried to plumb the sentiments of leaders feared to be militating for too quick a transition to popular rule (see Ministerie van Kolonien 1959–62; see also Drooglever 2009, 515–47). As for capabilities, it was only "euphemistically," the last governor of the colony remarked ruefully, that the Dutch even referred to a Papuan elite (see Ministerie van Kolonien 1962a).[7] The Dutch viewed the Papuans as impressionable children. The Indonesians viewed them as imperial puppets. Neither party to the dispute believed the Papuans were capable of acting in their own best interests. As a result, although the Dutch allowed—and even encouraged—Papuan leaders to give voice to a Papuan *we*, the pronoun appeared somehow empty to outsiders. Papuan leaders found it impossible to speak for their "nation" in international settings without others hearing Dutch voices coming from their mouths.[8]

Among Papuans, there have been two contrasting responses to this dilemma. One has been armed struggle, initiated in the mid-1960s by young Papuans who vowed to "buy our freedom with our own golden blood" (Ministerie van Kolonien 1962b). Over the decades, scores of young Papuans have fled to the forests and joined the OPM, the guerilla army begun early in the period of Indonesian rule (see Osborne 1985; Djopari 1993). The other response, I argue here, has been mobilized by elite activists and politicians who speak not of "our blood" but of "theirs." This elite's use of the third person is historically overdetermined: by the postwar discourse on Papuan primitivism, by Indonesian accusations of puppetry, by decades of repression—and cultivation—under the New Order regime. Elite Papuans have found it safer to speak about, rather than for, the territory's population, and they have gained authority by distancing themselves from their supposedly Stone Age kin. By referring to the Papuan people and their aspirations in the third person, nationalist leaders present their utterances as revealing, rather than creating, a nation. At the same time, they imaginatively adopt a transcendent perspective on their homeland, akin to that of the diplomats who decided West Papua's fate in 1962. The constative dimension of nationalist rhetoric looms large for understandable reasons in this setting. Historically, the Papuans' *we*-ness has been less problematic than their acceptance as agents capable of so-called rational-critical debate.

With its displaced subjects and contorted temporalities—has self-determination occurred already, or is it yet to come?—political discourse in Papua brings to the fore tensions anticipated in the American revolutionary model. Like their American predecessors, today's Papuan nationalists present themselves as poised between the international community and the national masses. They stand at the interface of powerful and potentially threatening audiences: in Jayapura and Wamena, as well as Jakarta, Brussels, Washington, and New York. Papua's third-person nationalism has been the result. But the complex interplay of pronouns in the video we are about to consider raises questions not only of audience but also of genre: when speaking in the voices of extranational others, what rhetorical styles and verbal and visual registers should one use? The United States Declaration of Independence arguably partakes of the genre of the legal brief, with "mankind" serving as jury and God as judge.[9] *Why Papua Wants Freedom* follows very different conventions. Papuan leaders are sensitive to the impact on global opinion of journalistic exposés documenting the human rights abuses and everyday indignities suffered by oppressed minorities. In addition to legal documents, West Papua's would-be founding fathers have invested in the production of documentaries: filmic representations of their people's history and dashed dreams, which demonstrate these leaders' power to represent. The video we now consider reveals the highly fraught field of interlocutors confronted by one group of contemporary nationalists, and the dilemmas and opportunities this field presents to those who would speak with them all.

"A Region Full of Mystery": The Third Person in the Video

Why Papua Wants Freedom was produced in 2002. One will recall that four years earlier, following the flag raisings in July 1998, church and nongovernmental organization leaders came together to form the Forum for the Reconciliation of Irian Jaya Society. FORERI, as it was dubbed, set up the

February 26, 1999, meeting where one hundred delegates presented President Habibie with a signed declaration calling for West Papua's separation from Indonesia. The FORERI Team of 100's trip to Jakarta enjoyed the Indonesian government's blessing and financial support, like other key events in the recent history of the movement: the Grand Consultation of February 23–26, 2000, and the Second Papuan National Congress, which was held from May 29 to June 4 of the same year and resulted in the formation of the Papuan Presidium Council and the election of Eluay as its leader. Two events proved central in setting the stage for the video: Indonesia's passage of a special autonomy law for Papua in early 2001 and the military-led crackdown in the territory discussed in chapter 4, which resulted in the jailing and eventual murder of Eluay later the same year.

In the fall of 2001, Yorrys Raweyai, the Suharto henchman, received an invitation to speak at a seminar in Jakarta and came to Mandowen, the presidium moderator, for help in writing the presentation. The paper met with an enthusiastic reception, and someone in the audience suggested that Raweyai expand it into a book, with the accompanying video compact disc (VCD) analyzed here. Raweyai took on this project, again with Mandowen's help. In early 2002, some five hundred people attending the book launch at the Hotel Borobudur in Jakarta and watched the video in its entirety.[10] Stocked and sold as a unit in Jakarta's major bookstores, the book and video quickly passed into the hands of elite Papuans, who brought them back to the territory.[11] I do not have sales figures, although one Papuan minister told me the package "sold super well" (*paling laku*).[12]

If I am correct about the appeal for Papuans of a discourse that constatively reveals their nation to extranational interlocutors, rather than performatively creating it anew, then video would seem to be a perfect medium for the Papuan nationalist movement. Recorded sounds and images cross global boundaries in ways that written words arguably cannot. Of course, the question of just how the third person could appear in a video merits contemplation, given the range of semiotic channels involved. Some possibilities come to mind by virtue of the formal qualities of film in general, and documentary in particular. Analysts of fiction film have explored how voice-over narration, which is usually male, "hovers" above the image track and the voices associated with it, including, most pointedly, the female scream (see Silverman 1988, 49). Documentary theorists have drawn similar conclusions concerning the transcendent nature of the authority claimed by such narrators, like the Javanese one in this video, whose utterances frame how viewers interpret what they see and hear (see

Nichols 1983). Although the play of identifications is ultimately far more complex, in both cases the image track and the voices associated with it are the *they*, at once excluded from and made the object of a dialogue between an invisible narrating *I* and spectating *you*. In a moment, I examine how the particular form of the images shown in the West Papuan video contributes to this result. But the first place to look for the third person in this production lies in the video-makers' treatment of the material they found at hand. That is, we need to attend to what—and how—the video makers repeat and cite.

The closing credits of *Why Papua Wants Freedom* thank Mandowen and Raweyai for providing materials from their "Visual Documentary Library." In addition to video clips, the presidium also provided texts to the video makers. A close scrutiny of the script suggests that the principle source in this regard was Alua's four-volume, presidium-sponsored *Series for Papuan Political Education*.[13] The presidium series refers to the Papuan nation almost entirely in the third person in the utterances voiced by its omniscient narrator.[14] But unlike the video, the series includes a plethora of inclusive and exclusive first-person plural pronouns within its abundant offerings of reported speech, including a quote from the declaration read to President Habibie on February 26, 1999: "We the people of West Papua desire to leave the unified Republic of Indonesia to be free and fully sovereign among other nations on the face of this earth" (Alua 2001, 38–39). The video entirely omits this declaration. Also missing, despite the video's loving attention to Eluay's imposing physical form, is any footage in which we actually hear the "Great Leader," rather than merely seeing him speak. There is no footage featuring interviews with named presidium members. The only unnamed presidium member who comments on the movement is Raweyai himself. Audible non-Papuans, by contrast, are all fully identified: Major General Abinowo, Trikora Commander; Retired Major General Samsuddin, Member of the National Human Rights Commission; and Indonesia's first president, Sukarno. The anonymous collective voices are implicitly Papuan: they sing a hymn and their national anthem, chant "freedom" (*merdeka*), whoop, whistle, shout, and scream.

But at the same time that the video excludes portions of the presidium archive, it also supplements it with music, special effects, and excerpts from earlier productions. Lingering on Papuan bodies in their most "traditional" form, the image track includes clips from ethnographic films; excerpts from television programs depicting such perennial attractions as Asmat paddling, Dani warfare, and highland pig feasts; a reenactment of a young man hunting with a bow and arrow; and endless close-ups of Papuan faces, young and old.[15] To the extent that the video offers an argument for separatism, it does so through a visual rhetoric that racializes the Papuans and plays up their primitive way of life.

But the assumption that *Why Papua Wants Freedom* offers an argument for separatism proves problematic when one takes a closer look at how the video's components work together. One must, indeed, look closely—and repeatedly—to appreciate all the visual and auditory ingredients that make up this complex mix. Here are a few examples from the opening sequence, which showcases the repertoire of techniques employed by the video to present West Papua as the object of an external gaze. Even before the narrator starts speaking, we get a sense of how the video will undo the movement's separatist aspirations by resolving the specter of disorderly violence into clearly articulated needs. One of the first things we notice is the soundtrack, which inserts us into the scene of Papuan nationalism from a distance. We begin in silence with the following frame:

Which fades to:

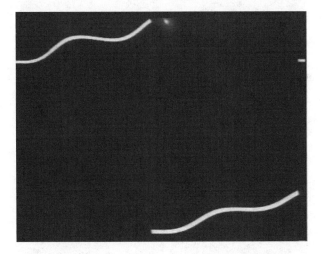

As the credit fades, we hear radio static. This is followed by drumming, and then the sounds of a crackling fire and shouting. The radio static hails us as a radio audience, akin to those that listen to the BBC, Radio Australia, and other global broadcasts; the sound effects give us a sense of "being there," even as they mark us as listening from afar.

Even more striking is the image track, which also distances the viewer from the object viewed. A key feature of the video is its giddy deployment of computer editing techniques: a juxtaposing, layering, and framing of images that presents them as objects to be manipulated rather than visions of the world.[16] One sometimes gets the impression that the video makers felt they simply had too much to show to include only one image per frame. These two frames are representative:

Within a yellow box, we find footage from the protests in Jakarta that led to President Suharto's resignation. A moving caption appears, à la Star Wars, from the bottom of the screen to tell us of the "democratic climate" that is "sweeping every nation-state, including Indonesia." The waving lines and twinkling light provide the visual equivalent of the radio static; as we "tune in" to the topic they unfurl into the West Papuan (Morning Star) and Indonesian (Red and White) flags. A black-and-white still photograph of marching soldiers provides a ghostly backdrop for the footage,

caption, and flags. Later, the same function is served by still close-ups of
Papuan faces, which become things one can pick up and move around
the screen. These close-ups are thinglike in another respect, as well: they
present Papuans as a limited set of types rather than as interlocutors with
whom one might converse.

Sound and image come together in the depiction of the Papuan nation
that emerges from this giddy mix. In these two frames, the video's protago-
nist comes into view:

The soundtrack has shifted from the crackling fire and shouting to the high
quavering tones of a violin. Like the theme from a suspense movie, the
music reaches a crescendo just as the video's title comes into focus. Pairs of

large yellow words appear in the foreground, cross, and then drop back to form a sentence: "WHY . . . PAPUA . . . WANTS . . . FREEDOM." Footage of running tribesmen appears in the yellow box. At just the moment when the title becomes legible, the image in the box cuts to a close-up of a "primitive" Papuan with a bone ornament through his nose. (Similar photographs appear in travel brochures intended to attract Western tourists.) Another close-up of a primitive Papuan provides a ghostly backdrop for a new series of scenes, now set to cheerful, vaguely world-beat music.

In these two frames, the footage in the yellow box depicts events in and around the sports stadium where the Second Papuan National Congress was held:

They illustrate more of the strategies through which the video refers to West Papua in the third person. The portrayal of large and amorphous crowds adds to the impression of the Papuan people as an amorphous whole, while shots of the people's backs convey a sense of closure. The unmistakable back portrayed in the frame on the right belongs to West Papua's self-proclaimed "Great Leader," the presidium chairman, Eluay. One effect of referring to the Papuan nation in the third person is to provide an impression of unity and coherence in a setting where competition for leadership is actually rife. In Eluay's impressive physique and confident comportment, the West Papuan leadership appears in a unified and bounded form. Eluay becomes another object to which the video can point.

The video goes stylistically overboard in order to claim an exorbitant power to circumscribe the West Papuan nation as an entity. As we have seen, various images of this nation congeal along the way. But in the end, a familiar portrait of the primitive Papuan comes into focus. These four frames bring the opening sequence to a close:

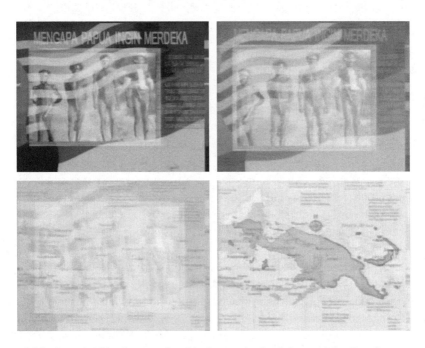

A black-and-white image of a ship forms the backdrop of the first frame, perhaps in a reference to the European explorers who "discovered" and named New Guinea. West Papua's inhabitants reminded these explorers, who reappear later in the video, of the African natives of the Guinea coast.

The most racialized figures of the sequence—men in penis gourds, standing erect on a ridge—appear in the yellow box, which expands before fading away. At the same time, an old-fashioned map of the archipelago comes into focus, with an icon of western New Guinea emerging from it. The soundtrack switches to a lighter, slower tune, played by flutes and drums. Gone is the suspense music; gone is the footage of roiling crowds. The narrator with the Javanese accent begins speaking. Giving a name to what we have been seeing, the word "Papua" slowly rolls off his tongue.

With this utterance, the documentary proper begins. Over the course of it, Papuan difference will come to serve as a resource for Indonesia's resurrection as a "reformed" nation-state. The cut to the man with the bone ornament through his nose holds the key to the video's implicit message. It is Indonesia's future that is at stake in its account of what "they"—the objectified Papuans—really "want."

This implicit message is legible throughout the video. The first narrated scenes deliver us from the streets of Jakarta to the vast natural expanses of Papua, a land "three times the size of Java" and "filled with mystery." "In general, the Papuan people possess a culture that has been able to preserve its existence for centuries," the narrator remarks. These words are accompanied by what appears to be old ethnographic footage, tinted pink, depicting men in penis gourds and women in fiber skirts making their way down a trail. The next line, "That is, the attitude that they should govern themselves," is spoken over a shot of young children cutting grass, their bare buttocks directed at the camera, in an oddly infantile image that undermines the statement with which it is paired. In some cases, the video intersperses portraits of Papuan people and practices with footage of sunsets, forests, and animals to highlight the natural beauty and integrity of Papuan life. In other cases, comments on the province's poor "human resources" appear in the company of the same genre of rural scenes, which become legible as signs of what "development" should leave behind.

But this message is also presented in a blatant form in the video's retelling of recent history. One learns that the 1998 demonstrations that followed Suharto's fall in West Papua were "often accompanied by violence," a vague construction that tells us nothing of who did what to whom. Following close-ups of various members of FORERI, the narrator lists options explored by the organization to address the conflict: "full independence," "broad autonomy within the Unitary Republic of Indonesia," "or the creation of a federal system, in which Irian Jaya would enjoy substantial autonomy." Rather than recounting how the organized movement came together behind the first option, "full independence," the scenes that follow, which depict Papuan nationalist leaders in restaurants, conference rooms, and convention halls, are set to cheerful music. The segment reaches a climax with an interview fragment in which Raweyai explains the presidium's agenda: "The Papuan Council is only enacting a mandate of the Congress. The two substances of this are first, regarding the demand for independence. Independence in the universal sense. It wants to be free from its ignorance, it wants to be free from the backwardness that . . ."[17] As elsewhere in the video, the narrator interrupts the pictured speaker, this time with a question: "Seriously, what do the people of Papua need?" Harking back to Indonesian promises made in the 1960s, the answer to this question turns out to be the special autonomy package offered by the new president, Megawati Sukarnoputri, and "more important still, a deeper understanding of the culture and customs of Papuan society, from an objective perspective, such that the government can avoid the mistakes that happened in the past" (see Drooglever 2009, 563). Moving from a still of the Indonesian presidential palace, the image track returns to the map of Indonesia pictured at the start of the video, with an icon of Papua emerging from it. But now Papua sinks back into it and disappears.

Idyllic nature scenes follow, and the video's theme song is given lyrics:

This life is a blessing
Free to the death
Not to be wasted
On the desires of the world.

This is our moment
To be liberated
From all ties
To worldly darkness.

We're free
Were released
Not by our courageous deeds
But only the Savior, Our Lord.

The theme song's lyrics sum up the video's message. Freed of separatist connotations, "we" the Papuans will be liberated from worldly desires and darkness, not from Indonesia. The video reveals the ambivalence inherent in the presidium's effort to stand within and beyond the Papuan nation. The voice of Papuan nationalism becomes the voice of the Indonesian state.

This outcome is, needless to say, curious. Papuan alterity becomes the object of "objective" understanding and intervention, with national shame paving the way for the consolidation of a multicultural nation-state (see Povinelli 2002). Although I was not in Papua at the time when the video was released, informants told me that *Why Papua Wants Freedom* was very popular. Both the VCD and the book had vanished from the bookstores I visited in Jakarta and Jayapura in 2003; shortly afterward, the Indonesian government banned several books on the movement. Nevertheless, during my six weeks in Papua, other films and books, as well as recordings, that Papuan friends and acquaintances judged to be even remotely related to the nationalist cause met with much interest and applause.[18] How can we explain this project's appeal to the presidium and its supporters, such as PaVo, which saw fit to screen *Why Papua Wants Freedom* at the meeting I attended? How do we account for its attraction to "regular folks" in Papua, who, as one presidium member told me, "all want to see" the video, just "love" the production, and even cheer as particular scenes unfold?

Clearly, there is more than one way to experience this work. A consultant who had watched *Why Papua Wants Freedom* with friends and relatives in Jayapura found it easy to explain its popularity: the video was a sources of delight because it offered "proof" that the struggle was being publicized far and wide.[19] He did not remember anyone noticing the narrator's Javanese accent. He laughed when I suggested that some might view it as evidence of the presidium's fluency in foreign talk. But he went on to tell me about a prophet whom presidium leaders had consulted, who supposedly could converse in the language of any foreigner she confronts.[20] She had asked Papuan leaders to set up a meeting with Kofi Annan, so she could convey the Papuans' aspirations in his own tribal tongue. *Why Papua Wants Freedom* may silence Papuan voices—those voices uttering the national *we*—but only to facilitate the presidium's assumption of a more potent foreign register. With its narrator quoting, however partially, the presidium's official documents and statements, the video allows Papuan leaders to profit from what is gained by speaking of one's nation in the third person: access to the (documentary) voice of God.

Rewind, Repeat

The story told in this chapter belongs to a specific place and time; some might argue that its implications are limited. But this is my point, in the most general sense: all nationalisms are limited—and facilitated—in historically specific ways that become apparent when we consider the extranational others they respond to and cite. The leaders of the contemporary movement I have considered take their voicing of extranational perspectives to such an extreme that their nationalist productions threaten to become unrecognizable as such. What makes *Why Papua Wants Freedom* an expression of Papuan nationalism, rather than a somewhat amateurish effort to present an "objective" picture of Papua's current predicament and contentious past? The fact that, as analyses of the US Declaration of Independence make clear, the performative creation of a nation has long entailed the conjuring of transcendentally extranational points of view. My analysis of the 1998 Biak flag raising in chapter 4 also suggested as much.

That the video, like a host of other "objective" reports and documentaries, appears to Papuans as an expression of their nationalist aspirations indicates the force of this paradox, which is fraught with consequences in this age of UN peacekeepers, humanitarian interventions, and preemptive strikes. Nation building has become the violent work of powerful outsiders, and those unable to voice their aspirations in internationally recognizable registers risk having others' aspirations foisted on them. But the problems of voice, genre, and history I have analyzed in this chapter also made their mark on earlier generations of nationalist texts. The founding documents of Latin American nations, for example, invoke a plethora of audiences and subjects. Among the earliest of such texts is the 1810 Declaration of the City Council of Caracas, which, rather than voicing the people's desires, depicts the people's unruly activities in a document that reads as realist reportage.[21] These problems continue to make their mark on nationalist movements outside of Papua, movements that in turn provide both models and a context for other struggles for sovereignty.

My findings suggest that the third person in contemporary nationalism marks not only the fields of power in which today's nationalist movements unfold but also the forms of authority and pleasure they promise to their participants. When we attend to the conjuring of audiences by such movements, we gain new insights into the dreams and desires that move people to risk joining in. When I asked a Papuan activist living in the United States why so many Papuans refer to the nation in the third person, he responded first with puzzlement, then enthusiasm: it must be because popular support for independence is not in question. As a result, the task of a good Papuan nationalist leader is less to call forth the nation than to translate its demands. Given this assumption, it makes sense that elite writers would feel little uneasiness—and, indeed, find much enjoyment—in speaking of the movement in a range of alien idioms, including the language of international law, the discourse of human rights, and even the rhetoric of Indonesian reform.

Clearly, third-person nationalism has important political stakes for those who compete for leadership of the Papuan nationalist movement. Outsiders, including anthropologists, find themselves drawn in to this contest, giving rise to a doubled ventriloquism: we speak for elite Papuans, who authorize their words by speaking just like us. During the week when I first viewed the video, I spent time with another friend and consultant, a Papuan exile who had not seen his homeland since 1962. The walls of his small living room were crowded with memorabilia from the struggle: portraits of Papuan leaders, newspaper clippings, a large plaque adorned with the West Papuan coat of arms adopted in 1961. The adjoining room was crammed with books and documents as well as audio- and videocassettes. When I visited one evening, my friend played a video featuring items on West Papua that had recently aired on Dutch television. As I sat sipping orange soda, I heard a whir and looked up to discover that my friend had his camera: he was videotaping me watching his video of Papuan images shown on TV.

Such scenarios are almost a cliché for today's anthropologists, who savor these ironic moments when the investigated become the investigators. But my friend was doing more than just turning the ethnographic tables. I had seen him armed with a video camera at the first meeting of "Indonesia Week," a series sponsored by Dutch advocacy groups, but he chose to sit out the PaVo event I described at the start of this chapter. Like other Papuans long in exile, my friend distrusted the presidium, which he viewed as compromised by the leaders' dependence on Indonesian patronage.[22] My friend described freedom as a distant land, and the various Papuan organizations as vessels competing to reach it. Customs officers would inspect the arriving ships, and those with unacceptable baggage would not be allowed to disembark.

My friend who had worked so hard to build an archive of depictions of the Papuans and their audiences would have something to show for his efforts. I knew he was in the midst of editing some of his footage and setting it to music. Was this something he would show to the outside world? "It is just for Papuans, really. Those living there. So they will know what we have done here. There will be proof." What kind of retrospective gaze did my friend anticipate in this footage of foreign documentaries and the foreigners who watched them? Could we call this fourth-person nationalism,[23] this utopian practice addressed to a sovereign West Papua, which would someday fix the global view from nowhere within its sights?

In chapter 8, the final essay in this collection, I will have more to say about how Papuan audiences react to this play of perspectives. But I can draw some conclusions from the analysis I have undertaken here. In this chapter, through a close reading of *Why Papua Wants Freedom* and its pronouns, I have explored the possibilities and pitfalls of third-person nationalism. The case of West Papua illuminates nationalism's founding exclusions—of subjects deemed unqualified to speak for themselves. But it also illuminates its founding *inclusions*—of subjects deemed too lofty to speak for any particular nation-state. Third-person nationalism fixes on the remainders of repetition—those other scenes and subjectivities, other settings for the "human reality of dialogue," that haunt nationalist words, images, and sounds. The pitfalls of this orientation are obvious: however welcome it may be to its Papuan producers and consumers, third-person nationalism reproduces the very mismatch in perceptions on which the conflict over western New Guinea long has turned. As the video makes clear, third-person nationalism has promoted the stereotype of Papuan primitivism, preserved the privileges of the Papuan elite, and provided fodder for an Indonesian multiculturalism that papers over very real conflicts and inequalities that plague this postauthoritarian nation-state. And yet the effort to translate Papuan nationalism into terms acceptable in Jakarta has not only allowed figures like Raweyai and Alua to weather subsequent Indonesian crackdowns on the movement.[24] It has also kept the movement's signs available for delectation back at home. Or so it would seem in this April 2000 passage from "Sago Pudding Stand," a column in the provincial daily featuring and directed at "ordinary Papuans."

"Whoaaaaaa . . . Grandpa, you are like really having fun. Coffee with a song and a smoke, and betel nut, too," said Pa Shaman when he saw Grandpa relaxing on the platform while moving to the music.

"This is what they call life in a world that is free [*merdeka*]. What else is there to do . . ." Grandpa Pimple replied. (Cenderawasih Pos 2000)

CHAPTER EIGHT

The Appeal of Slippery Pronouns

"What else is there to do?" asks Grandpa Pimple in "Sago Pudding Stand," that column in the provincial daily featuring this fictional Papuan's playful remarks on "life in a world that is free." "A lot," one is tempted to answer, after reading recent reports by journalists, academics, and human rights advocates on the situation in West Papua (see, e.g., King 2004; International Crisis Group 2006a; McGibbon 2006; Fernandes 2006; Survival International 2008; Singh 2008; Amnesty International 2008a, b, c). Over a decade into the so-called reform era, a far-reaching special autonomy law and four free and fair national elections notwithstanding, West Papua remains troubled. Vast inequities in income and health persist, with 3 percent of West Papuans now HIV positive. Illegal loggers plunder forests. Human rights violations still occur. To hide all these problems, the central government still restricts the travel of foreign journalists, diplomats, and aid workers in the province. Despite the fact that the special autonomy law sanctioned the use of the Morning Star flag as a "cultural symbol," demonstrators who dare to raise the flag still end up in jail; some end up tortured and even killed (see Amnesty International 2008a, b).

A Papuan nationalist looking back with nostalgia at the so-called Papuan spring of 1998–2000 might also feel there is a lot to do. "The dream of Papuan freedom is on the wane," reads a recent headline in a major Indonesian news magazine (see Gatra 2008). The article quotes remarks from Barnabas Suebu, the current governor of Papua and one of the drafters of a Papuan version of the special autonomy bill that Indonesian legislators used as the basis for the current law.[1] Suebu offered a sanguine explanation for the relative dearth of demonstrators who turned out on December 1, 2008, to celebrate the seventeenth anniversary of the introduction of the Morning Star flag. "The public has begun to experience the results of special autonomy in Papua," the governor noted, "so that demands to be freed from the Unitary Republic of Indonesia have diminished." The journalist elaborated: "Suebu used the metaphor that the flag was only the smoke, whereas the fire was poverty, injustice, and backwardness"—ills supposedly remedied by special autonomy. "When we put out the fire," Suebu told the journalist, "the smoke won't appear anymore."

The International Crisis Group has also played down the importance of the independence struggle in today's Papua. In July 2007, the organization issued a report titled "A Local Perspective on the Conflict," based on fieldwork in Boven Digoel, a district in the south (International Crisis Group 2007; see also International Crisis Group 2006c). The report's findings suggested that "the issues most commonly associated with Papua—the independence struggle, half-hearted implementation of special autonomy, and abuse by the military" are "not at the forefront of Boven Digoel residents' concerns." Instead, these residents spoke of tribal disputes sparked by recent events in the district: the loss of customary land to a plantation project, corruption in a recent election, and a series of ham-fisted security operations.[2] Suebu declared that the government's success in coping with Papua's problems has turned Papuan minds to concerns other than freedom. The International Crisis Group report asserts that the government's failure to solve local problems has had the same effect. Although they disagree on the mechanism, these assessments suggest that the Papuan pursuit of sovereignty has lost its allure as people turn their attention to the predicaments of daily life. As the previous chapters have suggested, and other analyses of the Papuan nationalist movement confirm, both Suebu and the International Crisis Group are correct to stress the range of practical issues that concern today's Papuans (see Mote and Rutherford 2001; Leith 2003; McGibbon 2004b; Chauvel 2005; Hedman 2007; Butt 2005; Kirksey 2012). But many Papuans—including, I would wager, some in Boven Digoel—still dream, however wistfully, of being free in the political as well as personal sense of the word. As this book neared completion in 2009 a fresh round of demonstrations signals that the movement is still very much alive.

The question is why. Why do Papuans continue to pursue national sovereignty when their chances of achieving it seem so slight? What is so appealing about the representational practices through which they envision and seek to achieve, to quote Grandpa Pimple, "life in a world that is free?" In this chapter, which opens yet another angle on the signs of West Papuan sovereignty in motion, I suggest that the second question holds the key to the first. At stake in the Papuans' pursuit of sovereignty is pleasure as well as control over their own affairs, exhilaration as well as an escape from terror and exploitation. For those engaged in the struggle for Papuan freedom, the pleasure and exhilaration associated with the movement's imaginings are a significant draw. In West Papua, as elsewhere, the proliferation of audiences spawns passions that propel the quest for sovereignty, passions that run the gamut from sorrow and anger to hope. This chapter thus speaks directly to one of this book's central arguments. By way of such passions, the sense that others are or could be paying heed both dogs and fuels sovereignty struggles wherever they occur.

In doing so, this chapter extends the exploration that I began in chapter 7, where I sought to account for Papuan nationalists' tendency to refer to their nation in the third person. In that chapter, my analysis of the video, *Why Papua Wants Freedom*, illuminated the authority that Papuan nationalists gain when they speak of their struggle in the voice of powerful outsiders. By speaking as "we the international community" rather than "we the Papuan people," leaders present themselves as having access to forces that can change their homeland's fate. Papuans take pride in the movement's diplomatic victories, but they also delight in the artful wielding of words, gestures, sounds, and images in speeches, texts, and videos that describe and aim for recognition from a wider world. In describing how Papuans in the audience for such productions feel when they imagine their movement being seen through sympathetic foreign eyes, friends and informants used the Indonesian term, *semangat* (literally "spirited"), which combines a sense of enthusiasm and excitement with confidence in one's ability to act. *Semangat* verges close to the affective states I discussed in chapter 2, where Freud's insights on humor helped me to analyze Dutch officials' reactions to the proliferation of audiences for their deeds. Whereas in that chapter I focused on the discomfort and even anguish felt by Dutch officials, here I focus on the pleasurable sense of potency that Papuans enjoy when they shift between pronouns and points of view. I show how this shifting can lead to an exhilarating, even giddy, feeling of expanded possibility as Papuans envision distant others sharing their sorrow, anger, and pain.

Building on the analytic tools that I developed in previous chapters, I use the word *slippery* to describe the pronouns and other elements of sign use that provide Papuans with this pleasurable sense of potency. Slipperiness is the indeterminacy that allows participants in an interaction to shift among what linguistic anthropologists and other scholars of sign use have called "footings," "voices," and "stances" (see Irvine 1996; Keane 1997, 2001; Agha 2007; Dickinson 2007; Shoaps 2009). These terms refer to the relationship between perceivable signs and the varied figures of person-hood that language users evoke and inhabit as they converse (see Goffman 1981; see also Bakhtin 1981; Vološinov 1986 [1973]). On the one hand, some of the signs discussed in this chapter are slippery because they are "shifters" (see Jakobson 1971). One voices a pronoun only to have it slip from one's grasp; the one who was "I" becomes "you" and later "she." Other deictic elements of language, such as verb tenses ("is" and "was") and demonstrative pronouns ("this" and "that"), share this trait with per-sonal pronouns; they anchor a speaker's words in the real time of inter-action by indexing—that is, pointing to by virtue of an assumed causal link—the circumstances in which these words present themselves. A shifter's function is metapragmatic: shifters turn back on themselves to refer to an aspect of the speech situation their utterance works to bring about. Shifters are slippery in the sense that they both convey a general meaning and serve as an index that interlocutors take up in succession as they talk.

On the other hand, like bivalence and heteroglossia, slipperiness is an irreducible aspect of all sign use. In the beginning of this book, I made the point that the interplay with an audience that George Herbert Mead (1965, 184) referred to as the "conversation of gestures" is constitutive of social action: the idea of an interpreting other into whose position one can shift is what makes the social social and a sign a sign. But every sign, from a sigh to a sculpture, not only presumes this conversation, it is also an ob-ject, a concrete thing with its own singular trajectory and traits (see Peirce 1986, 62, in Keane 1997, 8; see also Parmentier 1994). Taking this point seriously allows us to grasp how the slipperiness associated with shifters might extend more widely. Asif Agha (2007) has argued that even denota-tion, the general meaning of a word, arises out of a history of real-time interactions. Denotation is more a matter of statistical regularities than structural essences, notwithstanding the tendency of dictionaries and aca-demic disciplines to stabilize the definition of particular terms. Not only the particular things that a word refers to but also its general meaning can slip as interlocutors coordinate their understandings of the encounter in which they are engaged. This kind of slipperiness is sequential, mov-ing signs along a singular trajectory from one referent or denotational meaning to another. But what makes this phenomenon possible is a si-multaneous kind of slipperiness, an excess of potential stemming from a sign's material traits. Webb Keane (1997) has argued that all signs are underdetermined by virtue of their status as objects: our interpretations cannot exhaust the full range of meanings that an object can call to mind. Interpretation spotlights certain features while leaving others in shadow; no perspective can access the full range of possible viewpoints all at once. As we will see in the examples discussed in this chapter, the particular version of a pronoun uttered by an orator can evoke a plethora of imagined subjects and scenarios, a plethora of imagined points of view. By featuring a sound track that conflicts with its image track, a video can speak to at least three imagined audiences—one that hears, one that sees, and one that experiences the mismatch between the first two.

Pronouns and other signs are thus slippery in two respects: they shift in their reference over the course of their use, and they are subject to multiple interpretations all at once. What is distinctive about the texts I explore in this chapter is that they foreground both aspects of this trait. They encourage their audiences to reflect upon and enjoy the exhilarating sense of shifting from one figure of personhood to another. They showcase the underdetermined character of signs by drawing on a slippery mixture of visual and verbal styles, registers, and interpretive frames. Sliding from "we" to "we," these texts play with semiotic business as usual for the pleasurable sense of potency, the enlivening spiritedness, that this slipperiness can bring.

Papuan nationalism's slippery pronouns are politically efficacious because they are appealing, in both senses of the term: they appeal to potential supporters—they solicit their aid—and they please and encourage the Papuans who wield them. The same no doubt holds true for nationalisms elsewhere. But in West Papua slippery pronouns have a special charm. These pronouns bear witness to what Donald Brenneis (1987) has called a "cultural aesthetic" and Steven Feld (1988) has called a "groove": a taste for a particular way of using signs that cuts across an array of social arenas and expressive genres. The link between politics, pleasure, and potency is particularly clear in today's West Papua, where the nationalist movement has more or less gone underground. In previous chapters I have mentioned Eben Kirksey's writings, which focus on the most committed dreamers of Papuan freedom. Kirksey (2012) describes the Papuan movement as going through "rhizomic" phases when the freedom dream takes shelter in the private domain: it lives on in conversations over dinner, comments on a bus, and jokes told among friends (see also Deleuze and Guattari 1987). These phases have alternated with periods in which the movement has assumed institutional heft in the form of organizations like the Papuan Presidium Council.[3] Papuans today are as far as they have ever been from agreeing on which individuals and organizations can legitimately represent their nation. But no matter how bold or cautious particular individuals may be, many still enjoy imagining that day when a sovereign West Papua will suddenly step onto the world stage.

One place where Papuan nationalists and their supporters can indulge this pleasure is on YouTube. Announcing a new, viewer-generated form of television or "Tube," the very name of the website showcases a slippery pronoun. On the one hand, the name, YouTube, conjures a process of interpellation or hailing, in the sense Louis Althusser (1971) illustrated with the example of a policeman shouting, "Hey, you!" On the other hand, the name implies that even "you" can become the producer of videos—and often do, as amateur producers post video responses to videos by which they have been "hailed." Many in the West Papuan movement have heeded YouTube's call. When one searches the site for West Papua, dozens of titles pop up, from Australian and British documentaries to Papuan music videos to homemade coverage of recent demonstrations and cultural events. E-mail groups such as the Papuan Internal Forum and Kabar Irian ("News from Irian") publicize recent entries. Below each posting, the space for viewers' comments is generally filled with praise for the movement, along with an occasional slinging of insults (see YouTube 2008d, 2008e). If these remarks are any indication, a variety of individuals have produced and watched these videos: speakers of Indonesian, Dutch, and English; students; exiles and activists; and Indonesian loyalists and their Papuan foes.[4] Two 2008 postings provide a particularly clear illustration of how the sense that others are watching can fuel, as well as foil, the pursuit of sovereignty. They also illuminate the appeal of the slippage between subject positions that this pursuit has come to entail.

The first video consists of more or less unedited footage of Filep Karma, the leader of the Biak flag raising of 1998, giving a speech at another flag raising held in 2004 (see YouTube 2008c). The 2004 flag raising resulted in Karma's arrest and prosecution for treason; along with his co-organizer, Yusak Pakage, Karma is now languishing in jail. The demonstration ended with the shooting of several of Karma's supporters, when the Indonesian police moved in to break up the crowd (see Amnesty International 2008c). The second video is set to the Obama Song, an artifact of the 2008 presidential campaign that first aired in a star-studded music video that also appeared on YouTube (see 2008b). I have chosen these two productions to illustrate the range of rhetorical tools that Papuan activists use to make their case.[5] The first video appeals to the Papuan faithful and others with the language skills and knowledge to appreciate Karma's virtuosity, oratorical skill being a prerequisite for leadership in West Papua, as elsewhere in the Pacific (see Brenneis and Myers 1984; Duranti 1990). The second casts its net more widely, creatively juxtaposing photographs, drawings, and English- and Dutch-language labels with hip-hop musician will.i.am's remix of an Obama speech to appeal to an international community schooled in these references.

The disturbing images of Papuan victimhood showcased in the second video would scarcely seem to inspire confidence, let alone enthusiasm or enjoyment in viewers. Nevertheless, the second video belongs to the same imaginary world as does the first: a world where Papuans first appeal to then imaginatively join powerful audiences whose attention they seek to turn to their struggle. Each video invites viewers to listen with and watch over the shoulders of imagined others: from the Papuan faithful who joined Filep Karma in December 2004 to a distinctly American version of the "international community." The slippery pronouns that populate these videos—in the form of racialized, nationalized, and globalized versions of "we"—perform familiar political work: they conjure up a Papuan subject and call out to the legitimating constituencies that Papuan nationalism will need to succeed. But these slippery pronouns also allow the videos' viewers to imagine Papuan sovereignty as offering not only legitimacy but also delight. These two videos, which I analyze in their entirety, show us why, even in the darkest of times, the dream of Papuan freedom remains compelling—and, well, even fun.

This fun has serious ramifications. The events in American politics that overtook me as I completed this book provide an unlikely confirmation of the importance of attending to the role of audiences in the pursuit of sovereignty. As I point out at the end of this essay, the slippery pronouns so evident in West Papua recently made an appearance in US president-elect Barack Obama's campaign strategy. What one can learn from the struggle in West Papua can help us understand why this strategy worked. In 2008, Obama's audiences indulged in the thrills of identifying, however fleetingly, with the perspective of spectral others long marginalized from the political mainstream. They experienced a US version of Papuans call *semangat* or "spirit": the pleasure and potency entailed in inhabiting the slippery "we" of "yes we can." Commentators have argued that the slippery quality of Obama's "we" contributed to the election's historic outcome—that is, to the success of a quest for sovereignty that used the ballot box rather than rifles or human rights reports (see Remnick 2008). But before speculating on the sentiments that facilitated Obama's bid for office, let's consider how Papuan leaders have sustained their struggle in a setting where it seems particularly audacious to hope.

"The World Is Watching Now"

A good deal of water passed under the bridge in West Papua between the 1998 flag raising that I discussed in chapter 5 and the 2004 flag raising that was the occasion for the speech by Filep Karma documented in the first video, which was posted by westpapuaeurope in April 2008 (see YouTube 2008c; see also YouTube 2007b; YouTube 2008d). One must dip into this stream to grasp the significance of what Karma had to say. Between 1998 and 2000, Papuan nationalists mounted a series of public events that yielded unprecedented international attention to the troubles of their homeland. In 1999 the central government in Jakarta responded to the movement's successes by issuing a presidential instruction calling for Papua's division into three provinces (see International Crisis Group 2003; McGibbon 2004a). National leaders spoke in public of the need to improve services in the territory. But most observers assumed the administration's objective was to dilute support for Papuan independence. If this was, indeed, the strategy, it seems to have worked. Although rioting in Timika in 2003 forced the government to postpone the establishment of a Central Irian Jaya province, there was enough local support for the formation of West Irian Jaya—now confusingly known as West Papua—that this province now exists.

The presidential instruction to divide Papua collided head on with the central government's other strategy for suppressing the nationalist movement, that is, through the granting of special autonomy in 2001. Politicians from the greatly diminished Papua province headquartered in Jayapura objected vociferously to the loss of territory and the legal and administrative muddle caused by the conflicting policies. The loudest protests came from the Papua People's Assembly (Majelis Rakyat Papua, MRP), a consultative body created under the provisions of special autonomy. The MRP was designed to serve as the defender of traditional, religious, and women's rights for the entire region of western New Guinea. The body's most important function is the vetting of candidates for governor and lieutenant governor, who have to be indigenous Papuans according to the new law. Even as the MRP negotiated with the central government over West Irian Jaya's legal status, voters flocked to the polls to elect a governor for the new province (see International Crisis Group 2006a).

As I explained in chapter 1, decentralization has become a watchword in reform-era Indonesia. Throughout the archipelago, it has led to the exacerbation of ethnic tensions; Papua is no exception in this regard (see Aspinall and Fealy 2003; McGibbon 2004b, 2006). On the one hand, the debate between Papuan supporters and opponents of the division of the province has led to conflicts among Papua's many tribal and regional groups. On the other hand, special autonomy has deepened the rift between Papuans and non-Papuan migrants. Under the law, the province's indigenous inhabitants gained an opportunity to serve in government posts once staffed by non-Papuans. Governors, mayors, and district officers received access to larger budgets, thanks to the fact that the lion's share of tax revenues from resource extraction in Papua now supposedly remains in the province (see Tebay n.d.).[6] Yet reports of widespread corruption and competition for the spoils have soured the taste of freedom this new control over local affairs has afforded. It is not surprising to hear Papuans, like other Indonesians, complaining that decentralization has spawned a slew of "little Suhartos": figures deploying the same mixture of coercion, provocation, and patronage through which the former president ruled.

Papuan activists in support of what they call "full sovereignty and independence" have had little good to say about either policy. If anything, they are more dismissive of the "sell-outs" who have supported—and benefited from—the granting of special autonomy than they are of those who have backed the central government's attempt to divide and rule (see McGibbon 2004a). Critics of special autonomy point to the fact that the law has done little to change conditions on the ground (see Mote 2010). The situation in West Papua contrasts with that in Aceh, where, in the wake of the tsunami, which turned international attention to the troubled province, separatist leaders reached an agreement with Indonesia's central government that led not only to amnesty and the right to compete in regional elections for the Free Aceh Movement (Gerakan Aceh Merdeka, GAM) but also to the withdrawal of Indonesian troops from the province (International Crisis Group 2006b, 2008; Siegel 2010: 97–115). In Papua, the military remains entrenched, whether or not troop levels have grown.

These issues would have been on the mind of those who met on a sports field in Jayapura in 2004 to raise the West Papuan flag. These issues would also be on the mind of a well-informed viewer watching the 2008 YouTube video of Karma's speech, to which I turn now. A Papuan exile living in Oxford or an Australian scholar who has followed Papua's woes would no doubt recognize the setting. The scene is a soccer field in Abepura, a town close to Jayapura that houses several seminaries and the provincial university. There are goal posts in the distance beyond the fifty or so people visible to the handheld camera. These people are standing or squatting in a half circle; most are young Papuan men, although there are a few young women as well. One young man has a woven tote bag adorned with the Morning Star flag slung over his shoulder; another is wearing a baseball cap. Many of those on hand look like students. At the center of the frame is a middle-aged Papuan man, dressed in a tan civil service uniform; for his part, he looks like a typical "big foreigner," as Biaks would put it, save for certain key details: his bushy afro and braided beard, typical of men who have pledged not to shave or cut their hair until Papua is free, and the tag clipped to his shirt, which features the Morning Star flag. This is Filep Karma, five years after the Biak flag raising that brought him renown.

As we will see, Karma also orates like a typical big foreigner, with all the skill that my fieldwork in Biak has led me to expect of such a leader (see Rutherford 2003). One must watch as well as listen to the video carefully to capture the appeal of Karma's slippery pronouns and the "spirit" that fills his supporters when they imagine their world through another's eyes. One must pay heed to what Karma does with language—a language of gestures as well as of words—to capture how Karma transports the Papuans gathered around him into other settings and invites them to stand in other shoes. Several features of Karma's speech come to the fore in my analysis: (1) Karma's use of reported speech to call to mind outside audiences; (2) Karma's use of gesture to create a boundary between "there" and "here"; (3) Karma's use of repetition to foreground ethnic and national identities; (4) Karma's use of dialect, including Papuan versions of Indonesian personal pronouns, to create an incongruous affinity between West Papuans and outsiders who slip from seeing the Papuans' suffering to becoming Papuans themselves. The video gives us an opportunity to track a Papuan audience's reactions to these rhetorical moves.

Karma takes the stage with a call and response chant—

Karma: Papua!
Crowd: Free!
Karma: Papua!
Crowd: Free!
Karma: Papua!
Crowd: Free!

Then he switches gears to deal with logistical matters. The organizers have taken a collection—of the same sort taken in Papuan churches—and Karma offers some remarks as he turns the money over to the "servants of God" who have just led the group in worship. It is "God's right" to receive these contributions, Karma points out, and so it is only right for us to turn the money over to the pastors. Two portly men in white shirts step forward; smiling awkwardly, they raise their hands in a gesture of refusal; the sound track captures one pastor saying to the man trying to hand him the bundle of bills, "Save it for food and drink." The assembled men and women applaud this familiar ritual; like the churchgoers I knew on Biak, they seem to be enjoying this moment when their collective generosity is on display. The fact that the pastors insisted on returning the donations to the organizers for the benefit of the movement also goes over well. Karma takes the pastors' magnanimity as an occasion to launch into the next item on the agenda: his speech.

Karma: That's right . . . These guys [Indonesian: *dorang*] of ours spoke the truth a minute ago. They are faithful shepherds. Such a shepherd will say, "Before killing my sheep, kill me first." And in church at the pulpit, he or she will pray for the OPM Armed Forces [TNP-OPM] in the forest. Because the OPM Armed Forces are also his sheep. So, if there is a servant of God or a pastor who is afraid to pray at the pulpit for the OPM Armed Forces and only prays for the Indonesia Republic and its institutions, then we must ask, what is the status of his stewardship?

Someone in the crowd begins to clap; someone else softly shouts something. Karma, who is pacing as he speaks, turns. A serious look comes over his face.

Karma: Because God doesn't differentiate. God says "tend all the sheep." As for the sheep, there are some that are naughty, there are others that are not. We also have to consider the naughty ones. Naughty through whose eyeglasses? If we're seeing through Indonesian eyeglasses, maybe those of us gathered here are naughty sheep. But through Papuan eyeglasses, now, this is right.

A young man in a baseball cap nods; more people applaud.

Karma: But through God's eyeglasses, these are all His children. There are evil children, those that take others' wealth. These exist. But there are also children who suffer because their wealth is stolen. There you have it.

Karma turns; his face relaxes. Bringing his hands together, he moves on to the next topic.

In these opening remarks, Karma has already conjured a multiplicity of audiences to witness the event of his speech and the flag raising that would follow it. He has used rhetorical devices—the call and response cheer, the ritualized surrender of the offering—to fashion the individuals standing around him into a collective: a group of fans cheering the home team, a congregation gathered in church. (Later, these individuals will congeal into a dancing and singing group of celebrants hoisting long sticks into the air as they circle the flagpole, in a highland-Papuan-style dance.) At the same time, he has pointed to other possible observers: the Indonesian government, the broader Papuan public, and God. In the language of eyewear, Karma has referred to the varied perspectives that these observers might take on the demonstration. Now he turns to the core concern of his address: race, ethnicity, and the movement, which Karma also examines through different pairs of eyeglasses. Karma's approach to the matter differs from that demonstrated by the Papuan People's Assembly (MRP) a year after the flag raising. During the run-up to the gubernatorial election in Papua in November 2005, the MRP disqualified two candidates for lieutenant governor on the basis of not only of their parentage but also of their physical traits: their lack of "black skin and frizzy hair" (International Crisis Group 2006a, 9; see also Aspinall 2006). Karma, as we will see, proposes a far more nuanced approach to the substance of Papuan identity.

> Karma: Very good. Now. My friends . . . I also need to share some remarks with you about this. Our [*kitorang*] struggle today is being observed. We've already informed our friends on Java, and these friends already know everything. We [*kitorang*] are shouting "Freedom!" But on Java, someone with straight hair, an authentic Javanese, also cares about us. And so, over there, he or she is also shouting "Free Papua!" And this guy, at the moment Indonesia is seizing people to kill them . . . "Friend [*Sobat*], come here!" [Karma quotes the imagined Papuans calling out to this Javanese friend.] So what kind of person is this? That's right!

Karma nods emphatically as he asks this rhetorical question. People in the audience smile, murmur, and clap.

It is worth taking note of several features of Karma's performance in this section of the speech. Throughout the speech, Karma uses hand gestures to track a trajectory between "here"—in Papua—and variously defined and evaluated "theres." In general, when Karma speaks of Indonesia, he points toward the horizon behind his left shoulder; when he speaks of America and the world at large, he points toward the horizon behind his right shoulder. Since Karma uses his right hand, the first gesture is more awkward than the second; it forces him to reach across his chest. But in this section of the speech, which portrays the movement's Javanese friends, Karma breaks this rule: he points toward the horizon behind his right shoulder—the good horizon associated with the movement's Western allies. This indexical gesture and the one that follows give force to Karma's words. After pointing "there," Karma points back "here" to the ground at his feet. The sports field where Karma is standing was the scene of shootings in July 1998 when students demonstrated for independence in Abepura (see chapter 5). Likewise, to break up the 2004 flag raising, the security forces moved in. Many viewers watching Karma's speech on YouTube would recall both episodes of state violence. Karma is literally pointing at a place where human rights violations had occurred in the past and where, as it happened, they were about to occur again.

It is also worth taking note of Karma's voicing. Throughout this book, I have dwelt on the dialogic character of discourse: the haunting of our words by other's spectral voices, which we replicate or reply to in everything we say (see Bakhtin 1981; see also Vološinov 1986 [1973]). In this passage, and throughout his entire speech, Karma brings this haunting to the fore through his repeated use of reported speech. Particularly interesting is Karma's use of personal pronouns. Karma speaks in the Papuan dialect of Indonesia. In addition to the cadence commonly used in the province when friends gather to swap stories, Karma uses the colloquial terms for "he," *dorang*—roughly translated as "that guy" or "those guys"—and "we, *kitorang*—roughly "we guys"—as well as the vaguely folksy *sobat*, "comrade" or "friend." Karma speaks in this register, but he also, as we will see, represents it as the language of the many real or imagined non-Papuans whom he quotes.

Karma: And so, in order that we . . . Here, this is what I mean. We in the local environment, we should not always think that [the supporters of] Papuan freedom [*Papua Merdeka*] are only those of us who live here, those with frizzy hair and black skin. Rather, we need to open our minds to the idea that those who struggle for Papuan freedom are also people with straight hair, authentic Mena-donese people or authentic Javanese. Such a person sees, he has a conscious, he sees that this is not just, this is not right. Until he also shouts, "This is not right! Give the Papuans' rights back to them! Let them enjoy them! Enough already! That's the Papuans' prerogative!"

Karma stands with one hand pointing at the ground, and the other on his heart as he describes what compels the straight-haired people to struggle for Papuan freedom. The crowd murmurs as he closes with a nod and an emphatic, "That's right! This exists!"

In this passage, Karma portrays a hypothetical non-Papuan sympathizer using the Papuan version of the third-person possessive—*dia punya*—"that he has"—rather than the standard Indonesian construction—*-nya*. He also depicts a common Papuan expletive—*Sudah!* "Enough already!"—coming from the mouth of this "authentic" straight-haired Menadonese or Javanese person who can't help but shout, having been touched by what he or she has seen. This voicing is striking, given local stereotypes of these ethnic groups' speech styles. Papuans describe the Menadonese and Ja-vanese as "refined" (*halus*) and evasive—as speakers unlikely boldly to express an opinion, desire, or demand. In Karma's speech, the outsider who acts as an audience to the Papuans' troubles goes on boldly to attract an audience of his or her own. Significantly, he or she does this by shout-ing in a Papuan dialect. This slippage in identity is what comes of being touched: the Menadonese or Javanese with a conscience sympathizes—in-deed, identifies in terms of dialect—with those whose suffering he or she sees.

> Karma: When we were imprisoned, they also called. One called the governor. "Why is he jailed?" Now, they united with us. Or they sent news to the world.

Karma gathers his hands together when he says "joined in" and gestures to the right horizon when he says "to the world."

> Karma: "So, let's struggle for Papuan freedom for our younger siblings, so that we can all be prosperous people." Because up until now, this has been the decid-ing factor: Papua's wealth has been stolen and managed on Java.

This time, Karma reaches across his chest to the left horizon—the bad "elsewhere" that is this thieving version of Java.

In this phrase, there is a slippage between reported speech and assertion. "Hey let's struggle" is what the sympathetic Javanese or Menadonese
would say to the world. But Karma seemingly speaks in his own voice in
asserting that the "deciding factor" in Papua's troubles lies in the theft of
Papua's wealth.

> Karma: So we demonstrated in 1998 demanding independence. Those guys
> [*dorang*, presumably referring to members of the central government] were
> scared and said, "Hey, let's give you a little bit to eat over here." That little bit,
> our friends who are officials, they have eaten most of it of late. This is true. A
> person with frizzy hair. But he or she has a heart that is more Indonesian. More
> Indonesian.

Karma's rhetoric gains force through repetition; later passages in the
speech will echo and expand on the rhythm evident here. Beginning with
Karma's opening chant, what is repeated in many of these instances are
national and ethnic labels. These fall into a series whose starting point is
the "Papua" that will be "free." Karma's use of repetition invites listeners
to focus on and anticipate further references to ethnic and national identities. This strategy heightens the impact of other moments in Karma's
speech when he depicts the slipperiness of such identities: a change in
viewpoint can bring a change in dialect and even citizenship, as we will see.
These comments meet with the strongest reaction so far from the crowd.
People mutter, "It's too much!" and "Yes, the governor!" Attracted by the
chatter, the camera pans across the onlookers, before returning to Karma,
who is building up to a crescendo.

> Karma: So, when we are shouting that politics is the same as curly hair, we need
> to think again. That's my point!

The camera alights on Yusak Pakage, Karma's co-organizer, who is seated
on the ground. Karma goes on.

> Karma: So that we can enjoy great enough support. I'll give you an example.
> We can look at Brazil. When these guys play soccer, are they all black? Or are
> they all white? "Okay, you move to America!" [Karma imitates white and black
> Brazilians exiling one another.] No. "We are all Brazilian. We are all equally
> Brazilians." So you can imagine [Papuans saying] "Come on. All of us here
> are Papuan. So you have straight hair, what counts is that you shout for a free

Papua. So why don't you unite with us? It's okay if you are scared, then what's important is that you generate lots of big news for the newspapers, say, or maybe campaign to the outside world?" Like that.

This passage features more repetition: "all Brazilian . . . all equally Brazilian." Karma uses the Papuan word *kah* ("say" or "maybe") in the dialogue that he imagines future Papuans having with one another across the boundaries of race. This expression functions both as a question mark and a gentle critique. Karma both describes what he would like his listeners to imagine themselves saying in the future and says it, here and now. In the next passage, Karma also slips between discursive positions, this time to layer his own voice over the voice of the world.

> Karma: Because it is like this. The world is watching now. If we only think about race, sometimes these guys won't support us.

Karma points toward the ground and then pulls back his hand as he describes the world withdrawing its support.

> Karma: Because these guys are afraid that there will be killings. Take Africa. There are free nation-states, but one tribe kills another tribe. Another tribe kills yet another tribe. Now, we in Papua don't want this. There are 250 Papuan tribes. Do we want to be free just to kill each other?

In this passage, Karma speaks strategically, sketching out the image that will give the Papuan freedom movement the greatest possible traction among outsiders. His remarks allude to the relationship between audience and sovereignty at a time when international actors claim the authority to build others' nations and change others' regimes. But at the same time, he also speaks substantively about the free Papua he would like to see come into being. We don't want to look like Africa—and we don't want to be like Africa—he tells his listeners, not simply because this resemblance will damage our international reputation, but also because we Papuans wouldn't want to live in this kind of liberated place. The freedom of liberation, *merdeka*, should not lead to another kind of freedom, known in Indonesian as *kebebasan*, the license to do whatever one wants to do. Karma invites his supporters to imagine a scenario in which the world assesses the legitimacy of the Papuan struggle by viewing it through eyeglasses that Karma describes, and then dons. In a moment, Karma will take this gesture further: the Papuans themselves will assess the legitimacy of the world's claims. In other words, the Papuans will exercise the sovereign power to decide which nations deserve sovereignty and which do not.

> Karma: Later say, say it's like now. Someone from one tribe becomes the leader, then all the officials end up belonging to his tribe.

Remarks and laughter come from the crowd.

> Karma: It's true!!!

Louder laughter.

> Karma: And this isn't good. It's not good. It's not good. It's not good.

Karma's repetitive rhythm gains intensity; the audience responds with laughter. There are more remarks; someone mentions Sorong, the homeland of the governor serving at the time. Karma reacts to the comment.

> Karma: I'm sorry, but don't say Sorong because there are people from Sorong, Sorong people also want Papuan freedom.

Murmurs from the crowd.

> Karma: That's just certain elements [Indonesian: *oknum*]. Guys who put their own self-interest first. So, say, I get appointed so I appoint my father's younger brother, my son-in-law; I give all these relatives jobs as officials. Only this is not good behavior. So in order for Papua really to be free, let's not have a Biak president and only Biak ministers.

Louder laughter and catcalls from the onlookers; Karma's hypothetical situation is amusing, since Karma is himself a Biak and would no doubt be in the running for the position of president should Papua gain independence.

> Karma: That's no good. So, one guy rises . . . here's what I see. [We've got] a guy from Wamena. "Hey, why don't you take this position? Hey, [guy from] Paniai! Hey, [guy from] Serui! Hey, [guy from] Ayamaru! Whoever! Let's all sit together, manage things together." So the Papuan nation-state can prosper.

Here Karma is quoting a hypothetical Papuan president, calling out to individuals from several of Papua's major highland and coastal ethnic groups and inviting them to join his cabinet.

> Karma: So now we can learn from Indonesia's experience. I went to Jakarta, I asked a guy, "Sir, until now those who most frequently become president, who are they?" "Javanese." "And the ministers, most of them are which kind of people?" "Javanese." "And what about the beggars on the street, who are they?" "Javanese."

Karma speaks in a singsong tone. "Javanese," "Javanese," "Javanese." By the third repetition, the onlookers are laughing and clapping.

> Karma: They can't help those who are right before their eyes, then they promise special autonomy to benefit people way over there? That's bullshit.

More laughter and applause from the audience.

> Karma: That's trickery. Trickery, trickery. You should help the one right before your eyes to eat, you should give him or her food, give him or her clothing, give him or her a house. Welfare. Only after that should you promise [to help] those far away, only then can we work [for the distant people's benefit]. So, enough already. Special autonomy is enormous bullshit. The division of the province, it's all bullshit. What's true is Papuan freedom. Only that. What counts: Papuan freedom.

Still more repetition: trickery, trickery, trickery; bullshit, bullshit, Papuan freedom, Papuan freedom. Loud applause erupts from the crowd.

Moving from Karma's rhetoric to his theme, the crowd's warm reaction to this part of Karma's speech makes perfect sense; the most striking political rift in 2004 divided Papuans in favor of giving special autonomy a chance from those who took a hard line on independence. A group formed in the aftermath of the crackdown that followed the Papuan National Congress of 2000, the Papuan Customary Council (Dewan Adat Papua), expressed the sentiment of many Papuans in a demonstration held on August 12, 2005, in which it "symbolically handed Special Autonomy back to the central government" (International Crisis Group 2006a, 6–7). Karma has dismissed special autonomy not by way of an analysis of what is happening in West Papua—despite his earlier reference to corruption in the "local environment"—but by offering an account of a distant encounter. He quotes his own words and the words of a person who tells it like it is: who admits that the Javanese can't get their own house in order, as it were, let alone help the Papuans do the same for theirs. Papua goes from being "here"—the ground before Karma's feet—to being "far away"—the distant elsewhere to which Javanese leaders should turn only after the needy Javanese in their immediate proximity have been helped.

This conjuring of the view from a distant space segues seamlessly into the conjuring of the view from a future time. In the next section of the speech, Karma provides a new way of thinking about the relationship between "here" and "there" by portraying how Papuans will someday exercise the authority to inscribe or erase such distinctions. This section addresses a key function of a Papuan sovereignty-to-come: the naturalization—and denaturalization—of Papuan citizens.

> Karma: Also, in the future, this is what I'm envisioning. Later, Papua will not just be the Biak tribe, the Ayamaru, whatever, right? Among the people of the Papuan nation one will find straight hair and frizzy hair. Someone might be a Makassarese. But he or she will be a Papuan. Someone might be a person from Menado. But he or she will be a Papuan. Someone might be a person from Java. A Papuan.

> Say later, someone tries to become a Papuan citizen but is acting as a spy for Indonesia. "Friend [*Sobat*], I apologize. Here's the revocation of your Papuan citizenship. Here's your ticket home. If you want to follow Indonesia, then you should go home already."

This passage parallels Karma's earlier quotation, in which he imitates a Papuan calling for help from a straight-haired person from Java. Instead of "Friend, come here!" Karma has this Papuan say "Friend, go home!" Again, Karma's hand gestures distinguish between the good horizon— the one on the right—and the bad one—the one on the left. He reaches across his chest to point to the "there" to which the Indonesian spy must retreat. The men and women watching Karma nod, laugh, and even hoot with pleasure as Karma's image of the future takes shape. Pleasure fills their faces as Karma continues in a similar vein, expanding the reach of Papuan citizenship across the seas.

> Karma: So tomorrow, in the future, we the Papuan nation will consist of all kinds of ethnicities. Canadian ethnicity, American ethnicity, whatever. "I'm

happy to work for Papua; I want to be a Papuan national citizen." "Let's do it, friend [*sobat*]; you can become one. What counts is that you are really serious. Because if you become a spy, if you sell information to America, you'll go home to America over there."

Breaking the pattern described above, Karma points to the right horizon as he quotes a Papuan telling the American traitor to go home.

> Karma: Why? Who owns the Freeport mine?
> Crowd: America.
> Karma: America.

Karma invites the audience to respond then repeats its answer, "America." His voice rises in anger.

> Karma: Every day America watches Indonesia kill Amungme and Kamoro before his eyes. And America doesn't yell [for the Papuans'] rights. And America doesn't yell for rights. They look over at [Muslims?] way over there and make a stink about that. America is also a big cheater. It watched Suharto kill us and was silent. Because it saw Suharto do all this, but it had its mine . . .

The video ends.

Many of the ingredients of the struggle discussed in the preceding chapters make an appearance in this video: the role of the church and the transcendent audience to which it appeals for legitimacy; the hopes pinned to a watching world; the sovereignty attributed to a future Papua that will blur, but not erase the lines dividing there and here, them and us. As Karma's speech unfolds, the Papuan nation slides into a sovereign position. What were the "world's" assumptions about the proper role of race in the struggle become Karma's and "ours." The free Papuans will ultimately decide who gains admission to the Papuan nation on the basis of these assumptions. These future Papuans will divide the "naughty" audiences from the good ones. They will decide which onlookers are spies who merely act as though they were joining the Papuan nation, and which are friends who see this nation suffer, shout for its freedom, and slip into the struggle they observe. Given western New Guinea's troubled history, it is no accident that "America" is the final candidate for West Papuan citizenship named.

Significantly, the video holds clues to the appeal of this imaginative nationalist discourse. Members of the crowd show clear signs of possessing *semangat* or "spirit": enthusiasm, excitement, and confidence in their ability to act. There are two moments in the speech when the crowd erupts in laughter. The first occurs when Karma makes fun of tribalism using Biak as an example; he says what everyone is thinking, diagnosing a tendency that few Papuans can avoid indulging, whether or not they openly accuse their leaders of this crime. (Karma's comments on nepotism may have seemed particularly delicious, given that he himself is the son of a prominent official and could well owe his government position to this fact.) But the other moment occurs when Karma depicts a future in which Papuans enjoy a particularly vivid kind of sovereignty: the right to decide where the Papuan "we" begins and ends. The crowd's reaction reflects the pleasure and potency the onlookers take in envisioning this aspect of Papuan freedom. What the MRP was designed to do in a limited fashion—to decide who is Papuan enough to accede to high office—the free Papuans will do on a grand scale. Unlike the MRP, in deciding whom to admit to their nation, the Papuans will avoid racial criteria seen as anathema to the outside world. Karma allows his listeners to imagine what their movement might look like from the perspective of those in a position to pass judgment on its legitimacy. He invites them to imagine joining an audience with the power to determine the Papuans' fate.

Even more strikingly, Karma allows his listeners to overhear what members of this audience sound like when they speak. As I have suggested, the dialect that Karma uses when he quotes these audience members anticipates how close the identification between Papuans and these outsiders will turn out to be. Even when Karma is repeating the words of hypothetical Javanese or American sympathizers, he speaks in a Papuan dialect. Those listening to Karma slip between local and foreign "we's" yet remain on familiar ground. Instead of shifting among clearly defined alternatives, listeners can hear multiple voices in Karma's words. When powerful outsiders talk, they sound like Papuans. The language of rational critical debate is the Papuans' own tongue. Recall my argument in the previous chapter. The incongruity is amusing, but it is also uplifting for people all too often deemed incapable of speaking for themselves.

For YouTube viewers who happen on the video, Karma's speech invites overhearing and identification on yet another level. Such viewers would experience Karma's speech at a remove that in part realizes his dream: the movement has indeed been uploaded and made available to the world. But there are limits to the video's impact. Karma's speech is directed inward—literally to a circle of supporters acquainted not only with the issues Karma addresses but also with the registers and dialects Karma deploys. Karma speaks informally, in the first person, albeit in a first person whose location slips across the horizon to a distant elsewhere and someday. YouTube viewers can appreciate Karma's virtuosity only to the degree that they can place themselves in these supporters' shoes. The next video is directed outward, even if it inspires the same sense of *semangat* or "spiritedness" as that enjoyed by the Papuans on hand for Karma's speech. What Karma does through his oratorical artistry, this video does by other means: both fall into the same cultural aesthetic or groove. *The Obama Song for West-Papua* appeals to Papuan nationalists—and those whose support they seek to win—by offering a slippery and sometimes distressing mixture of images and sounds.

"Yes We Can"

In the future West Papua that Filep Karma sketched for his supporters, an American who works for Papua can become a Papuan citizen. In *The Obama Song for West-Papua*, a suitable candidate for such an honor makes an appearance: Barack Obama, then a presidential candidate, now president of the United States, whose victory inspired West Papuans no less than it did others around the world.[7] The United States presidential campaign coincided with local elections in Papua. Homemade Obama posters, copied from the Internet, adorned houses in Jayapura, and candidates for public office designed logos that resembled Obama's. An Obama Fan Club in Jayapura celebrated Obama's victory with a vehicle parade, much like those held by Indonesian political parties during election season. The convoy included a truck carrying a huge poster of Obama and a sound system that blared Papuan music and a cheer: "Long live Barack Obama, Long live black skin, Long live Papua, Long live Melanesia, Yes We Can" (KPKC Sinode GKI 2009). Malaikat007 ("Angel007"), who posted the *Obama Song for West-Papua* in February 2008, used the sound track from will.i.am's widely circulated *Obama Song* music video, which debuted on YouTube two weeks earlier (2008a). The work of an artist whose very name showcases a slippery pronoun, will.i.am's version features an array of celebrities, black, white, and brown, male and female, who are pictured singing or reciting stirring words from one of Obama's campaign speeches in near unison with the candidate.[8] The Papuan version keeps the heterophonic voices—voices that coincide without blending—but replaces the black-and-white footage with colored images relevant to the West Papuan struggle. The outcome is a pastiche of sounds and images, some perfectly matched, others strangely juxtaposed, that forces the slippery "we" of Obama's motto, "Yes We Can," to slide in a direction that presents Obama both as an audience and as a partisan to the West Papuan cause.

In doing so, the video reveals how passions born of the sense that others are watching have helped to sustain the quest for West Papuan sovereignty. The lion's share of the images—and the ones that jar most uncomfortably with Obama's uplifting words—depict victims of human rights violations: sad reminders of the "bare life" that analysts following Giorgio Agamben (1998) have identified as the target and hostage of sovereignty. For outsiders watching the video, these images cannot help but disturb. For Papuans watching the video and imagining outsiders doing the same, these images carry a different charge, as we will see. Some Papuan viewers would recognize the victims and recall the infractions that led to their suffering: from participating in a peaceful protest to engaging in armed acts of insurrection to simply being in the wrong place at the wrong time. This background knowledge would enable them to view the images as evidence of the arbitrary nature of Indonesian violence: whatever a Papuan does to fall afoul of the authorities, the sad result is always the same. This reading could lead to despair—to the conclusion, "no, we can't"—but for the feeling of expansiveness born of such viewers' awareness of the virtually unlimited access afforded by the video's presence on YouTube. Such viewers would see these photographs as depicting not generic human subjects, but particular individuals: individuals to be remembered, mourned, and potentially redeemed by their entry onto the world stage. As Alan Klima (2002) makes clear in his discussion of photographed corpses in Thailand, we cannot grasp the significance of such gruesome documents without taking into account local perspectives on the fact and force of their global circulation. Through the circulation of photographs of Papuan victims, Papuan viewers come to imagine sharing not just perspectives but also sentiments with a widening circle of sympathetic outsiders, who, like the good Javanese described by Karma, join them in "shouting" for the Papuans to be free.

The video opens with an image of Obama making a speech; the still photograph, like most of the images shown in the video, is framed by a black field. "Change We Can Believe In" reads the placard on the podium where Obama stands. Under this campaign slogan, just beyond the border of the image, the video's producers have added a phrase in blue letters: "a free west-papua."

The photograph and phrase dissolve into an American flag. The music starts, and the American flag is replaced by a smaller image of the Morning Star flag, which appears at the bottom of the black field. Above it, quadrant by quadrant, the same photograph shown in the first frame appears on the screen. The words, "4 west-papua" appear in white letters just below the flag.

This image vanishes in its turn, and another appears on the left half of the frame: the cover of an edition of *The New Internationalist* featuring a head shot of a distressed Papuan woman. The magazine's cover reads "West Papua"; below the woman's face appears a quote: "We will be free."

The lyrics begin:

"It was a creed . . ." A head shot of Obama speaking appears on the right side of the frame, his face slightly turned so that he is looking at—in Karma's words, perhaps, "seeing"—the magazine cover (and the distressed Papuan woman) on the left side of the frame.

". . . written into the founding documents . . ." Obama and the magazine cover vanish. An image of an archival document fills the center of the frame. Superimposed on the document are words in light pink, which gradually deepen into a vivid red: "new york agreement" and, below it, "act of free choice."

"... that declared the destiny ..." On the word "destiny" the document vanishes, and a photograph of a bearded, bare-chested Papuan man appears in the center of the frame. He is seated on the ground, and it takes a minute to realize that he has a bayonet piercing his stomach. Three smiling Indonesian soldiers ring the man; it seems they are holding him up. One gradually realizes that the man is a corpse, put on display by his jubilant killers. The photograph shows the OPM leader, Yustinus Murip, who was killed in November 2003 a day after appearing on Australian television in an interview in which he called for the pursuit of Papuan independence through peaceful means.[9] Officers released his photograph to the Indonesian press as proof that the army had managed to hunt him down. Here, the image serves as proof of the destiny written into West Papua's founding documents: a destiny of torture and murder. The other grisly pictures that follow in the next frames—in jarring contrast to the uplifting rhetoric of Obama's speech—serve to bring home this point. Recalling Karma's speech, these images show us what those who have "come" to West Papua must "see" in order to feel moved to declare "It's not right."

What then appears next to the photograph of the dead OPM commander confirms this impression. Four flags appear lined up in a column with the Dutch flag on top, the American flag under it, the United Nations flag below the American flag, and the Indonesian flag on the bottom. The Dutch word, "schuldig" ("guilty") appears in white letters in a red box above the Dutch flag.

"... of a nation. Yes we can." A map of New Guinea and the surrounding region replaces the flags and grisly photograph. No national borders appear on the map; rather, we see only the names of cities: Jakarta, Jayapura, Port Moresby, and Canberra. The seas are greenish blue and the landmasses are white, except for the western half of New Guinea, which is vivid green. This is the nation and the focus, if not exclusive locus, of the "we" who "can."

"It was whispered by slaves ..." The map is replaced by a photograph of a shirtless Papuan man, his face swollen and bruised. He is seated on the ground; a red pool—his own blood?—stands before him.

"... and abolitionists ..." Another photograph of a torture victim appears in the middle of the frame. This man has been photographed from behind to reveal (or, rather, to document) a back covered with lacerations.

" . . . as they blazed a trail toward freedom." Yet another photograph of a torture victim, a young man with a mustache whose face is swollen and whose lips are red with blood.

"Yes we can." The same man pictured in the previous frame reappears now, but from a slightly different angle. A hand appears behind his head; is it holding him up? The swelling now looks like decomposition; this could be another corpse.

"It was sung by immigrants . . ." Another photograph in the same vein as the previous three shows a man with longer hair, lying face down.

" . . . as they struck out from distant shores and pioneers who pushed westward . . ." The top half of a corpse lies in a coffin lined in white. We see a person's arms reaching down to arrange the remains, which seem very decomposed. Like several of the other photographs, this one has appeared in other videos produced by West Papuan activists. This is a photograph of a local health worker who was killed amid allegations that he was sleeping with the wife of a local government official. His execution took place during a violent "sweeping operation" by the security forces in Wasior that started after Papuan guerillas, perhaps incited by the military themselves, staged an attack on a police post (Kirksey 2012).

" . . . against an unforgiving wilderness." A head shot of another victim appears; the face is red and bruised.

"Yes we can. It was the call of workers . . ." This photograph takes us back to the remains being laid out in a white lined coffin. The health workers have assembled more of the corpse.

" . . . who organized; women who reached for the ballots; a President who chose the moon as our new frontier . . ." Another photograph of decomposed body parts, in this case lying on a table. The same white-sleeved arms are at work. In this photograph, we arrive at what Agamben (1998) would call "bare life" in all its materiality. There is no way to tell, other than from context, that this flesh was once a person.

" . . . and a King who took us to the mountaintop . . ." Finally, we see a photograph of someone who is still alive, if badly injured: a man whose naked back is marred by a large, red hole—a bullet wound—in the middle of his shoulder blade. He holds the hand of a man in a short-sleeved white shirt.

"... and pointed the way to the Promised Land." A new series of photographs fill the frame. We see protesters wielding three West Papuan flags. The photograph has been trimmed, collage style, to create a border around their shouting faces and raised fists.

"Yes we can to justice and equality." If the content of the previous image moved closer to the spirit of Obama's speech, this image cites his words. The "we" shouting "yes" is anticipated in the cutout faces and fists of the protesters. As Obama and the heterophonic voices miming his words articulate the slippery pronoun, a stylized drawing of the scales of justice on a mustard yellow backdrop comes into view. The words, "justice" and "equality" appear in white as the words are spoken.

"Yes we can, Yes we can, Yes we can." The United Nations flag appears on top of the West Papuan flag. The words "free west-papua" appear in a yellow box on the bottom of the United Nations flag. The words "yes" then "we" then "can" appear in white boxes in succession, first on the left side of the flag, then on the right side of the flag as the voices pronounce them. Again, the image track and the voice track converge.

"Yes we can. Yes we can." Another image rapidly appears. We see a white poster with many images on it: the Dutch, United States, United Nations, and Indonesian flags are in a row on top. The United Nations seal is below them. A stylized drawing of a hand, with the finger pointing at the viewer in the fashion of an "Uncle Sam Wants You" poster appears in the middle of the seal. The words "act of free choice" appear in red under the hand. There are three large and one small blood stains under it. Below this, side by side, are the West Papuan flag and a map-logo of West Papua decorated like the flag, with a stylized bird of paradise in its center. Left justified, the words "west papua" appear in black. Here, the "hailing" implied in the name of the website is literal. The "you" of "YouTube" is rendered into a "we." "You," whose conscience causes you to feel for those you see, are reminded of what you have to shout about. The next frame channels this urge, while producing a figure of the powerful audience the video aims to attract.

"Yes we can. Yes we can. Yes we can." The poster vanishes from the center. An image of the dead OPM commander, now the same size as the poster, appears on the left, but with the words "stop the killing" in red within a white ribbon embossed below his chest.

"Yes we can." Right next to the image of the man with the bayonet in his stomach appears a photograph of Obama orating at a podium. (This is a different image than used earlier, there is much more black in the background.) Obama is smiling slightly and pointing for emphasis; but here it looks like he is pointing at the face of the dead man.

"Oh." A stop sign suddenly appears at the end of Obama's finger. The word "genocide" is written lightly in black below the word "stop." Obama sees, then he points, then he "shouts" for West Papuan freedom; he recruits a vague and powerful "we" to champion the West Papuan cause.

The video continues in this fashion until the *Obama Song* soundtrack is almost over. The Papuan version fades out following the words "nothing can stand in the way of the power of millions of voices calling for change," illustrated by a photograph of a long line of highland warriors, standing side by side, that sweeps across a highlands field. (Like the gruesome pictures of Papuan victims of human rights violations, this photograph, which portrays a large troop of OPM fighters, has appeared repeatedly in the advocacy literature, not to mention malaikat007's other postings.) There are more photographs of protesters, occasionally shot in West Papuan or Indonesian settings, but more frequently shown marching down what look like the cobblestone streets of European city centers. There are also some photographs showing OPM rebels conducting national rituals in their forest strongholds. Taken as a whole, the video tells in photographs, graphics, words, and song the same narrative that Karma portrayed in his speech, albeit with a somewhat more hopeful ending. Here is an America that sees dead Papuans and shouts—eloquently and beautifully—on Papua's behalf. Here is a "we" defined by a commitment to social justice that crosses geographic and racial boundaries. And here, even with the disturbing images of torture and death, is something of the playfulness that pervaded Karma's oratory. This playfulness is captured in the stop sign that sprouts from Obama's finger and in the objectification of political ideals, slogans, and events, which appear, like so many laundry labels or poetry magnets, as moveable scraps of text. A simultaneous kind of slipperiness comes to the fore by virtue of the medium's material traits. As images appear and vanish, slipping into and out of sync with the sound track, they conjure different audiences: American, Papuan, European, and Indonesian. We are not faced with alternatives, but rather with multiple viewpoints that blend together, jostling for attention within the same frame.

The appeal of this video, with its slippery pronouns, runs deep. When I spoke with two Papuan intellectuals about it, one offered a moving discussion of the purpose of the gruesome photographs of Papuan victims of Indonesian state terror. These images are not just disturbing; their presence in the video is exhilarating, saddening, angering, and yet strangely comforting. Posted on YouTube, the video gives the victims' friends and relatives—and Papuans more generally—a space where they can visit those whom they have lost. YouTube provides the Papuan dead with a final resting place: "a cemetery in technology, a cemetery in the world." In this cemetery, Papuans can imagine meeting outsiders paying their respects to their loved ones. "If God moves the world's heart, these pictures can touch these people's hearts." The images of "spirited" crowds that follow visually portray the outcome of this encounter. The world shelters the dead and is touched by their suffering. The outcome is redemptive. The world slips into the Papuans' struggle, feels the Papuans' pain, and shouts for Papua to be free.

The comments left by YouTube viewers regarding these and other videos promoting the struggle provide further evidence of the sentiments inspired by these productions. Caught up in the same cultural aesthetic or groove as that exemplified in the two videos I have analyzed, these consumers of Papuan media play with equally slippery signs, beginning with the tag lines with which they sign their remarks. Viewers respond emphatically, shouting in writing, as it were. "Nice speech . . . Keep the Spirit.!!!!! We West Papuans will be Free. Papua Merdeka!!!!!!!" says abrui about a video that sets an English-language poem celebrating the movement to string band music and scenic photographs of village life (YouTube 2009h). Viewers praise the videos for their production values, as did 1974papua in this Dutch-language comment on a video combining house music and flashy graphics: "Ik moet echt die showbiz van jou lenen broer. respect" ("I must borrow this showbiz from you, brother, respect") (YouTube 2009b). Another video by the same poster inspired a string of comments on how Indonesia always twisted the facts of history. An English-language comment on the Indonesian government's "bull' sit people" who were "always trying to make others versions story about West Papua" inspired Dirrenk17 to post the following remarks in the Papuan dialect of Indonesia: "Maen tong trus . . . Sampe kam(Indonesian) Mati semua, kaya bangsa Mesir!!!" ("Keep playing us . . . Until you(Indonesian) are all Dead, like the nation of Egypt!!!") (YouTube 2009a). The video, which juxtaposes the Indonesian flag and anthem with captions contesting Indonesia's territorial claims, moved these viewers to slip between English and Papuan dialect voices endorsing the filmmaker's assault on the Indonesian version of history. Dirrenk17 colloquial "we"—*tong*, short for *kitorang*—speaks back to a "you(Indonesian)," who faces a destruction as sure as that which befell the Egyptians who would not "let our people go" (see YouTube 2009a). These comments register the range of ways in which viewers can register a "spirited" response: from exclamation marks, parentheses, and expletives to praise for a video maker's technical artistry paired with applause for the Papuan cause.

The dream of West Papuan nationalism lives on in phenomena like these YouTube videos. This dream allows viewers to imagine that Papuan victims of Indonesian violence did not die in vain. The public to whom they speak is not large. Less than three thousand people have watched the *Obama Song for West-Papua*, despite the fact that it was featured in the *San Francisco Bay View*, a prominent black paper. Those who have watched the video of Filep Karma's speech number even fewer. Nonetheless, these productions, like the scores of others made available on YouTube, preserve a space where West Papuans and their supporters can enjoy a glimpse of freedom, and activists like those who produced these videos can imagine attracting the world's gaze. Despite the movement's effective insularity, these productions bear witness to the thrill of imagining that things could be otherwise and that a more expansive Papuan "we" could result.

Other Specters, Other Audiences?

If it were not for the horrific evidence of Indonesian state violence that the *Obama Song for West-Papua* pairs with Obama's words, it might be tempting to chuckle at the YouTube video. But the video is not simply a clever knock-off. The original's political efficacy springs from a similar source. Obama's "message," maintained with great discipline throughout the campaign, rested on the slipperiness of the very "we" into which the video invites Papuans and their supporters to slide. Recall Filep Karma's deft insinuation of Papuan dialect into the mouths of "straight-haired" speakers. The equally deft rhetoric of the presidential candidate accomplished a similar operation, if recent analyses are correct. Writing in *The New Yorker* shortly after Obama's victory, David Remnick (2008) quotes at length from a speech that Obama gave following his victory in the Iowa caucuses of 2008. Obama opposes a doubting "they" to the faithful "we" and "you" of his grassroots supporters. "They said our sights were set too high. . . . But on this January night, at this defining moment in history, you have done what the cynics said we couldn't do. . . . We are one people. And our time for change has come." Consider the slippage—"they" holds steady but "you" becomes "we" in the course of Obama's uplifting exhortation. Yet there is more at stake here, having to do with the history indexed by Obama's style of speech.

Remnick describes what he calls "an astounding rhetorical move."

> Obama calls on the familiar cadences and syntax of the black church. He gestures towards what everyone is thinking about—the launching of a campaign that could lead to the first African American president. "This was the moment when we tore down the barriers that have divided us for too long," he says. "When we rallied people of all"—wait for it—"parties and ages." The displacement is deft and effective. We know that he means racial barriers—we can *feel* it—but the invocation is more powerful for being unspoken. The key pronoun is always "we," or "us."

In making sense of Obama's election victory, one must not overlook the strategic value of this inclusive gesture; it contributed to the building of a broad coalition of voters convinced that, compared to a McCain presidency, an Obama presidency would serve their needs. In the same fashion, one must not overlook the strategic value of the inclusive gestures made in Filep Karma's speech, in the *Obama Song for West-Papua*, and indeed in the various performances and practices analyzed in this book. A struggle like the movement for West Papuan freedom has no chance of prevailing unless its proponents can attract the support of powerful outsiders. To attract this support, such proponents must present their case in a way that signals their movement's endorsement by the people whom they claim to represent. And yet, as I also hope that the essays in this volume have made clear, this strategy only works because it has a strong affective charge. "We feel it," writes Remnick, suggesting that those who listened to Obama found themselves seduced by forces not unlike those that seduce those who listen to Papuan leaders like Filep Karma or watch productions like the Papuan version of the Obama song. Non–African American listeners slide into the position of an American "we" by way of pronouns etched in the history of the civil rights struggle. Difference is not erased in this movement but inhabits the "we" in a spectral fashion. What "we" feel is an exhilarating passage through otherness to a new sense of self. The will.i.am video intensifies this feeling by adding sonic and visual layers: the video pulls the viewer into a scene where singing and speaking flow together and apart, where audience and orator remain distinguishable even as they merge.

In Filep Karma's rhetoric, an equally exhilarating passage occurs within an imagined scenario acted out by sympathetic Javanese who speak of themselves in the language of the Papuan "we." The *Obama Song for West-Papua* works toward the same aesthetic end using different means. Throughout this book—and indeed throughout all of my writings on Papua—I have attempted to make sense of how Biaks and other Papuans have derived a pleasurable sense of potency from encounters with the foreign, whether these encounters occur in the mode of raiding or of taking on the perspective of someone else. I have shown how, by slipping among perspectives, Papuans imagine imbuing others with their passions, turning their horror, sorrow, and anger into a source of hope. This phenomenon has political implications, I have insisted; it is responsible for the remarkable staying power of the dream of West Papuan freedom in difficult times. I certainly would not want to understate the significant differences between the US and West Papuan contexts, but neither would I want to exoticize the people and happenings described in this book. That "feeling" that Remnick describes is not alien to the "feeling" felt by my Papuan friends and consultants. Or, rather, the slippage between familiarity and difference felt in both cases strikes similar chords.

Beyond these aesthetic parallels, there are historical ties that bind Obama's campaign to the campaign to free West Papua. Papuan activists are as quick to stress these ties as they are to stress Obama's skin color, which they see as a source of hope to "black skins" all over the world. Obama's mother married an Indonesian whom she met at the University of Hawai'i following her divorce from Obama's Kenyan father. Although the marriage did not last, Obama's mother's entanglement with Indonesia persisted; trained as an anthropologist, she devoted much of her career to programs for Indonesian women. Obama spent part of his childhood in a neighborhood of Jakarta. He and his mother arrived in 1967 not long after Suharto came to power and just before the Act of Free Choice. As Obama recounts in his autobiography, *Dreams from My Father*, his mother's husband had been a mild-mannered student at the time of the coup and massacres of 1965 (see Obama 2004). The new regime forced students studying abroad to come home and sent some of them to jail; they sent Obama's mother's husband to West Irian, where he served in the Indonesian army for several years. Obama remembers his stepfather's hardened attitude toward life. The strong will always devour the week, he told the nine-year-old Obama: it is better to be strong. Obama also remembers his mother's reaction to the cynicism and corruption that prevailed during the New Order's infancy: it was during these years that she instilled in Obama a "sense of empathy" and regaled him with tales of African American heroes like Martin Luther King (Obama 2004, 66).

At this time, neither Obama nor his mother had a clear understanding of the tumultuous events that had just transpired in Indonesia. One cannot help but imagine the specters that would have haunted his Jakarta neighborhood a few short months after Suharto's rise to power. Villagers suffered in the killings, but they also participated in the killings: communities like Obama's neighborhood were literally filled with ghosts. Those of us familiar with West Papua's history can't help but fill in the blanks in Obama's stepfather's résumé: equally grim scenes of repression and violence would have unfolded before the mild-mannered student's eyes during his tour in newly annexed West Irian, where OPM rebels had just begun to fight Indonesian rule. Obama's mother's response to all this was less to essentialize or romanticize Obama's African heritage than to introduce a new imaginary audience to the scene. In the place of Obama's stepfather's moral compromises—understandable, if not forgivable in his increasingly estranged wife's eyes—Obama's mother presented her son with a vision of moral consistency. Obama was growing up Indonesian, and the heroes of the civil rights struggle served as an antidote to New Order models. Out of the multiple vectors that have added up to Obama's biography, one can trace a line from his campaign rhetoric to his childhood in Jakarta, and from his childhood in Jakarta to the political events that gave rise to the troubles in West Papua. In this sense, the producers of the *Obama Song for West-Papua* may not be wrong when they sketch out their own version of the "founding documents" referred to in the song. The history of Obama's appropriation of the rhetoric he deployed to such advantage in his campaign springs from multiple sources. These may well have included the New York Agreement and the Act of Free Choice.

Why should we care, John F. Kennedy's CIA advisor Robert Komer asked in 1962, about the tiny indigenous population of western New Guinea, scattered across " a thousand miles of cannibal land?" (Monbiot 2005; see also Pemberton 1987; Survival International 2005; Banivanua-Mar 2008; Kirksey 2012). In sketching out the uneasy relationship between sovereignty and audience in West Papua, I have offered a portrait of what some might take to be an anomaly: a case that is too unusual to challenge the norm. But I hope that I have provided reasons for attending to the history of this seemingly exotic place. Pronouns slip and audiences proliferate in political settings like the United States, where the pursuit of sovereignty may seem less quixotic than in West Papua, but is vexed in its own specific ways. The verdict is still out on Obama's presidency. But his election changed the world in significant ways. West Papuan nationalists no longer seem so utopian in their aspirations, now that we have seen what a slippery pronoun can do.

Epilogue

CHAPTER NINE

Beasts and Sovereigns

On June 21, 2008, the following posting, which was originally in Indonesian, appeared in the Papua Internal Forum (PIF), a newsgroup open by invitation to Papuans and their supporters around the world. It was attached to a news story from one of the wire services reporting that the United Nations head of nuclear inspections had threatened to resign if Israel attacked Iran:

> It's a catastrophe that the symptoms of war have made the power of the nuclear bomb transform the lives of us members of humanity on the face of this ephemeral earth. If we honestly and justly acknowledge that we are the creation of God the Almighty, then why do there have to be wars that cost the lives of thousands, even millions of innocent people around the world? The second commandment of the LORD God is "Love your neighbor as yourself." In theory all Christians believe and abide by this law, but in practice is it not like that because personal interest forces us to break the law and kill and eliminate the souls of our fellow humans without philanthropy?

Divine sovereignty should trump the human struggle for sovereignty that leads men to "kill and eliminate the souls of our fellow humans without philanthropy." The sentiment expressed would scarcely seem controversial, especially among Papuan readers accustomed to the scattering of references to Scripture within discussions of contemporary events. Yet controversial it proved to be.

> I'm happy to hear statements like this, but I'd be even happier if there were news that "if we within the nation here announced the establishment of a transitional Papuan government" there would be support from other nations and within less than twenty-four hours there would already be "peacekeeping" or

at the very least "there would be support for peaceful dialogue in which the United Nations, the Netherlands, and Indonesia would review the results of the Act of Free Choice of 1969 brokered by Scandinavia, etc." Let's try to do this right.

This Indonesian-language reaction seemed mild enough, and others chimed in. PIF subscribers should keep their eyes on the prize, as it were, and not worry about nuclear war and the fate of humanity when their own problems were more pressing. Contributors provided examples—what they called "proof"—of the publicity that the subscribers should strive for by providing links and attachments: to a letter to the Australian prime minister written by the leader of an Australian advocacy association and a website called "Grime and Reason" that used the case of West Papua as an illustration of the shortcomings of Western philosophy and political thought. But the bomb came in the form of a diatribe from the original posting's author. Rather than drawing his readers' attention to God and his higher law, this author criticized the critics for thinking that announcing establishment of a transitional government would be enough to free the Papuans. The author recalled his many years of armed struggle as an OPM leader to authorize his views. The OPM

> is the mother organization that represents all of the Papuan people and that has led and sponsored the full scope of the struggle for the national liberation of West Papua and bravely and boldly stood before the eyes of all the people of West Papua and before all the eyes of the people of the international world including those within the colonial government of Indonesia in Southeast Asia and the kangaroo government of Australia in the area of the South Pacific. . . . My West Papuan brothers and sisters are wrong to think that West Papua's independence and full sovereignty are going to come from outside the country/the international community; the military strength of the OPM/TPN is the determining factor in all areas of the national struggle to grasp total victory and get the Indonesian government to roll up its mats and go home.

The author referred to the OPM's recent operations in the highlands, which sparked a harsh response from Indonesian troops. "For that reason there is some attention from humanitarian groups around the world." It was an unexpected ending to a debate that this PIF contributor himself had begun with a plea for the equivalent of "Peace on Earth, Good Will to Men." But even within this posting, the ultimate locus of "supreme and absolute power" remained debatable. The OPM/TPN's "military strength" was "the determining factor in all areas of the national struggle." But the point of OPM/TPN violence was to provoke an Indonesian reaction that attracted the attention of the world's "humanitarian groups."

"The eyes of all the West Papuan people." "All the eyes of the people of the international world." In the preceding chapters, we have seen how officials, missionaries, and nationalists have staked their standing—and sometimes their lives—on their ability to catch all these eyes. But we have also seen something of the pleasure that comes from swimming in a sea of global communications, as these PIF subscribers do for hours every day. Papuan nationalists are scarcely alone in wanting wide exposure for their struggle. There are real stakes in a movement's ability to win global attention in an era when international institutions have taken on functions once reserved for nation-states. But as I hope the preceding essays have made clear, this situation is less novel than one might think. The uneasy relationship between sovereignty and audience has been there all along.

I have had to define sovereignty in general and stark terms in order to grasp this uneasy relationship. I have had to look for the pursuit of sovereignty in settings not usually considered "political," from mission stations to the newsletters of colonization societies, from Biak villages to the latest offerings on YouTube. Ironically, by associating sovereignty with supremacy, I have created space for the analysis of the roles that audiences come into play in these settings. The very notion of supremacy implies a relationship to others and a division of the indivisible power that thinkers like Bodin and Hobbes urged sovereigns to seek. In insisting that to speak of sovereignty is to speak of supremacy—of a potency above and beyond that of potential rivals—is not to belie, but rather, to get to the heart of what anthropologist Jessica Cattelino's Seminole consultants were talking about when they told her that sovereignty is the "right to 'make social decisions, cultural decisions: how to live'" (Cattelino 2008, 140). The fact that one sovereign enters into a contract with another does not necessarily diminish that sovereign's supremacy; that is, if this sovereign still sovereignly agrees to the contract's terms. There are multiple ways of asserting supremacy in the face of the interdependency that Cattelino rightly insists is an irreducible element of sovereignty as it is lived. One way might entail downplaying influences from extraneous forces in order to claim a monopoly on the forces that cause the would-be sovereign to act. Another way might entail positing these extraneous forces as all consuming and the would-be sovereign as the privileged conduit of powers from afar. Such is the way of asserting sovereignty that one sees in the Koreri movement, whose leaders claimed to embody the power of foreignness. Such is the way of asserting sovereignty that we also see in the less dramatic episodes of activism depicted in this book: episodes in which Papuan nationalists manage to redefine their situation by identifying with a perspective that trumps the Indonesian party line. Our first PIF contributor combines both these ways of asserting sovereignty. On the one hand, he claims that it is not the "international community," but the OPM, West Papua's armed "mother organization," that will bring West Papuans "independence and full sovereignty." On the other hand, he insists that the OPM's potency lies in its capacity to draw the world's gaze.

My insistence on the bonds that link sovereignty and audience has arisen from my long-standing attempt as an anthropologist to address the question of how people deal with difference, including the alterity that haunts and sustains every effort to inhabit a self. I began wrestling with this question in my first book on West Papua, *Raiding the Land of the Foreigners* (2003), and I have continued to wrestle with it in these essays. I refer to wrestling for a good reason: difference is not something that one can ever pin down. One is only left with its figures and traces, which come in various forms. In this book I have paid close heed to the figure of unseen watchers, but other figures of difference have made an appearance as well. The widespread opinion that West Papuans are not quite civilized, rational, and responsible enough to govern themselves has played an important role in New Guinea's history. In closing, I would like to reflect further on this aspect of the Papuan other whose imagined gaze, I have suggested, has fueled efforts to exert supreme and absolute power.

This reflection takes us back to an issue raised by George Orwell's short story, "Shooting an Elephant," which I discussed at the opening of this book. The short story's narrator is a colonial police official in Burma who finds himself forced to kill a domesticated elephant that has run wild through a village when an "immense crowd of natives" gathers around him and his rifle. In chapter 1, I devoted most of my attention to the human audiences confronted by the narrator: the natives, with their "two thousand wills pressing me forward, irresistibly," the Europeans of various stripes whom the narrator imagines reacting to what he has done. I said less about the pressure exerted by the suddenly docile elephant's gaze.

In *The Beast and the Sovereign*, a translation of the late philosopher Jacques Derrida's seminar held from 2001 to 2003, animals like this elephant loom, well, large (see Derrida 2009). Derrida took up the figures of beasts and bestiality that have populated discussions of sovereignty, from Aristotle to Agamben. The beast and the sovereign, Derrida noted, share certain traits. Both exist outside the law: the sovereign creates the law from a position that transcends it; the beast supposedly lacks language and reason and, hence, the capacity to commit crime. Derrida's discussion called into question the sheer division between the human and nonhuman that European treatments of politics and ethics have tended to presume. The classical Western definition of man depends on dichotomies that undergird social hierarchies: humans respond, animals react; humans have reason, animals have instinct, with primitives, women, and the lower classes appearing as relatively more animal in their traits. When we challenge these dichotomies, a new space opens for thinking about the relationship between the proliferation of audiences and the passions entailed in the pursuit of sovereignty, that incessant form of one-upmanship that Derrida saw as sovereignty's dynamic. A new space also opens for thinking about the encounter between would-be sovereigns and subjects, like the Papuans or the Papuans' God, deemed to stand either beyond or beneath the reach of the law.

On February 27, 2002, as part of this project, Derrida analyzed a poem by the early twentieth-century poet, D. H. Lawrence. "Snake" depicts an encounter with an animal that reveals the hidden affinities between the beast and the sovereign, while staging an encounter with an audience that breaks down the barriers that define humanity.

> A snake came to my water-trough
> On a hot, hot day, and I in pyjamas for the heat,
> To drink there.
>
> In the deep, strange-scented shade of the great dark carob-tree
> I came down the steps with my pitcher
> And must wait, must stand and wait, for there he was at the trough before me.

As Derrida points out, the poem opens with a scene of hospitality: the narrator defers to the snake, the first comer for whom he "must wait, must stand and wait." But the most interesting part of the poem for my purposes arrives in the next section, when the narrator is accosted by voices that challenge this imperative. The snake is "earth-brown, earth golden from the burning bowels of the earth," the narrator notes, "on the day of Sicilian July, with Etna smoking."

The voice of my education said to me
He must be killed,
For in Sicily the black, black snakes are innocent, the gold are venomous.
And voices in me said,
If you were a man
You would take a stick and break him now, and finish him off.

But must I confess how I liked him
How glad I was he had come like a guest in quiet, to drink at my water-trough
And depart peaceful, pacified, and thankless,
Into the burning bowels of this earth?

Was it cowardice, that I dared not kill him?
Was it perversity, that I longed to talk to him?
Was it humility, to feel so honoured?
I felt so honoured.

After describing how the snake "looked around like a god, unseeing, into the air, and slowly turned his head," the narrator describes a sudden change in his emotional state.

And as he put his head into that dreadful hole,
And as he slowly drew up, snake-easing his shoulders, and entered farther,
A sort of horror, a sort of protest against his withdrawing into that horrid
    black hole,
Deliberately going into the blackness, and slowly drawing himself after,
Overcame me now his back was turned.

The narrator threw a log at the snake, forcing him to withdraw "with un-dignified haste."

And immediately I regretted it.
I thought how paltry, how vulgar, what a mean act!
I despised myself and the voices of my accursed human education.
And I thought of the albatross,
And I wished he would come back, my snake.
For he seemed to me again like a king,
Like a king in exile, uncrowned in the underworld,
Now due to be crowned again.

And so, I missed my chance with one of the lords
Of life.
And I have something to expiate;
A pettiness.

Derrida's discussion of the poem focuses on an ethical question with political implications. The poem affirms an ethic of hospitality grounded in responsiveness to the other, which can be a figure as maximally different from the self as the snake is from the narrator. By the poem's end, this most lowly of animals has become a god, a king, and a lord of life, leading Derrida to ask, "are we going to reconstitute a logic of sovereignty, a scene of sovereignty, by simply displacing sovereignty from me to the other . . . or should the idea of sovereignty in general be contested here?" (2009, 244–45).[1] In the face of this difficult question, one thing is clear: passions born of all the others competing for his allegiance are what move the poem's narrator to act. Honored by the snake, the narrator nonetheless sees himself from the perspective of his "accursed human education"; caught between audiences, he is torn between reverence and fear. When the snake withdraws into the earth, the narrator, overcome by horror, throws the log. The narrator's violence follows a path I have described in this book. The blow falls at the moment when the snake's face no longer faces the narrator; this is when the voices of the narrator's human education drown out all the others. In striking the snake, the narrator does not simply obey his imagined human interlocutors; rather, he reacts in a visceral, almost automatic way to the shift in the conversation of gestures that occurs when the snake turns away. No longer an audience, this nonhuman witness no longer defines what counts as the ethical in this scene.

As the poem's final stanza makes clear, the narrator is immediately filled with remorse. Suddenly, what has just occurred appears as a crime. This is but another example of how the quest for sovereignty feeds off of encounters with multiple audiences; it is not in response to the other, but to the tension among a plurality of others, that blows fall and laws are formed. I cannot help but think of the disturbing, yet moving photographs from the *Obama Song for West-Papua* and the small sample of Papuan victims they portray. What Agamben calls "bare life" is the corpse of an audience. This corpse carries the memory of a point of view, a gaze registered and rejected, but available for revival, as when the narrator reconsiders his "mean act" in throwing the log at the snake. Derrida's question about sovereignty and difference returns to haunt us. Do we contest the very idea of sovereignty when we attend to the uneasy relationship between sovereignty and audience? Or is sovereignty just another word for the force that brings multiple audiences into view, for better or worse, compelling would-be sovereigns to act?

Ethnography is neither poetry nor fiction. Poetry and fiction may well provide us with a subtler sense of the dynamics I have tried to capture through more limited, empirically grounded means. Far less than the poet or fiction writer, let alone the philosopher or political theorist, do I enjoy a mandate to describe what sovereignty—or ethics—should be. Still, I hope this book's essays have offered a starting point for further reflection by tracing the effects, in a particular setting, of the uneasy relationship between sovereignty and audience. D. H. Lawrence's snake, George Orwell's elephant, and the primitive Papuan, not to mention that Biak ancestor, the Itchy Old Man: they all participate in this dimension of the real-world interdependencies that bedevil every quest for supreme and absolute power. If the poet or the ethnographer can imagine such figures, then those who seek sovereignty in this interconnected world should be able to, too. Dutch officials, Indonesian politicians, United Nations envoys, United States legislators, not to mention Papuan nationalists: they all should be able imagine others whose gaze disturbs familiar hierarchies, beings reduced to "bare life" who could in fact be "lords of life," audiences who may have a claim to sovereignty after all.

References

Aa, P. J. B. C. Robidé van der. 1879. *Reizen naar Nederlandsch Nieuw-Guinea ondernomen op last der Regeering van Nederlandsch-Indie in de jaren 1871, 1872, 1875–1876.* 's Gravenhage: Martinus Nijhoff.

Adas, Michael. 1987. *Prophets of Rebellion: Millenarian Protest Movements against the European Colonial Order.* Cambridge: Cambridge University Press.

———. 1989. *Machines as the Measure of Men: Science, Technology, and Ideologies of Western Dominance.* Ithaca, NY: Cornell University Press.

Adriani, Nicolaüs. 1916. "Het Christaniseeren eener Taal." *Elitheto Orgaan der Nederlandsche Studenten Vereeniging* 71 (December): 102–20.

Agamben, Giorgio. 1998. *Homo Sacer: Sovereign Power and Bare Life.* Translated by Daniel Heller-Roazen. Stanford, CA: Stanford University Press.

Agence France-Presse. 1998. "Jakarta Ready to Hold Dialogue on Irian Jaya: MP." October 19.

———. 1999. "Irian Jaya Man Jailed over Separatist Protest." January 31.

———. 2000. "Irian Jaya Congress Organisers Suspected of Treason." June 20.

Agha, Asif. 2007. *Language and Social Relations.* Cambridge: Cambridge University Press.

Althusser, Louis. 1971. "Ideology and Ideological State Apparatuses (Notes towards an Investigation)." In *Lenin and Philosophy.* London: New Left Books.

Alua, Agus. 2000. *Papua Barat dari Pankuan ke Pankuan: Suatu Ikhtisar Kronologis.* Seri Pendidikan Politik Papua no. 1. Jayapura: Sekretariat Presidium Dewan Papua/Biro Penelitian STFT Fajar Timur.

———. 2001. *Dialog Nasional Papua dan Indonesia, 26 Februari 1999: "Kembalikan Kedaulatan Rakyat Papua Barat, Pulang dan Renungkan Dulu."* Seri Pendidikan Politik Papua no. 2. Jayapura: Sekretariat Presidium Dewan Papua/Biro Penelitian STFT Fajar Timur.

———. 2002a. *MUBES Papua 2000, 23–26 Februari: "Jalan Sejarah, Jalan Kebenaran."* Seri Pendidikan Politik Papua no. 3. Jayapura: Sekretariat Presidium Dewan Papua/Biro Penelitian STFT Fajar Timur.

———. 2002b. *Kongres Papua 2000, 29 Mei–04 Juni: "Mari Kita Meluruskan Sejarah Papua Berat."* Seri Pendidikan Politik Papua no. 4. Jayapura: Sekretariat Presidium Dewan Papua/Biro Penelitian STFT Fajar Timur.

Amnesty International. 1991. "Indonesia: Continuing Human Rights Violations in Irian Jaya." Country Dossier ASA 21/06/91, Microform E151.

———. 1999. "Fear for Safety/Threats and Intimidation: Hermanus Wayol, Don Flassy, Workers at ELS-HAM, a Local Human Rights Organization." AI Index: ASA 21/16/99. March 9.

———. 2008a. "Indonesia: Investigate Police Shooting of Peaceful Papuan Protester." Amnesty International Public Statement. ASA21/017/2008. August 18. At http://www.amnesty.org/en/library/info/ASA21/017/2008/en.

———. 2008b. "Ill-treatment of Papuan prisoner must be investigated." Amnesty International Australia. September 26. At http://www.amnesty.org.au/news/comments/17815/.

———. 2008c. "Priority Cases: Filep Karma and Yusak Pakage, Prisoners of Conscience." Amnesty International. At http://www.amnestyusa.org/individuals-at-risk/priority-cases/filep-karma-and-yusak-pakage/page.do?id=1101238.

Andaya, Leonard Y. 1993. *The World of Maluku: Indonesia in the Early Indonesian Period.* Honolulu: University of Hawai'i Press.

Anderson, Benedict R. O'G. 1990 [1966]. "The Languages of Indonesian Politics." In *Language and Power: Exploring Political Cultures in Indonesia,* 123–51. Ithaca, NY: Cornell University Press.

———. 1990 [1972]. "The Idea of Power in Javanese Culture." In *Language and Power: Exploring Political Cultures in Indonesia,* 17–77. Ithaca, NY: Cornell University Press.

———. 1990. "Further Adventures of Charisma." In *Language and Power: Exploring Political Cultures in Indonesia,* 78–93. Ithaca, NY: Cornell University Press.

———. 1991. *Imagined Communities: Reflections on the Origins and Spread of Nationalism.* New York: Verso.

Anonymous. 1886. *Dojasi Ko Disen Sjoom faro Mansren Allah Roem Skola ro Farkoor ma Roemsi Kobena.* Andaij: De Johanna's Zending Pers.

———. 1887. *Dojasi Kiawer Kwaar ro Woois Woranda be Woois Noefoor.* 2nd ed. Andaij: De Johanna's Zending Pers.

———. 1995 [1898]. "Kort verslag omtrent de Afdeeling Noord Nieuw Guinea over de maand November." In *Topics Relating to Netherlands New Guinea in Ternate Residency Memoranda of Transfer and Other Assorted Documents.* Irian Jaya Source Materials No. 13, edited by Jeroen A. Overweel, 85–92. Leiden: DSALCUL/IRIS.

———. 1911. *Kakòfein ma Kakajik kuker Fàrkor,* 40. Batavia: Drukkerij Papyrus/H. M. van Dorp.

———. n.d. "Raport tentang Koreri." Unpublished manuscript. Files of F. C. Kamma, Hendrik Kraemer Institute, Oegstgeest, the Netherlands.

Aragon, Lorraine V. 2000. *Fields of the Lord: Animism, Christian Minorities, and State Development in Indonesia*. Honolulu: University of Hawai'i Press.

Asad, Talal. 1993. *Genealogies of Religion: Discipline and Reasons of Power in Christianity and Islam*. Baltimore: Johns Hopkins University Press.

Aspinall, Edward. 2006. "Selective Outrage and Unacknowledged Fantasies: Re-Thinking Papua, Indonesia, and Australia." Australia Policy Forum 06-15A. May 4. At http://www.globalcollab.org/Nautilus/australia/apsnet/policy-forum/2006/0615a-aspinall.html/. Accessed March 1, 2009.

Aspinall, Edward, and Greg Fealy. 2003. "Introduction: Decentralisation, Democratisation and the Rise of the Local." In *Local Power and Politics in Indonesia: Decentralisation and Democratisation*, edited by Edward Aspinall and Greg Fealy, 1–14. Singapore: Institute of Southeast Asian Studies.

Associated Press. 1998. "Activists Rally in Indonesian Region." July 4.

Astaga.com. 2000. "Makar, DPR Tolak Deklarasi Merdeka Papua." June 7.

Austin, J. L. 1976. *How to Do Things with Words*. London: Oxford University Press.

Baal, Jan van. 1989. *Ontglipt Verleden*. Vol. 2. Franeker: Van Wijnen.

Baaren, Theodorus Petrus van. 1968. *Korwars and Korwar Style: Art and Ancestor Worship in North-West New Guinea*. The Hague: Mouton.

Bakhtin, Mikhail M. 1981. "Discourse in the Novel." In *The Dialogic Imagination: Four Essays*, edited by Carl Emerson and Michael Holquist, translated by Michael Holquist, 259–422. Austin: University of Texas Press.

Ballard, Chris. 1997. "Irian Jaya." *The Contemporary Pacific* 9 (2): 468–74.

———. 2002a. "The Signature of Terror: Violence, Memory, and Landscape at Freeport." In *Inscribed Landscapes: Marking and Making Place*, edited by B. David and M. Wilson. Honolulu: University of Hawai'i Press.

———. 2002b. West Papua. *The Contemporary Pacific* 14 (2): 467–76.

Banivanua-Mar, Tracey. 2008. "'A Thousand Miles of Cannibal Lands': Imagining Away Genocide in the Re-Colonization of West Papua." *Journal of Genocide Research* 10 (4): 583–602.

Barker, Joshua. 1999. "Surveillance and Territoriality in Bandung." In *Figures of Criminality in Indonesia, the Philippines, and Colonial Vietnam*, edited by Vicente Rafael, 95–127. Ithaca, NY: Cornell Southeast Asia Program Publications.

———. 2001. "State of Fear: Controlling the Criminal Contagion in Suharto's New Order." In *Violence and the State in Indonesia*, edited by Benedict R. O'G. Anderson, 20–53. Ithaca, NY: Cornell Southeast Asia Program Publications.

Barkun, Michael. 1996. "Introduction: Understanding Millennialism." In *Millennialism and Violence*, edited by Michael Barkun, 1–9. London: F. Cass.

Bataille, Georges. 1987. *Eroticism*. Translated by M. Dalwood. London: Marion Boyars.

———. 1990. "Hegel, Death, and Sacrifice." In *On Bataille*, edited by Allan Stoekl, 9–28. Yale French Studies 78. New Haven, CT: Yale University.

————. 1991. *Consumption*. Vol. 1 of *The Accursed Share: An Essay on General Economy*. Translated by Robert Hurley. New York: Zone Books.

Bauman, Richard. 1983. *Let Your Words Be Few: Symbolism of Speaking and Silence among Seventeenth-Century Quakers*. Cambridge: Cambridge University Press.

Bauman, Richard, and Charles L. Briggs. 1990. "Poetics and Performance as Critical Perspectives on Language and Social Life." *Annual Review of Anthropology* 19: 59–88.

————. 2000. "Language Philosophy and Language Ideology: John Locke and Johan Gottfried Herder." In *Regimes of Language: Ideologies, Polities, and Identities*, edited by Paul V. Kroskrity, 139–204. Santa Fe, NM: School of American Research Press.

Becker, Alton. 1995. *Beyond Translation: Essays toward a Modern Philology*. Ann Arbor: University of Michigan Press.

Beekman, Elke. 1989. "Driekleur en Kruisbanier, De Utrechtsche Zendingsvereeniging op Nederlands Nieuw-Guinea, 1859–1919." PhD diss., Erasmus University.

Benjamin, Walter. 1968 [1923]. "The Task of the Translator: An Introduction to the Translation of Baudelaire's Tableaux Parisiens." In *Illuminations: Essays and Reflections*, edited by Hannah Arendt, translated by Harry Zohn, 69–82. New York: Schocken Books.

————. 1978 [1920–21]. "Critique of Violence." In *Reflections: Essays, Aphorisms, Autobiographical Writings*, edited by Peter Demetz, translated by Edmund Jephcott, 277–300. New York: Schocken Books.

Benveniste, Émile. 1971. *Problems in General Linguistics*. Coral Gables, FL: University of Miami Press.

Berg, G. W. H. van den. 1981. *Baalen Droefheid: Biak—Nederlands Nieuw-Guinea sche(r)tsenderwijs*. The Hague: Moesson.

Berlant, Lauren. 1991. *The Anatomy of National Fantasy: Hawthorne, Utopia, and Everyday Life*. Chicago: University of Chicago Press.

————. 1996. *The Queen of America Goes to Washington City: Essays on Sex and Citizenship*. Durham, NC: Duke University Press.

Bertrand, Jacques. 2007. "Papuan and Indonesian Nationalism: Can They Be Reconciled?" In *Dynamics of Conflict and Displacement in Papua, Indonesia*, edited by Eva-Lotta E. Hedman. Refugee Studies Centre Working Paper No. 42, 16–31. Department of International Development, University of Oxford.

Bestuur, Director Binnenlandsch. 1892. "Director Binnenlandsch Bestuur to the Governor-General 6-2-1892." Historische nota in Algemeene Rijksarchief. Col., vb. 8-12-1897 (33).

Bhabha, Homi. 1983. "The Other Question." *Screen* 24 (6): 18–36.

Blom-Hansen, Thomas, and Finn Stepputat. 2001. "Introduction: States of Imagination." In *States of Imagination: Ethnographic Explorations of the Postcolonial*

State, edited by Thomas Blom-Hansen and Finn Stepputat, 1–40. Durham, NC: Duke University Press.

———. 2006. "Sovereignty Revisited." *Annual Review of Anthropology* 35: 295–315.

Blussé, Leonard. 1986. *Strange Company: Chinese Settlers, Mestizo Women, and the Dutch in VOC Batavia.* Verhandelingen van het Koninklijk Instituut voor Taal-, en Volkenkunde, 122. Dordrecht: Foris Publications.

Bodin, Jean. 1992. *On Sovereignty.* Edited by Julian H. Franklin. Cambridge: Cambridge University Press.

Bohannon, Paul. 1955. "Some Principles of Exchange and Investment among the Tiv." *American Anthropologist* 57: 60–70.

Bonay, E. J. n.d. "Sejarah Kebangkitan Nasionalisme Papua" (A History of the Rise of Papuan Nationalism). Unpublished manuscript. Leiden: KITLV Historical Documents.

Bourdieu, Pierre. 1977 [1972]. *Outline of a Theory of Practice.* Translated by Richard Nice. Cambridge: Cambridge University Press.

———. 1981. *Language and Symbolic Power.* Edited and translated by John B. Thompson. Cambridge: Polity Press.

Bowen, John R. 1993. *Muslims through Discourse.* Princeton, NJ: Princeton University Press.

Brenneis, Donald. 1987. "Performing Passions: Aesthetics and Politics in an Occasionally Egalitarian Community." *American Ethnologist* 14 (2): 236–50.

Brenneis, Donald Lawrence, and Fred R. Myers, eds. 1984. *Dangerous Words: Language and Politics in the Pacific.* New York: New York University Press.

Brundige, Elizabeth, Winter King, Priyneha Vahali, Stephen Vladeck, and Xiang Yuan. 2004. "Indonesian Human Rights Abuses in West Papua: Application of the Law of Genocide to the History of Indonesian Control." A paper prepared for the Indonesian Human Rights Network by the Allard K. Lowenstein International Human Rights Clinic. Yale Law School. At http://www.law.yale .edu/documents/pdf/Intellectual_Life/West_Papua_final_report.pdf. Accessed March 9, 2009.

Bruyn Kops, G. F. de. 1850. "Bijdrage tot de kennis der Noord- en Oostkusten van Nieuw Guinea." *Natuurkundig Tijdschrift voor Nederlandsch Indië* 1: 164–235.

Bull, Malcolm. 1995. "On Making Ends Meet." In *Apocalypse Theory and the Ends of the World*, edited by Malcolm Bull, 1–17. Oxford: Oxford University Press.

Burridge, Kenelm. 1960. *Mambu: A Melanesian Millennium.* London: Methuen.

———. 1969. *New Heaven, New Earth: A Study of Millenarian Activities.* Oxford: Basil Blackwell.

Buset Foker LSM. 1998. "Perkembangan Kasus Irian Jaya." July 8.

Butt, Leslie. 2005. "'Lipstick Girls' and 'Fallen Women': AIDS and Conspiratorial Thinking in Papua, Indonesia." *Cultural Anthropology* 20 (3): 412–41.

Campo, Joseph Norbert Frans Marie à. 1986. "Een Maritiem BB: De Rol van de

Koninklijke Paketvaart Maatschappij in de integratie van de koloniale staat." In *Imperialisme in de Marge: De afronding van Nederlands-Indië*, edited by Jurrien van Goor, 12–78. Utrecht: Hes.

———. 2002. *Engines of Empire*. Hilversum: Verloren.

Cannell, Fenella. 1999. *Power and Intimacy in the Christian Philippines*. Cambridge: Cambridge University Press.

———. 2006. "Introduction: The Anthropology of Christianity." In *The Anthropology of Christianity*, edited by Fenella Cannell, 1–50. Durham, NC: Duke University Press.

Cannell, Fenella, ed. 2006. *The Anthropology of Christianity*. Durham, NC: Duke University Press.

Caton, Steven C. 2006. "What Is an 'Authorizing Discourse'?" In *Powers of the Secular: Talal Asad and His Interlocutors*, edited by David Scott and Charles Hirschkind. Stanford, CA: Stanford University Press.

Cattelino, Jessica R. 2008. *High Stakes: Florida Seminole Gaming and Sovereignty*. Durham, NC: Duke University Press.

Cenderawasih Pos. 1998a. P. 1. July 14.

———. 1998b. Pp. 1, 4. July 25.

———. 1998c. "Lagi Sembilan Mayat Ditemukan di Biak Timur." P. 1. July 29.

———. 1998d. "Masih Dalam Penyelidikan." P. 1. July 29.

———. 1998e . "Korban Tsunami PNG di Biak Ditemukan Mencapai 28 Orang." P. 1. August 1.

———. 2000. "Warung Papeda: Tutup Lobang deng Bae." P. 9. April 7.

Chatterjee, Partha. 1986. *Nationalist Thought and the Colonial World: A Derivative Discourse?* London: Zed Books.

Chauvel, Richard. 1998. "West New Guinea: Perceptions and Policies, Ethnicity and the Nation State." In *Australia in Asia: Episodes*, edited by Anthony Milner and Mary Quilty. Oxford: Oxford University Press.

———. 2005. *Constructing Papuan Nationalism: History, Ethnicity, Adaptation*. Policy Studies 14. Washington, DC: East-West Center Washington.

Chauvel, Richard, and Ikrar Nusa Bhakti. 2004. *The Papua Conflict: Jakarta's Perceptions and Policies*. Policy Studies 5. Washington, DC: East-West Center Washington.

Cheah, Pheng. 1999. "Spectral Nationality: The Living on [*sur-vie*] of the Postcolonial Nation in Neocolonial Globalization." *Boundary 2: A Journal of Postmodern Literature* 26 (3): 225–52.

Cheah, Pheng, and Suzanne Guerlac, eds. 2009. *Derrida and the Time of the Political*. Durham, NC: Duke University Press.

Clough, Patricia Ticineto. 2007. *The Affective Turn: Theorizing the Social*. Durham, NC: Duke University Press.

Cohen, Ted. 2008. *Thinking of Others: On the Talent for Metaphor*. Princeton, NJ: Princeton University Press.

Coleman, Simon. 2000. *The Globalisation of Charismatic Christianity: Spreading the Gospel of Prosperity*. Cambridge: Cambridge University Press.

Collins, James. 1996. "Socialization to Text: Structure and Contradiction in Schooled Literacy." In *Natural Histories of Discourse*, edited by Michael Silverstein and Greg Urban. Chicago: University of Chicago Press.

Comaroff, Jean. 2007. "Beyond Bare Life: AIDS, (Bio)Politics, and the Neoliberal Order." *Public Culture* 19 (1): 197–219.

Comaroff, Jean, and John Comaroff. 1991. *Of Revelation and Revolution: Christianity, Colonialism, and Consciousness in South Africa*. Vol. 1. Chicago: University of Chicago Press.

———. 2004a. "Criminal Justice, Cultural Justice: The Limits of Liberalism and the Pragmatics of Difference in the New South Africa." *American Ethnologist* 31 (2): 188–204.

———. 2004b "Criminal Obsessions, After Foucault: Postcoloniality, Policing, and the Metaphysics of Disorder." *Critical Inquiry* 30: 800–824.

———. 2006a. "Figuring Crime: Quantifacts and the Production of the Un/real." *Public Culture* 18 (1): 207–44.

Comaroff, Jean, and John Comaroff, eds. 2006b. *Law and Disorder in the Postcolony*. Chicago: University of Chicago Press.

Commissie voor Nieuw-Guinea. 1862. *Nieuw Guinea: Ethnographisch en Natuurkundig Onderzocht en Beschreven in 1858*. Uitgegeven door het Koninklijk Instituut voor Taal-, Land- en Volkenkunde van Nederlandsch Indie. Amsterdam: Frederik Muller.

Cooley, Charles Horton. 1983 [1922]. *Human Nature and the Social Order*. Piscataway, NJ: Transaction Publishers.

Couperus, Louis. 1921. *The Hidden Force: A Story of Modern Java*. Translated by Alexander de Mattos. New York: Dodd, Mead.

Daley, Paul. 2000. "Concern as Indonesia Dispatches Troops to West Papua." *The Age*, August 10. At http://www.hamline.edu/apakabar/basisdata/2000/08/10/0091 .html. Accessed January 22, 2011.

Davies, Matthew N. 2001. *Indonesian Security Responses to Resurgent Papuan Separatism*. Strategic Defence Studies Centre Working Paper No. 361. Melbourne: Strategic and Defence Studies Centre, Australian National University.

De Bruyn, Jan Victor. 1948. "Jaarverslagen 1947 en 1948 van Onderafdeling Biak." Nienhuis Collectie van de Department van Bevolkingszaken. Nummer Toegang 10–25, Stuk 188. The Hague: Algemeene Rijksarchief.

De Kolonist. 1933. 1 (1): 1.

Deleuze, Gilles. 1990. *The Logic of Sense*. Edited by Constantin V. Boundas. Translated by Mark Lester. New York: Colombia University Press.

———. 1994. *Difference and Repetition*. Translated by Paul Patton. New York: Columbia University Press.

Deleuze, Gilles, and Félix Guattari. 1987. *A Thousand Plateaus: Capitalism and*

Schizophrenia. Translated by Brian Massumi. Minneapolis: University of Minnesota Press.

Democracy Now. 2006. "Amy Goodman Recounts the East Timor Massacre Fifteen Years Ago." Democracy Now: The War and Peace Report. November 13. At http://www.democracynow.org/2006/11/13/amy_goodman_recounts_the_east_timor. Accessed July 7, 2010.

De Nieuw-Guineaer. 1930. "Toegepast historica." *De Nieuw-Guineaer* 1 (9): 4.

———. 1931a. "Het leven in de Papoea kampoeng Sam Sanggasse in Zuid Nieuw Guinea." *De Nieuw-Guineaer* 1 (11): 4.

———. 1931b. "Waar de landbouw bloeit, daar bloeit de staat." *De Nieuw-Guineaer* 1 (11): 13.

———. 1931c. "Communisme." *De Nieuw-Guineaer* 1 (11): 2.

———. 1931d. "Ondervinding meesteress." *De Nieuw-Guineaer* 1 (11): 4.

———. 1931e. "Eeuwige bezwaren." *De Nieuw-Guineaer* 1 (11): 9.

———. 1931f. "Een lied uit 1930." *De Nieuw-Guineaer* 2 (1): 6.

———. 1931g. "Waar de landbouw bloeit, daar bloeit de staat." *De Nieuw-Guineaer* 2 (1): 14.

———. 1931h. "De landbouw en andere mogelijkheden voor den Indo-Blijver." *De Nieuw-Guineaer* 2 (2): 3.

———. 1931i. "Verschilpunten tussschen de VKNG en SIKNG." *De Nieuw-Guineaer* 2 (2): 7.

———. 1931j. "Java en Nieuw-Guinea." *De Nieuw-Guineaer* 2 (3): 15.

———. 1931k. "Waarom associatie." *De Nieuw-Guineaer* 2 (4): 3–5.

———. 1931l. "Java en Nieuw-Guinea." *De Nieuw-Guineaer* 2 (5): 8.

———. 1931m. "De landbouw en andere mogelijkheden voor den Indo-Blijver." *De Nieuw-Guineaer* 2 (9): 5–6.

———. 1932a. "De Indo en de Agr. Zaken." *De Nieuw-Guineaer* 3 (3): 6.

———. 1932b. "Onze leidende principe." *De Nieuw-Guineaer* 3 (5): 14.

———. 1934. "Indo-Zionism." *De Nieuw-Guineaer* 5 (5): 4.

Derix, Jan. 1987. *Bapa Papoea: Jan P. K. Van Eechoud, Een Biografie*. Venlo: Van Spijk.

Derrida, Jacques. 1974. *Of Grammatology*. Translated by Alan Bass. Baltimore: Johns Hopkins University Press.

———. 1978a. "From Restricted to General Economy: A Hegelianism without Reserve." In *Writing and Difference*, translated by Gayatri Spivak, 251–77. Chicago: University of Chicago Press.

———. 1978b. *Spurs: Nietzsche's Styles*. Translated by Barbara Harlow. Chicago: University of Chicago Press.

———. 1981. *Dissemination*. Translated by Barbara Johnson. Chicago: University of Chicago Press.

———. 1982. "Signature, Event, Context." In *Margins of Philosophy*, translated by Samuel Weber, 307–30. Chicago: University of Chicago Press.

———. 1986. "Declarations of Independence." Translated by Thomas Keenan and T. Pepper. *New Political Science* 15: 11.

———. 1995. *The Gift of Death*. Translated by David Wills. Chicago: University of Chicago Press.

———. 1996. "Force of Law: the 'Mystical Foundations of Authority.'" In *Deconstruction and the Possibility of Justice*, edited by Drucilla Cornell, Michel Rosenfeld, and David Gray Carlson, 3–67. New York: Routledge.

———. 2005. *Rogues: Two Essay on Reason*. Translated by Pascale-Anne Brault and Michael Naas. Stanford, CA: Stanford University Press.

———. 2009. *The Beast and the Sovereign*. Translated by Geoffrey Bennington. Chicago: University of Chicago Press.

Dickinson, Jennifer A. 2007. "'Go [Expletive] a Girl for Me': Bivalent Meaning, Cultural Miscues, and Verbal Play in Ukrainian Migrant Labor Stories." *Journal of Linguistic Anthropology* 17 (2): 231–45.

Dirks, Nicholas B. 2006. *The Scandal of Empire: India and the Creation of Imperial Britain*. Cambridge, MA: Harvard University Press.

Djopari, John R. G. 1993. *Pemberontakan Organisasi Papua Merdeka*. Jakarta: Gramedia Widiasarana Indonesia.

Drooglever, Pieter. 1980. *De Vaderlandse Club, 1929–1942: Totoks en de Indische politiek*. Franeker: Wever.

———. 2005. *Een Daad van Vrije Keuze: De Papoea's van Westelijk Nieuw-Guinea en de Grenzen van het Zelfbeschikkingsrecht*. Den Haag: Instituut voor Nederlandse Geschiedenis.

———. 2009. *An Act of Free Choice: Decolonization and the Right to Self-Determination in West Papua*. Oxford: One World Publications.

Drooglever, Pieter, ed. 2008. "Papers Presented the Seminar on the Act of Free Choice." Held in the Hague November 15, 2005, on the occasion of the book launch of P. J. Drooglever, *Een Daad van Vrije Keuze: De Papoea's van Westelijk Nieuw-Guinea en de Grenzen van het Zelfbeschikkingsrecht* (An Act of Free Choice: The Papuans of Western New Guinea and the Limits of the Right to Self-Determination). The Hague: Institute of Netherlands History.

Duara, Prasenjit. 2003. *Sovereignty and Authenticity: Manchuku and the East Asian Modern*. Lanham, MD: Rowman and Littlefield.

Duranti, Alessandro. 1990. "Politics and Grammar: Agency in Samoan Political Discourse." *American Ethnologist* 17 (4): 646–66.

Durkheim, Émile. 1965 [1915]. *The Elementary Forms of the Religious Life*. Translated by Joseph Ward Swain. New York: Free Press.

Dutton, Tom. 1995. "Language Contact and Change in Melanesia." In *The Austronesians: Historical and Comparative Perspectives*, edited by Peter Bellwood et al., 207–9. Canberra: Australian National University.

Dutton, Tom, and Darrell Tryon, eds. 1994. *Language Contact and Change in the Austronesian World*. Berlin: Mouton de Gruyter.

Elisha, Omri. 2008. "Moral Ambitions of Grace: The Paradox of Compassion and Accountability in Evangelical Faith-Based Activism." *Cultural Anthropology* 23 (1): 154–89.

Ellen, R. F. 1986. "Conundrums about Panjandrums: On the Use of Titles in the Relations of Political Subordination in the Moluccas and along the Papuan Coast." *Indonesia* 41 (April): 47–62.

Elmberg, John-Erik. 1968. *Balance and Circulation: Aspects of Tradition and Change among the Mejprat of Irian Barat.* Stockholm: Ethnographical Museum.

ELS-HAM. 1999. "Nama Tanpa Pusara, Pusara Tanpa Nama: Laporan Pelanggaran HAM di Biak, Irian Jaya." Report from Lembaga Study dan Advokasi Hak Asasi Manusia (ELS-HAM). Jayapura, July 10.

———. 2003. "Semua Warga Biak yang Terlibat Separatis OPM Diancam Menyerah Sebelum Batas waktu yang Ditetapkan Berakhir." *Elsham News Report*, July 28.

Engelke, Matthew Eric. 2007. *A Problem of Presence: Beyond Scripture in an African Church.* Berkeley: University of California Press.

Engelke, Matthew Eric, and Matt Tomlinson, eds. 2006. *Limits of Meaning: Case Studies in the Anthropology of Christianity.* Oxford: Berghahn Books.

Engels, Friedrich, and Karl Marx. 1978. *The Marx-Engels Reader.* Edited by Robert Tucker. New York: W. W. Norton.

England, Vaudine. 2000a. "Fight for Dream of Freedom." *South China Morning Post*, August 13.

———. 2000b. "Symbolic Ritual Flagged for Trouble." *South China Morning Post*, August 13.

Engster, Daniel. 2001. *Divine Sovereignty: The Origins of Modern State Power.* DeKalb: Northern Illinois University Press.

Errington, Joseph. 1998a. "Indonesian('s) Development: On the State of a Language of State." In *Language Ideologies: Practice and Theory*, edited by B. Schieffelin, Kathryn A. Woolard, and Paul V. Kroskrity, 271–84. Oxford: Oxford University Press.

———. 1998b. *Shifting Languages: Interaction and Identity in Javanese Indonesia.* Cambridge: Cambridge University Press.

———. 2001. "Colonial Linguistics." *Annual Review of Anthropology* 30: 19–39.

Fanon, Frantz. 1967. *Black Skin, White Masks.* New York: Grove Press.

Fatie, John. n.d. "Obama, Papua dan Indonesia." Unpublished manuscript.

Fautngil, Christ, Frans Rumbrawer, and Bartolomeus Kainakaimu. 1994. *Sintaksis Bahasa Biak.* Jakarta: Pusat Pembinaan dan Pengembangan Bahasa, Departemen Pendidikan dan Kebudayaan.

Feld, Steven. 1988. "Aesthetics as Iconicity of Style, or 'Lift-up-over Sounding': Getting into the Kaluli Groove." *Yearbook for Traditional Music* 20: 74–113.

Feldman, Martha. 2007. *Opera and Sovereignty: Transforming Myths in Eighteenth-Century Italy.* Chicago: University of Chicago Press.

Fernandes, Clinton. 2006. *Reluctant Indonesians: Australia, Indonesia, and the Future of West Papua*. Melbourne: Scribe Short Books.

Feuilletau de Bruyn, W. K. H. 1916. Militaire Memorie der Schouten-eilande. August 31, 1916. Nummer Toegang 10–25, Stuk 183. Nienhuis Collectie van de Department van Bevolkszaken Hollandia Rapportenarchief. The Hague: Algemeene Rijksarchief.

———. 1920. *Schouten en Padaido-eilanden. Mededeelingen Encyclopaedisch Bureau* 21. Batavia: Javaasche Boekhandel.

———. 1933. "Economische ontwikkelingsmogelijkheiden van Noord-Nieuw-Guinea in het bijzonder door kolonisatie van Europeanen en Indo Europeanen." *Koloniale Studiën* 17: 514–39.

———. 1936–37. "De bevolking van Biak en het kolonisatievraagstuk van Noord Nieuw-Guinea." *Tijdschrift Nieuw-Guinea* 1 (1–6): 169–77.

———. 1947–48. "Boekbespreking: Het Noemfoorschen Woordenboek van J. L. en F. J. F. van Hasselt." *Tijdschrift Nieuw-Guinea* 8 (1–6): 189–90.

Firma de Acta de la Declaración de la Independencia de Venezuela. 1881. At es.wikisource.org/wiki/Firma_del_Acta_de_la_Declaraci%C3%B3n_de_ Independencia_de_Venezeula. Accessed July 3, 2006.

Fliegelman, Jay. 1993. *Declaring Independence: Jefferson, Natural Language, and the Culture of Performance*. Stanford, CA: Stanford University Press.

Foucault, Michel. 1979 [1975]. *Discipline and Punish: The Birth of the Prison*. Translated by Alan Sheridan. London: Penguin.

———. 1991. "Governmentality." In *The Foucault Effect: Studies in Governmentality*, edited by Graham Burchell, Colin Gordon, and Peter Miller. London: Harvester Wheatsheaf.

———. 1998 [1976]. *The Will to Knowledge*. Vol. 1 of *The History of Sexuality*. New York: Penguin.

Fraassen, Christian Frans van. 1987. "Ternate, de Molukken en de Indonesische Archipel." 2 vols. PhD diss., Leiden University.

Freud, Sigmund. 1960. *Jokes and Their Relation to the Unconscious*. Translated by James Strachey. New York: W. W. Norton.

———. 1963. *Sexuality and the Psychology of Love*. Edited by Philip Rieff. New York: Collier Books.

Furnivall, John S. 1939. *The Fashioning of Leviathan*. Reprinted from *The Burma Research Society Journal* 29 (1). Rangoon: Zabu Meitswe Pitaka Press.

———. 1944. *Netherlands India: A Study in the Plural Economy*. Cambridge: Cambridge University Press.

———. 1956 [1948]. *Colonial Policy and Practice*. New York: New York University Press.

Gal, Susan. 1998. "Multiplicity and Contention among Language Ideologies: A Commentary." In *Language Ideologies: Practice and Theory*, edited by Bambi B. Schieffelin, Kathryn A. Woolard, and Paul V. Kroskrity, 317–32. Oxford: Oxford University Press.

Galis, K. W. 1946. Dagboek over April 1946. Nummer Toegang 10–25, Stuk 179. Nienhuis Collectie van de Department van Bevolkingszaken Hollandia Rapportenarchief. The Hague: Algemeene Rijksarchief.

Garnaut, R., and C. Manning. 1974. *Irian Jaya: The Transformation of a Melanesian Economy*. Canberra: Australian National University Press.

Garrett, Paul B. 2004. "Language Contact and Contact Languages." In *Handbook of Linguistic Anthropology*, edited by Alessandro Duranti, 43–73. Oxford: Blackwell.

Gatra. 2008. "Tuntutan Papua Merdeka Berkurang." December 3.

Geertz, Clifford. 1973. "Religion as a Cultural System." In *The Interpretation of Cultures: Selected Essays*. New York: Basic Books.

———. 1981. *Negara: The Theater State in Nineteenth-Century Bali*. Princeton, NJ: Princeton University Press.

Geissler, J. G. 1870. *Bijbelsche Geschiedenissen van F.L. Zahn, vertaald in de Papoesch-Noefoorsche Taal (Faijasi rijo Refo Mansren Allah Bieda kiawer kwaar ro woos Woranda be woos Noefoor)*. Utrecht: Kemink en Zoon.

Gellner, Ernest. 1983. *Nations and Nationalism*. Ithaca, NY: Cornell University Press.

Generale Synode der Nederlandse Hervormde Kerk. 1956. Oproep van de Generale Synode der Nederlandse Hervormde Kerk tot bezinning op de verantwoordelijkheid van het Nederlandse volk inzake de vraagstukken rondom Nieuw-Guinea. No. 825.35/3690. June 27. The Hague.

Giay, Benny. 1986. *Kargoisme di Irian Jaya*. Sentani, Irian Jaya, Indonesia: Region Press.

———. 1995a. "The Conversion of Weakebo: A Big Man of the Me." *Journal of Pacific History* 34 (2): 181–90.

———. 1995b. *Zakheus Pakage and His Communities: Indigenous Religious Discourse, Socio-Political Resistance, and the Ethnohistory of the Me of Irian Jaya*. Amsterdam: Amsterdam University Press.

———. 2000. *Menuju Papua Baru: Beberapa pokok pikiran sekitar Emansipasi Orang Papua*. Jayapura: Deiyai/Elsham Papua.

Giay, Benny, and Jan A, Godschalk. 1993. "Cargoism in Irian Jaya Today." *Oceania* 63: 33–44.

Giay, Benny, and Yafet Kambai. 2003. *Yosepha Alomang: Pergulatan Seorang Perempuan Papua Melawan Penindasan*. Jayapura: Elsham Papua.

Goffman, Erving. 1981. "Footing." In *Forms of Talk*, 124–59. Philadelphia: University of Pennsylvania Press.

Golden, Brigham Montrose. 2003. "Political Millenarianism and the Economy of Conflict: Reflections on Papua by an Activist Anthropologist." *Asian Social Issues Forum*. At www.asiasource.org/asip/papua_golden.cfm. New York: The Asia Society.

Goor, Jurrien van., ed. 1986. *Imperialisme in de Marge: De Afronding van Nederlands-Indië*. Utrecht: Hes.

Gouda, Frances. 1993. "The Gendered Rhetoric of Colonialism and Anti-Colonialism in Twentieth-Century Indonesia." *Indonesia* 55 (April): 1–23.

———. 1995. *Dutch Culture Overseas: Colonial Practice in the Netherlands Indies, 1900–1942*. Amsterdam: University of Amsterdam Press.

Goudswaard, A. 1863. *De Papoewa's van de Geelvinksbaai*. Schiedam: H. A. M. Roelants.

Gow, Peter. 2006. "Forgetting Conversion: The Summer Institute of Linguistics Mission in the Piro Lived World." In *The Anthropology of Christianity*, edited by Fenella Cannell, 211–39. Durham, NC: Duke University Press.

Guardian Weekly. 1998. "Fishermen Find Bodies Off Indonesian Coast." P. 4. August 9.

Gunning, J. W. 1908. "De Beteekenis der Christelijke Zending voor onze Koloniën." In *Zending in Nederlandsch Indië*. Reprinted from *De Tijdspiegel* (November).

Habermas, Jürgen. 1991. *The Structural Transformation of the Public Sphere: An Inquiry into the Category of Bourgeois Society*. Translated by Thomas Burger. Cambridge, MA: MIT Press.

Hacking, Ian. 2006. "Making Up People." *London Review of Books*, August 17. At http://www.lrb.co.uk/v28/n16/hack01_.html. Accessed March 9, 2009.

Hadisumarta, Mgr. F. X., O. Carm. 2001. "Keuskupan Manokwari-Sorong Gerak dan Perkembangannya." In *Bercermin pada wajah-wajah keuskupan Gereja Katolik Indonesia*, edited by Dr. F. Hasto Rosariyanto. Yogyakarta, Indonesia: Kanisius.

Haenen, Paul. 1991. "Weefsels van Wederkerigheid: Sociale Structuur bij de Moi van Irian Jaya." PhD diss., Katholieke Universiteit van Nijmegen.

Haga, A. 1884. *Nederlandsch Nieuw Guinea en de Papoesche eilanden: Historische bijdrage*. 2 vols. Batavia: Bruining; 's Gravenhage: Nijhoff.

Handelingen Volksraad. 1931–32. Statement by Feuilletau de Bruyn. *Handelingen Volksraad*: 873, 1121.

———. 1935–36a. Statement by van Sandick, Chairman of the Vaderlandse Club Colonization Study Committee in the Netherlands. *Handelingen Volksraad*: 17.

———. 1935–36b. Statement by Roep, Member of the Politiek Economisch Verbond. *Handelingen Volksraad*: 62.

Hartweg, Friedrich. 1926. Letter to the Board of September 23, 1926. UZV K31, D12. Oegstgeest: Archives of the Hendrik Kraemer Institute.

———. 1927. Letter to the Board of February 7, 1927. UZV K31, D 12. Oegstgeest: Archives of the Hendrik Kraemer Institute.

Hasselt, F. J. F. van. 1900. *The Book in Which We Learn about Insulinde (Soerat ko farkoor ro Insulinde)*. Np.

———. 1905. *Spraakkunst der Nufoorsche Taal*. Den Haag: Martinus Nijhoff.

———. 1936–37. "Het Noemfoorsch als Eensheidstaal op het Noordwestelijk Deel van Nieuw Guinea." *Tijdschrift Nieuw-Guinea* 1 (1–6): 114–17.

————. n.d.a. "Geschiedenis van het Zendingsonderwijs op Noord-Nieuw-Guinea." SI: sn. pp. 43–57. Offprint in KITLV.

————. n.d.b. *Petrus Kafiar: Een Bladzijde uit de Nieuw-Guinea Zending.* Utrecht: Utrechtsche Zendings-Vereeniging.

Hasselt, J. L. van. 1868. *Allereerste Beginselen der Papoesch-Mefoorsche Taal.* Utrecht: Kemink and Zoon.

————. 1876. *Holland-Noefoorsch en Noefoorsch-Hollandsch Woordenboek.* Utrecht: Kemink and Zoon.

————. 1885. *Garra: Faija Kiawer ro Woranda be Woos Noefoor.* Andaij: Johanna's Zending Pers.

————. 1888. *Gedenkboek van een Vijf-en-Twintigjarig Zendelingsleven op Nieuw-Guinea (1862–1887).* Utrecht: Kemink and Zoon.

————. 1893. *Noefoorsch-Hollandsch Woordenboek.* 2nd ed. Utrecht: Kemink and Zoon.

————. 1909. *Nacht en Morgen: Herinneringen uit een Zendelingsleven op Nieuw-Guinea.* Utrecht: J. van Boekhoven.

Hasselt, J. L. van, and F. J. F. van Hasselt. 1947. *Noemfoorsch Woordenboek.* Amsterdam: J. H. de Bussy.

Hedman, Eva-Lotta E., ed. 2007. *Dynamics of Conflict and Displacement in Papua, Indonesia.* Refugee Studies Centre Working Paper No. 42. Department of International Development, University of Oxford.

Hegel, Georg Wilhelm Friedrich. 1977 [1807]. *The Phenomenology of Spirit.* Translated by A. V. Miller. Oxford: Oxford University Press.

Henderson, William. 1973. *West New Guinea: The Dispute and Its Settlement.* Seton Hall: Seton Hall University Press.

Herder, Johan Gottfried. 1966 [1772]. "Essay on the Origin of Language." In *On the Origin of Language: Jean-Jacques Rousseau, Essay on the Origin of languages; Johann Gottfried Herder, Essay on the Origin of Language,* translated by John H. Moran and Alexander Gode, 87–166. Chicago: University of Chicago Press.

Hernawan, J. Budi, and Theo van den Broek. 1998. "Dialog Nasional Papua: Sebuah Kisah 'Memoria Passionis.'" *Tifa Irian.* March 12. Internet posting March 25, 1998.

Hill, Hal, and Anna Weidermann. 1989. "Regional Development in Indonesia: Patterns and Issues." In *Unity and Diversity: Regional Economic Development in Indonesia since 1970,* edited by Hal Hill, 3–54. Oxford: Oxford University Press.

Hobbes, Thomas. 1986. *The Leviathan.* Edited by C. B. Macpherson. Middlesex: Penguin.

————. 1998 [1651]. *The Leviathan.* Edited by J. C. A. Gaskin. Oxford: Oxford University Press.

Hobsbawm, E. J. 1990. *Nations and Nationalism since 1780.* Cambridge: Cambridge University Press.

Hoffman, John. 1979. "A Foreign Investment: Indies Malay to 1901." *Indonesia* 27 (April): 65–92.

Honig, Bonnie. 1991. "Declarations of Independence: Arendt and Derrida on the Problems of Founding a Republic." *American Political Science Review* 85 (1): 97–113.

Hoskins, Janet. 1996. "Introduction: Headhunting as Practice and Trope." In *Headhunting and the Social Imagination in Southeast Asia*, edited by Janet Hoskins, 1–49. Stanford, CA: Stanford University Press.

Human Rights Watch. 1998a. "Indonesia Alert: Trouble in Irian Jaya," July 6.

———. 1998b. "Indonesia: Human Rights and Pro-Independence Actions in Irian Jaya." December.

———. 1998c. "Irian Jaya Detainees Denied Family Visits, Medical Care," July 9.

———. 2000. "Human Rights and Pro-Independence Actions in Papua, 1999–2000." May.

———. 2007. "Out of Sight: Endemic Abuse and Impunity in Papua's Central Highlands." *Human Rights Watch* 19, no. 10 (C). July.

Humphrey, Caroline. 2007. "Sovereignty." In *A Companion to the Anthropology of Politics*, edited by David Nugent and Joan Vincent, 418–36. Oxford: Blackwell.

IHRSTAD/ELS-HAM. 2000. "Mass Mobilisation to Defend the State Underway in West Papua." August 31.

Indonesian Observer. 2000a. "Gus Dur Hopeful of Halting Separatism." August 21.

———. 2000b. "Papua Leader Meets Police Summons." June 27.

Inside China. 1998. "Indonesian Church Groups: Two Shot Dead in Irian Jaya." July 10.

Inside Indonesia. 2007. "News Briefs." At http://insideindonesia.org/content/view/469/29/.

International Crisis Group. 2003. "Dividing Papua: How Not to Do It." *Asia Briefing* 24. April 9. At http://www.crisisgroup.org/home/index.cfm?l=1&id=1764.

———. 2006a. "The Dangers of Shutting Down Dialogue." *Asia Briefing* 47. March 23. At www.crisisgroup.org/home/index.cfm?id=4042.

———. 2006b. "Aceh: Now for the Hard Part." *Asia Briefing* 48. March 29.

———. 2006c. "Papua: Answers to Frequently Asked Questions." *Asia Briefing* 53. September 5.

———. 2007. "Indonesian Papua: A Local Perspective on the Conflict." *Asia Briefing* 66. July 19.

———. 2008. "Indonesia: Pre-Election Anxieties in Aceh." *Asia Briefing* 81. September 9.

Irvine, Judith. 1996. "Shadow Conversations: The Indeterminacy of Participant Roles." In *Natural Histories of Discourse*, edited by Michael Silverstein and Greg Urban, 131–59. Chicago: University of Chicago Press.

Irvine, Judith T., and Susan Gal. 1995. "The Boundaries of Languages and Disciplines: How Ideologies Construct Difference." *Social Research* 62 (4): 967–1001.

————. 2000. "Language Ideology and Linguistic Differentiation." In *Regimes of Language: Ideologies, Polities, and Identities*, edited by Paul V. Kroskrity, 35–84. Santa Fe, NM: School of American Research Press.

Ivy, Marilyn. 1995. *Discourses of the Vanishing: Modernity, Phantasm, Japan*. Chicago: University of Chicago Press.

Jakarta Post. 1998. "Irianese Want More Than Pledge of Dialog." January 23.

————. 1999. "Irianese Leaders Want Control of Their Land." February 27.

————. 2000a. "Government Adamant Irian Will Remain in Indonesia." June 6.

————. 2000b. "House Officially Rejects Irian's Independence." June 7.

————. 2000c. "Papuans Allowed to Hoist Morning Star Flag." June 8.

Jakobson, Roman. 1971. "Shifters, Verbal Categories, and the Russian Verb." In *Selected Writings*, vol. 2, 130–47. The Hague and Paris: Mouton.

Jourdan, Christine. 1991. "Pidgins and Creoles: The Blurring of Categories." *Annual Reviews in Anthropology* 20: 187–209.

Kabar Irian. 1999. "West Papuans Demanding for Free West Papua." February 17.

Kahin, Audrey R., ed. 1985. *Regional Dynamics of the Indonesian Revolution: Unity from Diversity*. Honolulu: University of Hawai'i Press.

Kahin, George McTurnan. 1952. *Nationalism and Revolution in Indonesia*. Ithaca, NY: Cornell University Press.

————. 2003. *Southeast Asia: A Testament*. London: Routledge Curzon.

Kamma, F. C. 1947–49. "De verhouding tussen Tidore en de Papoese eilanden in legende en historie." *Indonesië* (1): 361–70, 536–59; (2): 177–88, 256–75.

————. 1972. *Koreri: Messianic Movements in the Biak-Numfor Culture Area*. The Hague: Martinus Nijhoff.

————. 1976. *"Dit Wonderlijk Werk": Het Probleem van de Communicatie tussen Oost en West Gebaseerd op de Ervaringen in het Zendingswerk op Nieuw-Guinea (Irian Jaya) 1855–1972: Een Socio-missiologische Benadering*. Vol. 1. Oegstgeest: Raad voor de Zending der Nederlands Hervormde Kerk.

————. 1977. *"Dit Wonderlijk Werk": Het Probleem van de Communicatie tussen Oost en West Gebaseerd op de Ervaringen in het Zendingswerk op Nieuw-Guinea (Irian Jaya) 1855–1972: Een Socio-missiologische Benadering*. Vol. 2. Oegstgeest: Raad voor de Zending der Nederlands Hervormde Kerk.

————. n.d. *Pembangunan Djemaaat: Tentang Kepenatuaan*. Hollandia: Panitia Pembangunan Djemaat.

Keane, Webb. 1997. *Signs of Recognition: Powers and Hazards of Representation in an Indonesian Society*. Berkeley: University of California Press.

————. 2001. "Voice." In *Key Terms in Language and Culture*, edited by Alessandro Duranti, 268–71. Oxford: Blackwell.

————. 2007. *Christian Moderns: Freedom and Fetish in the Mission Encounter*. Berkeley: University of California Press.

Kelly, John D., and Martha Kaplan. 2001. *Represented Communities: Fiji and World Decolonization*. Chicago: University of Chicago Press.

Kermode, Frank. 1967. *The Sense of an Ending*. Oxford: Oxford University Press.

———. 1995. "Waiting for the End." In *Apocalypse Theory and the Ends of the World*, edited by Malcolm Bull, 250–63. Oxford: Oxford University Press.

Kern, H. 1916 [1886]. *Maleisch-Polynesische Taalvergelijking*. Vol. 4, part 1 of *Verspreide Geschriften*, 243–343. 's Gravenhage: Martinus Nijhoff.

———. 1917 [1885]. "Over de Verhouding van het Nufoorsch tot de Maleisch-Polynesische talen." Vol. 6, part 1 of *Verspreide Geschriften*, 37–76. 's Gravenhage: Martinus Nijhoff.

Kerr, Douglas. 2004. "In the Picture: Orwell, India and the BBC." *Literature and History* 13 (1). At http://www.netcharles.com/orwell/articles/bbc-orwell-india.htm. Accessed December 30, 2008.

Kierkegaard, Søren. 1983 [1843]. "Repetition." In *Fear and Trembling/Repetition*, edited and translated by Howard V. Hong and Edna H. Hong, 125–232. Princeton, NJ: Princeton University Press.

———. 1985 [1843]. *Fear and Trembling*. Translated by Alastair Hannay. London: Penguin.

———. 1992 [1846]. *Concluding Unscientific Postscript to Philosophical Fragments*. Translated by Howard V. Hong and Edna H. Hong. Princeton, NJ: Princeton University Press.

Kilvert, Andrew. 1999. "Irian Jaya Has a Dream: It May Become a Nightmare." *Sydney Morning Herald*, December 1.

King, Peter. 2002. "Morning Star Rising? Indonesia Raya and the New Papuan Nationalism." *Indonesia* 73 (April): 89–127.

———. 2004. *West Papua and Indonesia: Independence, Autonomy, or Chaos?* Sydney: University of New South Wales Press.

Kipp, Rita Smith. 1993. *Dissociated Identities: Ethnicity, Religion, and Class in an Indonesian Society*. Ann Arbor: University of Michigan Press.

Kirksey, Eben. 2012. *Freedom in Entangled Worlds*. Durham, NC: Duke University Press.

Kirsch, Stuart. 1996. "Refugees and Representation: Politics, Critical Discourse, and Ethnography along the New Guinea Border." In *Mainstream(s) and Margins: Cultural Politics in the 90s*, edited by Michael Morgan and Susan Leggett, 222–36. Westport, CT: Greenwood Press.

Klein, W. C. 1937. *Nieuw-Guinee*. 3 vols. Amsterdam: J. H. de Bussy.

Klima, Alan. 2002. *The Funeral Casino: Meditation, Massacre, and Exchange with the Dead in Thailand*. Princeton, NJ: Princeton University Press.

Klinken, Gerry van. 2001. "The Maluku Wars: Bringing Society Back." *Indonesia* 71 (April): 1–26.

Kompas Online. 1998. "Habibie Setuju Berdialog dengan Tokoh Irian Jaya." October 27.

———. 1999a. "President Habibie tentang Irian Jaya: Renungkan Lagi Tuntutan Kemerdekaan Itu." February 28.

————. 1992b. "Pemerintah Tolak Tuntutan Kemerdekaan Papua Barat." March 15.

Koopman, Joop W., and Arend H. Huusman. 2007. *Historical Dictionary of the Netherlands*. Plymouth: Scarecrow Press.

KPKC Sinode GKI. 2009. "Penggemar Obama Di Jayapura Konvoi Kendaraan." January 29.

Krohn-Hansen, Christian. 1994. "The Anthropology of Violent Interaction." *Journal of Anthropological Research* 50 (4): 367–81.

Kroskrity, Paul V. 2000. "Regimenting Languages: Language Ideological Perspectives." In *Regimes of Language: Ideologies, Polities, and Identities*, edited by Paul V. Kroskrity, 1–34. Santa Fe, NM: School of American Research Press.

Kulick, Don. 1992. *Language Shift and Cultural Reproduction: Socialization, Self, and Syncretism in a Papua New Guinean Village*. New York: Cambridge University Press.

La Biblioteca de las Culturas Hispánicas. 1810. Acta del 19 de Abril de 1810. At www.cervantesvirtual.com/servlet/SirveObras/04700741222647284199079/p0000001.htm#1_1. Accessed July 3, 2007.

Langeler, J. W., and L. A. C. M. Doorman. 1918. *Nieuw-Guinee en de exploratie der "Meervlakte": De Aarde en haar Volken*. Project Gutenberg e-Book. At http://www.gutenberg.org/files/20167/20167-h/20167-h.htm. Accessed January 24, 2011.

Lanternari, Vittorio. 1963. *The Religions of the Oppressed: A Study of Modern Messianic Cults*. London: MacGibbon and Kee.

Larkin, Emma. 2005. *Finding George Orwell in Burma*. London: Penguin.

Lawrence, Peter. 1971. *Road Belong Cargo*. Prospect Heights, IL: Waveland Press.

Leach, Edmund. 1983. "Melchisedech and the Emperor: Icons of Subversion and Orthodoxy." In *Structuralist Interpretation of Biblical Myth*, edited by Edmund Leach and D. Alan Aycock, 67–88. Cambridge: Cambridge University Press.

Lee, Benjamin. 1997. *Talking Heads: Language, Metalanguage, and the Semiotics of Subjectivity*. Durham, NC: Duke University Press.

Leith, Denise. 2003. *The Politics of Power: Freeport in Suharto's Indonesia*. Honolulu: University of Hawai'i Press.

Lev, Daniel. 1985. "Colonial Law and the Genesis of the Indonesian State." *Indonesia* 40 (October): 57–74.

Liddle, R. William. 2008. "Obama dan Reformasi Indonesia." *Kompas*. November 7.

Lijphart, Arend. 1966. *The Trauma of Decolonization: The Dutch and West New Guinea*. New Haven, CT: Yale University Press.

Liklikwakoe, P. n.d. "Tentang agama Koreri (Manseren)." Unpublished manuscript. Files of F. C. Kamma, Hendrik Kraemer Institute, Oegstgeest, the Netherlands.

Lindstrom, Lamont. 1984. "Big Men and the Conversational Marketplace of Tanna (Vanuatu)." *Ethnos* 53 (3–4): 159–89.

————. 1990. *Knowledge and Power in a South Pacific Society*. Washington, DC: Smithsonian Institution Press.

————. 1993. *Cargo Cult: Strange Stories of Desire from Melanesia and Beyond.* Honolulu: University of Hawai'i Press.

LiPuma, Edward. 2002. "Cultures of Circulation: The Imaginations of Modernity." *Public Culture* 14 (1): 191–213.

Locher-Scholten, Elsbeth. 1981. *Ethiek in Fragmenten: Vijf Studies over Koloniaal Denken en Doen van Nederlanders in de Indonesische Archipel, 1877–1942.* Utrecht: HES.

————. 1994. "Dutch Expansion in the Indonesian Archipelago around 1900 and the Imperialism Debate." *Journal of Southeast Asian Studies* 25 (1): 91–111.

————. 1998. "'So Close and Yet So Far': The Ambivalence of Dutch Colonial Rhetoric on Javanese Servants in Twentieth-Century Indonesia." In *Domesticating the Empire: Race, Gender, and Family Life in French and Dutch Colonialism*, edited by Julia Clancy Smith and Frances Gouda, 131–54. Charlottesville: University of Virginia Press.

Locke, John. 1993. *Political Writings.* Edited by David Wootton. Indianapolis: Hackett.

————. 1997 [1689]. *An Essay concerning Human Understanding.* Edited by Roger Woolhouse. London: Penguin.

Lomnitz, Claudio. 2000. "Nationalism as a Practical System: Benedict Anderson's Theory of Nationalism from the Vantage Point of Spanish America." In *The Other Mirror: Grand Theory through the Lens of Latin America*, edited by Miguel Angel Centeno and Fernando López-Alves, 329–59. Princeton, NJ: Princeton University Press.

Lorentz, H. A. n.d. *Eenige maanden onder de Papoea's.* Privately published edition dedicated to Prof. Dr. C. E. A. Wichmann, Leader of the New Guinea Expedition of 1903.

Madji, Alex. 2006. "MRP, Monster yang Menakutkan?" *Suara Pembaruan Daily,* January 16.

Maier, Hendrijk M. J. 1990. "Some Genealogical Remarks on the Emergence of Modern Malay Literature." *Journal of the Japan-Netherlands Institute* 2: 159–77.

————. 1993. "From Heteroglossia to Polyglossia: The Creation of Malay and Dutch in the Indies." *Indonesia* 56 (October): 37–65.

Malley, Michael S. 2003. "New Rules, Old Structures, and the Limits of Democratic Decentralization." In *Local Power and Politics in Indonesia: Decentralisation and Democratisation*, ed. Edward Aspinall and Greg Fealy, 102–18. Singapore: Institute of Southeast Asian Studies.

Manning, Chris, and Michael Rumbiak. 1989. "Irian Jaya: Economic Change, Migrants, and Indigenous Welfare." In *Unity and Diversity: Regional Economic Development in Indonesia since 1970*, edited by Hal Hill, 77–106. Oxford: Oxford University Press.

Markell, Patchen. 2003. *Bound by Recognition.* Princeton, NJ: Princeton University Press.

Marx, Karl. 1967. *Capital*. Vol. 1, *The Process of Capitalist Production*. Edited by
Frederick Engels. Translated by Samuel Moore and Edward Aveling. New
York: International Publishers.

Massumi, Brian. 2002. *Parables of the Virtual: Movement, Affect, Sensation*. Durham, NC: Duke University Press.

Mauss, Marcel. 1967. *The Gift: Forms and Functions of Exchange in Archaic Societies*. Translated by Ian Cunnison. New York: W. W. Norton.

Mazzarella, William. 2010. "The Myth of the Multitude, or, Who's Afraid of the
Crowd?" *Critical Inquiry* 36 (Summer): 697–727.

Mbembe, Achille. 2001. *On the Postcolony*. Berkeley: University of California
Press.

McDonald, Hamish. 2000. "Testing Time Ahead as Jakarta Tries to Pull Down
Papua Flag." *Sydney Morning Herald*, August 18.

McGibbon, Rodd. 2003. "Between Rights and Repression: The Politics of Special
Autonomy in Papua." In *Local Power and Politics in Indonesia: Decentralisa-
tion and Democratisation*, edited by Edward Aspinall and Greg Fealy, 194–216.
Singapore: Institute of Southeast Asian Studies.

———. 2004a. *Secessionist Challenges in Aceh and Papua: Is Special Autonomy the
Solution?* Policy Studies 10. Washington, DC: East-West Center Washington.

———. 2004b. *Plural Society in Peril: Migration, Economic Change, and the Papua
Conflict*. Policy Studies 13. Washington, DC: East-West Center Washington.

———. 2006. *Pitfalls of Papua: Understanding the Conflict and Its Place in
Australia-Indonesia Relations*. Lowy Institute Paper 13. Double Bay, New South
Wales, Australia: Lowry Institute for International Policy.

Mead, George Herbert. 1965. "Self." In *The Social Psychology of George Herbert Mead*, edited by Anselm Strauss, 199–246. Chicago: University of Chicago
Press.

Media Indonesia. 1999. "Irian Governor Calls for 'Special Autonomy.'" March 11.

Mehta, Uday. 1999. *Liberalism and Empire: A Study in Nineteenth-Century British
Liberal Thought*. Chicago: University of Chicago Press.

Mertz, Elizabeth. 1996. "Recontextualization as Socialization: Text and Pragmat-
ics in the Law School Classroom." In *Natural Histories of Discourse*, edited by
Michael Silverstein and Greg Urban, 229–52. Chicago: University of Chicago
Press.

Mewengkang, Jus F., MSC. 2001. "Arah Dasar Keuskupan Agung Merauke." In
Bercermin pada wajah-wajah keuskupan Gereja Katolik Indonesia, edited by
Dr. F. Hasto Rosariyanto. Yogyakarta, Indonesia: Kanisius.

Miedema, Jelle. 1984. *De Kebar 1855–1980: Sociale Structuur en Religie in de Vo-
gelkop van West-Nieuw-Guinea*. Verhandelingen van het Koninklijk Instituut
voor Taal-, Land- en Volkenkunde 105. Dordrecht: Foris Publications.

Mietzner, Marcus. 2003. "Business as Usual? The Indonesian Armed Forces and
Local Politics in the Post-Soeharto Era." In *Local Power and Politics in Indone-*

sia: Decentralisation and Democratisation, edited by Edward Aspinall and Greg Fealy, 245–58. Singapore: Institute of Southeast Asian Studies.

————. 2006. *The Politics of Military Reform in Post-Suharto Indonesia: Elite Conflict, Nationalism, and Institutional Resistance*. Policy Studies 23. Washington, DC: East-West Center Washington.

Milbank, John. 1990. *Theology and Social Theory: Beyond Secular Reason*. Oxford: Blackwell.

Ming, Hanneke. 1983. "Barracks Concubinage in the Indies." *Indonesia* 35 (April): 65–95.

Ministerie van Kolonien. 1959–62. Kabinet Gouverneur van Nederlands Nieuw-Guinea, Serie C, 1959–1962, ARA 2.10.36.13, inv. 17. Nationaal Archief, The Hague.

————. 1962a. Letter from Gouverneur Platteel to Bot. April 11, 1962. 2.10.2/361/2, Ministerie van Kolonien, inv. 5, folder 50. Nationaal Archief, The Hague.

————. 1962b. Letter from Si. Rumasew, Hollandia, to Tuan2 Ketua Partei Poloik DVP, PPM, March 8, 1962, Ministerie van Kolonien, inv. 19. Nationaal Archief, The Hague.

Mitchell, Timothy. 1988. *Colonizing Egypt*. Cambridge: Cambridge University Press.

Monbiot, George. 2005. "In Bed with the Killers: BP Is Working with a Genocidal Government." *The Guardian*. May 3. At http://www.arena.org.nz/wpbpoil.htm.

Mooiy, D. n.d. "Perhambatan Koreri." Unpublished manuscript. Files of F. C. Kamma, Hendrik Kraemer Institute, Oegstgeest, the Netherlands.

Morris, Rosalind. n.d. "'62, '73, '84: In the Groove of Nationalism, or Recordings on the Question of Belonging." Unpublished paper.

Mosse, G. L. 1985. *Nationalism and Sexuality: Middle-Class Morality and Sexual Norms in Modern Europe*. Madison: University of Wisconsin Press.

Mote, Octovianus. 2010. "Crimes against Humanity: When Will Indonesia's Military Be Held Accountable for Deliberate and Systematic Abuses in West Papua?" Testimony before US House Committee on Foreign Affairs. At http://foreignaffairs.house.gov/111/mot092210.pdf.

Mote, Octovianus, and Danilyn Rutherford. 2001. "From Irian Jaya to Papua: The Limits of Primordialism in Indonesia's Troubled East." *Indonesia* 72 (October): 115–40.

Mrazek, Rudolf. 1994. *Sjahrir: Politics and Exile in Indonesia*. Ithaca, NY: Cornell University Southeast Asia Program Publications.

Mühlhäusler, Peter. 1986. *Pidgin and Creole Linguistics*. Oxford: Blackwell.

Multatuli. 1987 [1860]. *Max Havelaar; Or, the Coffee Auctions of a Dutch Trading Company*. Translated by Roy Edwards. London: Penguin.

Nagel, Thomas. 1986. *The View from Nowhere*. New York: Oxford University Press.

Nederlandsch Indië. 1934. May 15: 1–6.

New York Times. 2008. "Barack Obama's New Hampshire Primary Speech." January 8. At http://www.nytimes.com/2008/01/08/us/politics/08text-obama.html?_r=1&pagewanted=all.

Nichols, Bill. 1983. "The Voice of Documentary." *Film Quarterly* 36 (3): 17–30.

Nieuwenhuys, Robert. 1982. *The Mirror of the Indies: A History of Dutch Colonial Literature*. Translated by Frans van Rosevelt. Amherst: University of Massachusetts Press.

Niezen, Ronald. 2003. *The Origins of Indigenism: Human Rights and the Politics of Identity*. Berkeley: University of California Press.

Nugent, David. 2007. "Governing States." In *A Companion to the Anthropology of Politics*, edited by David Nugent and Joan Vincent, 198–215. Oxford: Blackwell.

Obama, Barack. 2004. *Dreams from My Father: A Story of Race and Inheritance*. New York: Three Rivers Press.

———. 2006. *The Audacity of Hope: Thoughts on Reclaiming the American Dream*. New York: Three Rivers Press.

Office for Justice and Peace, Jayapura Diocese. 2000. "Description of Problems in Papua: Presentation by Catholic Church leaders in Papua in a personal meeting with President Abdurrahman Wahid Jakarta." Unpublished Internet posting. June 27.

Ong, Aihwa. 2006. *Neoliberalism as Exception: Mutations in Citizenship and Sovereignty*. Durham, NC: Duke University Press.

Ontwikkeling van en kolonisatie in Nieuw-Guinea. 1934. Rapport van de studiecommissie ingesteld door de Vaderlandsche Club in Nederland. The Hague.

Onze Toekomst. 1933. "De politieke tendenz in onze beweging." *Onze Toekomst* 6 (53): 2.

———. 1935a. *Onze Toekomst* 8 (15): 2.

———. 1935b. *Onze Toekomst* 8 (40): 1.

Orwell, George. 1950 [1936]. "Shooting an Elephant." In *Shooting an Elephant and Other Essays*. London: Secker and Warburg. At http://www.orwell.ru/library/articles/elephant/english/e_eleph. Accessed December 30, 2008.

———. 2003 [1942]. "Rudyard Kipling." In *The Complete Works of George-Orwell*. At http://www.george-orwell.org/Rudyard_Kipling/0.html. Accessed December 30, 2008.

Osborne, Robin. 1985. *Indonesia's Secret War: The Guerilla Struggle in Irian Jaya*. Sydney: Allen and Unwin.

———. 1986. "The OPM and the Quest for West Papuan Unity." In *Between Two Nations: The Indonesia–Papua New Guinea Border and West Papuan Nationalism*, edited by R. J. May, 49–64. Bathurst, Australia: Brown.

Overweel, Jeroen A., ed. 1995. *Topics Relating to Netherlands New Guinea in Ternate Residency Memoranda of Transfer and Other Assorted Documents*. Irian Jaya Source Materials No. 13. Leiden: DSALCUL/IRIS.

Oxford English Dictionary. 1991. *The Compact Oxford English Dictionary*. 2nd ed. Oxford: Oxford University Press.

Paczulla, Jutta. 2007. "'Talking to India': George Orwell's Work at the BBC, 1941–1943." *Canadian Journal of History*. At http://findarticles.com/p/articles/mi_qa3686/is_200704/ai_n19434996/print?tag=artBody;col1. Accessed December 30, 2008.

Paget, Roger K., ed. 1975. *Indonesia Accuses! Soekarno's Defense Oration in the Political Trial of 1930.* Kuala Lumpur: Oxford University Press.

Paine, Thomas. 1974 [1794]. *The Age of Reason.* Edited by Philip Sheldon Foner. New York: Citadel Press.

Parmentier, Richard. 1994. *Signs in Society: Studies in Semiotic Anthropology.* Bloomington: Indiana University Press.

Pattynama, Pamela. 1998. "Secrets and Danger: Interracial Sexuality in Louis Couperus's *The Hidden Force* and Dutch Colonial Culture around 1900." In *Domesticating the Empire: Race, Gender, and Family Life in French and Dutch Colonialism,* edited by Julia Clancy-Smith and Frances Gouda, 84–107. Charlottesville: University of Virginia Press.

Peirce, Charles Sanders. 1986. *Writings of Charles Sanders Peirce: A Chronological Edition.* Edited by Max H. Fisch et al. Vol. 3. Bloomington: Indiana University Press.

Peluso, Nancy. 1992. *Rich Forests, Poor People: Resource Control and Resistance in Java.* Berkeley: University of California Press.

Pemberton, Gregory. 1987. *All the Way: Australia's Road to Vietnam.* Sydney: Allen and Unwin.

Pemberton, John. 1994. *On the Subject of "Java."* Ithaca, NY: Cornell University Press.

Picanussa, J. n.d. "Soetoe Ibarat dari Hikajat Manseren Manarmaker (Manseren Konori)." Unpublished manuscript. Files of F. C. Kamma, Hendrik Kraemer Institute, Oegstgeest, the Netherlands.

Piliang, Indra Jaya. 2008. "Andai Obama WNI." *Harian Seputar Indonesia,* November 8. At http://indrapiliang.com/2008/11/08/andai-obama-wni/. Accessed January 24, 2011.

Pitchforth, Simon. 2008. "Metro Mad: Papuan for President?" *The Jakarta Post,* November 9. At http://www.thejakartapost.com/news/2008/11/09/metro-mad-papuan-president.html. Accessed January 24, 2011.

Portier, K. 1994. "Tussenstation 'Nieuw-Guinea.'" In *Het onbekende vaderland: De repatriering van Indische Nederlanders (1946–1964),* edited by W. Willems and L. Lucassen, 129–47. The Hague: 's Gravenhage.

Povinelli, Elizabeth A. 2002. *The Cunning of Recognition: Indigenous Alterities and the Making of Australian Multiculturalism.* Durham, NC: Duke University Press.

Prai, Jacob Hendrik. 2006. Pidato oleh Jacob Hendrik Prai—D. D. E. Kepala Missi Politik OPM/TPN Urusan Luar Negeri (International) pada Pesta Perayaan Memperingati HUT ke 35 Kemerdekaan Bangsa Papua Barat pada tanggal 1 juli 2006 di Markas Besar OPM/TPN Dalam Negeri Papua Barat alias Irian Jaya

Nama Simbol Perjuangan Politik Pemerintah Kolonial RI. Malmö, Sweden: Organisasi Papua Merdeka, The Political Mission of OPM, the Department for External Affairs. At http://dir.groups.yahoo.com/group/PPDi/message/13704. Accessed September 15, 2009.

Pratt, Mary Louise. 1991. "Arts of the Contact Zone." *Profession* 91: 33–40.

Rabkin, Eric S. 1983. "Introduction: Why Destroy the World?" In *The End of the World*, edited by E. S. Rabkin, Martin H. Greenberg, and Joseph D. Olander, vii–xv. Carbondale: Southern Illinois University Press.

Rafael, Vincente L. 1988. *Contracting Colonialism: Translation and Christian Conversion in Tagalog Society under Early Spanish Rule*. Ithaca, NY: Cornell University Press.

Rappaport, Roy A. 1999. *Ritual and Religion in the Making of Humanity*. Cambridge: Cambridge University Press.

Raweyai, Yorrys T. 2002. *Mengapa Papua Ingin Merdeka*. Jayapura: Presidium Dewan Papua. With accompanying video compact disc.

Remnick, David. 2008. "The Joshua Generation: Race and the Campaign of Barack Obama." *The New Yorker*, November 17. At http://www.newyorker.com/reporting/2008/11/17/081117fa_fact_remnick?currentPage=all. Accessed January 24, 2011.

Reuters. 1998a. "Focus: Indonesian Troops Tackle Fresh Irian Rally." July 7.

———. 1998b. "Indonesian Activists Say Five Missing in Irian." August 7.

———. 1998c. "Indonesians Dismantle Irian Separatist Flag Pole." July 8.

Riches, David. 1991. "Aggression, War, Violence: Space/Time and Paradigm." *Man* 26: 287.

Robbins, Joel. 2001. "Secrecy and the Sense of an Ending: Narrative, Time, and Everyday Millenarianism in Papua New Guinea and in Christian Fundamentalism." *Comparative Studies in Society and History* 43 (3): 525–51.

———. 2004. *Becoming Sinners: Christianity and Moral Torment in a Papua New Guinea Society*. Berkeley: University of California Press.

———. 2007. "Continuity Thinking and the Problem of Christian Culture." *Current Anthropology* 48 (1): 5–38.

Robert F. Kennedy Center. 2004. "The Papua Report." Robert F. Kennedy Memorial Center for Human Rights Indonesia Support Group. January. At http://wpik.org/Src/Papua_Report_1_04.pdf.

Rodgers, Denise. 2006. "The State as a Gang." *Critique of Anthropology* 26 (3): 315–30.

Roest, J. L. D. van der. 1912. *Lief en Leed uit de Zending op Nieuw Guinea*. Lichtstralen op den Akker der Wereld series. Rotterdam: Bredee.

Rooden, Peter van. 1996. "Nineteenth-Century Representations of Missionary Conversion and the Transformation of Western Christianity." In *Conversion to Modernities: The Globalization of Christianity*, edited by Peter van der Veer, 65–88. New York: Routledge.

————. 2003. "Long-Term Religious Developments in the Netherlands, 1750–2000." In *The Decline of Christendom in Western Europe, 1750–2000*, edited by Hugh McLeod and W. Ustorf, 113–129. Cambridge: Cambridge University Press.

Rooijen, W. van. 1989. "Toean Baroe, de nieuwe heer, Nieuw-Guinea, 1949–1962: Beleid, onderzoek en beeldvorming." PhD diss., University of Amsterdam.

Rosenberg, C. B. H. von. 1875. *Reistochten naar de Geelvinksbaai op Nieuw-Guinea in de Jaren 1869 en 1870.* 's Gravenhage: Martinus Nijhoff.

Runawery, Clemens. 2009. "An Open Letter to Mr. Barack Obama, President of the United States of America." Unpublished document. February 11.

Rush, James R. 2007 [1990]. *Opium to Java: Revenue Farming and Chinese Enterprise in Colonial Indonesia.* Ithaca, NY: Cornell University; Jakarta: Equinox Publishing.

Rutherford, Danilyn. 1996. "Of Birds and Gifts: Reviving Tradition on an Indonesian Frontier." *Cultural Anthropology* 11 (4): 577–616.

————. 1998. "Love, Violence, and Foreign Wealth: Kinship and History in Biak, Irian Jaya." *Journal of the Royal Anthropological Institute* 4 (2): 255–81.

————. 2000. "The White Edge of the Margin: Textuality and Authority in Biak, Irian Jaya, Indonesia." *American Ethnologist* 27 (2): 312–39.

————. 2001. "Intimacy and Alienation: Money and the Foreign in Biak." *Public Culture* 13 (2): 299–324.

————. 2003. *Raiding the Land of the Foreigners: The Limits of the Nation on an Indonesian Frontier.* Princeton, NJ: Princeton University Press.

————. 2006. "The Bible Meets the Idol: Writing and Conversion in Biak, Irian Jaya, Indonesia." In *The Anthropology of Christianity*, edited by Fenella Cannell, 240–72. Durham, NC: Duke University Press.

————. 2007. "Der Tanz, Durkheim und das Freimde: Eine Rückkehr zum Comeback der Tradition in Biak" (Dance, Durkheim, and the Foreign: Revisiting the Revival of Tradition in Biak). In *Tanz als Anthropologie*, edited by Gabriele Brandstetter and Christoph Wulf, 288–306. Berlin: Wilhelm Fink.

————. 2009. "Sympathy, State-Building, and the Experience of Empire." *Cultural Anthropology* 24 (1): 1–32.

Ryter, Loren. 2001. "Pemuda Pancasila: The Last Loyalist Free Men of Suharto's Order?" In *Violence and the State in Suharto's Indonesia*, edited by Benedict Anderson, 124–55. Ithaca, NY: Cornell Southeast Asia Program Publications.

Salim, I. F. M. 1973. *Vijftien Jaar Boven Digoel: Concentratiekamp in Nieuw Guinea, Bakermat van Indonesische Onafhankelijkheid.* Amsterdam: Uitgeverij Contact.

Saltford, John. 2000. "United Nations Involvement with the Act of Self-Determination in West Irian (Indonesian West New Guinea) 1968–1969." *Indonesia* 69 (April): 71–92.

————. 2002. *The United Nations and the Indonesian Takeover of West Papua, 1962–1969.* London: Routledge Curzon.

Sankoff, Gillian. 1977. "Multilingualism in Papua New Guinea." In *Language, Culture, Society, and the Modern World*. Vol. 3 of *New Guinea Area Languages and Languages Study*, edited by S. A. Wurm. Pacific Linguistics Series C, No. 40. Pp. 265–307. Canberra: Research School of Pacific Studies, Australian National University.

Sassen, Saskia. 2006. *Territory, Authority, Rights: From Medieval to Global Assemblages*. Princeton, NJ: Princeton University Press.

Saussy, Haun. 2001. "In the Workshop of Equivalences: Translation, Institutions, and Media in the Jesuit Re-Formation of China." In *Religion and Media*, edited by Hent de Vries and Samuel Weber, 163–81. Stanford, CA: Stanford University Press.

Savage, Peter. 1978. "The National Liberation Struggle in West Irian: From Millenarianism to Socialist Revolution." *Asian Survey* 18 (10): 981–95.

Scheiner, Charles. 2000. "International Federation Warns of West Papua–East Timor Parallels in Letter to Indonesia's President." Press release from United Nations representative of the International Federation for East Timor. Unpublished Internet posting. June 13.

Schieffelin, Bambi. 2000. "Introducing Kaluli Literacy: A Chronology of Influences." In *Regimes of Language: Ideologies, Polities, and Identities*, edited by Paul V. Kroskrity, 293–327. Santa Fe, NM: School of American Research Press.

Schijfsma, J. H. 1936. "Kolonisatie vrouw in Nieuw-Guinea." In *Indisch Vrouwen Jaarboek*. Jogjakarta: Kolff-Buning.

Schmitt, Carl. 2005 [1922]. *Political Theology: Four Chapters on the Concept of Sovereignty*. Translated by George Schwab. Chicago: University of Chicago Press.

Schrauwers, Albert. 2000. *Colonial Reformation in the Highlands of Central Sulawesi, Indonesia, 1892–1995*. Toronto: University of Toronto Press.

Searle, John. 1965. "What Is a Speech Act?" In *Language and Social Context*, edited by Pier P. Gigioli, 136–54. London: Penguin.

Sekretariat Presidium Dewan Papua. 2000. "Laporan Hasil Kongres II Papua Barat: Mari Kita Melurauskan Sejarah Papua Barat." Sekretariat Presidium Dewan Papua. Port Numbay [Jayapura]. July 1.

SEM-L Archives. 2008. May 19. At https://listserv.indiana.edu/cgi-bin/wa-iub.exe?A2=ind0805C&L=SEM-L&D=0&P=2546. Accessed March 2, 2009.

Sharp, Nonie, with Markus Wonggor Kaisiëpo. 1994. *The Morning Star in Papua Barat*. North Carlton, Australia: Arena.

Shiraishi, Takashi. 1990. *An Age in Motion: Popular Radicalism in Java, 1912–1926*. Ithaca, NY: Cornell University Press.

Shoaps, Robin A. 2002. "'Pray Earnestly': The Textual Construction of Personal Involvement in Pentecostal Prayer and Song." *Linguistic Anthropology* 12 (1): 34–71.

———. 2009. "Moral Irony and Moral Personhood in Sakapultek Discourse and

Culture." In *Stance: Sociolinguistic Perspectives*, edited by Alexandra Jaffe. Oxford: Oxford University Press.

Sidel, John T. 1998. "Macet Total: Logics of Circulation and Accumulation in the Demise of Indonesia's New Order." *Indonesia* 66 (October): 159–96.

———. 1999. *Capital, Coercion, and Crime: Bossism in the Philippines*. Stanford, CA: Stanford University Press.

———. 2003. "Other Schools, Other Pilgrimages, Other Dreams: The Making and Unmaking of Jihad in Southeast Asia." In *Southeast Asia over Three Generations: Essays Presented to Benedict R. O'G. Anderson*, edited by James T. Siegel and Audrey R. Kahin, 347–82. Ithaca, NY: Cornell Southeast Asia Program Press.

———. 2006. *Riots, Pogroms, Jihad: Religious Violence in Indonesia*. Ithaca, NY: Cornell University Press.

Siegel, James T. 1997. *Fetish, Recognition, Revolution*. Princeton, NJ: Princeton University Press.

———. 1998. *A New Criminal Type in Jakarta: Counter-Revolution Today*. Durham, NC: Duke University Press.

———. 2006. *Naming the Witch*. Stanford, CA: Stanford University Press.

———. 2010. *Objects and Objections of Ethnography*. New York: Fordham University Press.

Siegel, Jeff. 2008. *The Emergence of Pidgin and Creole Languages*. Oxford: Oxford University Press.

Silverman, Kaja. 1988. *The Acoustic Mirror: The Female Voice in Psychoanalysis and Cinema*. Bloomington: Indiana University Press.

Silverstein, Michael. 1976. "Shifters, Linguistic Categories, and Cultural Description." In *Meaning in Anthropology*, edited by Keith H. Basso and H. A. Selby, 11–55. Albuquerque: University of New Mexico Press.

———. 1993. "Metapragmatic Discourse and Metapragmatic Function." In *Reflexive Language: Reported Speech and Metapragmatics*, edited by John Lucy, 33–58. Cambridge: Cambridge University Press.

———. 1996. "Monoglot 'Standard' in America: Standardization and Metaphors of Linguistic Hegemony." In *The Matrix of Language: Contemporary Linguistic Anthropology*, edited by Donald Brenneis and Ronald K. S. Macauley, 284–306. Boulder, CO: Westview Press.

———. 1997. "The Improvisational Performance of Culture in Realtime Discursive Practice." In *Creativity in Performance*, edited by R. Keith Sawyer, 265–312. Greenwich, CT: Ablex.

———. 2000. "Whorfianism and the Linguistic Imagination of Nationality." In *Regimes of Language: Ideologies, Polities, and Identities*, edited by Paul V. Kroskrity. Santa Fe, NM: School of American Research Press.

Silverstein, Michael, and Greg Urban, eds. 1996. *Natural Histories of Discourse*. Chicago: University of Chicago Press.

Simmel, Georg. 1978. *The Philosophy of Money*. Edited by David Frisby. Translated by Tom Bottomore and David Frisby. 2nd ed. London: Routledge.

Singh, Bilveer. 2008. *Papua: Geopolitics and the Quest for Nationhood*. New Brunswick, NJ: Transaction Publishers.

Smeele, Rogier. 1988. "De Expansie van het Nederlandse Gezag en de Intensiviering van de Bestuursbemoeienis op Nederlands Nieuw-Guinea 1898–1942." PhD diss., Institute of History, Utrecht University.

Smirnoff, Victor M. 1980. "The Fetishistic Transaction." In *Psychoanalysis in France*, edited by Serge Lebovici and Daniel Widlöcher, 303–31. New York: International Universities Press.

Smith, Robert Ross. 1953. *The Approach to the Philippines*. Vol. 3 of *The US Army in World War II: The War in the Pacific*. Washington, DC: Office of the Chief of Military History.

Soeharto. 1969. *Presidential Message at the Year's End*. Jakarta: Department of Information, Republic of Indonesia.

Soeparno. 1977. *Kamus Bahasa Biak-Indonesia*. Jakarta: Pusat Pembinaan dan Pengembangan Bahasa, Departemen Pendidikan dan Kebudayaan.

Somba, Nethy Dharma. 2006. "Boycott Threat Looms for West Irian Elections." Jakarta Post.com, March 8.

Special Autonomy Legislation. 2001. Bill of Law of the Republic of Indonesia No. 21 Year 2001 on Special Autonomy for the Papua Province. At http://www.papuaweb.org/goi/otsus/files/otsus-en.html. Accessed January 24, 2011.

Spitulnik, Deborah. 1998. "The Language of the City: Town Bemba as Urban Hybridity." *Journal of Linguistic Anthropology* 8 (1): 30–59.

Spitzer, Leo. 1990. *Lives in Between*. Cambridge: Cambridge University Press.

Spyer, Patricia. 1996. "Serial Conversion and Conversion to Seriality: Religion, State, and Number in Aru, Eastern Indonesia." In *Conversion to Modernity: The Globalization of Christianity*, edited by Peter van der Veer, 171–98. New York: Routledge.

Starrenburg, D. B. 1916. "Moeilijkheden op Onderwijsgebied." In *Berigten van de Utrechtsche Zendingsvereeniging* 1 (January): 4–5. Utrecht: Kemink and Zoon.

———. 1939. *Kerk der Hope. Bijdrage tot kennis der Nieuw-Guinea-Zending*, series 9, number 5. Amsterdam: Nederlandsch Jongelings-Verbond.

Steinberg, David Joel, ed. 1987. *In Search of Southeast Asia: A Modern History*. Rev. ed. Honolulu: University of Hawai'i Press.

Stoler, Ann Laura. 1985. *Capitalism and Confrontation in Sumatra's Plantation Belt, 1870–1979*. New Haven, CT: Yale University Press.

———. 1989a. "Making Empire Respectable: The Politics of Race and Sexual Morality in 20th-Century Colonial Cultures." *American Ethnologist* 16 (4): 634–60.

———. 1989b. "Rethinking Colonial Categories: European Communities and the Boundaries of Rule." *Comparative Studies in Society and History* 3 (1): 134–61.

————. 1995. *Race and the Education of Desire: Foucault's History of Sexuality and the Colonial Order of Things*. Durham, NC: Duke University Press.

————. 2009. *Along the Archive Grain: Epistemic Anxieties and Colonial Common Sense*. Princeton, NJ: Princeton University Press.

Strathern, Marilyn. 1988. *The Gender of the Gift: Problems with Women and Problems with Society in Melanesia*. Berkeley: University of California Press.

Suara Pembaruan. 1998. "Akibat Kurusuhan di Irja 16 Ditahan, 20 Dirawat." July 8.

————. 1999. "Tokoh Irja Bertemu untuk Amankan 1 Desember." November 25.

Sukarno. 1961. *Toward Freedom and the Dignity of Man: A Collection of Five Speeches by President Sukarno of the Republic of Indonesia*. Jakarta: Department of Foreign Affairs, Republic of Indonesia.

Survival International. 1998a. "Urgent Action Needed: People Shot in Biak, West Papua/Irian." July 6.

————. 1998b. "Update from Biak." July 9.

————. 2005. "CIA Named Papua a Cannibal Land." May 3. At http://www.survival-international.org/news/452. Accessed January 24, 2011.

————. 2008. "HIV/AIDS set to soar in West Papua." Survival International: The Movement for Indigenous People. November 18. At http://www.survival-international.org/news/3937. Accessed January 24, 2011.

Sutjipto, S. H., Brigadir Djendral TNI. 1965. "Irian Barat: Agama dan Revolusi Indonesia." Pidato disampaikan oleh Sekretaris Koordinator Urusan Irian Barat/Sekretaris Umum Musjawarah Pembantu Pemimpin Revolusi/Ketua Gabungan V Komando Operasi Tertinggi di "Pekan Pengenalan Tudjuan dan Upaja Revolusi Indonesia" bagi Rochaniawan dan Rochaniawati Daerah Propinsi Irian Barat disponsori Sekretariat Koordinator Urusan Irian Barat, Jakarta, 2–10 Juni, 1965. Jakarta: Projek Penerbitan Sekretariat Koordinator Urusan Irian Barat.

Swadling, Pamela. 1996. *Plumes from Paradise: Trade Cycles in Outer Southeast Asia and Their Impact on New Guinea and Nearby Islands until 1920*. Boroko: Papua New Guinea National Museum/Robert Brown.

Sydney Morning Herald. 1998a. "Irian Tribes Defy Slaughter." July 8.

————. 1998b. "Indonesia's Black Death." November 11.

Tapol. 1980. "OPM Is 'The Kiss of Death,' Says MP." *Tapol Bulletin* 43 (January): 5.

————. 1981. "Former Governor of West Irian Interviewed by TAPOL." *Tapol Bulletin* 48 (November): 9–10.

————. 1998. "Situation Tense in Biak." July 5.

————. 1999. "Critical Days in West Papua." November 25.

Taylor, Jean. 1984. *The Social World of Batavia*. Madison: University of Wisconsin Press.

————. 2003. *Indonesia: Peoples and Histories*. New Haven, CT: Yale University Press.

Tebay, Vience. n.d. "Pengalaman Berdemokrasi di Papua." Unpublished paper.

Teutscher, H. J. 1961. "Pembangunan Djemaat: Katechismus Ketjil tentang Kerd-jasamaan." Unpublished manuscript.

Theweleit, Klaus. 1987. *Women, Floods, Bodies, History*. Vol. 1 of *Male Fantasies*. Edited by S. Conway. Minneapolis: University of Minnesota Press.

Tichelman, G. L. 1946. *NSB deportatie naar Oost en West*. Amsterdam: Uitgever.

Timmer, Jaap. 2000. "Living with Intricate Futures: Order and Confusion in Imyan Worlds, Irian Jaya, Indonesia." PhD diss., Centre for Pacific and Asian Studies, University of Nijmegen, the Netherlands.

Toer, Pramoedya Ananta . 1982. *Tempo Doelo: Antologi Sastra Pra-Indonesia*. Jakarta: Hasta Mitra.

———. 1992. *House of Glass*. Translated by Max Lane. New York: Penguin.

Tomlinson, Matt. 2009. *In God's Image: The Metaculture of Fijian Christianity*. Berkeley: University of California Press.

Toorn, Maarten C. van den. 1975. *Dietsch en volksch: Een verkenning van het taalgebruik der Nationaal-Socialisten in Nederland*. Gronigen: H. D. Tjeenk Willink.

Tryon, Darrell T., and Jean-Michel Charpentier. 2004. *Pacific Pidgins and Creoles: Origins, Growth and Development*. Berlin: Mouton de Gruyter.

Tsing, Anna Lowenhaupt. 1993. *In the Realm of the Diamond Queen: Marginality in an Out-of-the-Way Place*. Princeton, NJ: Princeton University Press.

Tsuchiya, Kenji. 1986. "Kartini's Image of the Javanese Landscape." *East Asian Cultural Studies* 25 (1–4): 59–86.

———. 1987. *Democracy and Leadership: The Rise of the Taman Siswa Movement in Indonesia*. Translated by Peter Hawkes. Honolulu: University of Hawai'i Press.

———. 1990. "Javanology and the Age of Ranggawarsita: An Introduction to Nineteenth-Century Javanese Culture." In *Reading Southeast Asia*, edited by Takashi Shiraishi, 75–109. Ithaca, NY: Cornell University Southeast Asia Program Publications.

Tuck, Richard. 1991a. "Introduction." In *Leviathan / Thomas Hobbes*, xi–xlv. Cambridge: Cambridge University Press.

Tuck, Richard, ed. 1991b. *Leviathan / Thomas Hobbes*. Cambridge: Cambridge University Press.

Tucker, Robert C., ed. 1978. *The Marx-Engels Reader*. New York: W. W. Norton.

Tuzin, Donald F. 1997. *The Cassowary's Revenge: The Life and Death of Masculinity in a New Guinea Society*. Chicago: University of Chicago Press.

Ukur, Dr. F., and Dr. F. L. Cooley. 1977. *Benih Yang Tumbuh VIII: Suatu Survey Mengenai Gereja Kristen Irian Jaya*. Jakarta: Lembaga Penelitian dan Studi Dewan Gerja-gereja di Indonesia; Ende, Flores, Indonesia: Percetakan Arnoldus.

Urban, Greg. 2001. *Metaculture: How Culture Moves through the World*. Minneapolis: University of Minnesota Press.

Urcioli, Bonnie. 1996. *Exposing Prejudice: Puerto Rican Experiences of Language, Race, and Class*. Boulder, CO: Westview Press.

Utrechtsche Zendingsvereeniging. 1926. "Het Maleis op onze Scholen." Confer-

ence report from Miei. Received March 30. UZV 13. Oegstgeest, the Netherlands: Archives of the Hendrik Kraemer Institute.

Vademecum voor Nederlands-Nieuw-Guinea. 1956. Rotterdam: New Guinea Institute in cooperation with the Ministry of Overseas Territories.

Van Den Broek, Theo, and Alexandra Szalay. 2001. "Raising the Morning Star."
Journal of Pacific History 36 (1): 77–91.

Van der Veur, Paul. 1955. "Introduction to a Socio-Political Study of the Eurasians
of Indonesia." PhD diss., Cornell University.

———. 1966. *The Search for New Guinea's Boundaries*. Canberra: Australian National University Press.

Van Staden, Miriam. 1998. "Where Does Malay End and Tidore Begin?" In *Perspectives on the Bird's Head of Irian, Jaya, Indonesia: Proceedings of the Conference, Leiden, 13–17 October 1997*, edited by Jelle Miedema, Cecilia Odé, and
Rien A. C. Dam, 691–718. Amsterdam: Rodopi.

Velde, Henk te. 1992. *Gemeenschapszin en plichtsbesef: Liberalisme en nationalisme
in Nederland, 1870–1918*. 's Gravenhage: Sdu Uitgeverij Koninginnegracht.

Vlasblom, Dirk. 2004. *Papoea: Een Geschiedenis*. Amsterdam: Mets and Schilt.

Vološinov, V. N. 1986 [1973]. *Marxism and the Philosophy of Language*. Translated by
Ladislav Matejka and I. R. Titunik. Cambridge, MA: Harvard University Press.

Wal, S. L. van der. 1965. *De Volksraad en de staatkundige ontwikkeling van
Nederlands-Indië*. Gronigen: Wolters.

Warner, Michael. 1990. *The Letters of the Republic: Publication and the Public Sphere
in Eighteen-Century America*. Cambridge, MA: Harvard University Press.

———. 1991. "The Mass Public and the Mass Subject." In *Habermas and the Public
Sphere*, edited by Craig Calhoun. Cambridge, MA: MIT Press.

———. 2005. *Publics and Counterpublics*. New York: Zone Books.

Watson, C. W. 2000. *Of Self and Nation: Autobiography and the Representation of
Modern Indonesia*. Honolulu: University of Hawai'i Press.

Weber, Max. 1948. *From Max Weber: Essays in Sociology*. Edited by H. H. Gerth
and C. W. Mills. New York: Oxford University Press.

———. 1978. *Economy and Society*. Edited by G. Roth and C. Wittich. Berkeley:
University of California Press.

———. 1990a [1948]. "Bureaucracy." In *From Max Weber: Essays in Sociology*,
edited by H. H. Gerth and C. W. Mills, 196–244. London: Routledge and Kegan
Paul.

———. 1990b [1948]. "Politics as a Vocation." In *From Max Weber: Essays in Sociology*, edited by H. H. Gerth and C. W. Mills, 77–128. London: Routledge and
Kegan Paul.

Weber, Samuel. 2001a. *Institution and Interpretation*. Stanford, CA: Stanford University Press.

———. 2001b. "Religion, Repetition, Media." In *Religion and Media*, edited by Hent
de Vries and Samuel Weber, 43–55. Stanford, CA: Stanford University Press.

Wedeen, Lisa. 2008. *Peripheral Visions: Publics, Power, and Performance in Yemen*. Chicago: University of Chicago Press.

West Papuan Peoples' Representative Office. 2004. "Background and Progress Report: On the Campaign for 'A UN Internal Review Of Its Conduct' in the Act of Free Choice 1969 in West Papua." December. At http://www.westpapua.net/docs/papers/free/wppro/briefing04a.doc. Accessed January 25, 2011.

Widodo, Amrih. 2003. "Changing the Cultural Landscape of Local Politics in Post-Authoritarian Indonesia: The View from Blora, Central Java." In *Local Power and Politics in Indonesia: Decentralisation and Democratisation*, edited by Edward Aspinall and Greg Fealy, 179–94. Singapore: Institute of Southeast Asian Studies.

Wild, Colin, and Peter Carey, eds. 1988. *Born in Fire: The Indonesian Struggle for Independence*. Athens: Ohio University Press.

Wing, John, with Peter King. 2005. "Genocide in West Papua? The Role of the Indonesian State Apparatus and a Current Needs Assessment of the Papuan People." A report prepared for the West Papua Project at the Centre for Peace and Conflict Studies, University of Sydney, and ELSHAM Jayapura, Papua. At http://www.arts.usyd.edu.au/centres/cpacs/docs/WestPapuaGenocideRpt05.pdf. Accessed March 9, 2009.

Winkler, P. E. 1935. *Blank Nieuw-Guinea: Een Nieuw Stamland voor het Nederlandsche Volk*. Utrecht: Nederlandsche Nationaal Socialistische Gegeverij.

Woods, Jackie. 2000. "Megawati Bad News for Papua Independence Hope, Activist Says." *Kyodo News*, August 10. Reprinted on Peace Movement Aotearoa website. At http://www.converge.org.nz/pma/wpapua5.htm. Accessed January 21, 2011.

Woolard, Kathryn A. 1998. "Simultaneity and Bivalency as Strategies in Bilingualism." *Journal of Linguistic Anthropology* 8 (1): 3–29.

Woolard, Kathryn A., and Bambi B. Schieffelin. 1994. "Language Ideology." *Annual Review of Anthropology* 23: 55–82.

Worsley, Peter. 1968. *The Trumpet Shall Sound*. New York: Schocken Books.

Xinhua News Service. 2000. "Indonesia's Assembly Assigns President to Curb Separatism." August 15.

Yampolsky, Philip, and Danilyn Rutherford, eds. 1996. *Music of Biak, Irian Jaya: Wor, Church Songs, Yospan*. Vol. 10 of *Music of Indonesia*. Washington DC: Smithsonian Institute/Folkways Records, compact disc.

YouTube. 2007a. *West Papua Bintang Kejora at Papua Presidium Council 2007*. Posting by westpapuaeurope. December 21. At http://www.youtube.com/watch?v=_MyfH7Y4yyQ&feature=channel. Accessed January 25, 2011.

———. 2007b. *Demonstrating for independence in Jayapura 2004*. Posting by westpapuaeurope. December 21. At http://www.youtube.com/watch?v=uyeJeh1lZ9I&feature=channel. Accessed January 25, 2011.

———. 2008a. *Yes We Can—Barack Obama Music Video*. Posting by WeCan08.

February 2. At http://www.youtube.com/watch?v=jjXyqcx-mYY. Accessed January 25, 2011.

———. 2008b. *obama song for west-papua.* Posting by malaikat007. February 18. At http://www.youtube.com/watch?v=8MoJH5mGH7o. Accessed January 25, 2011.

———. 2008c. *Filep Karma: Freedom for West-Papua Speach, 2004.* Posting by westpapuaeurope. April 6. At http://nl.youtube.com/watch?v=ul-wTo9p9Bc&feature=related. Accessed January 25, 2011.

———. 2008d. *West-Papua flagraising (abepura 1 December 2004).* Posting by westpapuaeurope. April 6. At http://www.youtube.com/watch?v=J1qzKu1Nkjc. Accessed January 25, 2011.

———. 2008e. *West Papua Music: The Sound of the Morningstar.* Posting by abrui. September 15. At http://www.youtube.com/watch?v=7--7_JjpPl8&feature=channel. Accessed January 25, 2011.

———. 2008f. *West Papua music: Kyamadu.* Posting by abrui. September 17. At http://www.youtube.com/watch?v=t6OrddffyYE&feature=related. Accessed January 25, 2011.

———. 2008g. *Viktor Kaisiepo, West Papua.* Posting by Inmyname. September 25. At http://www.youtube.com/watch?v=gp-TRGM8rQU&feature=related. Accessed January 25, 2011.

———. 2008h. *FREE WEST PAPUA.mp4.* Posting by SAIselecta. November 21. At http://www.youtube.com/watch?v=r9pgiGgEnlA&feature=related. Accessed January 25, 2011.

———. 2008i. *West Papua.wmv.* Posting by Elrich2109. December 6. At http://www.youtube.com/watch?v=A5VVcMV3eac&feature=related. Accessed January 25, 2011.

———. 2009a. *Proklamasi: Papua tidak termasuk.* Posting by Manyouri. January 20. At http://www.youtube.com/watch?v=foUqEVMUqQc&feature=channel.

———. 2009b. *Status of Papua.* Posting by Manyouri. February 16. At http://www.youtube.com/watch?v=eWVbvt-1kmE. Accessed January 25, 2011.

Zerner, Charles. 1990. "Community Rights, Customary Law, and the Law of Timber Concessions in Indonesia." In Jakarta Forestry Studies UTF/IN/065. Jakarta.

Zimmer, Benjamin G. n.d. "'To Know Foreign Tongues, Ask the Polyglot': Sundanese Visions of Linguistic Difference on the Eve of Dutch Colonialism." Paper presented in Adventures in Heteroglossia: Navigating Terrains of Linguistic Difference in Local and Colonial Regimes of Knowledge, a session at the American Anthropological Association 100th Annual Meeting, December 2, 2002, Washington, DC.

Žižek, Slavoj. 1993. "The Obscene Object of Postmodernity." In *Looking Awry: An Introduction to Jacques Lacan through Popular Culture,* 141–53. Cambridge, MA: MIT Press.

Notes

Chapter One

1. Thinkers from John Locke to Erving Goffman to Jacques Lacan have made versions of this point. See also Keane 1997; Silverstein 1997.

2. I'm told that the Papuan slang for "rifle" is *alat negara*, literally "instrument of state." Eben Kirksey, personal communication, April 28, 2009.

3. These were Law No. 22/1999 on Regional Governance and Law No. 25/1999 on Fiscal Balance between the Center and the Regions. See Aspinall and Fealy 2003.

4. See Agamben 1998, 21. For Agamben, language, like law, lies on an otherworldly plane that is withdrawn from what he calls the "concrete instance." But one could argue that a sign's ability to signify rests precisely on its haunting by other "concrete instances": imagined moments, past and present, when a sign has functioned in the same way. See chapter 7. See also Comaroff 2007 for a related critique.

5. For Peirce, signs also function as symbols, which are linked to their object by convention, and as icons, which are linked by resemblance.

Chapter Two

1. I would like to thank Jim Siegel for suggesting this contrast.

2. Sandra Macpherson, David Levin, and Jacqueline Goldsby helped me clarify this point.

3. On the history of colonial governance in western New Guinea, see Haga 1884; Kamma 1947–49, 1976, 1977; Van der Veur 1966; Salim 1973; Smeele 1988; Beekman 1989; and Baal 1989.

4. Haga 1884 reflects the degree that the VOC period remained on Dutch officials' minds.

5. Hartweg's relationship with his superiors only worsened with time. After his young daughter died in a dysentery epidemic, he left Biak abruptly, and we hear

little of him in official mission histories, even if North Biaks in the early 1990s still remembered his visits to their communities.

Chapter Three

1. A. A. Mussert, chairman of the Dutch National Socialist movement, 1935, quoted in Lijphart 1966, 87.

2. Henceforth, the terms "European" or *blijver*, denote "legally European." I use the term *totok* for pure-blooded whites.

3. The following account is drawn from Van der Veur 1955, 351–69; Lijphart 1966, 69–89; Drooglever 1980, 193-209.

4. De Nieuw-Guineaer 1931f describes the Indo's recognition "in father's fatherland" as the "noblest product" of the Indies. See also De Nieuw-Guineaer 1934.

5. De Nieuw-Guineaer 1930 offers a satirical view of the founding of the Netherlands by relating the early Batavians' history and character to that of the Indo-Blijvers.

6. See Stoler 1985 on the history of the penal sanction.

Chapter Four

1. International press reports on the incident include Sydney Morning Herald 1998a, 1998b; Inside China 1998; Associated Press 1998; Reuters 1998a, 1998b, 1998c; Guardian Weekly 1998; Agence France-Presse 1998. For local coverage, see Cenderawasih Pos 1998c, 1998d, 1998e; Kompas Online 1998; Suara Pembaruan 1998; Jakarta Post 1998. See also Human Rights Watch 1998a, 1998b, 1998c; Survival International 1998a, 1998b; Tapol 1998; Buset Foker LSM 1998; ELS-HAM 1999, 2003.

2. See Human Rights Watch 1998c for the oath in its entirety.

3. Karma was convicted and sentenced to six and a half years in prison. See Agence France-Presse 1999.

4. The Indonesian military was also using arms supplied by the United States. See Drooglever 2009, 374.

5. See Savage 1978, 985–87; Djopari 1993, 72–73; Saltford 2002; Drooglever 2005, 2009. The New York Agreement called for an open consultation with the province's population on the methods to be used to ascertain their desires. It also called for freedom of speech and freedom of assembly. The Indonesian authorities honored neither of these provisions. Although the settlement called for UN supervision, the only observers allowed to be on hand for the plebiscite were a Bolivian diplomat— who spoke no Indonesian—and a skeletal staff.

6. See Agence France-Presse 1998; Kompas Online 1998; Jakarta Post 1998; see also chapter 7.

7. See chapter 6.

8. I was told that the West Biaks agreed to play their part in the drama only after the commander promised to let them recover the remains of loved ones killed by the military.

9. Karma reputedly also had documents relating to the Act of Free Choice.

10. See Rabkin 1983, ix; Kermode 1967 on the impossibility of narrating the end of all creation.

11. See Human Rights Watch 2000; England 2000a; Alua 2000, 2001, 2002a, 2002b; Ballard 2002b; King 2004; Chauvel and Nusa Bhakti 2004; McGibbon 2004b, 2006; Chauvel 2005; Fernandes 2006; Office for Justice and Peace, Jayapura Diocese 2000; Kirksey 2012.

Chapter Five

1. Australia took over the administration of the German and British territories on the eastern half of New Guinea after World War I. In the 1950s, Dutch and Australian diplomats discussed the possible creation of a Melanesian federation. See Drooglever 2009, 335–40. On West Papuan refugees in Papua New Guinea, see Kirsch 1996.

2. Ethical Theology received the endorsement of the neo-Orthodox Calvinist theologian and Dutch prime minister Abraham Kuyper. Kuyper created the breakaway Dutch Reformed Churches (Nederlandse Gereformeerde Kerken), the Free University in Amsterdam, and the Anti-Revolutionary Party. See Rooden 1996, 2003; see also Keane 2007, 100–101.

Schrauwers has taken Adriani and Kruyt's work in central Sulawesi as exemplifying the aims and methods of Protestant missionaries throughout the Indies. But see Aragon 2000.

3. Malay Bible translations date as far back as the seventeenth century. Missionaries also used Portuguese and Dutch. See Hoffman 1979, 72; Blussé 1986, 156–71; Maier 1993, 45.

4. For similar examples from St. Lucian Kwéyòl, see Garrett 2004, 55.

5. Each Noefoorsch entry was followed by glosses from Ambonese Malay, islands such as Windessi and Roon, and multiple Biak villages.

6. This may be why that Tobati man mentioned in chapter 2 cried out a seemingly French word when he met the Dutch explorers.

Chapter Six

1. For related arguments concerning language use, see chapter 5.

2. Interview, Seth Rumkorem, Wageningen, October 14, 2002.

3. Interview, Wageningen, October 14, 2002.

4. According to Rumkorem, a group of Catholic villagers staged a crucifixion, promising that the victim would rise in three days, at which time Papua would be free. Other villagers tried to recruit the guerrillas to submit to a scheme in which they would lay down their arms, pray, and sound a trumpet outside the provincial capital, Jayapura, which, like Jericho, would fall.

5. Zachi Sawor remembered the names of the two Biak students who were the first to call themselves *amber*. He told me that the practice began in the 1960s as a joke. Interview, Wageningen, October 11, 2002.

6. They had to compete with Ambonese Christians, who flooded into Netherlands New Guinea after the Indonesian Republic crushed a separatist rebellion in the southern Moluccas.

7. Henderson (1973, 90) notes that the Protestant church was the first institution in the colony to entrust the average Papuan "with the promotion of his [*sic*] own interests via a democratic system."

8. Although Catholic leaders in Jaya supposedly engaged in a similar lobbying effort, their initiative was much less open. Interview with Nicolaas Jouwe, Leiden, October 17, 2002.

9. In September 2003, a former GKI officer explained this policy.

10. Some analysts have gone so far as to argue that the rise of reformist Islam in the 1990s represented an attempt on the part of elite Muslims to compete with elite Christians on the same terrain. See Sidel 2003; see also Schrauwers 2000, 14.

11. Some Papuans left the GKI as a result of these incidents. Interview with Nicolaas Jouwe, Leiden, October 17, 2002.

12. Interview, Wageningen, October 14, 2002.

13. Interview, Seth Rumkorem, Wageningen, October 14, 2002.

14. Interview, Nicolaas Jouwe, Leiden, October 17, 2002.

15. Interview, Washington DC, October 3, 2002.

16. Interview, Washington DC, October 3, 2002.

17. Personal communication, Eben Kirksey, May 6, 2009.

18. In fact, Koru Konsup, who founded a proindependence community deep in the forest in West Biak, has no weapons. The community's main activities are marching and prayer. See Kirksey 2012.

Chapter Seven

1. Other speakers included Yusan Yeblo, from Papuan Women's Solidarity Group, and Jerry Imbiri, the student representative on the Papuan Presidium Council.

2. To test my suspicions, I tabulated the various types of *we* that appeared in the Indonesian language e-mail postings I received from the Papua Internal Forum between May 13 and July 28, 2003. These postings included not only articles but also comments by participants. Only 89 out of 1,100 uses of the Indonesian first-person plural pronoun referred to a West Papuan as opposed to a more generalized

collective subject. I discuss the significance of the use of Papuan dialect "we's"—
kamorang and *kitorang*—in chapter 8.

3. This paucity may stem in part from the fact that speakers and writers of
Indonesian and related languages tend to avoid self-reference. See Becker 1995;
see also Watson 2000, 106–29. Nevertheless, a national *we* features prominently in
official Indonesian rhetoric. See Wild and Carey 1988; Sukarno 1961; Paget 1975;
Soeharto 1969.

4. For other examples, see Giay 2000; Raweyai 2002; Alua 2000, 2001, 2002a,
2002b; Bonay n.d.

5. This complicity would be particularly troubling to those who subscribe to
"Standard Average European" language ideologies. See Bauman and Briggs 2000;
see also Silverstein 2000, 113.

6. Legality is a problem beyond the scope of this chapter, but the relevance of
Warner's argument should be clear. It is not simply the creation of an identity that
Derrida is accounting for, but the validation of a form of action formerly justified
by appeals to the divine right of kings.

7. Even in the company of such Papuan leaders as Nicolaas Jouwe, Markus
Kaisiëpo, and Herman Womsiwor—all quadrilingual in Dutch, English,
Melayu, and their local languages, with Womsiwor also fluent in Japanese—the
governor doubted that there were any Papuans capable of keeping up with the
correspondence involved in running the government.

8. United Nations representatives ignored New Guinea Council Members who
traveled to New York to participate in the 1961 debate over the Dutch-backed Luns
Plan, which would have placed the territory under United Nations administration
(see Drooglever 2009, 548–94). Not long afterward, Papuan leaders failed to gain
entry to the negotiations leading up to the New York Agreement (see Drooglever
2009, 561). For their part, the Dutch had little patience for Papuans who didn't toe
the party line. Eliëzer Bonay, the New Guinea Council representative from Serui,
received a stern dressing down in The Hague and later in Hollandia for entering
into discussions with Indonesian diplomats during the trip to New York. Frits
Kirihio, a Papuan student attending university in the Netherlands, went so far as
to meet with President Sukarno in early January 1962. The Dutch foreign ministry
promptly withdrew his fellowship (see Drooglever 2009, 555, 564).

9. Michael Silverstein, personal communication, October 28, 2004.

10. Willy Mandowen, interview with the author, New York, December 10,
2002.

11. Shortly afterward, segments of the production were aired on television.
Following that, the book and VCD have circulated overseas through events such
as the forum I attended. Raweyai reportedly has distributed copies of the book to
foreign guests. Eben Kirksey, personal communication, November 23, 2002.

12. Anonymous, interview by the author, Chicago, February 4, 2003. The
minister's copy made the rounds in the neighborhood as well as in the local army
barracks, where his nephew is stationed.

13. The series is a joint publication of the presidium and the Catholic seminary in Jayapura that Alua directs (see Alua 2000, 2001, 2002a, 2002b).

14. The one exception comes from a preface where Alua explains the purpose of the series: "We Papuans have to learn from history, because history represents a very valuable source of learning and a model for a nation struggling for its future" (see Alua 2001, ii). But the series is also meant to educate Indonesian readers more generally (see Alua 2002a, iii).

15. One gets a sense of the source of these images from the closing credits, which thank the television production studios MetroTV, Indosiar, and TVRI, as well as the individuals Claudio van Planta and W. Barmes.

16. Rihan Yeh helped me work through this point.

17. Raweyai makes his appearance when "Papuan intellectuals" first are mentioned.

18. These productions included a recording of Papuan-language hymns sung by a German pastor and a film by Garin Nugroho, an internationally renowned Indonesian director. *Aku Ingin Menciummu Sekali Saja* (I Only Want to Kiss You Once) is set in Jayapura against the backdrop of the Papuan National Congress and Eluay's death.

19. Anonymous, interview with the author, February 4, 2003.

20. So far, she had demonstrated this talent by speaking Mandarin to a Chinese visitor.

21. See La Biblioteca de las Culturas Hispánicas 1810. See also Firma de Acta de la Declaración de la Independencia de Venezuela 1881. Lomnitz 2000, 351 points out that the particular internal and external relations of dependency that structured these colonial societies shaped their nationalism to an extent that Benedict Anderson's depiction of the "modularity" of "creole nationalism" fails to capture. I owe these insights to Stephen Scott, who assisted me by conducting a careful analysis of thirty-seven founding documents from Latin America.

22. His real enmity was reserved for PaVo, for the seemingly petty reason that the organization has succeeded in winning Dutch government funding.

23. On the fourth person, see Deleuze 1990, 141.

24. In 2006, Alua was elected chair of the Papua People's Assembly (Majelis Rakyat Papua, MRP), the "customary" advisory council of traditional, religious, and women leaders convened as part of the central government's special autonomy package (see Madji 2006; see also chapter 8). That same year, Raweyai ran for governor of West Irian Jaya, a new province split off from Papua, many argue in an effort to divide and conquer the nationalist movement (see Somba 2006).

Chapter Eight

1. Suebu also served as governor in the early 1990s; in the late 1990s he was Indonesia's ambassador to Mexico. The document crafted by Suebu and other

moderate provincial leaders was far more bold and far-reaching than the bill that became law. Among other things, it held out the possibility of a referendum on Papua's political status. See Bertrand 2007.

2. According to the report, other factors included the loss of customary land rights to palm oil production and the machinations of an OPM leader with suspicious ties to the district's security forces.

3. See also Wedeen (2008) on the "episodic" nature of nationalism in Yemen.

4. A representative participant is "abrui," who has his or her own YouTube channel. "Abrui" is thirty-seven years old and lives in The Hague. For "interests and hobbies" "abrui" lists: "Nothing only Freedom.!!!" See http://www.youtube.com/user/abrui.

5. See also YouTube 2007a (unnarrated footage of a dance troupe performing at a political gathering); YouTube 2008f (a sequence of still photographs progressing from picturesque village scenes to images of torture victims and shots of Papuan activists); YouTube 2008g (the Netherlands-based activist, the late Viktor Kaisiëpo, standing in front of the United Nations headquarters and calling for the inclusion of "the indigenous people of the world" in the Millennium Development Goals); YouTube 2009a (a series of graphics that "correct" the Indonesian national anthem by indicating that the republic should never have included West Papua); YouTube 2009b (cartoons, maps, and snippets of English-language text to advance the argument that the Act of Free Choice should be overturned set to an English-language rap song).

6. The provincial government retains 80 percent of the tax revenues gained from forestry and mining and 70 percent of the tax revenues gained from natural gas (see Special Autonomy Legislation 2001).

7. Obama's election inspired flights of imagination in Indonesia. On whether a Papuan could follow Obama's lead and become Indonesia's president, see Liddle 2008; Pitchforth 2008; Piliang 2008; Fatie n.d. Papuan nationalist leaders both in exile and living in Papua have written letters to the new president urging him to take up their cause. See, e.g., Runawery 2009. For songs in Obama's honor from around the world, see SEM-L Archives 2008.

8. The video uses the speech Obama gave after losing the New Hampshire primary to Hillary Clinton. For a full text, see New York Times 2008.

9. Octovianus Mote, personal communication, January 7, 2009. See also Robert F. Kennedy Center 2004.

Chapter Nine

1. For Derrida, the very idea of sovereignty turns on an impossible quest for "ipseity" or "self-sameness." See Derrida 2005; see also Cheah and Guerlac 2009.

Index